W9-CQM-075

The
Standard Concert Guide

GEORGE P. UPTON

AND FELIX BOROWSKI

THE STANDARD CONCERT GUIDE

BLUE RIBBON BOOKS

GARDEN CITY, NEW YORK

1940
BLUE RIBBON BOOKS
14 WEST 49TH STREET, NEW YORK, N. Y.

This book is also published in combination with The Standard Opera Guide under the joint title: The Standard Opera and Concert Guide.

CL
Printed in the United States of America

THIS VOLUME IS DEDICATED

to

FREDERICK A. STOCK

CONDUCTOR OF

THE CHICAGO SYMPHONY ORCHESTRA

PREFACE

To the Revised Edition

THE STANDARD CONCERT GUIDE was first issued in 1908. The following year Mr. Upton brought out the Standard Concert Repertory, a work in which he tilled much of the ground that had been cultivated in its predecessor. Realizing that the needs of the average listener would be met more effectively by combining the material of both volumes, the author merged the Standard Concert Repertory in the earlier book when the necessity for a new edition became apparent in 1917. Mr. Upton was a pioneer — in English-speaking countries, at least — in assisting concert-goers to a better understanding of orchestral music, the oratorio, the cantata, etc. His books enjoyed a large sale because it was realized that the pleasure which was to be derived from symphonic art was heightened when the listener knew something about the music to which he lent his ears. The public which desired this knowledge was, in extent, infinitesimal in 1917 as compared with the public which desires it now. Not only have orchestras multiplied exceedingly in recent years, but the recording instruments and, particularly, the radio have created a multitude of listeners — a multitude so vast that its size would stagger belief if only it could be known. It has been to meet the demands of thousands of music-lovers, who wish to listen intelligently, that this new edition of the Standard Concert Guide has been called into being. The book has been greatly enlarged by the addition of many works to the concert repertory since the second edition was issued from the press. Some of the compositions which were given an honored place in the earlier volume have been removed from this, for they have been relegated to that pathetic backwater in which lie, forgotten or neglected, the things that the world finds out-moded and of no account. It should be said, however, that a number of works of the lighter order, which were not included by Mr. Upton in his edition of the Standard Concert Guide and whose popularity has been long-continued, have been given a place in this edition. For the present the Standard Concert Guide aims to satisfy, not only the fastidious listener who believes that the ultimate word in art has been said by Honegger and Stravinsky, but that lover of fine tune who enjoys the music of Massenet, of Victor Herbert, of Flotow, as it comes to him, perhaps, "over the air." Also the thousands of young people who play in the high school orchestras have been taken into consideration. Their enjoyment of the overtures to "William Tell," "Masaniello," "Mignon" and other mellifluous classics will undoubtedly be heightened by knowledge concerning the history and meaning of those works.

The present editor of the Standard Concert Guide has reverently left Mr. Upton's contributions unchanged, except for the correction of a few dates and minor details. His own additions have been signed with his initials.

FELIX BOROWSKI.

CONTENTS

CONTENTS

CONTENTS

CONTENTS

CONTENTS

CONTENTS

CONTENTS

CONTENTS

CONTENTS

CONTENTS

CONTENTS

CONTENTS

CONTENTS

CONTENTS

CONTENTS

CONTENTS

APPENDIX

THE STANDARD CONCERT GUIDE

D'ALBERT

1864 –

Overture to Der Improvisator

EUGENE D'ALBERT, who was born at Glasgow, has contributed many operas to the German stage, of which "Der Improvisator" ("The Improvisatore") is the sixth. The work was first produced at the Royal Opera, Berlin, February 26, 1902, its story having been derived from Victor Hugo's "Angelo, Tyran de Padoue," a drama which also provided the basis of César Cui's "Angelo" and Ponchielli's "La Gioconda."

The overture to "Der Improvisator," which Arthur Smolian, who wrote a short biography of d'Albert, asserts should be labelled "Carnival in Padua," begins with a brief Introduction (Sehr lebhaft) in D major, 6-8 time, the principal subject soon following in the violoncellos. The tarantelle-like figure is worked out more or less extensively and eventually leads to the second subject — also given to the violoncellos — in B major, the tarantelle-like figure still persisting in the wood winds. A short development section follows, this being in its turn succeeded by the customary recapitulation and a Coda — the latter returning to the material of the Introduction.

F. B.

ALFVÉN

1872 –

Symphony No. 3, in E Major

1. Allegro con brio.
2. Andante.
3. Presto.
4. Allegro con brio.

THE Swedish composer, Hugo Alfvén. wrote four symphonies of which the third is the best known and most frequently performed. Its inner meaning is best told in the composer's own words:

"My Symphony No. 3 was written in Italy. It is a paean in praise of all the joys of life, sunshine and the joy of living. The last movement is imbued with an intense longing for home; I dreamed I was a knight in a far-off land, who in a heedless gallop is making for home — a wild ride, now through sunny landscapes, now through dark abysses — until I have reached the goal of my dreams."

The opening motive of the first movement appears at once in full orchestra and after its statement passage work connects it with the second theme also in full orchestra. A section of it follows in the wood winds to the accompaniment of strings and horns. The usual exposition, development and recapitulation close the movement.

The opening theme of the second movement, a charming melody, is stated in the wood winds, and taken up later in the strings, muted, followed by a new subject for strings and wood winds. The second theme is announced by the clarinet, followed by the first theme in the wind instruments. After its recapitulation in the flutes, the first theme closes the movement.

In the third movement, the opening theme is heard in the first violins and after development is followed by a subject in the oboes and bassoons. The first theme recurs followed by the subject of the Trio in the clarinets and horns to the pizzicato accompaniment of the strings. Recapitulation closes the movement.

The final movement is announced by the trumpet, followed by a passage in the strings with one section of it in the first violins against the basses and horns. The wind instruments give out the second theme, with string tremolo accompaniment, reaching a climax. After a new passage in the strings and wood winds, exposition and recapitulation occur and the work comes to a close with the trumpet call which opened the first movement. The composer has "reached the goal of his dreams."

Rhapsody, Midsommarvaka

Hugo Alfvén's Swedish rhapsody, "Midsommarvaka" ("Midsummer Vigil") is written in two divisions, Allegro moderato, and Allegro con brio. The opening theme of the first division is stated by the clarinet with pizzicato accompaniment in the strings. The flute and oboe, and next the bassoon, repeat it, and it disappears at last in the strings. A new subject follows in the bassoons and horns which is developed in conjunction with the opening theme. A slow section follows in which the English horn with 'cello accompaniment gives out a new theme, repeated by the horn and strings. A fresh theme of a lively character appears in the strings, which, after development, is followed by the Allegro con brio, the violins announcing the subject with accompaniment of basses and bassoons. A counter theme appears in the horns and again in muted trumpet, the rhapsody closing with a stirring Coda. The piece was produced in 1908.

AUBER

1782 — 1871

Overture to Masaniello

"MASANIELLO," or "La Muette de Portici" (the title under which it was produced) was Auber's one grand opera. The work, written to a libretto by Scribe and Germain Delavigne, was produced at the Opéra, Paris, February 29, 1828. Scribe had probably not been unacquainted with an English opera, "The famous history of the rise and fall of Masaniello" which, written by Samuel Akeroyde to a text by D'Urfey, was printed in 1700. Masaniello, it may be said, was not a character of fiction. His name was properly Tommaso Annello and in 1647 he headed a revolt at Naples against the Duke of Arcos, the Spanish viceroy, that action having been dictated by the loss of his scanty possessions, which were sold to pay a fine imposed upon his wife for having brought a bag of flour into the city. The revolt was so successful that the viceroy was forced to abolish the taxes which had been imposed on food and other necessities of life. But when the insurrectionists disbanded Masaniello was assassinated by the ruler's adherents.

Auber's opera, which makes use of the episode of the rebellion, had not a little to do with fanning the flames of revolution in France and Belgium in 1830. The July Revolution in Paris was influenced by it — Adolphe Nourrit, who was the creator of the part of Masaniello, sang "La Parisienne" at each performance of the work — and its representation at Brussels on August 25, 1830, actually caused the riots which drove the Dutch from Belgium and brought about the independence of the country. In America "Masaniello" was first given in New York (in English), November 28. 1831.

The overture to "Masaniello" begins (Allegro assai, 4-4 time) with stormy material in the full orchestra, this having been derived from the music at the opening of the fourth act of the opera. A slow section (Andante, B flat major, 6-8 time) follows, its theme being given out by the clarinet and bassoon in octaves. The original tempo (Allegro) and mood return and lead to the main movement (in G minor), in which the principal theme's first phrase is given to the strings and answered by the wood winds. A triplet figuration for the first violins follows, being accompanied by pizzicatos in the strings, a fortissimo passage for the full orchestra succeeding it. The section then passes into the second subject, in D major, whose theme, taken from the chorus "Honneur et gloire" in the fourth act, is heard in the wood winds and first violins, the full orchestra accompanying piano. The principal subject is then brought forward in a recapitulation, the second theme following, in G major. The overture closes with a Coda, in which instruments of percussion (the side drum and bass drum) play important parts.

F. B.

Overture to Fra Diavolo

"Fra Diavolo, ou l'Hôtellerie de Terracine," opéra comique in three acts, was written to a text by Scribe and produced for the first time at the Opéra Comique, Paris, January 28, 1830. The work was based upon the adventures of a Calabrian bandit, Michele Pezza, whose soubriquet was Fra Diavolo, and who, after having been pardoned in 1790, became a colonel in the Neapolitan army. He was captured by the French at Naples in 1806, during the Napoleonic wars, and hanged. Fra Diavolo had interested other dramatists than Scribe. A play bearing his name was produced by Cuvelier and Franconi at Paris in 1806 and a German version had been given, under the title "Die Räuber in den Abruzzen," at Vienna in 1822. Scribe himself drew some of the incidents in the work from Lesueur's "La Caverne."

The overture, which. like Rossini's "La Gazza Ladra," is

of military character, opens (also like the opera just named) with a solo for the side drum (Allegro maestoso, D major, 4-4 time). A solo violin and viola bring forward the subject of a march, played as if from a distance. The music gradually becomes louder. Instruments are added from time to time, giving the impression of a band approaching nearer and nearer. A triplet figuration for the violins ensues. The music becomes louder and louder, eventually culminating in a fortissimo tutti for the full orchestra, which presents a march subject. The opening material returns, the music gradually dying away. Following a pause, the main section (Allegro, D major, 6-8 time) brings forward a passage of military character for the trumpet. The full orchestra bursts in fortissimo with a brilliant subject. This is developed noisily and leads to the second theme, in A major, presented by the wood winds. The melody of this, as well as the material following it, was taken by Auber from the finale in the opening act of the opera. Development and recapitulation follow and the overture closes with a brilliant and sonorous Coda (Presto).

F. B

BACH

1685 – 1750

The Saint Matthew Passion

THE St. Matthew Passion is written in two parts, between which the sermon intervened in olden times. It includes portions of chapters XXVI and XXVII of the Gospel according to St. Matthew. The *dramatis personæ* are Jesus, Judas, Peter, Pilate, the Apostles, and the People, or *Turbæ,* and the narrative is interpreted by reflections addressed to Jesus, forming two choruses ("The Daughter of Zion") and ("The Faithful"). They are sometimes given by the chorus, and sometimes by single voices. The chorales are selected from those which were in common use in the Lutheran Church. The Gospel text is in recitative form throughout, the part of the Evangelist, or narrator, being assigned to a tenor voice, while those of the persons incidentally introduced are given to other singers. In the dialogue, wherever the words of Jesus occur, the accompaniment is furnished by a string quartet, which serves to distinguish them from the others, and invests them with a peculiar gentleness and grace. The incidental choruses, sung by the people and the Apostles, are short and vivacious in character, many of them being in madrigal form. The chorales, fifteen in number, as has already been said, were taken from the Lutheran service. One of them, which Bach also liberally used in his "Christmas Oratorio," beginning "Acknowledge me, my Keeper," appears five times in the progress of the work, forming the keynote of the church sentiment, and differently harmonized on each occasion. Another ("O blessed Jesus") is twice used — once where the Savior announces that he will be crucified after the Feast of the Passover, and again in the scene at Gethsemane. The whole work is written for double chorus, the two choruses singing the harmony of the chorales, accompanied by the instruments, while the congregation sing the tune in unison. Each chorus has its own orchestra and its own organ accompaniment. The double orchestra is composed of oboes, flutes, and stringed instruments. Drums and brass instruments are not used, the sentiment of the work, in Bach's estimation, not being fitted for them, sweetness and expressiveness of tone rather than power being required.

The first part opens with a reflection sung by double chorus ("Come, ye Daughters, weep for Anguish"), the first exhorting believers to weep over the sinful world, the second responding with brief interrogations, and at last taking part in the sorrowful strains of the first. Interwoven with these is an independent instrumental melody, the whole crowned with a chorale sung by the sopranos ("O Lamb of God all blameless!"), followed by still another ("Say, sweetest Jesus"), which reappears in other parts of the work variously harmonized. The double chorus and chorales form the introduction, and are followed by recitative and a chorale ("Thou dear Redeemer") and a pathetic aria for contralto ("Grief and Pain"), relating the incident of the woman anointing the feet of Jesus. The next number is an aria for soprano ("Only bleed, Thou dearest Heart"), which follows the acceptance by Judas of the thirty pieces of silver, and which serves to intensify the grief in the aria preceding it. The scene of the Last Supper ensues, and to this number Bach has given a character of sweetness and gentleness, though its coloring is sad. As the disciples ask "Lord, is it I?" another chorale is sung ("'Tis I! my Sins betray me"). Recitative of impressive character, conveying the divine injunctions, leads up to a graceful and tender aria for soprana ("Never will my Heart refuse Thee"), one of the simplest and clearest, and yet one of the richest and most expressive melodies ever conceived. After further recitative and the chorale ("I will stay here beside Thee"), we are introduced to the scene in the Garden of Gethsemane. It is introduced by a short instrumental prelude, Zion, represented by the tenor voice, and the Believers by the chorus, coming in after a few bars and alternating with extraordinary vocal effect. It prepares the way for the two great movements which close the first part, an aria for soprano and alto ("Alas! my Jesus now is taken") and a double chorus ("Ye Lightnings, ye Thunders!"). The two solo voices join in a lament of a most touching nature, accompanied by the chorus exclaiming in short, hurried phrases ("Let Him go! Hold! Bind Him not!"), until at last the double chorus bursts in like a tempest, accompanied with the full power of the instruments, expressing the world's indignation at the deed which is to be committed. The first part concludes with the chorale ("O Man, bewail thy great Sin!").

The second part opens with an aria for contralto, full of the deepest feeling ("Alas! now is my Jesus gone"). The trial scene before Caiaphas and the threefold denial of Peter follow, leading up to the expressive aria for alto, with violin obligato ("Oh, pardon me, my God!"). The work now rapidly progresses to its beautiful finale. The soprano recitative in response to Pilate's question ("He hath done only Good to all"), the aria for soprano ("From Love unbounded"), the powerful contralto recitative ("Look down, O God!"), the chorale ("O Head, all bruised and wounded!"), the contralto aria with chorus ("Look where Jesus beckoning stands"), and the peaceful, soothing recitative for bass ("At Eventide, cool Hour of Rest") are the principal numbers that occur as we approach the last sad but beautiful double chorus of the Apostles ("Around Thy Tomb here sit we weeping") — a close as peaceful as the setting sun; for the tomb is but the couch on which Jesus is reposing, and the music dies away in a slumber-song of most exalted beauty.

Magnificat in D

The Magnificat in D — known as the "Great Magnificat," to distinguish it from the smaller — is considered one of the grandest illustrations of Bach's genius. It was composed for Christmas Day, 1723. For the occasion of this festival Bach expanded the Biblical text into four vocal numbers; but in describing the work it is only necessary to give it as it is now generally sung.

The work is written for a five-part chorus, with organ and orchestral accompaniment. After a concerted introduction, foreshadowing the general character of the music, it opens with the chorus ("Magnificat Anima mea"), in fugal form. It is followed by an aria for second soprano ("Et exultavit Spiritus meus: in Deo salutari meo"), which is in the same key and has the same general feeling as the opening chorus, that of Christmas rejoicing, and in turn is followed by an aria for first soprano ("Quia respexit Humilitatem Ancillæ suæ"), leading directly to the chorus which takes up the unfinished words of the soprano ("Omnes Generationes"), each part overlaying the other as it enters, and closing in canon form in grave and colossal harmony. Its next number is an aria for bass ("Quia fecit mihi magna"), of a simple and joyous character, followed by a melodious duet for alto and tenor ("Et Misericordia"), with violin and flute accompaniment, setting forth the mercy of God, in contrast with which the powerful and energetic chorus ("Fecit Potentiam") which succeeds it is very striking in its effect. Two beautiful arias for tenor ("Deposuit, Potentes de Sede") and alto ("Esurientes implevit Bonis") follow, the latter being exquisitely tender in its expression, and lead to the terzetto ("Suscepit Israel Puerum suum: recordatus Misericordiæ suæ"), arranged in chorale form, and very plaintive and even melancholy in style. A stupendous five-part fugue ("Sicut locutus est") follows it and leads to the triumphant ("Gloria"), closing the work, a chorus of extraordinary majesty and power.

The Christmas Oratorio

The "Christmas Oratorio" was written by Bach in 1734, the subject being taken fror texts in Luke and Matthew pertaining to the Nativity. It is not an oratorio in the modern sense; but the justification of its appellation as such is to be found in Bach's own title, "Oratorium tempore nativitatis Christi."

As the entire six parts are very rarely given, a general review of their character will better suit the reader's purpose than a detailed review of each. The entire vocal score embraces no less than sixty-four numbers. In the first three parts, the connecting narratives, recited by the Evangelist, are assigned to tenor and bass, and declare the events associated with the birth of our Lord — the journey to Bethlehem, the birth in the manger, the joy of Mary, and the thanksgiving over the advent of the Lord — the choral parts being sung by the shepherds. The fourth part relates the naming of Jesus, and outlines His career in a grand expression of faith and hope. The fifth illustrates the visit of the three kings, the anxiety of Herod when he hears of the advent of the Lord, and the assurances given him to allay his fears. In the sixth, the visitors depart to frustrate Herod's designs, and choruses of rejoicing over the triumph of the Lord close the work.

The first two parts are the only ones which need special notice for the purposes of the concert-goer. The first opens with a brilliant prelude, introduced by the drum, which Bach, like Beethoven, sometimes treated as a solo instrument. It preludes the narrative bidding Zion prepare to meet her Lord — a simple, touching melody, followed by the chorale ("How shall I fitly meet Thee and give Thee welcome due?"), set to the old Passion-hymn ("O Haupt voll Blut und Wunden") — a solemn and even mournful melody, which at first appears incongruous in the midst of so much jubilation. The composer's evident intention was to impress the hearer with the fact that the object of the divine advent on earth was the Passion of our Lord. At the close of the work the same chorale appears, but with another meaning. It is there an exultant expression of Christ's victory over sin and death. As the chorale dies away, the narrative is resumed, leading up to another chorale ("For us to Earth He cometh poor"), combined with an orchestral symphony and bass recitative. The next number is a bass aria with trumpet accompaniment ("Lord Almighty, King all glorious"), and is followed by a chorale set to the words of Luther's Christmas hymn, which also occurs in other parts of the work, differently harmonized to suit the nature of the situation, and with which the first part closes.

The second part opens with one of the most delightful instances of Bach's orchestration, a pastoral symphony. Like the symphony of the same style in Handel's "Messiah," it is simple, graceful, and idyllic in character, and pictures the shepherds watching their flocks by night on the plains of Bethlehem. At its conclusion the Evangelist resumes his narrative, followed by the chorale ("Break forth, O beauteous, heavenly Light"), preluding the announcement of the angel ("Behold, I bring you good tidings"). It is followed by the bass recitative ("What God to Abraham revealed, He to the Shepherds doth accord to see fulfilled"), and a brilliant aria for tenor ("Haste, ye Shepherds, haste to meet Him"). The Evangelist gives them the sign, followed by the chorale which closed the first part, in another form ("Within yon gloomy Manger lies"). The bass recitative ("O haste ye then") preludes the exquisite cradle-song for alto ("Sleep, my Beloved, and take thy Repose"). This lovely song brings us to the close, which is an exultant shout from the multitude of the heavenly host, singing "Glory to God in the highest."

Suite No. 2

The Suite No. 2, in B minor, is one of the most characteristic and popular of the set. Its various members are an Overture, Rondo, Sarabande, Bourrée, Polonaise, Minuet, and a little closing movement in free style, called "Badinerie." The overture consists of an introductory Adagio, followed by a four-part fugue, at the close of which the movement ends with another Adagio similar to the first.

The other sections are dance forms. The second is a Rondo,

a familiar movement, in which the main theme is several times repeated, sometimes in strict style and again with elaborate embellishment. The third is a Sarabande, originally a Spanish dance for a single performer, accompanied by the castanets, and slow and stately in character. The fourth is a Bourrée, another old-time dance, very lively in style. In this section one Bourrée follows the other, as was the usual custom. The fifth is a Polonaise, a familiar dance form. A peculiarly noticeable passage is the trio, in which the basses have the melody, accompanied by an elaborate flute obligato. The sixth, the Minuet, is a graceful dance form, like all Minuets. It is constructed in two parts, both repeated, and is dominated by a refined and dainty theme. The Minuet form is peculiarly interesting, from the fact that after its introduction by Lully, the French composer, it was frequently employed in sonatas, overtures, and other concert pieces. It was also a movement in the symphony form until the time of Beethoven, who substituted the Scherzo in its place. The old suites usually close with a Gigue, but this suite ends with a very light, playful piece in 2–4 time, denominated "Badinerie" or "Tändelei," signifying sportiveness. With this merry badinage the beautiful suite comes to its close.

Suite No. 3

The movements of Bach's Third Suite, in D, are the Overture, Air, two Gavottes, Bourrée, and Gigue. The Overture begins with a Grave, which leads to the Vivace, a free fugue, after the development of which the Grave occurs, but with different treatment. The Vivace as a whole and the second Grave complete the Overture. The Air, second movement, is the most familiar and beautiful feature of the suite and is often played by solo violin with piano accompaniment, as "Air for the G String." It is a continuous flow of sweet melody, its two strains being several times repeated. The two Gavottes, which correspond to the Minuet and Trio of the old symphonies, and constitute the third movement of the Suite, are very characteristic. The second, which is given out in unison in the whole orchestra, is followed by a repetition of the first and is entirely independent of it. The fourth movement, Bourrée, is gay and sprightly in character. The Gigue, which concludes the suite, as its name indicates, is a still livelier and more rollicking dance than any of the others and leaves the listener in a genial mood.

Suite No. 4

The movements of Bach's Fourth Suite, in D, are Overture, Bourrées 1 and 2, Gavotte, Minuets 1 and 2, and Réjouissance. The Overture is in the usual form. The first Bourrée is constructed in two parts, both repeated, with this distinction, that in the first part the wood winds have the theme with string accompaniment, and in the second the strings have the theme with wood wind accompaniment. The second Bourrée contains solos for oboe and bassoon with string accompaniment. The Gavotte and Minuets closely resemble these forms in the other suites. The last movement, like that of Suite No. 2, is in triple time, very bold in style, and sprightly as a dance movement. Its name, "Réjouissance" (merriment), like "Badinerie," which is affixed to the last movement of the Second Suite, does not refer to the form but to the nature of the music. The most remarkable feature of these suites is that they are bright, cheerful, and even gay in character, and that they were written by Bach at a time of great anxiety and trouble.

Prelude, Chorale and Fugue

The Prelude, Chorale and Fugue is a composite work. The Prelude in C sharp minor is taken from Bach's "Well-Tempered Clavichord" and the Fugue is for the organ in G minor. J. J. Abert, the German composer, in his setting transposed the Prelude to D minor and between it and the Fugue has placed a Chorale in G minor for two trumpets, four horns and three trombones. The theme of this Chorale also appears in the Fugue. In the original, the Fugue has a very elaborate prelude which is not included in Abert's arrangement. This favorite concert number was first performed in this country by Theodore Thomas in 1876.

Mass in B Minor

Bach wrote in all five Masses, of which the B minor Mass is undoubtedly the greatest. The fact that Bach was a Lutheran has caused some misunderstanding as to his employment of a liturgy which is associated with the Roman Catholic church. It should be remembered, however, that when at the time of the Reformation, Luther arranged the form of service for his followers, he did not put aside the Mass of the Roman church from which he had seceded. The Mass was retained, with the exception of the Offertory, which was replaced by the sermon; and in Bach's day Protestant composers occupied themselves with the Kyrie, Gloria, Credo, Sanctus and Agnus Dei as frequently as their Roman Catholic colleagues did.

Bach composed the Kyrie and Gloria of his B minor Mass in 1733 and those movements he sent, with a letter of dedication, to Sigismund III, who was the reigning monarch of Saxony (in which Bach was living) and who later also became King of Poland. The Mass is a work of enormous dimensions, for although it contains the subdivisions which have just been mentioned, Bach, instead of making each a single movement, caused each one to contain several sections. Thus the Kyrie contains three movements, the Credo eight, etc. It should be said that not a little of the material in the B minor Mass was drawn by its composer from other works, most of it from his Church Cantatas. The Mass, as a complete entity, was not published until 1845 and no performance of it as a whole was given until 1834, when it was interpreted at the Berlin Singakademie. The complete manuscript autograph score is in the State Library, Berlin. The sections of the Mass are as follows: I. Kyrie Eleison, a five-part chorus, constituting a solemn supplication to God for mercy. It also comprises a duet for soprano and mezzo-soprano. II. Gloria, a section containing eight movements: Chorus, Gloria in excelsis; Aria, Laudamus Te; Chorus, Gratias agimus tibi; Duet, Domine Deus; Chorus, Qui tollis peccata mundi; Aria, Qui sedes; Aria, Quoniam tu solus sanctus; Chorus, Cum sancto spiritu. III. Credo, containing the following divisions: Chorus, Credo in unum Deum; Chorus, Patrem omnipotentum; Duet, Et in unum Dominum; Chorus, Et incarnatus est; Chorus, Crucifixus etiam pro nobis; Chorus, Et resurrexit tertia die; Aria, Et in Spiritum sanctum; Chorus, Confiteor unum baptisma. IV. Sanctus, comprising three divisions — Chorus, Sanctus, sanctus, sanctus; Chorus, Osanna in excelsis; Aria, Benedictus qui venit. V. Agnus Dei, written in two movements; Aria, Agnus Dei and Chorus, Dona nobis pacem.

F. B.

Concerto No. 1

The six concertos for orchestra by Bach were composed as the result of a commission from Christian Ludwig, Margrave of Brandenburg — hence the frequently employed appellation for them, Brandenburg concertos. The Margrave was an enthusiastic amateur and he maintained an orchestra which in terpreted for his pleasure the large collection of concertos — mostly by the admired Italian composers of his day — which he spent a number of years in forming. It should be remembered that the word "concerto" was employed in the 18th century, not in the sense of a brilliant composition for a solo instrument, but for a combination of instruments or even voices. In writing his examples of this form Bach employed as varied a combination as possible. The completed set of concertos was sent by Bach to the Margrave of Brandenburg in 1721 and he accompanied it with a letter couched in the somewhat servile terms which, in his day, authors and composers addressed those who were their social superiors. After the death of Christian Ludwig, the manuscripts of Bach's concertos passed into the possession of his pupil, Johann Philip Kirnberger. who bequeathed them to Princess Amalia of Prussia sister of Frederick the Great, who was herself a composer. They are now in the State Library, at Berlin.

The first Concerto is in F major. Upon the manuscript Bach wrote the following title: *Concerto Imo a 2 Corni di Caccia, 3 Hautbois et Bassono, Violino piccolo concertato, 2 Violini una Viola e Violoncello col Basso continuo.* The Corno di caccia is our modern French horn. The Violino piccolo was a small sized violin which was used as a solo instrument and tuned a fourth higher than the ordinary instrument.

The first concerto contains four movements, the first of which is without any indication of tempo, but is without doubt an Allegro moderato. It is in 2-2 time. The second movement is an Adagio in D minor, 3-4 time, its theme being given out by the oboe. The third movement is an Allegro in 6-8 time, whose subject is set forth by the first violins and first oboe, the violino piccolo playing a prominent part. A Minuet closes the concerto.

F. B.

Concerto No. 2

Like the first of the set of six concertos, this second one is in F major. The title on the manuscript score is as follows: *Concerto 2do à I Tromba, I Flauto, I Hautbois, I Violino concertati è 2 Violini, I Viola è Violone in Ripieno col Violoncello è Bassò per il Cembalo.* In explanation of this title it may be said that "tromba" signifies trumpet; "flauto," flute and 'hautbois," oboe. The concertos of the eighteenth century contained as a rule parts for solo performers who were known as "concertino," the accompanying instrumentalists being called "ripieno." Bach's "I Violino concertati" thus signifies the solo violinist. The "cembalo" was the harpsichord which always formed part of the orchestra in Bach's day and from which the conductor gave the tempo and kept the musicians together.

The movements of the second concerto are as follows: I. Allegro moderato, F major, 4-4 time; II. Andante, D minor, 3-4 time; III. Allegro assai, F major, 2-4 time. The concerto is frequently performed in an edition made by Felix Mottl for modern orchestra.

F B.

Concerto No. 3

Upon the manuscript score of the third concerto Bach wrote the following title: *Concerto 3 à tre Violini, tre Viole e tre Violoncelli col Basso per il Cembalo.* It will be seen from this enumeration of instruments that the concerto is for stringed orchestra. In its original form the work contained only two movements — I. Allegro in G major, 2-2 time and II. Allegro, G major, 12-8 time. It has sometimes been the custom of conductors to insert a slow movement of some kind by Bach between the two Allegros in order to provide contrast. The first movement of this concerto was also employed by Bach for the opening section of his Whitsunday cantata, "Ich liebe den Höchsten von ganzen Gemüthe."

F. B.

Concerto No. 4

Bach's title for his fourth concerto — as set forth upon the autograph score — was the following: *Concerto 4to a violini principale, due Fiulte d'Echo, due violini, una viola e violone in Ripieno, violoncello e continuo.* Exactly what was meant by "Fiulte d'Echo" has never been made clear. There are no such instruments as "Echo flutes" — for it was two flutes that Bach intended to be used in the performance of his work; moreover, he stated on his score that the instruments were to be flutes à bec. The latter were instruments provided with a mouthpiece like a whistle, but they have long been superseded by the other species of flute which, known as flauto traverso, is that which is familiar to us to-day. The concerto is in three movements, the first of which (Allegro, G major) is in three divisions, the first and third made of the same material. The second movement (Andante, E minor) is based on a theme given to the solo instruments with the harmony sustained by the lower strings. The Finale, (Presto, G major) brings forward the main theme in the violas and later in the solo violin, afterward to be taken up by the full orchestra.

F. B.

Concerto No. 5

Bach's fifth concerto was composed for a flute, solo violin, strings and harpsichord. The title which the master placed upon his manuscript score ran thus: *Concerto 5to à une Traversière, une Violon principale, une Violino è una Viola in ripieno, Violoncello, Violòne è Cembalo concertato.* The Traversière to which Bach alluded was the flute held transversely — as it is held now-a-days — in distinction to the flute à bec, which was played with a mouthpiece and held like, say, an oboe. The "violon principale" signifies a solo violin, the other instruments, indicated by the words "in ripieno" accompanying. The "cembalo concertato" indicated that the harpsichord, instead of merely filling in as ordinarily it did in the 18th century, was given a brilliant part.

There are three movements in the concerto, the first being an Allegro in D major, 2-2 time. In this the harpsichord — or the piano — has a difficult and brilliant part to play. The slow movement (Affetuoso, B minor, 4-4 time) is expressively written as a trio for the flute, solo violin and cembalo. The Finale, Allegro, D major, 6-8 time, is remarkable among the movements by Bach for the interpretative directions which the master put in it in order to guide the players.

F. B.

Concerto No. 6

Bach's sixth concerto was originally written for two viole da braccio, two viole da gamba, violoncello and harpsichord. Both the viola da gamba and the viola da braccio are now obsolete. The former was a six stringed instrument held between the knees like a violoncello and played with a bow more nearly resembling that employed today by performers on the double bass. Bach was devoted to this instrument, which was already becoming obsolete in his own time. The viola da braccio was the ancestress of the viola of modern times, but possessed five strings. In order to perform Bach's sixth concerto in modern times it is necessary, since the two previously mentioned instruments are no longer used, to replace them with others which are more or less similar. The viola da gamba is, therefore, generally replaced by a violoncello and the viola da braccio by a viola. The concerto contains three movements. The first, in B flat major, 2-2 time, was not provided by Bach with any tempo indication, but is generally played Allegro moderato. The second movement, Adagio ma non tanto, is in E flat major, but modulates at its close to lead without coming to a definite pause to the last movement (Allegro, 12-8 time) in B flat major.

F. B.

BALAKIREV

1836 — 1910

Symphonic Poem, Thamar

THE composer Balakirev belonged to the New Russian School of which César Cui and Rimsky-Korsakov were the founders and ardent champions, but his music is not so well known in the Western World as that of some of his associates. "Thamar" is his work which has made the deepest impression. Its story is taken from a poem by the Caucasian poet Lermontoff and is one of the favorite Russian myths. Briefly, Queen Thamar, a beautiful creature but a demon of cruelty, dwells in a tower overlooking the river Terek. It is her habit to invite passing travelers to her banquets, and the next day their bodies may be found in the Terek. Among them is her lover.

The music begins with passages describing the roar of the river in the distance, followed by phrases indicating the warning voices of spirits and in which is now and then heard the call of a sweet, far-away voice. New themes in folk-song style are introduced to represent the responses to the Queen's call. These themes are repeated and intensified, at last reaching a fortissimo climax in which the full orchestra joins. The roll of drums announces the approach of a warrior who is attracted by the weird melodious strain of Thamar's song. Passages follow describing the revelry at the banquet and the ominous silence as it dies away. The roar of the river is heard again, and through it the Queen's farewell, followed by a theme which tells of approaching happiness when the warrior and his love shall meet again. Though "Thamar" is purely program music, it is strictly constructed, but notwithstanding this conventionality of form it is infused with the lavish color and Oriental spirit which characterize nearly all the works of this school.

BANTOCK

1868 –

Fifine at the Fair

"FIFINE at the Fair," described in the score as "orchestral drama," is a musical setting of Browning's poem of that name, the composer adding to the title an explanatory phrase — "a defense of inconstancy." It opens with a prologue for strings, picturing the ocean of life with a man swimming in it and a butterfly fluttering over it, the latter being the type of womanly nature. The prologue is expressive of passionate aspiration for woman. At its close there is a radical change and the festivities of the fair are set forth in carnival style. Fifine appears and exerts her fascinating charms to captivate the man, closing with a beautiful cadenza for clarinet. Elvine next appears, the type of nobler and higher womanhood, her appeal delightfully set forth in the strings, horns and clarinets. The man is unfaithful to Elvine and she leaves him. The work closes with an Epilogue, describing the reunion of Elvine and the man and the disappearance of Fifine. In the poem this reunion is effected by death, but the composer more practically unites the pair in marriage, Elvine having forgiven her consort, and it is to be presumed they lived happily ever after. The piece had been written in 1902, and produced ten years later.

BARTÓK

1881 -

Suite No. I, Op. 3

BELA BARTÓK, born at Nagyszentmiklós, Hungary, is, with Zoltán Kodály, the principal representative of modern Hungarian music. Educated at the Royal Hungarian Academy of Music at Budapest, Bartók made a special and extensive study of the folksong of his native land and employed it in his own works. The first suite for orchestra was composed in December, 1905. The hearing of the suite will be made more interesting if it is remembered that Bartók's idiom is that of the ultra-modern composer. "We miss," wrote Michel Calvocoressi in an article on the Hungarian master, "landmarks by which we were wont to steer. Extensions of the tonal range, new associations of chords, unusual sequences of meters and intervals are enough to make us feel as though tonality, harmony, rhythm and melody told us nothing of the musician's purpose. But if that purpose is dictated by, and carried out under the guidance of genuine imagination, we shall find it far less difficult to grasp than we might think at first."

The suite contains the following five movements: I. Allegro vivace, E major, 2-4 time; II. Poco Adagio, A minor, 3-4 time; III. Presto, C major, 3-4 time; IV. Moderato, A minor, 2-4 time; V. Molto vivace, E major, 3-4 time.

F. B.

Dance Suite

Bartók's Dance Suite was composed in 1923 for a celebration at Budapest of the fiftieth anniversary of the union of the cities Buda and Pesth, a musical festival which was held November 19 of that year. The suite contains six independent sections which are not self-contained but run into each other without any pause. In order to provide a certain unity the composer employs a theme — which occasionally he terms "Ritornello" — which is heard at the end of the first and second sections and toward the end of the finale.

F. B.

BAX

1883 –

Symphonic Poem, The Garden of Fand

ARNOLD BAX, who was born at London, England, gained his musical education at the Royal Academy of Music, where he was a pupil of Frederick Corder in composition, and of Tobias Matthay in piano-playing. Of Irish descent, through both his father and his mother, Bax has been largely influenced in his music by Celtic things. Upon finishing his studies in London, he betook himself to Ireland and lived for long periods in the western division of that country. Later he lived in Dublin.

"The Garden of Fand" was written in 1916 and first produced at a concert of the Chicago Symphony Orchestra, Chicago, October 29, 1920. In order to clarify the significance of the title it should be explained that while Fand is the heroine of the ancient Irish saga, "The Sickness of Cuchullin," the symphonic poem bears no specific relation to the saga. The composer communicated the meaning of his work as follows:

"The Garden of Fand is the sea itself. At the outset of the work the composer seeks to create the atmosphere of the enchanted Atlantic, utterly calm and still beneath a fairy spell. Upon its surface floats a small ship bearing a few human voyagers adventuring from the shores of Erin towards the sunset dream, as St. Brendan and the sons of O'Connor and Maeldune had adventured before them. The little craft is borne on beneath a sky of amethyst and pearl and rose until, on the crest of an immense wave, it is cast onto the shores of Fand's miraculous island. Here in eternal sunlight unhuman revelry continues unceasingly between the ends of time. The travelers are caught, unresisting, into the maze of the dance. A pause comes, and Fand sings her song of immortal love, claiming the souls of her hearers forever. The dancing and feasting begin again, and finally the sea, rising, overwhelms the whole island, the people of the Sidhe riding in rapture upon the ridges of the green and golden waves, and laughing carelessly amidst the foam at the fate of the over-rash mortals, lost forever in the unfathomable depths of ocean. The sea subsides again, the veils of twilight cloud the other world, and the Garden of Fand fades from our sight."

"The Garden of Fand" is scored for the following orchestra: Two flutes, piccolo, two oboes, three clarinets, two bass clarinets, two bassoons, four horns, three trumpets, three trombones, bass tuba, kettle-drums, two harps and strings.

F. B.

Symphonic Poem, November Woods

"November Woods" was composed in 1917 and was given its first production at a concert of the Hallé Orchestra, Manchester, England, November 18, 1920. In an article on the music of Bax, published in the Musical Times, London, in 1919, Edwin Evans gave the following description of the symphonic poem:

"'November Woods' is a picture of storms and driving leaves and the sere and dank atmosphere of autumn. Mingled with this is the mood of human loneliness and regret, which is finally absorbed in the restlessness and turmoil of nature. The composer himself regards it as his best orchestral work, and the one by which he would elect to be represented if asked to make a choice."

The symphonic poem is scored for three flutes, piccolo, two oboes, English horn, three clarinets, bass clarinet, two bassoons, double bassoon, four horns, three trumpets, three trombones, tuba, kettle-drums, bass drum, cymbals, glockenspiel, celesta, two harps and strings.

F. B.

BEETHOVEN

1770–1827

Symphony No. 1, in C Major. Op. 21.

1. Adagio molto. Allegro con brio.
2. Andante cantabile con moto.
3. Menuetto e Trio.
4. Adagio. Allegro molto e vivace.

THE date of Beethoven's First Symphony has not been definitely ascertained. Sketches of its finale are found as early as 1795, though the work was not performed until April 2, 1800, at a concert in Vienna, conducted by the composer. The symphony, in the key of C major, does not begin with the common chord of C, but with a seventh chord in C, resolving into F major, at that time an unheard-of proceeding.

The short introduction leads us in twelve measures to the first movement, with this principal theme—

The flutes take up the cadence and lead through C and C sharp into a repetition of the theme one step higher in D minor, bringing it the third time in a slightly altered form on the dominant chord of G and leading back into the principal key of C. The second theme—

includes in its melody another of Beethoven's idiosyncrasies, namely, the syncopations at *a,* while the broken chords in the staccato accompaniment foreshadow his preference for decided figures in his basses.

The second part opens with the principal theme in A major, which after some modulations is reiterated fortissimo and in unison by the whole orchestra. The chromatic step C, C sharp, for the winds, which we found in the beginning, leading into a repetition in D minor, is now extended to a quasi-chromatic scale, running through an octave and a half, and leading in a steady crescendo into the dominant and thus back to the second theme, which appears now in the original key of C. Near the close of the movement, Beethoven very ingeniously gives us a reminder of his opening chords and their resolution by using the principal theme in part, overlaying it in the winds with a seventh chord. The treatment throughout is simple and clear.

The Andante cantabile con moto opens with the following melody:

answered in canon by the violas and 'cellos. The opening step C to F, enlarged to a sixth, G to E, makes the second phrase of the movement a natural sequence of the first. In the last eight measures of the first part, Beethoven again steps out of the beaten track of using the kettle-drum only as a kind of metronome, by giving it a rhythmic phrase accompanying a triplet figure in the violins. The step C to F, in connection with the pulsating beat of the drum, furnishes the composer the material for the opening of the second part of the Andante, which is worked out with the utmost delicacy and closes with one of those dynamic contrasts of which Beethoven was so fond.

The Minuet was the composer's most serious attempt to impress his individuality upon a form which had been so strongly defined by his predecessors, and which, as the representative of the dance Minuet, seemed to have been almost exhausted by Haydn and Mozart. Beethoven, recognizing the fitness of a bright and sprightly movement between the Andante and the last movement of the sonata form, aimed at once to break through the form of the Minuet proper and create the Scherzo and Trio, which he afterward developed so successfully. The movement under consideration, although entitled "Minuet," is really a Scherzo. Its beginning reveals those characteristics of the composer which further study of his works forces us to admire the most in him — simplicity and strength. Look at the opening:

Its tonal design appears to be nothing but the scale of G major, but what does it become under the hands of the young master?

The second part of the Minuet is remarkable for its modulation, and there is something infinitely humorous in the measures which follow this *tour de force:*

until their pianissimo comments are cut short by the statement of the opening scale fortissimo. The Trio is very simple and chiefly based on the interchange of the wind and string choirs, and the Minuet, da capo, closes the movement.

The Finale opens with a few bars of Adagio. After a hold on G, the first violins rush off in their mad dance:

The opening phrase of the Allegro is a violin figure, pure and simple, and the scale runs of the second part are but threads compared with the scale which we found overlaying the harmonic structure of the opening of the Minuet. The second theme of the Finale is the following:

coquettishly set off against the steady basses and entirely in keeping with the spirit of the whole.

In the First symphony Beethoven still clings to the accepted musical forms; hence the occasional phrases which remind us of Haydn and Mozart. And yet the symphony shows us in embryo all those qualities which made Beethoven the greatest symphonic writer the world has thus far produced.

Symphony No. 2, in D. Op. 36

1. Adagio molto. Allegro con brio.
2. Larghetto.
3. Scherzo and Trio. Allegro.
4. Allegro molto.

Beethoven's Second Symphony was completed in the year 1802, and was first heard at the Theater an der Wien, April 5, 1803. It begins, like the first, with an introductory Adagio, although of much greater length. The sturdy opening on a hold on D, in unison by the whole orchestra, is at once followed by an exquisite phrase for the oboes and bassoons. Similar contrasts prevail until the opening of the Allegro con brio. The theme is given out by the 'cellos, and in the repeat—

the basses softly join them. The last part of the motive is somewhat emphasized by repeating the step of a third on the quarter notes at *a*, to a connecting melody in the winds, until the strings take up the first part of the theme given above, and carrying it up into the seventh, enlarge the scope for a sweeping violin figure, which with a pronounced staccato phrase serves as a connection with the second theme:

This theme is scarcely inferior in its jubilant expression to any similar outburst in Beethoven's later works. This feeling is intensified in the repeat by a trill-like figure in the violins, which now runs into this motive:

until after a number of abrupt chords fortissimo the full orchestra stops on a diminished seventh chord, followed by three-quarters rest, during which in place of some crashing resolution, a soft murmur strikes the ear from the strings:

and not until after a crescendo of eight measures are we gratified with a satisfactory closing. The second part deals chiefly with the same material, a new feature being added by the counter-movement of a broken scale against the theme:

and the constant tossing about of the motive:

The second half of the second theme furnishes the composer the material for the following exquisite phrase:

The close is exceedingly bold, the basses rising in a slow chromatic scale throughout an octave from D to D, the violins trying to counterbalance it by the other extreme of gigantic strides. The movement ends with a feeling of exultant joy and happiness.

The Larghetto is one of the loveliest slow movements Beethoven ever wrote, and is a special favorite in the concert-room. The opening theme —

given out by the strings and repeated by the winds, is a flowing cantilena of exceeding beauty, uninterrupted by any staccato or even any well-marked incision in the phrasing. The second phrase —

only intensifies the general feeling expressed in the first. A long dialogue follows, which hardly needs musical quotation to be thoroughly understood by the attentive listener.

The Scherzo here appears under its own name. It is built up on a short motive of three notes repeated over and over again, first by the basses, then by the violins, and again by the horns, after which the oboes bring it reversed, at one time fortissimo and again piano, but ever tripping along staccato until the violins in the second part indulge in a temporary sweep of descending scale, followed by a reminder of the leading figure of the first Allegro:

The three-note motive however soon carries the day. The Trio begins with a short phrase in oboes and bassoons, played twice and ending in D. The violins follow with a determined stroke on the third (F sharp) and turn the note into the tonic of the chord of F sharp, eventually quieted down on the same F sharp.

The Finale expresses the same happy mood that characterizes the preceding movements. The opening motive is thoroughly characteristic and piquant:

Then follows a longer period, in which the winds carry the melody while the strings furnish an apparently monotonous staccato accompaniment. In the further working up, that part of the motive containing the trill is also more extensively employed. Right here we have also an instance where the composer exchanges humor for downright fun. Imagine the beginning of the following quotation:

fortissimo, supported by the whole orchestra, closing at *a* with a sforzando crash, followed by the weazened little gasp of the first violin pianissimo, then by a pause and a repetition of this whimpering appoggiatura, finally after a second pause the whole orchestra breaking in at *b* with the opening motive, forte. The close is worked out into a Coda of considerable length, starting from two successive holds with a new rhythmic figure, which, however, soon merges into the general whirl of joyous mirth pervading the whole movement.

Symphony No. 3, in E Flat (Eroica). Op. 55.

1. Allegro con brio.
2. Marcia funèbre. Adagio assai.
3. Scherzo and Trio. Allegro vivace.
4. Finale. Allegro molto.

Beethoven first projected the Third Symphony in 1802 and finished it in 1804. "Eroica" is likely to mislead the hearer if he supposes the music to be of a martial character, and we therefore add the complete title of the work as it first appeared in print: "Sinfonia Eroica, composta per pesteggiare il sovvenire di un grand' Uomo, dedicata," etc.; ("Composed to celebrate the memory of a great man"), namely, the hero in its widest sense. The first manuscript copy, however, bore the following inscription:

Sinfonia grande,
Napoleon Buonaparte,
1804 in August:
del Sigr.
Louis Van Beethoven.
Sinfonia 3. *Op. 55.*

The fly-leaf of the copy, which the composer retained, had the words "Luigi van Beethoven" at the top, and "Buonaparte" at the bottom. It is known that Beethoven watched with deep interest the revolution in France. One man attracted his attention and kindled his enthusiasm. Napoleon Bonaparte had appeared like a sun above the sea of confusion and mediocrity, rising rapidly but steadily until it seemed he would be the foremost hero of the republic, but when Beethoven first heard of the "*Vive l' Empereur*" he took the score of his "Eroica," tore its title-page in two, and threw the work on the floor. His idol was shattered, and the symphony was finally published in memory of "un grand' Uomo."

The first movement has a number of themes in the highest degree characteristic. The main theme is given out at the very beginning by the 'cellos in a quiet manner, but after twenty-four measures we encounter the syncopations which play so decided a part in this great picture of strife. A tender episode for the winds, repeated by the strings, interrupts the turmoil, but after a short repose a rapid crescendo leads again to the clashing syncopations. A similar treatment is adopted in the second part, the whole forming one of the most remarkable pieces of orchestral writing ever accomplished.

The Adagio appeals more directly to the listener, with its sad melody in C minor and its heartfelt tones of melancholy. This solemn dirge, designated by the composer "Marcia Funèbre," is followed by the Scherzo, Allegro vivace. The contrast in the heading of the two movements would naturally suggest startling incongruities in the music; but it is one of the greatest achievements of Beethoven's genius that he surmounts the difficulty in a way which does not admit of an idea of unfitness.

The Scherzo begins with a pianissimo staccato, which has something mysterious in its character, moving four measures in the step of a secunda only, and that on the lower notes of the violins. Not until the fifth measure does the melody rise into the higher octave, and only in the ninth measure do we find a hint of the lighter character of the Scherzo in a short group of connected descending notes. Even the second part moves in a similar manner of steps and half-steps always pianissimo. It is not until the middle of this part that it breaks forth with a sudden fortissimo, and not even then without a reminiscence of the syncopations of the first Allegro.

The Trio, with its horn passage, finally dispels the gloomy character of all that precedes, and calls up more peaceful visions.

The last movement, Allegro molto, begins with a dominant seventh chord in the form of a cadenza, after which the theme enters pizzicato. This melody, in its intervals, is really a fundamental bass, and is worked up in the form of variations, ever and anon interrupted by a hold on the dominant chord, until a new theme appears, happier and brighter than any, dominating the last part of the movement. It gives room to a severe treatment of the first theme in strict counterpoint, only to reappear in a Poco andante of some length, which without warning breaks into the final Presto fortissimo that brings the work to a close.

The principal theme of the first movement is given out by the 'cellos as quoted at *a:*

The second subject at *b* is in fine contrast with the first, and is thrown about from instrument to instrument. The episode given out by the winds, as mentioned above, is indicated at *c:*

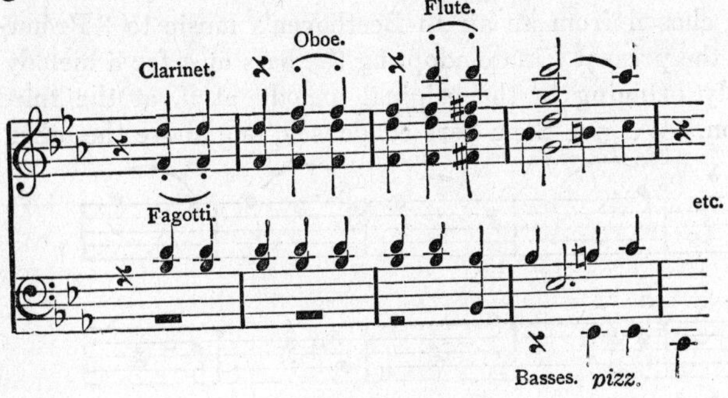

Another prominent theme starts in about the middle of the second part, as at *d:*

followed by that remarkable passage in the basses at *e.* The melody of the Adagio we give at *f*

with its counterphrase at *g.* The main theme of the Finale is a subject chosen from an air in Beethoven's music to "Prometheus," the present Finale adopting the bass at *a* for a melody, and only bringing in the original melody at *b,* at the third variation. We give them here condensed, one above the other:

Symphony No. 4, in B Flat. Op. 60

1. Adagio. Allegro vivace.
2. Adagio.
3. Menuetto. Allegro vivace. Trio, un poco meno allegro.
4. Allegro ma non troppo.

The Fourth Symphony, written in 1806, lies like a gleam of sunlight between the heroic Third and majestic Fifth.

The symphony begins with the customary slow introduction, which opens in this mysterious manner to a long-held B flat in the wind instruments:

and is followed by the Allegro vivace, at an accelerated pace:

While the violins are indulging in mysterious whisperings, the bassoon skips around nimbly, until it is silenced by a crescendo of four measures, and the rush of the opening of the Allegro is repeated. A mocking syncopated phrase now occurs, followed by a little conversation between the bassoon, oboes, flutes, and violins, until a unison figure in the strings, of a peculiarly buoyant character in its harmonic design and well calculated for a fine crescendo —

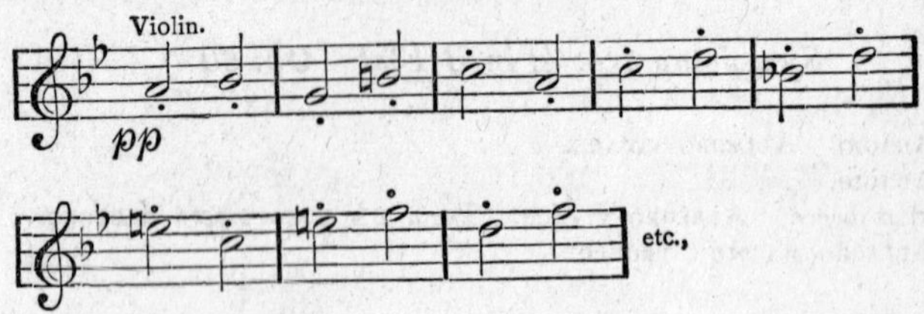

brings us to a little canon —

in its very simplicity admirably in keeping with the general character of the music. A mysterious tremolo pianissimo for the violins is followed by a syncopated figure in the violins forcing the repetition of the first part. The second part, though dealing essentially with the same thematic material, is exceedingly rich in harmonic changes and transpositions. This part also contains an unaccompanied, unbroken scale, started by the first violins and carried down into the basses, always pianissimo, breaking into an upward sweep through a diminished seventh chord and landing again within four measures on a high D in the flutes. This sets the kettle-drum to growling, and while it keeps up its rumbling for twenty-six measures, the scattered forces are called back one by one until they unite in the opening theme fortissimo.

In the Adagio the following measure, given out by the second violins —

is used by the composer as the chief design for his accompaniment throughout. A lovely air —

enters at the second measure, marked "cantabile," sung by the violins. It is repeated in the wind instruments, to which is also given the greater part of the second phrase. Just at the close the opening motive claims its right for the first time as a solo for the kettle-drum.

The Minuet differs in its form somewhat from any of Beethoven's former third movements, inasmuch as it is divided into five sections instead of three. The principal motive shows what care Beethoven bestowed upon these movements. The jostling, pushing effect of the first part of the opening phrase, offset by the sweeping legato answer, is all he needed for the Minuet proper; but how wonderfully these means are employed when we come to look at their distribution, as far as harmony and color are concerned! The Trio consists of a short phrase for the wind instruments, interrupted by a playful remark of the violins—

repeated on three ascending steps, with a short trill toward the end imparting a peculiar elegance to the dainty dialogue. The final repeat of the Minuet proper winds up with the following:

The last movement starts off merrily with the violins:

followed by a figure of limited compass. The close is playfully dramatic. After a general call to order, followed by a pause of one measure, the first violins make their adieux, answered by the bassoon and finally by the violas. At last all rush off helter-skelter, shouting fortissimo:

Symphony No. 5, in C Minor. Op. 67

1. Allegro con brio.
2. Andante con moto.
3. Allegro (Scherzo).
4. Allegro. Presto.

The Fifth Symphony was finished in 1808, although its composition had occupied Beethoven's attention for many years before. At its first performance, at Vienna, it was numbered on the program as the Sixth; and the Pastoral appeared as the Fifth. Both were finished in the same year, but the priority of the C minor is clearly established by Beethoven's own numbering in the autograph.

The C minor Symphony is probably the best known and most admired of the nine, perhaps because it is the most human in its qualities. Beethoven himself has left us a clew to its meaning, namely, that it pictures the struggle of the individual with Fate, the alternations of hope and despair, and the final triumph. In speaking of the first four notes of the opening movement, Beethoven said, some time after he had finished the symphony: "So pocht das Schicksal an die Pforte" ("Thus Fate knocks at the door").

In the Fifth, as in the Third Symphony, we find that concentration of thought and labor which makes these two musical poems so all-powerful and overwhelming in their effect. It is not marked by a spontaneous flow of musical phrases lightly strung together, or by mere toying with musical forms; but each motive represents a concentrated essence of thought which, once heard, makes an indelible impression, and apparently admits of no change. We give only a few quotations, but bearing them in mind, the listener will be able to follow the development of this passionate outpouring of a passionate mind while brooding over its fate:

The holds at *a* occur frequently, as well as the abrupt chords leading up to a pause. The persistency with which the theme at *b* is repeated and carried upward in a steady crescendo, only to vent its rage in those terrible three notes, dropping into a third below and cut short by two abrupt chords, well depicts the persistent struggle of a great mind with the misfortunes of life. After the statement of inexorable fate by the horns at *c*, it almost seems as if the mortal were appealing for mercy; but the pitiless cry at the five-fold repetition of the four notes at *d* grows unendurable, and, stung to the quick, he hurls his defiance against the gods. A period of exhaustion characterizes a passage in which the winds alternate with the strings during thirty-two measures, in short chords ever drooping until roused again to life and strife by the motive at *c*, given in unison by the whole orchestra. The last motive, at *f*, may simply be described as a hammer and anvil.

Of the Andante we quote only the principal phrases:

The opening is given out by the violas and 'cellos, while the phrase at *b* is always started by the winds, breaking into a sudden fortissimo at *d* and enriched at every repeat by a more animated figure in the violins. The first phrase breathes sweet consolation, while the second points onward and upward, with a bold transition at *d* assuring the sufferer triumph and happiness. The measures preceding this outburst produce a thrilling effect by the use of the ominous ninth below the melody, which in the second violins and violas raises the ghost of the Fate motive of the first part with its three strokes indicated at *c*.

The Allegro Scherzo starts out with a timid question—

but in the answer it seems as if the youthful hero had grappled with the decrees of Fate and boldly turned the point of the weapon against his foe. The three strokes of the first movement which started on an up-beat are now defiantly turned into , and boldly carry the day. The second part of the Scherzo, in the key of C major, which represents the Trio, opens with a strong and boisterous passage in the 'cellos and basses, gradually reinforced by the violins, and carried to a joyful climax, from which a gradual decrescendo leads back into the first part.

After the hold the now victorious triple beat starts pianissimo in the clarinets and changes from instrument to instrument, but always pianissimo, as if intended thoroughly to repress any premature exultation. The kettle-drum finally takes up the beat, and for forty-eight measures persistently furnishes the rhythm. The violins begin an upward sweep, always pianissimo and in ever-widening intervals, until it reaches the dominant seventh chord, when with a short crescendo the jubilant march of the last Allegro, in the key of C major, common time, begins:

The upward sweep from the sixth measure, ending twice on the octave, is in its third repetition carried a third higher, as if breaking all bounds, and naturally flows into a dotted rhythmic figure which only increases the excitement. After a perfect whirl on the dominant chord of G for twenty measures, the violins having a tarantella-like figure in triplets, the movement is suddenly interrupted by an episode of fifty-four measures in triple time, recalling the Scherzo in its rhythm, but in reality only a prolongation of the dominant chord, which was cut short at its climax so as to make a more deliberate change at the repetition of the grand march of joy.

Symphony No. 6, in F (Pastoral). Op. 68

1. Allegro ma non troppo. (The Cheerful Impressions excited on arriving in the Country.)
2. Andante molto moto. (By the Brook.)
3. Allegro. (Peasants' Merrymaking.)
4. Allegro. (Thunder-storm.)
5. Allegretto. (The Shepherd's Song; Glad and Thankful Feelings after the Storm.)

The Pastoral Symphony was composed by Beethoven in 1808, and was first performed at a concert given in Vienna,

December 22 of the same year. The composer has left his own explanation prefixed to each movement. In the sketches it is entitled "Sinfonie caracteristica. Die Erinnerungen von dem Landleben" ("Symphony Characteristic. Memories of Country Life"), and the following note is appended: "Man überlässt dem Zuhörer sich selbst die Situationen auszufinden" ("The hearer must find out the situations for himself"). When the symphony was completed, however, Beethoven gave explicit descriptions of the meaning of each movement, prefaced, however, with the significant caution: "Mehr Ausdruck der Empfindung als Malerei" ("Rather expressive of sensations than painting") — or actual description.

This symphony, in fact, is the masterly expression of that happy and contented feeling which the lover of Nature experiences during a ramble in the country. The motives employed are apparently of the simplest kind, but demonstrate the evolution of intense thought. They are short and close in design, and to a great extent lean on the tones of the hunting horn. We quote a few that will attract the hearer's attention:

The first movement, of which the above are the themes, is an Allegro ma non troppo, and is in keeping with the general description we have given of the music.

The Andante molto moto gives voice to the listless dreaming of the wayfarer who is resting at the bank of the brook. The monotonous accompaniment, sustained through nearly the entire movement by the strings, is of a flowing figure, containing a gentle rise and return to its level. The first violins give out the principal melodic theme, while the wind instruments respond with the second phrase. Short figures abound, flitting about among the different instruments, sometimes in imitation, again in euphonious thirds or sixths, and at times a brief trill or the short snapping of pizzicato notes. Its effect is that of the evening air alive with songs of birds and the buzz of insects. In the last twelve measures of this movement, the composer even introduces the bird-songs — a proceeding which has been pronounced childish and utterly unworthy of Beethoven, but which to the unprejudiced listener seems to belong in its connection.

The third movement, representing the Minuet, introduces the purely human element. The first eight measures usher in the country people tripping briskly along. In the next phrase we approach the dance proper with its "band accompaniment." The minuet-like movement is interrupted by a short Tempo d'allegro, which seems like the change to another dance, though being rather more boisterous it comes to a close by two short pauses, as if to give the dancers a chance to catch their breaths before returning to the triple time of the Minuet closing the movement.

The next movement, an Allegro in A flat, is entitled "Thunder-storm," and brings before us the lowering sky, the distant rumbling of thunder, the sultry air, and the storm breaking forth in all its fury. It soon passes over, however. Without interruption, the closing measure leads into the last movement — the shepherd's song of joy, and his feeling of relief from the dangers of the tempest. The motives are formed from the representative intervals of the instruments chiefly used by shepherds, and move in the steps of the chord rather than in the successive notes of the scale, although the middle section of the movement brings the violins to the front with just such runs as were excluded from the first part, which more strictly represent the song of the shepherd. The movement closes with one of those dynamic contrasts in which Beethoven delighted. After the horn once more sings the principal theme—

softly, and while the violins are twining around it in a descending figure, the whole orchestra breaks in suddenly and without any preparation on the closing chord fortissimo, as indicated above.

Symphony No. 7, in A Major. Op. 92

1. Poco sostenuto. Vivace.
2. Allegretto.
3. Presto. Presto meno assai.
4. Finale. Allegro con brio.

The Seventh Symphony, which vies in popularity with the Fifth, was finished in the year 1812, and was first performed December 8, 1813, at a concert in Vienna. Of all the Beethoven symphonies, it is the most romantic, as well as the most happy. The composer left no clew to its meaning, though we know from his letters that he esteemed it as one of his best works. Richard Wagner, with his keen insight into the subjectivity of music, declares that it is the apotheosis of the dance, the ideal embodiment in tones of the bodily movement—a definition which admirably applies to the symphony, as nearly all its motives are ideally perfect dance rhythms.

The introduction is almost a movement in itself, and contains one of the happiest and most delicate phrases to be found anywhere in Beethoven's music, as follows:

This episode occurs twice, preceded and followed by ascending scales running through two octaves, which are significant for the very staccato manner in which they are given. The last part of the above quotation is reiterated during a short crescendo, and suddenly resolves into the note E, given out by all the instruments fortissimo and repeated during the remaining ten measures of the introduction and the first four bars of the following Vivace, in various rhythms. At the entrance of the new movement it has the dotted rhythm of the quail-call, which is the predominating feature of the whole movement:

The opening suggests the dancing along of a bevy of happy girls followed by a reckless plunge into hilarity. Sudden pianissimos followed by fortissimos, harmonic changes for which there is no time to prepare in the general rush — these are the characteristics of the first part. The ill-tempered outbreak at the end of this part is repeated at the beginning of the second, only the flutes scream a third higher than before; then a pause, and the violins move off again pianissimo, while the basses come in with a long scale in the same rhythm. The Coda contains one of those phrases which by their monotonous repeats partake somewhat of the nature of a pedal point; and on the other hand remind us of the peculiarity of Slavonic music, in which this monotonous repeat of one figure plays so characteristic a part. The basses support a steady crescendo from pianissimo to fortissimo during twenty-two measures with this figure:

The Allegretto, which takes the place of the slow movement, is built up on the following rhythmic figure: | ♩ ♫ | ♩ ♩ |. The melody of the first part moves within the interval of a third, and is of the simplest construction. The movement itself is constructed on a long crescendo as gradual as it is persistent, and irresistible in its natural strength. The second part opens with this lovely melody:

accompanied in triplets by the violins. A short interlude of staccato scales brings us back to the first theme, which is now worked up in the accompaniment in the style of a variation. Then the A major episode is repeated. The Coda, after a few sudden dynamic transitions, falls back on the original theme and dies away in a pianissimo.

The Scherzo, marked "Presto," opens with the simple device of moving through the intervals of the chord of F, but stamped by the master's hand with the form at *a:*

followed by a descending scale motive, *b*. The third motive, growing out of *c*, furnishes by the repetition of the half-steps the principal material for the middle section of the second part. The last four measures of the Presto dwell on a prolonged A held by all the instruments, bringing in some part of the orchestra throughout the whole Trio, which changes into the key of D major. This A, suspended in mid-air as it were, with only an occasional pulsation into the G sharp below, sheds an air of serenity over the whole which greatly enhances the restfulness of the melodic theme:

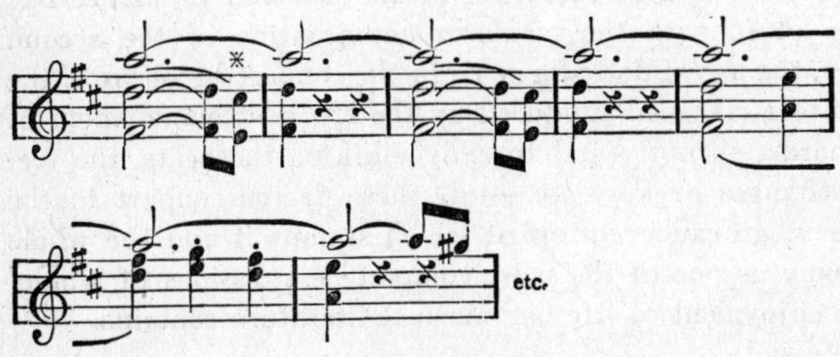

The second part contains a most peculiar effect for the second horn, which on a low A and G sharp in different rhythms for twenty-six measures leads to a fortissimo repeat of the main theme, the trumpets ringing out the sustained A, supported by the kettle-drums. An interlude leads back to the Presto. The Trio is then played again, followed by another repeat of the Presto and a short Coda, reminding one of the Scherzo in the Fourth Symphony.

The last movement, Allegro con brio, takes up the joyous strain of the first movement and opens with a whirling figure in the violins, supplemented by a figure accompanied by full, short strokes of the string instruments. It is in the dance rhythm throughout, justifying Wagner's characterization already quoted. Berlioz and Ambros call the symphony a rustic wedding; Marx, Moorish knighthood; Oulibishev, a masked ball, and Bischoff, a sequel to the Pastoral Symphony.

The following two motives complete the material for this movement:

The lightness and grace of the theme at *a* and the dance-like rhythm at *b*, with the mazurka accentuation of the second quarter, the use of dotted groups in the connecting phrases, the almost martial tread produced by the frequent employment of full chords, abruptly and forcibly marking the beats, the frequent changes of key, etc. — all these factors impart to the movement an exuberant spirit which stamps it and the whole symphony as one of the most complete expressions of whole-souled enjoyment of life our musical literature contains.

Symphony No. 8, in F. Op. 93

1. Allegro vivace e con brio.
2. Allegretto scherzando.
3. Menuetto e Trio.
4. Finale. Allegro vivace.

The Eighth Symphony was written in 1812 at Linz, whither Beethoven had repaired upon the advice of his physician for the benefit of his health. It was composed at a sad period of his life, for besides his sufferings from shattered health he was engaged in a most unpleasant lawsuit forced upon him by his unworthy sister-in-law and undertaken in the interest of a graceless nephew. Notwithstanding these depressing events the symphony is one of the brightest, most cheerful, and most humorous works that he ever conceived. He speaks of it himself in a letter as the "Kleine Sinfonie in F," not that it was little, but to distinguish it from the "Grosse Sinfonie in A" (the Seventh) composed in the same year.

As if serious preparation were unnecessary he plunges at

once into the work and opens the first Allegro with the main theme:

An intermediate phrase leads into the second theme which, containing a short ritardando, is then repeated in the wind instruments, and after a series of modulations runs into a motive for the full orchestra:

The first part closes with the following skipping figure:

which is in reality only an extension into the octave of the motive of *b*. The latter is frequently utilized during the second part in connection with the motive from the opening phrase, which is employed with all the art of the contrapuntist either in imitations or enlarged into longer phrases for the basses, which during seventy-six measures really dominate the melody and finally rest on the octave skip at *e*. Then follows a pianissimo passage, which leads in canon form through a crescendo to a hold, after which a Coda brings the first movement to a close.

The slow movement is again supplanted by an Allegretto scherzando. It is the well-known —

which depends on its staccato character and fine instrumentation for its daintiness, and has only one legato phrase in the whole movement.

The Minuet appears this time in its own true character, and develops the stately dance with its gliding figures to perfection. The third part, or Trio, has this opening for the horns —

The Minuet is then repeated.

The last part opens with this tremulous figure for the violins, pianissimo:

The second theme is the following cantilena:

After a jubilant fortissimo about the middle of the movement, the music is interrupted by frequent rests, the triplet figure gliding past, stopping short, then rushing on again to a second hold, after which a new design is introduced in a descending scale in the strings, and is opposed in the wind instruments by a similar scale, ascending. These scales move quietly and pianissimo in semibreves, while the triplet figure is flitting about here and there until the scale motive is brought in, fortissimo. The main themes are once more hastily touched, and the movement exhausts itself in a long repetition of the final chord, as if trying to reach the longed-for rest.

Symphony No. 9, in D Minor (Choral). Op. 125

I. Instrumental

1. Allegro ma non troppo, un poco maestoso.
2. Scherzo, molto vivace; Trio, presto.
3. Adagio molto e cantabile.
4. Recitative, Presto; Allegro ma non troppo, etc.
5. Allegro assai.

II. Vocal

1. Recitative.
2. Quartette and Chorus: Allegro assai.
3. Tenor Solo and Chorus: Allegro assai vivace; Alla marcia.
4. Chorus: Andante maestoso.
5. Chorus: Allegro energico, sempre ben marcato.
6. Quartette and Chorus: Allegro ma non tanto.
7. Chorus: Prestissimo.

The Ninth, or "Choral," Symphony, written in 1823, the last of the immortal group, stands prominently out among all other works of its class by its combination of voices and instruments. Before its composition, Beethoven had been preparing the way for such a union. In the Choral Fantasie, written in 1808, he advanced upon the idea by employing a chorus in the Finale; but in the Choral Symphony he made a still bolder advance, and introduced a chorus with variations on a colossal scale. There is a striking resemblance between the two in the choral parts, and Beethoven himself describes the symphony as being "in the style of the Pianoforte Choral Fantasie, but on a far larger scale." Schiller's "An die Freude," the "Ode to Joy," was selected by Beethoven for the Finale.

The symphony is without introduction proper. There is a prologue introducing the first subject, "always pianissimo," in which the instruments seem to be feeling their way. It begins with an incomplete chord, 'cello, second violin, and horns, the first violins following *sotto voce*. After a repetition the real work begins. Against the background of the second violins and 'cellos, strengthened by the sustained tones of the horns, clarinets, and flutes, the violins, tenors, and contrabasses appear in broken phrases. Then the wind instruments come in one by one, and at last with a mighty crescendo the whole orchestra in unison sweeps into the first subject:

The great crescendo dies away, but the titanic crash is renewed again and again whenever the theme occurs. The second subject—

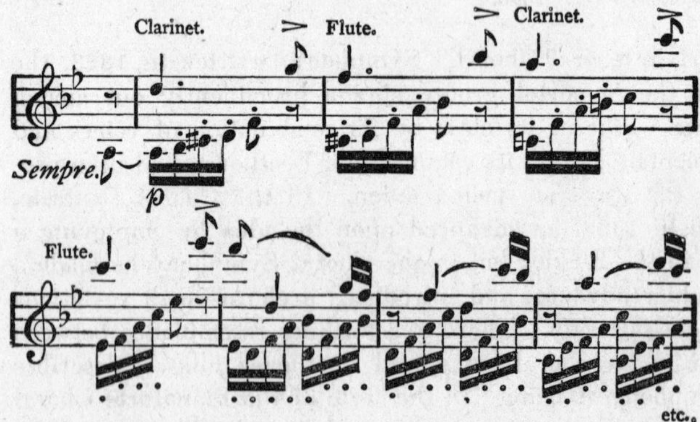

is in striking contrast with the first, being tranquil and gentle in its inception. At its conclusion, the violins announce another energetic phrase, at last reaching an episode from which is developed a brief but very melodious passage followed by a second episode for the strings in unison, that leads on to the close of the first part of the movement, ending fortissimo and in unison. This division is not repeated. In its place Beethoven proceeds with the working out of his materials, the orchestral parts moving independently of each other and frequently opposed, yet forming well-developed parts of a grand whole, until the Coda is reached. The old subjects and episodes are worked up with profound skill; but before he closes, a new and darker subject appears in the strings, companion to a threnody sung by the reeds, the strings repeating a chromatic passage through and above which is heard the wail of the oboes, until the movement closes with a powerful outburst.

After twelve bars of prelude the orchestra is fairly launched into the Scherzo, as follows:

in which all the instruments successively join with spirited and brilliant effect. The wind instruments follow with a second theme, accompanied by the strings, which, after repetition, leads up to still other tuneful motives given out by the winds. The Scherzo closes pianissimo, but at last the horns and trombones joyfully announce the Trio with its charming pastoral opening:

A vivacious subject for violas and 'cellos follows the first, and then the horns join in the principal theme until the Coda is reached, in which the whole orchestra enters with the utmost joyousness.

The third movement changes to celestial rest and serenity, and is among the noblest, purest, and most grandly beautiful hymns of joy the great master has written. It is made up of two distinct subjects differing in every musical respect, which are alternately developed until the second disappears. The first for delicious repose and ethereal sweetness can hardly be excelled in the whole realm of musical art. It is taken by the quartet of strings with interludes by the clarinets and horns, as follows:

After the strings have finished the melody, and the first part of the movement comes to a close, the time changes as well as the key, and the second violins and tenors announce the following subject in unison:

The transition from this serene movement to the Finale is a startling one. The wind instruments and drums, reinforced by the double-bassoon, break out in a most clamorous fanfare, which is interrupted by a recitative passage for the double-basses. Again the recitative is heard, and again the clamor; but at last there is an instant's hush. The opening bars of the first three movements appear, alternating with recitative, but these evidently are not wanted. At last the final theme is foreshadowed, quietly and almost timidly, until the 'cellos and basses vigorously and unmistakably give it out in the setting of the "Hymn of Joy":

Next the violas and 'cellos take the theme, then the first violins, and at last the whole orchestra in full force. After its variation, the ominous clamor which introduced the Presto is heard again. This time it is not interrupted by the basses, but by the solo barytone intoning the recitative ("O Brothers, these Tones no longer! Rather let us join to sing in cheerful measures a Song of Joyfulness"). The same voice sings the Hymn, accompanied by the oboes and clarinets, and is followed by the chorus, at first without the sopranos, and alternating with the solo quartet ("Hail thee, Joy, from Heaven descending, Daughter from Elysium!").

Now the orchestra resounds with martial strains in which the percussion instruments are used with powerful effect, introducing the tenor solo, with chorus, in a variation of the theme, "Joyful like her Sons so glorious." The next number is also for chorus, and its solemnity and religious sentiment finely contrast with the martial clang of its predecessor. It is at first given out by the male voices, the female voices following ("Millions, loving, I embrace you"). Following this comes a chorus full of spirit, with a lively accompaniment, based upon the two related themes that have been employed ("Hail thee, Joy, from Heaven descending, Daughter from Elysium," etc.). The solo quartet again intones the Hymn, alternating with chorus ("Hail thee, Daughter from Elysium, thine Enchantments bind together"). The time is gradually accelerated to a Prestissimo, and voices and orchestra in full volume close the work with the triumphant shout:

"Millions, loving, I embrace you,
All the world this kiss I send," etc.

The Fidelio Overtures

Beethoven's only opera, "Fidelio," was first produced in Vienna, November 20, 1805, under the title of "Leonora," with the overture now known as "Leonora No. 2." Subsequently the opera was shortened and produced with a new overture, the "Leonora No. 3." After a few performances it was withdrawn, but in 1806, anticipating its production under the name of "Fidelio," he wrote a third overture, usually called "Leonora No. 1." The performance did not take place however, but in 1814 a revision of the opera was given in its present form as "Fidelio," with an entirely new overture. The chronological sequence of these overtures is as follows: Leonora No. 2 in C, op. 72, 1805; Leonora No. 3 in C, op. 72, 1806; Leonora No. 1 in C, op. 138, 1807; Fidelio in E, op. 72, 1814. To avoid confusion, the overtures will be considered in this order.

Leonora Overture No. 2. Op. 72

The overture played at the first performance of "Fidelio" was the "Leonora No. 2," as already stated. Its principal numbers are an Adagio introduction, in which Florestan's aria ("In the Spring Days of Youth") from the second act appears; an Allegro containing the principal themes of the "Leonora No. 3," with the two trumpet calls; an Adagio episode reproducing the Florestan aria, which eventually gives way to a new theme developed in the violins and leading up to a stirring, vigorous Coda and Finale. It is stated by some authorities that the overture was withdrawn because the wind instrument parts were found to be too difficult. Others, however, are of opinion that after the first performance of the opera Beethoven was dissatisfied because the overture did not clearly express his ideas. However this may be, it is certain that he recast it, condensed the leading subjects, added fresh themes, and made a new overture, known as "Leonora No. 3."

Leonora Overture No. 3. Op. 72

The title-page of this majestic overture, which is a model for all dramatic preludes, bears the inscription, "Ouverture à grand orchestre de l'opera 'Leonore,' par L. van Beethoven." It opens with an Adagio in C major, fortissimo, in full orchestra, followed by a scale passage which some critics conjecture describes the descent into the gloomy depths of Florestan's dungeon. Following this passage, the clarinet and bassoon sing Florestan's dungeon aria, "In the Springtime of Youth," with string accompaniment. Immediately mysterious preludings are heard in the strings, accompanied by lighter work in the flutes and first violins and bits from the Florestan theme given out by the basses. A short climax is followed by an outburst of the full orchestra, leading to the Allegro. It opens pianissimo, with the first theme announced by the first violins and 'cellos in octaves. Its development leads to a fortissimo in which the theme is elaborated at considerable length. The second theme is introduced in the horns, thence passing to the first violins and flute. As the development draws to a close a climax is reached, after which ensues a dramatic episode of great power, in which the trumpet calls each time announce the approaching deliverance, followed by a fervid and impressive song of thanksgiving. The third section of the overture opens piano, with a flute solo. A crescendo follows, after which the theme is repeated fortissimo and developed most elaborately. The second theme now reappears, followed by development of a figure from the first theme, leading to the Coda, and closing the overture with an overwhelming outburst of gladness and triumph.

Leonora Overture No. 1. Op. 138

The Leonora Overture No. 1, is a posthumous work. As it is almost entirely unknown in the modern concert-room its analysis becomes unnecessary. After its completion Beethoven had doubts of its effectiveness, and accordingly tested it with a small orchestra. It was much too light for the opera, and in consequence it was laid aside and was not played in public during the composer's lifetime, its first performance having taken place in Vienna in 1828, and Beethoven died in 1827. The composer gave it the title of "Characteristic Overture in C." In its general construction it resembles the Fidelio Overture in E, op. 72.

Fidelio Overture. Op. 72

The libretto of "Fidelio" was revised and the score remodeled in 1814. It was Beethoven's original intention to revise the Overture No. 1 for it, but he ultimately changed his purpose and wrote the overture known as the "Fidelio." It was played for the first time at the Kärnthnerthor Theater, Vienna, May 23, 1814. The overture opens with a short unison Allegro in the string and wind instruments, followed by an Adagio in the horns and clarinet. The opening measures are then repeated and the Adagio reappears, the horn theme being taken in the wind instruments. After development the theme returns in the wood winds, and again appears for the horn, leading to the main Allegro of the overture. The wind instruments sound a crescendo chord and the first theme is outlined by the second horn, answered by clarinet, and then developed by full orchestra. The strings give out the second theme, which is briefly treated. In the closing section of the overture the first theme is heard in the horns, accompanied by violin passages. At the conclusion of the Allegro development the Adagio episode returns, leading to the Presto Coda, in which a familiar phrase from the first theme is worked up to a climax of exultation closing an overture which has been called "an example of perfect beauty." Of the four overtures, however, the No. 3 will always remain an example of supreme beauty and symmetry as well as of dramatic power.

Overture to Prometheus. Op. 43

The Prometheus Overture was written for the ballet of the same name, produced for the first time at the Imperial Hof Theater, Vienna, in 1801, and announced as "'Die Geschöpfe des Prometheus' ('The Creations of Prometheus'), an heroic-allegorical ballet in two acts." The overture opens with a brief but impressive Adagio, followed by a melody for oboe. A slow movement leads to an Allegro, opening with a quick passage in the first violins, accompanied by the other strings. After a vigorous repeat the second subject appears in the wind instruments. The theme is briefly treated and followed by some vigorous passages. The violin theme repeats and leads to an impressive subject in the basses. The themes are then repeated in order and a stirring Coda closes the overture.

Overture to Coriolanus. Op. 62

The overture to "Coriolanus" was written in 1807 and was first publicly performed in Vienna in December of the same year. It was not composed as a prelude to Shakespeare's tragedy of "Coriolanus," but to a drama by the German poet, Heinrich Josef von Collin, to whom the overture is dedicated. The story, only one passage of which is illustrated in the overture, follows history, the main incidents being the alliance which the defiant Roman patrician, Coriolanus, made against the city after his banishment, the pleading of his mother, wife, and children that he should return to his allegiance, his abandonment of the allies, and his tragic death.

The overture is written in a single movement and without an introduction. It opens with a unison in the strings, followed by a sharply sounded chord in full orchestra. After a double repetition and two more chords, the principal theme is announced, indicative of the heroic character of Coriolanus and the spirit of unrest which has possessed him. It is given out by the violins and violas and after a somewhat brief development is followed by a beautiful second theme which typifies the gentler and tenderer attributes. Later on, a third theme enters, a fugue in the violins worked up with an arpeggio in the violas and 'cellos, the development of which closes the first section of the movement. The second consists of a repetition of the same materials with some variations. The development leads to an intensely passionate and dramatic Coda, descriptive of the death of Coriolanus. There have been few, if any, more effective finales than the tragic ending of this overture, with its fragmentary allusion to the opening theme, its gradual ebbing away, and, at the last, those three soft notes which clearly are the last pulsations of the dying hero.

Overture to Egmont. Op. 84

The overture and incidental music to Goethe's "Egmont" were written by Beethoven in the years 1809-1810. The plot of the drama follows the historical narrative of the life of the Count of Egmont, the Flemish nobleman, who, although a Catholic, opposed the government which Philip sought to establish in the Netherlands, and became one of the associates of William of Orange in his struggle for Netherlandish liberty. By a treacherous conspiracy on the part of the infamous Duke of Alva, he was captured and executed, September 9, 1567.

The overture opens with a short Andante introduction, followed by a theme in Sarabande tempo given out in full harmony by the strings. Wood winds and strings reply in a subdued strain, leading to a fortissimo in full orchestra, followed by an impressive repetition of portions of the Sarabande. The wood wind passages return again, followed by a new passage, pianissimo in the first violins, accompanied by a tremolo in the other strings and a repetition of the Sarabande in the basses. The Allegro, or main section of the overture, opens with a crescendo, at the close of which the strings give out the first theme. Then follows passage work, leading to the second theme, bearing close relation to the Sarabande, which is given out fortissimo by the strings. The development leads to a tremendous climax. The Coda is composed of entirely new material. The close is a jubilant, mighty fanfare in full orchestra.

Overture to King Stephen. Op. 117

In 1811 the managers of the New Theater at Pesth commissioned the poet Kotzebue to prepare a trilogy, based upon Hungarian historical subjects, suitable for the occasion of its opening, and engaged Beethoven to compose the vocal and instrumental music to accompany it. Both poet and composer accepted the task. The full title of Beethoven's score is "King Stephen, Hungary's first Benefactor, a Prologue in one act by Kotzebue, Music by Ludwig van Beethoven, written for the Opening of the New Theater in Pesth, February 9, 1812."

The overture commences with four calls in the trumpets, horns, bassoons, and strings, followed by a march theme announced by the flute, accompanied by the wood winds, horns, and strings, pizzicato. The march is interrupted by four more calls, and then is resumed, leading to the main section of the overture. A theme of a martial character begins in the wood winds and horns. After its development, a second theme is introduced, which is the first phrase of the vocal theme in the finale of the Ninth Symphony, showing how persistently Beethoven was haunted by the ideas which finally were worked out in the Choral Symphony. The march theme then returns, and the two themes of the Presto are brilliantly developed. A stirring Coda brings the overture to its close.

Overture, The Consecration of the House. Op. 124

The overture "Consecration of the House" is in reality the second overture to "The Ruins of Athens." The success of that allegory at the opening of the New Theater in Pesth led to an adaptation of the same play for the opening of the Josephstadt Theater in Vienna, October 3, 1822. Beethoven revised the music and added a final chorus with violin solo and ballet, besides substituting the new overture for the original one. It is also known as the "Overture in Handel's Style."

The overture opens with an introduction set to the rhythm of a stately festal march, as if heard in the distance. As the imaginary procession approaches nearer, the march intensifies in distinctness and volume, closing with trumpet fanfares and kettle-drum beats announcing the arrival. An imitation passage follows, describing the hurrying and excitement of the crowd by runs in the bassoon, extending to the violins. The trumpets and drums resume, leading to an interlude connecting with the body of the overture an Allegro in fugato style. The Allegro is long and devoted entirely to the working out of the theme, both in single and double counterpoint, the theme appearing in the first violins, flute, and oboe, and a counter theme in the second violins and clarinets, the whole coming to a most brilliant and effective close.

Choral Fantasie in C Minor. Op. 80

[For Piano, Orchestra, and Chorus]

1. Adagio (Piano).
2. Finale, Allegro.
   a. Allegro (Orchestra).
   b. Meno Allegro (Piano and Orchestra).
   c. Allegretto, ma non troppo (Chorus).

Beethoven's sketch-book shows that some of the materials for the Choral Fantasie were collected as early as 1800, though it was not given until December 22, 1808, when Beethoven himself produced it. It is written in two general sections; an

Adagio and Allegro, for piano solo, orchestra, solo quartet, and chorus. While the work is very beautiful and effective in itself, it derives special interest from its being the prototype of the Choral Symphony. The Fantasie was first published in 1811, under the title of "Fantasie für das Pianoforte, mit Begleitung des ganzen Orchesters und Chor" ("Fantasie for pianoforte with accompaniment of full orchestra and chorus"), and was dedicated to Maximilian Joseph, king of Bavaria. The poem which forms the subject of the Finale was written by Kuffner, and is devoted to the praise of music.

The Adagio with which the work opens is a fantasie for piano alone, after which the Finale begins with an Allegro in C minor, the opening theme of which is given out pianissimo by the basses in a very grave and dignified manner and subsequently developed in canon form in the violins. The oboes and horns now introduce a new theme which is taken up by the piano with accompaniment of the horns, the melody being adapted from one of Beethoven's songs ("Seufzer eines Ungeliebten"). First the piano and then the other instruments repeat this theme with variations, after which the entire orchestra brings it to a close in firm and stately style. A short phrase by the piano preludes a development of the first section of the melody through an Allegro, an Adagio, and a march tempo, at the end of which the piano introduces a new phrase closing with an arpeggio. A genuine contest ensues between the piano and the basses, which comes to an end as the wind instruments give out the leading theme, which is first taken up by the solo voices with piano accompaniment and then by full chorus and orchestra, bringing the work to a brilliant and powerful close.

Oratorio, The Mount of Olives. Op. 85

Beethoven wrote but one oratorio, "Christus am Oelberge" ("Christ on the Mount of Olives"). It was begun in 1800 and finished during the following year. The text is by Huber, and was written, with Beethoven's assistance, in fourteen days.

The first performance of the work in its entirety took place at Vienna, April 5, 1803, at the Theater an der Wien.

The oratorio is written for three solo voices, Jesus, Peter, and a Seraph, and chorus and orchestra. The narrative opens with the agony in the garden, followed by the chant of a Seraph reciting the divine goodness and foretelling the salvation of the righteous. In the next scene Jesus learns His fate from the Seraph, yields Himself to approaching death, and welcomes it. The soldiers enter in pursuit, and a tumult ensues as the Apostles find themselves surrounded. Peter draws his sword and gives vent to his indignation; but is rebuked both by Jesus and the Seraph, and together they conjure him to be silent and endure whatever may happen. The soldiers, discovering Jesus, rush upon Him and bind Him. The disciples express their apprehension that they too will suffer; but Jesus uncomplainingly surrenders Himself, and a chorus of rejoicing completes the work.

The score opens with an Adagio introduction for instruments which is of a very dramatic character. The first number is a recitative and aria for tenor, sung by Jesus ("All my soul within Me shudders"), and is simple and touching in expression. The Seraph follows with a scene and aria ("Praise the Redeemer's Goodness"), concluding with a jubilant obligato with chorus ("O triumph, all ye Ransomed!"). The next number is an elaborate duet between Jesus and the Seraph ("On Me then fall Thy heavy Judgment"). In a short recitative passage, Jesus welcomes death; and then ensues one of the most powerful numbers in the work, the chorus of soldiers in march time ("We surely here shall find Him"), interspersed with the cries of the people demanding His death, and the lamentations of the Apostles. At the conclusion of the tumult a dialogue ensues between Jesus and Peter ("Not unchastised shall this audacious Band"), which leads up to a trio between Jesus, Peter, and the Seraph, with chorus ("O, Sons of Men, with Gladness"). The closing number, a chorus of angels ("Hallelujah, God's almighty Son"), is introduced with a short but massive symphony leading to a jubilant burst of "Hallelujah," which finally resolves itself into a glorious fugue. In all sacred music it is difficult to find a choral number which can surpass it in majesty or power.

Missa Solennis in D Major. Op. 123

The immortal "Missa Solennis" of Beethoven occupied him three years in composition. He had intended it to be sung at the installation of Archduke Rudolph as Bishop of Olmutz, in 1820, but it was finished too late and its first complete performance took place in Russia. The Mass has the five principal divisions, the Kyrie, Gloria, Credo, Sanctus and Agnus Dei. The Kyrie begins with a majestic introduction by orchestra and organ. After a pause, the strings introduce a phrase and after a few bars the chorus with organ and full orchestra intone the Kyrie three times, with solo voices making a solemn appeal. The "Christe eleison," based upon the Scripture motives, leads to a new movement, introduced by orchestra and then taken successively by soloists and chorus. The Kyrie then returns.

The opening theme of the Gloria is one of sacred enthusiasm. It is first given out by organ and orchestra, then taken up by one section of the chorus after the other, all at last uniting in a unison, "In Excelsis Deo." As it comes to a tranquil close, the basses, followed by the whole chorus, sing the "et in Terra Pax." The Gloria theme is heard again in the orchestra, followed by the "Laudamus Te" sung in unison. After a pause the chorus chants the "Adoramus" and the basses in both orchestra and chorus intone the "Glorificamus Te." The beautiful "Gratias agimus" follows successively by solo tenor, the other parts and chorus. The Gloria motive returns and leads to an impressive choral climax, "Pater omnipotens." The "Qui tollis" which shortly follows and the "Quoniam Tu solus sanctus," by the tenors and "Quoniam Tu solus Dominus" are followed by a mighty fugue which closes the Gloria with the full power of organ, orchestra and chorus.

The Credo, preceded by a short symphonic passage, is announced in three sections of the chorus successively and closes with a fugue on the words "Et Vitam venturi," followed by a majestic Coda. The Sanctus opens with an orchestral introduction followed by the movements "Pleni sunt Coeli" and "Osanne," the latter leading to a prelude which prepares the way for the beautiful Benedictus. At the last measure of the Benedictus a violin solo with flute accompaniment begins, leading to the chorus. The basses give out the Benedictus, the violin continuing. The soloists also take up the theme, and the movement comes to a close with the soloists, chorus and orchestra intoning the theme.

The Agnus Dei is sombre in color, and its expression very intense. The "Dona nobis Pacem" is extremely melodious, but the flow of the melody is soon interrupted by the rolling of drums and the ring of trumpets. The alto soloist declaims the Agnus Dei. The drums and trumpets are again heard. The tenor and soprano soloists repeat the appeal. The chorus shouts "Miserere nobis," but the tumult soon passes and the original theme returns. A martial symphonic passage follows and at last the "Missa Solennis" closes beautifully and restfully.

BERLIOZ

1803–1869

Romeo and Juliet

[Dramatic symphony, with choruses, solos, chant and prologue in choral recitative]

"ROMEO AND JULIET," entitled as above by Berlioz, was written in 1839. The work opens with a fiery introduction, representing the combats and tumults of the two rival houses of Capulet and Montague, and the intervention of the Prince. It is followed by a choral recitative for four altos, tenors and basses ("Long smouldering Hatreds"), with which is interwoven a contralto solo ("Romeo too is there"), the number closing with a passionate chorus ("The Revels now are o'er"). A beautiful effect is made at this point by assigning to the alto voice two couplets ("Joys of first Love") which are serious in style but very rich in melody. A brief bit of choral recitative and a few measures for tenor — Mercutio's raillery — lead up to a dainty scherzetto for tenor solo and small chorus ("Mab! bright Elf of Dreamland"), and a short choral passage brings this scene to a close.

The second scene, which is for orchestra only, an impressive declamatory phrase developing into a tender melody, representing the sadness of Romeo and set in tones against the brilliant dance music in the distance accompanying the revel of the Capulets, is one of the most striking effects Berlioz has accomplished, and illustrates his astonishing command of instrumentation.

The third scene represents Capulet's garden in the stillness of night, the young Capulets passing through it, bidding each other adieu and repeating snatches of the dance music. As their strains die away in the distance the balcony scene between Romeo and Juliet is given by the orchestra alone in a genuine love-poem full of passion and sensuousness.

The fourth scene is also given to the orchestra, and is a setting of Mercutio's description of Queen Mab. It is a Scherzo, intensely rapid in its movement and almost ethereal in its dainty, graceful rhythm. The instrumentation is full of subtle effects, particularly in the romantic passages for the horns.

In the fifth scene we pass from the tripping music of the fairies to the notes of woe. It describes the funeral procession of Juliet, beginning with a solemn march in fugue style, at first instrumental, with occasional entrances of the voices in monotone, and then vocal ("O mourn, O mourn, strew choicest Flowers"), the monotone being assigned to the instruments. It preludes a powerful orchestral scene representing Romeo's invocation, Juliet's awakening, and the despair and death of the lovers.

The Finale is mainly for double chorus, representing the quarrel between the Montagues and Capulets in the cemetery and the final reconciliation through the intercession of Friar Laurence, whose declamatory solos are very striking, particularly the air, "Poor Children mine, let me mourn you."

Symphonie Fantastique. Op. 14

1. Adagio. (Reveries and Passions.)
2. Le Bal. (The Ball.)
3. Scène aux Champs. (Scene in the Fields.)
4. Marche du Supplice. (Journey to Execution.)
5. Songe d'un Nuit de Sabbat. (Dream in a Witches' Sabbath Night.)

The "Symphonie Fantastique," also entitled by its composer "Episode in the Life of an Artist," was written by Berlioz in 1829. Every movement of this strange work is prefaced by a regular program and accompanied by notes which call the hearer's attention beforehand to the scenes which the music is intended to describe. To describe the symphony it is hardly necessary to do more than to tell the bizarre story of an episode in the life of an artist, which is a very nightmare of passion.

In the opening movement he introduces a young musician madly in love with a woman of ideal perfection, represented by a musical figure which he calls the "idée fixe." The whole movement is based upon this "fixed idea," representing the vague longings of love. The theme haunts the music as the vision of the ideal woman haunts the artist.

The second movement introduces us to a ball, but even in the midst of the festivity, and listening to the sensual strains of the waltz, the face of the loved one haunts the artist. From a technical point of view this movement shows the great skill of the composer in the symphonic treatment of a waltz rhythm, but the brilliant dance music is ever and anon interrupted as the melody which belongs to the loved one asserts itself through the bewitching strains.

The third movement, "Scène aux Champs," is one of quiet pastoral beauty, though it gathers gloom as it proceeds and closes in ominous darkness and silence. The lover is in the fields at evening and hears the shepherds' answering songs, sung by the oboe and horn. The charm of the spot, its peaceful repose, the gentle approach of evening, and the rustic chants call up the vision of the loved one and inspire him with hope, which soon clouds over again as darkness comes on. One of the shepherds repeats his song, but the other does not answer. The low rumble of a storm is heard in the distance, and the despairing lover gives way to melancholy.

In the fourth movement, "Marche du Supplice," persuaded that his affection is not reciprocated, the frenzied lover takes poison with the intention of suicide, but the drug instead of killing him only produces a stupor filled with wild hallucinations. He imagines that he has killed his mistress and is the witness of his own execution. The march to the scaffold begins amid the chanting of the "Dies Iræ," the tolling of bells, and the mournful roll of muffled drums. Even the rush of the multitude and the tramp of their feet are heard in this realistic music. The fatal melody, however, does not leave him even here. It is constantly heard in the gloom until it is cleft in twain by the sharp stroke of the headsman's axe.

The last movement, which is really a continuation of the fourth, pictures the lover in the midst of the witches and demons who have gathered to witness his burial, which takes place accompanied by a wild orgy reminding one of the chorus of demons in the composer's "Damnation of Faust."

Harold in Italy. Op. 16

1. Harold aux Montagnes. Scènes de Mélancolie, de Bonheur, et de Joie. (Harold in the Mountains. Scenes of Melancholy, Happiness and Joy.)
2. Marche de Pèlerins, chantant la Prière du Soir. (March of Pilgrims, singing the Evening Prayer.)
3. Sérénade d'un Montagner des Abruzzes á sa Maitresse. (Serenade of a Mountaineer of the Abruzzi to his Mistress.)
4. Orgie des Brigands. Souvenir des Scènes Précédentes. (Orgy of Brigands. Recall of preceding Scenes.)

"Harold in Italy" was written in 1834, and first produced at the Paris Conservatory, November 23 of the same year. The story of the symphony is the story of what Harold witnesses in his wanderings. The restless, melancholy exile beholds Nature in her loveliest as well as her most majestic aspects, but they fail to cheer him. He is in the midst of a band of happy and devoted pilgrims journeying along to worship at some shrine, but religion no more than Nature can calm his troubled spirit. He witnesses a mountaineer serenading his mistress beneath her window, but the simple love-scene has no charm for him. In despair he joins the bandits, and rushes into one of their orgies, where at last all his better thoughts and nobler feelings are lost in a vortex of dissipation and frenzy.

The first movement ("In the Mountains") is divided into two sections, an Adagio expressive of Harold's melancholy, and a strongly contrasting Allegro signifying his transient feeling of happiness and joy. The Adagio opens with a characteristic phrase in the basses and 'cellos, to which the bassoon adds a theme in chromatic progression. This is relieved by a second theme, at first taken by the wood winds and then developed by the viola, typifying the reflective character of Harold, as it does throughout the rest of the work. The harps and clarinets accompany the monologue as it moves on toward the second section of the movement. Four times the viola seeks to make the change, and at last seizes the joyous melody of the Allegro, and the music flows on to the close brightly and gracefully, richly colored, and always original and characteristic.

The second movement ("March of the Pilgrims") is one of the most charming numbers Berlioz has written. The march themes are very simple, but the composer has invested them with a peculiar charm by their sweetness and grace as well as by the richness of the instrumentation. The music is also very descriptive, and a pleasing effect is made by crescendo and diminuendo as the pilgrims approach, file past, and slowly disappear in the distance. The pretty scene closes with an evening prayer.

The third movement ("The Serenade") is a fit sequel to the second in its general character. It opens in genuine pastoral style, the horn and oboe giving a Tyrolean effect to the music and leading up to a quaint and very refined serenade in slower time. But even in the serenade of the mountaineer, as in the march of the pilgrims, the unrestful and sad plaint of the viola is heard.

In the last movement ("The Orgy") Berlioz gives free rein to his audacity and love of the horrible, and ends the career of Harold, like that of the artist in the "Symphonie Fantastique," in a wild and crashing hurly-burly of sound intended to picture a foul and frenzied orgy. The movement opens with reminiscences of preceding themes, woven together with great skill. Among them is the Harold theme, announcing his presence, and the march of the pilgrims taken by two violins and 'cellos in the wings, indicating their passage in the distance. As if Harold had turned for a moment and longingly listened to the beautiful melody, wishing that he were with them, the viola replies to it. It is only a snatch, however, for at once the furious orgy begins which drowns every reminiscence.

Overture to Les Francs Juges. Op. 3

In 1827 Berlioz, at that time struggling with poverty, debts, domestic troubles, and disappointed hopes, wrote an opera, "Les Francs Juges" ("The Vehmic Judges"). Berlioz himself called it "a hymn of despair," a fitting designation, as it depicts all of rage, as well as of piteous appeal for mercy, and black despair that the human heart can contain. The Francs Juges, like the German Vehmgerichte, were the vigilance committees and lynching mobs of the barbarous times when the laws were powerless. Edicts were issued in secret and mercilessly enforced. The penalty was always death.

The overture begins with an introduction, mainly in the strings, followed by a brief pianissimo passage, which leads to a majestic theme given out by the brasses. After elaboration a string passage enters for the violins. This is also elaborated, and during the elaboration is heard what may be called the Vehmic phrase of three notes, given out by the trombones and ophicleide with awful power. This is followed by the second subject, after which a passionate interlude, which suggests the despair of the accused, leads to the middle section, which opens with a chorale in the wind instruments, against a theme in the strings and blasts by the trombones and percussion instruments, full of fury and mystery. After a short interlude the second subject returns with counter themes in the 'cellos and flute. The tumult is renewed, the trombones sounding the ominous phrase already referred to. At last the din dies away and the second subject reappears, this time in fugal form. In the working up of this fugue and the subject-matter the whole orchestra engages in a fortissimo outbreak, which is continued until a short Coda brings the overture to a close.

Overture, Le Carnaval Romain. Op. 9

Berlioz's opera, "Benvenuto Cellini" met with an unfortunate reception when first performed in Paris in 1838. The

"Carnaval Romain," intended as an introduction to the second act, was written in 1843 and first performed the following year at a concert given by Berlioz in Paris. The principal theme is taken from the Saltarello, in the closing scene of the first act of the opera. The overture begins with this theme, given out by the violins with response at first in the flute, oboe, and clarinet, and then in the horns, bassoon, trumpet, and cornet. After a sudden pause and some light passage work in the strings, wood winds, and horns, the movement changes to a theme taken from an aria of Benvenuto's in the first act, given out by the English horn. The subdued melody is next taken by the violas, passing to the horns and violas. Interwoven with this romantic melody is heard a dance passage in the wood winds and brasses, also in the percussion instruments. Gradually the dance passage dies away, giving place to the Andante theme, but anon the time changes, and the strings begin the Saltarello, completing the main section of the overture. The entire development now runs on this movement with the Andante heard at intervals in contrast, and worked up in close harmony. The Saltarello dominates the Finale at a rushing pace. The overture is brilliant throughout and full of the gay, bustling scenes of the carnival.

Overture to King Lear. Op. 4

The overture to "King Lear," written in 1831, was inspired by Shakespeare's tragedy. It opens with an introduction setting forth a vigorous theme. A lighter one follows in the oboe with string accompaniment, next taken up by horns and trombones, the introduction closing with the first theme. The principal movement opens with a passionate theme followed by a tender melody in the oboe. The principal theme and a portion of the oboe melody are developed, leading to a recapitulation of the whole matter of the overture, variously treated, and a strenuous Coda closes the overture.

Overture to Benvenuto Cellini. Op. 23

The composition of an opera on Benvenuto Cellini, the great Italian artist and goldsmith, occurred to Berlioz as early as 1834, but he did not begin work on the overture until the end of 1837. "The strange career of Benvenuto Cellini," he wrote, "had made such an impression on me that I stupidly concluded that it would be both dramatic and interesting to other people. I therefore asked Léon de Wailly and Auguste Barbier to write me a libretto on it. I must own that even our friends thought it had not the elements essential to success, but it pleased me, and even now I cannot see that it is inferior to many others that are played daily."

The forebodings of Berlioz's friends were well justified by the failure which waited upon "Benvenuto Cellini" when the opera was produced at the Opéra, Paris, September 3, 1838. The overture evoked great applause, but the curtain had scarcely been raised upon the opening scene when the audience began to express its disapproval. Many left the theater; those who remained laughed derisively and some made noises in imitation of the cries of wild animals. Two more performances were given, but while there was no further demonstration, the theater remained empty.

The overture was published as a separate piece and dedicated by Berlioz to his friend Ernest Legouve, who had advanced him a sum of 2,000 francs whereby he might find leisure to complete the work. The opera as a whole was dedicated to the Grand Duchess of Weimar. The overture begins (Allegro deciso con impeto, 2-2 time). After twenty-two measures of this the time changes to Larghetto, 3-4 time, in which appears a pizzicato passage for the basses based upon the air from the third act, "A tous péchés pleine indulgence." The wood winds then bring forward a new idea which, in the opera, appears as the Harlequin's air in the carnival scene. This is taken up by the strings and there are suggestions of the Larghetto in the wood winds with a return to the Harlequin theme. This leads into the main movement, Allegro deciso con impeto, whose principal subject is heard in the wood winds with a syncopated accompaniment in the strings. A sonorous transitional passage leads to the second theme, in D major, first given to the wood winds and later taken up by the violins and violas. Development now takes place. The theme which opened the overture returns fortissimo and, later, the subject of the Larghetto recurs. It is this which brings the overture to an end.

F. B.

Requiem. Op. 5

In 1836 Berlioz was requested by M. de Gasparin, French Minister of the Interior, to write a requiem commemorating the victims of the July Revolution; but the work was not given to the public until 1837. It embraces ten numbers: I, Requiem and Kyrie ("Requiem æternam dona eis"); II, III, IV, V, and VI, including different motives taken from the hymn, "Dies Iræ"; VII, "Offertorium"; VIII, "Hostias et Preces"; IX, "Sanctus"; X, "Agnus Dei."

After a brief but majestic instrumental introduction, the voices enter upon the "Requiem" — a beautiful and solemn strain. The movement is built upon three melodies set to the words "Requiem æternam," "Tu decet Hymnus," and the "Kyrie," the accompaniment of which is very descriptive and characteristic. The "Kyrie" is specially impressive, the chant of the sopranos being answered by the tenors and basses in unison, the whole closing with a dirge-like movement by the orchestra.

The "Dies Iræ" is the most spirited as well as impressive number of the work. It is intensely dramatic in its effects; indeed, it might be called theatrical. The first part will always be remarkable for the orchestral arrangement. After the climax of the motive, "Quantus tremor est futurus," there is a pause which is significant by its very silence; it is the hush before the storm. Suddenly from either angle of the stage or hall, in addition to the principal orchestra in front, four smaller bands of trombones, trumpets, and tubas crash in with overwhelming power in the announcement of the terrors of the day of judgment. At its culmination the bass voices enter in unison upon the words "Tuba mirum," in the midst of another orchestral storm, which is still further heightened by an unusual number of kettle-drums. It is a relief when the storm has passed over, and we come to the next verse ("Quid sum miser"), for the basses and tenors, though mostly for the first tenors. It is a breathing spell of quiet delight and leads to the Andante number ("Rex tremendæ Majestatis"), which is sung fortissimo throughout, and accompanied with another tremendous outburst of harmonious thunder in crashing chords, which continues up to the last eight bars, when the voices drop suddenly from the furious fortissimo to an almost inaudible pianissimo on the words "Salve me." The next verse ("Quærens me") is an unaccompanied six-part chorus in imitative style, of very close harmony. The "Dies Iræ" ends with the "Lachrymosa," the longest and most interesting number in the work. It is thoroughly melodic, and is peculiarly strengthened by a pathetic and sentimental accompaniment, which, taken in connection with the choral part against which it is set, presents an almost inexhaustible variety of rhythms and an originality of technical effects which are astonishing. Its general character is broad and solemn, and it closes with a return to the "Dies Iræ," with full chorus and all the orchestras.

The next number is the "Offertorium," in which the voices are limited to a simple phrase of two notes, which is not changed throughout the somewhat long movement. It never becomes monotonous, however, so rich and varied is the instrumentation. The "Hostias et Preces," assigned to the tenors and basses, displays another of Berlioz's eccentricities, the accompaniment at the close of the first phrase being furnished by three flutes and eight tenor trombones. The "Sanctus," a tenor solo with responses by the sopranos and altos, is full of poetical, almost sensuous beauty, and is the most popular number in the work. It closes with a fugue on the words ("Hosanna in Excelsis"). The final number is the "Agnus Dei," a chorus for male voices, in which the composer once more employs the peculiar combination of flutes and tenor trombones. In this number he also returns to the music of the opening number, "Requiem æternam," and closes it with an "Amen," softly dying away.

The Damnation of Faust. Op. 24

The "Damnation of Faust, dramatic legend," as Berlioz calls it, was written in 1846. It is divided into four parts, the first containing three, the second four, the third six, and the fourth five scenes, the last concluding with an epilogue and the apotheosis of Marguerite. It was first produced in Paris in November, 1846, and had its first hearing in the United States, February 12, 1880.

The opening scene introduces Faust alone on the Hungarian plains at sunrise. He gives expression to his delight in a tender, placid strain ("The Winter has departed, Spring is here"). It is followed by an instrumental prelude of a pastoral character, in which are heard fragments of the roundelay of the peasants and of the fanfare in the Hungarian march, leading up to the "Dance of Peasants," a brisk, vivacious chorus ("The Shepherd donned his best Array"), beginning with the altos, who are finally joined by the sopranos, tenors, and basses in constantly accelerating time. The scene then changes to another part of the plain and discloses the advance of an army, to the brilliant and stirring music of the Rákoczy march.

The second part (Scene IV) discloses Faust alone in his chamber. He sings a soliloquy, setting forth his discontent with worldly happiness, and is about to drown his sorrow with poison, when he is interrupted by the Easter Hymn ("Christ is risen from the Dead"), a stately and jubilant six-part chorus, in the close of which he joins. As it comes to an end he continues his song ("Heavenly Tones, why seek me in the Dust?"), but is again interrupted by the sudden apparition of Mephistopheles, who mockingly sings ("Oh, pious Frame of Mind"), and entraps him in the compact. They disappear, and we next find them in Auerbach's cellar in Leipsic, where the carousing students are singing a rollicking drinking-song ("Oh, what Delight when Storm is crashing"). The drunken Brander is called upon for a song, and responds with a characteristic one ("There was a Rat in the Cellar Nest"), to which the irreverent students improvise a fugue on the word "Amen," using a motive of the song. Mephistopheles compliments them on the fugue, and being challenged to give them an air, trolls out the lusty *Lied* ("There was a King once reigning, who had a big black Flea"), in the accompaniment of which appear some very realistic effects. Amid the bravas of the drunken students Faust disappears, and is next found in the flowery meadows of the Elbe, where Mephistopheles sings a most enchanting melody ("In this fair Bower"). Faust is lulled to slumber, and in his vision hears the chorus of the gnomes and sylphs ("Sleep, happy Faust"), a number of extraordinary beauty and fascinating charm. Its effect is still further heightened by the sylphs' ballet in waltz time. As they gradually disappear, Faust wakes and relates to Mephistopheles his vision of the "angel in human form." The latter promises to conduct him to her chamber, and they join a party of soldiers and students who will pass "before thy Beauty's dwelling." The Finale of the scene is composed of a stirring soldiers' chorus ("Stoutly-walled Cities we fain would win") and a characteristic students' song in Latin ("Jam Nox stellata"), at first sung separately and then combined with great skill.

The third part begins with a brief instrumental prelude, in which the drums and trumpets sound the tattoo, introducing a scene in Marguerite's chamber where Faust sings a passionate love-song ("Thou sweet Twilight, be welcome"). At its close Mephistopheles warns him of the approach of Marguerite and conceals him behind a curtain. She enters, and in brief recitative tells her dream, in which she has seen the image of Faust, and discloses her love for him. Then while disrobing she sings the ballad ("There was a King in Thule"). As its pathetic strains come to a close, the music suddenly changes and Mephistopheles in a characteristic strain summons the will-o'-the-wisps to bewilder the maiden.

It is followed by their lovely and graceful minuet, in which Berlioz again displays his wonderful command of orchestral realism. This is followed by Mephistopheles, closing with a chorus of mockers which indicates the coming tragedy.

The fourth part opens with the romance ("My Heart with Grief is heavy"), the familiar "Meine Ruh' ist hin" of Goethe, sung by Marguerite, and the scene closes with the songs of the soldiers and students heard in the distance. In the next scene Faust sings a somber and powerful invocation to Nature ("O boundless Nature, Spirit sublime!"). Mephistopheles is seen scaling the rocks, and in agitated recitative tells his companion the story of Marguerite's crime and imprisonment. He bids him sign a scroll which will save him from the consequences of the deed, and Faust thus delivers himself over to the Evil One. Then begins the wild "Ride to Hell," past the peasants praying at the cross, who flee in terror as they behold the riders, followed by horrible beasts, monstrous birds, and grinning, dancing skeletons, until at last they disappear in an abyss and are greeted by the chorus of the spirits of hell in a tempest of sound, which is literally a musical pandemonium ("Has! Irimiru Karabras," etc.) in its discordant vocal strains, mighty dissonances, and supernatural effects in the accompaniment. A brief epilogue ("On Earth") follows, in which Faust's doom is told, succeeded by a correspondingly brief one ("In Heaven") in which the seraphim plead for Marguerite. The legend closes with ("Marguerite's glorification"), a jubilant double chorus, announcing her pardon and acceptance among the blest.

BIZET

1838 – 1875

Dramatic Overture, Patrie. Op. 19

THE Dramatic Overture, "Patrie," dedicated to Massenet, was written by Bizet as the result of a commission given to him by Pasdeloup in 1873. As its name suggests, it is an appeal to the martial spirit of the country.

The overture opens with a dashing military theme, fortissimo, in full orchestra. After brief development it reappears pianissimo, also in full orchestra. After some subsidiary passages the trombones give out a martial call, answered by explosive concussions of the drums against violin tremolos, after which the theme returns fortissimo, again subsiding to pianissimo modulations, preparing the way for the entrance of the second theme in the violins, clarinet, and bassoon, accompanied by the double basses, the new theme being in the nature of a folk song. After brief development, followed by a stirring passage in the brass section, the second theme returns fortissimo in full orchestra, leading to a powerful climax. A pause ensues, after which the third theme enters in the violas and 'cellos with accompaniment of the brasses and double basses. The new theme is elaborately developed and is followed by a fourth in the violas, clarinet, and English horn with arpeggio accompaniment by the muted violins, leading to a return of the martial first theme, pianissimo, developed to a powerful climax. The subsidiary passage after the first theme, and the second and fourth themes, return in regular order, each of them greatly enriched, and close the overture with an impressive burst of harmony.

Suite No. 1, L'Arlésienne

The suite "L'Arlésienne" is one of the two which Bizet arranged as incidental music to Daudet's play of the same name. It is written in four movements: 1, Allegro deciso; 2, Minuet, Allegro giocoso; 3, Adagietto; 4, Carillon — Allegro moderato.

The Prelude, in march time, opens with a vigorous theme given out in unison by the wood winds, horns, and violins. After repetition in the wood winds, the clarinet having the harmony, the theme is worked up and followed by a subject, varying the theme. It is then taken up fortissimo in full orchestra and gradually dies away. An intermezzo follows, with a peculiar alternating accompaniment in the clarinet. The movement comes to its close with a charming melody in the muted strings, accompanied by the wood winds and brasses. The second movement is a Minuet in the usual form with a trio in imitation of the bagpipe, and the third, a tender romanza for the muted strings. The last movement, Carillon, as its title suggests, imitates a bell chime. The bells sound an accompaniment, a repetition of three notes, against a sprightly little dance theme in the violins and other instruments, which is followed by a pastoral subject of a quaint sort. At its conclusion the carillon effect is reproduced and the suite comes to its close.

Little Suite, Children's Games. Op. 22

The "Little Suite" ("Jeux d'Enfants"), first written for piano (four hands) in 1872, was arranged for orchestra by Bizet and first performed at Paris in 1873. The first movement ("Trumpeter and Drummer"), with its crescendo and decrescendo, pierced with brisk trumpet calls and accompanied by the rattle of drums in the distance, clearly describes the approach and gradual disappearance of a troop of soldiers. The second movement ("The Doll") is a dainty, gentle little melody for the muted strings with responses in the wood winds over a berceuse accompaniment in the 'cellos, also muted. The third movement ("The Top") is described as an imitation of the spinning of that toy, its whizzing being depicted in the violins, accompanied by a dance melody given out now by the wood winds and again by the strings pizzicato. The fourth movement ("Little Husband, Little Wife") is a subdued domestic dialogue between the first violins ("Husband") and 'cellos ("Wife"), the nature of which may be left to the imagination of the hearer. That it is an agreeable one is sufficiently evident. In the last movement ("The Ball") this charming little suite comes to its close with a picturesque and lively dance by full orchestra. Daintiness, delicacy, and piquant melodic charm are its most salient features.

BLOCH

1880 –

Symphony, Israël

ERNEST BLOCH was born at Geneva, the son of a Jewish merchant in that city who, perceiving that his child possessed musical gifts, gave him opportunities to develop them. He studied first at Geneva with Jaques-Dalcroze, the founder of eurhythmics. Later Bloch was sent to Brussels, where he became a pupil in violin-playing of Ysaÿe. Three years later he went to Germany and studied at Frankfort with Ivan Knorr. For a time Bloch lived in Paris. He then (in 1909-1910) conducted at Lausanne and Neufchâtel and taught (1915) composition in the conservatory at Geneva. In 1915 he obtained an engagement to conduct the orchestra during the tour which the dancer, Miss Maud Allan, was to make in America. Bloch remained with the tour only a short time. Leaving it to go to New York, he lived for two years in straitened circumstances and, until Dr. Karl Muck brought out Bloch's Three Jewish Poems at Boston, utterly unknown. In 1917 a concert of his works was given by the Friends of Music in New York and, in 1920, Bloch's growing reputation procured for him the position of director of the Institute of Musical Art at Cleveland. He left that in 1925 to go to San Francisco.

The symphony "Israël" was composed between 1912 and 1916 at Geneva, Switzerland. The work was to have been written in two parts — the first part consisting of a Prelude, *Allegro agitato* and *Andante moderato*. The second part has not yet been completed (in 1930). The music is, in effect, an expression of the sorrows of Israel, an expression deepened by the horrors of the Great War. The second part will — if Bloch ever completes it — express joy in the redemption of the Jewish people.

The first production of "Israël" was given at a concert conducted by the composer in New York, May 3, 1917. The symphony, which comprises the movements mentioned above, is played without pause. In the closing section (Andante moderato) the voices of two sopranos, two altos and a bass are employed, sometimes merely humming and sometimes using a text, which begins: "Adonai, my Elohim."

F. B.

America, an Epic Rhapsody in Three Parts

Bloch's Epic Rhapsody, "America," was written in 1926-1927 for the competition for a prize of $3,000 instituted by the periodical *Musical America*. Ninety-two manuscripts were submitted by American composers and "America" was unanimously chosen by the judges — Frederick Stock, Walter Damrosch, Serge Koussevitzky, Leopold Stokowski and Alfred Hertz. A simultaneous production of the work was agreed upon — December 21, 1928 — by those conductors, respectively in Chicago, New York, Boston, Philadelphia and San Francisco.

Bloch has said that the first idea of the work came to him when the steamer upon which he came to America arrived in New York harbor in 1916. He was desirous, he said, of composing an anthem "which should rightfully belong to and reflect the country for which it might stand." His friends remaining lukewarm to such an aspiration, Bloch allowed the idea to sleep undisturbed for a decade. Meanwhile the study of Walt Whitman's works brought forward the plan once more, now in 1925. The following year the anthem occurred to Bloch in San Francisco and the plan of making an American epic began to fructify. The work was completed in 1927.

The score of "America" is dedicated to the memory of Abraham Lincoln and Walt Whitman, "whose visions," runs an inscription in the volume, "have upheld its inspiration.' "This symphony," the inscription continues, "has been written in love for this country; in reverence for its past, in faith for its future." A quotation also is made of Walt Whitman's apostrophe: "O America, because you build for mankind, I build for you." On a flyleaf there stands the following matter:

"The ideals of America are imperishable. They embody the future *credo* of all mankind; a union, in common purpose and under willingly accepted guidance, of widely diversified races, ultimately to become one race, strong and great. But, as Walt Whitman has said, 'To hold men together by paper and seal or by compulsion, is no account. That only holds men together which aggregates all in a living principle, as the hold of the limbs of the body or the fibres of plants.'

"Though this symphony is not dependent on a program, the composer wants to emphasize that he has been inspired by this very ideal.

"The anthem which concludes the work, as its apotheosis, symbolizes the destiny, the mission of America. The symphony is entirely built upon it. From the first bars it appears, in root, dimly, slowly taking shape, rising, falling, developing, and finally asserting itself, victoriously, in its complete and decisive form.

"It is the hope of the composer that this anthem will become known and beloved, that the audience will rise to sing it, becoming thus an active and enthusiastic part of the work and its message of faith and hope."

"America" is in reality a species of musical commentary on the history of the country and it accomplishes that purpose, in part at least, by the use of tunes which have had national significance. There are three movements. The first brings forward the Indians and the early life of America; the landing of the Pilgrims, the hardships which afflicted them. The second movement depicts the struggle in the Civil War between the North and South and the misery which followed that conflict. The third movement sets forth America of the present day, with its noise and turbulence, its prosperity and the inevitable collapse and the reconstruction and apotheosis.

The opening section bears the following inscription: ". . . . 1620 — The Soil — The Indians — (England) — The Mayflower — The Landing of the Pilgrims." It begins with a theme given out by the bassoon and lower strings over a tremolo in the strings. This theme has an Indian character. Other Indian characteristics are developed and a theme, which may be identified as "The Call of America," is heard. There are suggestions of an old English march given out by the trumpet, followed by the "Call of America," the first two measures of which are derived from the anthem which comes at the end. There follows a section specified as "Struggles and Hardships," in which an old chanty comes to notice in the violoncello and horn. Soon the opening phrase of the anthem is shouted forth fortissimo and this is succeeded by the hymn "Old Hundred." The movement ends softly and tranquilly.

The second movement bears the following: "1861–1865 — Hours of Joy — Hours of Sorrow." There is also a quotation from Walt Whitman: "I hear America singing, the varied carols I hear. . . . Each singing what belongs to him or her, and to none else. . . . Singing with open mouths their strong melodious songs." The movement begins Allegretto, A minor, 6-8 time, with the tune of a southern ballad in the English horn. After suggestions of "The Call of America" there comes a negro song, "Row After Row," a dreamy lullaby, "Old Folks at Home," "Pop Goes the Weasel" and "Hail Columbia." After a climax a Creole folk song (in the oboe) is heard and following it come snatches of Civil War songs — "John Brown's Body," "The Battle Cry of Freedom," etc. The anthem subject becomes more insistent and clamorous. Yet the mood subsides and the movement comes to a close sadly and quietly.

The final movement is headed: "1926 . . . . The Present — the Future." Here, too, a quotation is made from Walt Whitman: "As he sees the farthest he has the most faith." The movement opens with a syncopated version of the "America" motive — a dance scene filled with rhythm and verve. Negro songs occasionally make their appearance. "The Turmoil of the Present Time" now forms a new section; there is a great climax, but suddenly the turmoil subsides and the mood of the opening motive of the Rhapsody reappears. Development takes place. The hymn "Old Hundred" recurs and the motto theme becomes more and more insistent. Finally, as the culmination of a great climax, the anthem is sung and played. At the very end "Yankee Doodle" is heard.

F. B.

BOIELDIEU

1775 – 1834

Overture to La Dame Blanche

IN 1811 Boieldieu, one of the last composers of the old classical period in France, made a success with his opera "Jean de Paris," and singularly enough, though he wrote many operas afterwards, did not meet with further success until "La Dame Blanche" appeared in 1825. The story of the opera is adapted from Sir Walter Scott's "Monastery" and "Guy Mannering." It relates the dishonesty of the steward Gaveston, in charge of the Laird of Avenel's castle, his intimidation of the villagers in its vicinity by the story of a spectral White Lady whose statue is in the castle, and the manner in which Anna, an orphan whom the Laird has befriended, thwarts the steward's villainy by personating the White Lady and saves the property for the rightful heir.

The overture recites the principal theme of the opera, beginning with the motive of the first finale, followed by the ballad of the White Lady and the chorus from the same act. The Allegro section begins with the drinking-song, followed by many of the charming arias, ballads, and choruses of the opera. It is stated that the overture was written in a single evening, with the assistance of Adam and Labarre, two of the composer's pupils, Boieldieu writing the introductory section, and the others the remainder. The overture is also interesting by its introduction of the ballad of "Robin Adair" — as the song of the Clan Avenel. All its effects are made in the lightest and daintiest manner and almost entirely without utilizing the brasses.

BOLZONI

1841 – 1919

Minuet

GIOVANNI BOLZONI lives in contemporary musical history only in the popularity of this little piece. Born at Parma, he studied in the conservatory of his native town and began his career as a violinist, later filling various positions as opera conductor and, finally, as director of the Liceo Musicale Giuseppe Verdi at Turin, a position which Bolzoni held from 1889 until his death in 1919. This musician wrote five operas, a symphony, four overtures and a large amount of chamber music. The Minuet, which so frequently figures on the programs of popular orchestral concerts, was originally composed for string orchestra and was first performed at a concert of the Orchestral Society, of Milan, at La Scala, where it met with remarkable success.

F. B

BORODIN

1834 – 1887

Symphony No. 1, E Flat Major

1. Allegro.
2. Scherzo. Prestissimo.
3. Andante.
4. Allegro molto vivo.

THE first symphony by Borodin was finished in 1867 and first performed in Petrograd in 1869. The introduction to the first movement suggests the opening theme, which does not make its appearance however until several measures later, when it is given out by the second violins. It is next taken up by the wood winds, with string accompaniment. Lighter passages follow, leading to the second theme, stated by the wood winds. After development, a rhythm for the kettle-drums, which appeared in the introduction, recurs and is finally heard in the clarinet. The recapitulation contains the principal theme, followed by the second subject, partial development of the first theme and the drum figure. A fortissimo passage, followed by a slow section, brings the movement to its close.

The Scherzo is laid out in three parts. The first begins with a staccato in the strings, then taken up by the wood winds. The second is the trio in which all the previous material is developed, leading into the third part, which repeats the first.

The third movement begins with a melody for the 'cellos, followed by the flute and English horn with accompaniment of muted violins. A new section then appears with a passage for the 'cellos, the English horn following with a suggestion of the first theme to viola accompaniment, closing with a repetition of two notes on the kettle-drums, the violins playing a figure which was heard in the opening. The first melody then returns fortissimo in full orchestra and a Coda closes the movement.

The last movement opens with a vigorous subject for the strings, leading by a short passage to the second theme. The second subject appears in the strings and is then taken by the wood winds. Development follows and a recapitulation of all this material brings the movement to a close, fortissimo.

Symphony No. 2, B Minor

1. Allegro.
2. Scherzo.
3. Andante.
4. Allegro.

Borodin's Second Symphony was begun in 1871, finished in 1876, and was first heard in Petrograd in 1877. The first movement opens with a vigorous unison in the strings, reinforced by bassoons and horns, the theme forming the foundation of the whole movement. The second division is announced by the wood winds, the two alternating and leading to the second subject, presented by the 'cellos and subsequently by the wood winds. After the first theme is repeated by full orchestra, development begins, leading to the recapitulation fortissimo. A Coda, constructed on the theme, closes the movement.

The second movement opens with a theme for first and second horn followed by a passage in the strings in unison, which alternates with the first theme until the Trio is reached. A melody follows for the clarinet with harp and triangle accompaniment and a Coda closes the movement pianissimo.

A solo for clarinet opens the third movement, followed by a plaintive folk song for the horn, passing in modified form to the wood winds. A new passage follows, leading up to a climax and the clarinet solo, with which the movement began, closes the movement. The third leads directly into the fourth movement, the opening theme being announced by full orchestra. The second subject appears in the clarinet, followed by flute and oboe, with accompaniment of harp and strings. The first theme is then developed by the three trombones and tuba, followed by the strings and wood winds. The second subject follows and recapitulation of the opening material closes the movement.

On the Steppes of Central Asia

The symphonic sketch, "Dans les Steppes de l'Asie Centrale" ("On the Steppes of Central Asia") was written in 1880 for a series of *tableaux vivants* presented upon the occasion of the twenty-fifth anniversary of the reign of Alexander Second. The movement of the poem is an Allegretto, constructed upon two contrasting themes. It is free in form and an admirable example of program music. The program itself is printed upon the score and renders musical analysis unnecessary, as the music lucidly and unerringly suggests the development of the situation. The program reads:

> "Over the uniform sandy Steppes of Central Asia come the unwonted sounds of a peaceful Russian song. From the distance are heard the stamping of horses and camels and the peculiar sound of an Oriental melody. A native caravan draws near. It pursues its way, safe and free from care, through the boundless desert under the protection of Russian arms. It moves farther and farther off. The song of the Russians and the melody of the Asiatics combine to form a common harmony, the echo of which is gradually lost in the air of the Steppe."

The imitative characteristics of program music could hardly be more clearly expressed than they have been in this popular symphonic poem, or sketch, which is always welcome on the concert stage.

Dances from Prince Igor

Borodin first conceived the plan of an opera on the Epic of the Army of Igor in 1869. The people with whom the plot of "Prince Igor" was concerned were the Polovetsi, a race inhabiting Central Asia, and to do justice to his subject,

Borodin made minute researches into their history and characteristics. The composer did not, however, live to finish his opera. In 1887 he died, while dancing at a fancy dress ball which he was giving at St. Petersburg, and "Prince Igor" was completed by his friends Rimsky-Korsakov and Glazounov. The first performance of the opera was presented at St. Petersburg, November 4, 1890. In America it was first given December 30, 1915, at New York. The dances occur in the second act of the opera, some of their musical material having been given to Borodin by the traveler, Hunfalvi, who had spent some time among the tribes of Central Asia. The scene in which the dances take place is the Polovetzian camp, where Prince Igor, who has been captured by the Polovetsi, is interned as an honored prisoner of war. As given in the opera house the Polovetzian dances include choral music, but this is usually omitted in the concert room.

F. B.

BRAHMS

1833 – 1897

Symphony No. 1, in C Minor. Op. 68

1. Un poco sostenuto. Allegro.
2. Andante sostenuto.
3. Un poco allegretto e grazioso.
4. Adagio piu andante. Allegro moderato ma con brio.

BRAHMS waited until he was forty-three years of age before he produced his first symphony. Rumors of its coming preceded it many years, but when the composer was questioned about them he only remarked that there had been one C minor (Beethoven's Fifth), and there was no need of another. In the Autumn of 1876, however, it made its appearance, and created an enthusiasm which found its most flattering expression in Von Bülow's remark: "We have at last a Tenth symphony."

The symphony opens with a short introduction, of an agitated and somewhat melancholy but harmonious character and based upon the two themes of the Allegro, from which it is separated by four measures of prelude. It is in reality a clear, general statement of the movement, the principal theme of which is given out by the violins, accompanied by a chromatic phrase for the 'cello and bassoon, which appears again with a phrase derived from the first theme for its accompaniment, thus admirably preserving the unity of the movement. The second subject, full of hopeful aspiration, is taken by the oboes, clarinets, bassoons, and horns, treated as we have already indicated, and supplemented by a new melody in the oboes, supported by a sustained passage in bassoons, violas, and 'cellos, one measure of which is used in imitation between the clarinet, horn, flute, and bassoon, producing a quieter and more restful feeling. A new figure for the strings, however, soon recalls the old unrest, and thus the first section of the Allegro closes. After the repeat and the working out of the movement a fine effect is made by a long decrescendo, leading up to a passage which begins almost in a whisper and is developed by degrees to a tremendous fortissimo. The movement closes with a Coda in the same time and general character as the opening, developed with constantly increasing power.

The second movement opens with an exquisitely melodious theme in the strings, followed by an intensely passionate second theme, also in the strings, accompanied by a phrase from the opening melody — a form of treatment already observed in the Allegro movement. After this the first theme returns, this time, however, for the oboe, with response by the clarinet and an accompaniment of staccato chords for the violins and violas. In the close of the movement the first melody is divided as a solo between the violin and flute, with a charming accompaniment, and characterized by genuine romantic sentiment.

The third movement is introduced with a sweet and graceful melody for the clarinet, followed by an equally graceful subject for clarinet and flute. The third melody is also announced by the clarinet and finished by the flute and oboe with string accompaniment. The Trio is in strong contrast with the opening of the movement. At its close the first section is not repeated, as is customary in a Scherzo, whose place the movement occupies, but its themes are developed with charming grace and skill in a Coda.

The Finale is the most powerful and dramatic section of the work, and is evidently intended as a summary of the whole symphony. It is composed of an Introduction, Adagio, più andante, and an Allegro. The Introduction opens with three descending bass notes of highly tragic expression, gradually increasing in power, which are subsequently utilized for accompaniment in the Allegro; and the violins give out a very dramatic phrase, which also forms the opening theme of that movement. All through this majestic Adagio, which seems to be an alternation between hope and fate, and this is intensified when with an acceleration of the time and change of key to C major the horns and trombones are introduced, the former uttering a most passionate theme and the latter filling in a solid background of mysterious harmony. The opening theme of the Allegro recalls the choral melody of Beethoven's Ninth Symphony. It is introduced in the strings, assisted by the horn and bassoons, and is then repeated by the wind instruments accompanied pizzicato in the strings. Its effect is magical. To the preceding gloom, mystery, and passion succeeds a spirit of joyousness and healthy contentment. The work concludes with reminiscences of the preceding themes.

Symphony No. 2, in D Major. Op. 73

1. ALLEGRO MA NON TROPPO.
2. ADAGIO MA NON TROPPO.
3. ALLEGRETTO GRAZIOSO.
4. ALLEGRO CON SPIRITO.

The Second Symphony of Brahms was finished in 1877. Only a year had intervened since his *début* in this important field of music, but the second work is widely different from the first in its general character. It is distinguished by cheerfulness, repose, and almost pastoral simplicity, and betokens peaceful existence. Less dignified perhaps in its purpose, certainly less pedagogic in its structure and working out, it is none the less interesting for the beauty of its themes, the strength of its contrasts, the sustained character of the various movements, and the unity of the work.

The first movement suggests pastoral simplicity and repose. The opening subject is beautifully set for the wind instruments, and is thoroughly melodious, the horns fairly giving out festive strains. The second theme sings itself most sweetly and gracefully in the 'cellos and viola. In the working out, however, a more passionate key is struck and the idyllic character of the movement is disturbed. Then follows a succession of passages which are almost stormy in their effect, so strong are the brasses and blaring even to dissonance; but the angry waters are calmed again when the first theme returns, this time on the oboes, and the movement glides peacefully along to the Coda, in which the horn is used with fascinating effect, and a peculiar tone-color is given by the quaint pizzicato string accompaniment that follows.

The second movement is somewhat sphinx-like as to its real purport. The themes are less clearly stated. The form is more unique, but the workmanship shows the same consummate perfection that characterizes all this composer's work. Unquestionably there is a deep meaning underlying it, both in the form itself and in its expression, which we may leave to the hearer to interpret.

This criticism does not apply, however, to the third movement, for here everything is clear and full of cheerfulness, even to the verge of frolicsome gayety. It is made up of two sections, an Allegretto and a Presto. In beauty and vivacity it resembles the opening movement and strongly partakes of the Haydn spirit. It begins with an exquisite pastoral melody for the reeds, which is most deliciously treated and full of charming variety. It then rushes on to the Presto, which is a merry rustic dance in itself, abounding with sparkling humor and even boisterous gayety. Then comes a repetition of the Allegretto, which brings the happy scene to its close.

The Finale is full of reminiscences of preceding themes which are handled with great skill. After treating them in variations and with constantly changing shades of tone-color, sustaining them with all the strength of a master, he seems to give a free rein to his powers and the movement rushes on with constantly increasing vigor and spirit to a brilliant and sonorous close.

Symphony No. 3, in F Major. Op. 90

1. Allegro con brio.
2. Andante con moto.
3. Poco allegretto.
4. Allegro.

Brahms' Third Symphony, first performed at one of the concerts of the Vienna Philharmonic Society, December 2,

1883, is undoubtedly the most popular of the series for the reason that it is clearer in its general construction than the others. At the same time, while less complicated and elaborate in its development, it is not lacking in ideas of a thoroughly poetical kind and in great variety of color.

The first movement opens with a short prelude of powerful chords by the wind instruments, introducing the first theme, a majestic melody, which is given out by the violins, accompanied by the violas and 'cellos, and supported by the trombones. The theme, which is peculiarly brilliant and even heroic in its style, is treated with masterly skill as it progresses from a steady and peaceful flow to the highest point of vigor and majesty. In the transition to the second theme, however, announced by the clarinets, occurs a more restful period; and the theme itself, which is graceful and pastoral in style, imparts a serious, earnest character to the movement, which is still further enforced by the skilfully constructed Coda.

The second movement might almost be termed a rhapsody, as it is very short and is not elaborated after the customary manner. The greater part of the movement indeed rests upon and grows out of the opening theme, which is a simple but graceful and joyous melody, in strong contrast with the epic character of the work. This theme is taken alternately by the wind instruments, violas, and 'cellos, and is freely treated in variations, which give beautiful tone-color to it. It has a brief rest while the clarinets and bassoons give out a resonant, stirring phrase as if foreshadowing what is to come. It is hardly pronounced enough, however, to be called a second theme. The first subject at once returns and goes on to the end in a series of delightfully contrasted effects.

The third movement, which takes the place of the ordinary Scherzo, is mostly serious in its style, and really fixes the general character of the symphony. Its principal theme, a genuine sample of the *Lied,* is given out by the 'cellos, at first fanciful, tender, and full of simple grace, then reminiscent and contemplative, and at last dreamy; to which succeeds a passage for the wind instruments, soothing and almost suppliant.

The Allegretto dies away in soft chords which lead to the Finale — a passionate, agitated, and sombre movement, yet heroic, elevated, and strong in its style. The theme with which it opens rushes past with all the haste and mystery of a vision in a dream, and then reappears in a new harmonic form, only to grow more sorrowful and gloomy with the entrance of the trombones preluding a new phrase, for now the sentiment changes and we have in its place a passionate conflict. Through the fierce and determined phrases of the violins, however, is heard the steady, jubilant song of the 'cellos. As they announce the victory the gloom disappears, and gives place to peace and rest once more, dignified and ennobled by the heroic theme of the first movement.

Symphony No. 4, in E Minor. Op. 98

1. Allegro non assai.
2. Andante moderato.
3. Presto giocoso.
4. Allegro energico e patetico.

The Fourth Symphony is universally recognized as the most individual of all Brahms' works of this class. In the simplicity and originality of its themes, and in the subjective character of its ideas, as well as in its development, it bears the unmistakable impress of its composer.

The first movement opens with a melodious theme of unusual length which is treated in a masterly but intricate style. It is a wayward fancy, now cheerful, and again serious, but coming to a sombre close as the second theme enters in the same general manner. As the movement draws to an end its melodious character grows more joyous, strong, and dramatic, and the development leaves little to desire in the way of pleasing variety and artistic effect.

The second movement is almost akin to the *Lied* in the gracefulness and sweetness of its melody, its warmth of tone, and refined, *spirituelle* character; and the third, in rondo form, is full of animation and good humor, and yet is dignified in style and strong in expression, as befits the serious purpose of the composer, who always has a lofty object in view.

The Finale, a development of the Passacaglia form, is a model of earnest, serious, artistic workmanship, every measure of it revealing the conscientious and scientific scholar. It opens with a succession of massive chords introducing a stately first theme which frequently reappears. A melodious flute solo intervenes, and then the development begins, in which the subjects are given out in a broad and restful manner and treated with a richness of color and refinement of style, as well as a perfection in workmanship, which have rarely been excelled.

Academic Festival Overture. Op. 80

The cheerful, breezy, jovial "Academic" Overture was written by Brahms as a tribute of gratitude to the University of Breslau for conferring upon him the degree of Doctor of Philosophy. It, as well as the "Tragic" Overture, was produced in that city in 1881 under his own leadership. The overture is clearly enough identified with the University functions and particularly with the students' "Commersbuch." The whole overture is built up on themes taken from that memorable collection of German student songs now famous the world over, and some of them pleasantly familiar to our own colleges.

The overture begins at once with a stately theme announced in the strings pianissimo, horns, bassoons, and drums. After its development at some length, a subsidiary passage leads to the first of the student themes "Wir hatten gebauet ein stattliches Haus" ("We had built a Stately House"), taken in the basses and wood winds. After some transition passages reference is made to the opening theme, which finally leads to the second of the student songs, "Der Landesvater" ("The Country's Father"). This is followed by another subsidiary passage in the wood winds, closing the first part of the overture. The next section begins with the "Fuchs Lied" ("Fox Song") sung by the bassoons and clarinets with full orchestral accompaniment, which is carried from one group of instruments to another in a jolly manner. In the closing section all the student songs return, but with different modes of development, and lead at the close to the "Gaudeamus igitur," given in full force by the orchestra and bringing the overture to a triumphant conclusion.

Tragic Overture. Op. 81

It is a long remove from the briskness and geniality of the "Academic" Overture to the "Tragic" Overture with its dark and passionate themes and solid musical workmanship. The "Tragic," though written first, bears a later opus number. Both were composed in 1880 and given for the first time in the following year. It has no program beyond the significance of its title. Two themes, the one expressing intensely passionate sentiment and the dread of some impending catastrophe, and the other fitful gleams of hope, seem to dominate the overture and to represent the two contending forces in the human struggle, and the ultimate victory over fate rather than any special tragedy. The first subject is given out in the wood winds, the oboe being prominently accompanied by the strings and the other subject by the brasses. The whole overture is devoted to this struggle and its alternating phases. Musically the composer has not only gone beyond the overture limits, but also beyond those of the symphony, in his treatment of the themes and in the unusual amount of subsidiary matter which he introduces and elaborates as part of the principal material, by reason of its contrapuntal connection with it. Hence the overture is in somewhat irregular form, because of the long and intricate development of these themes and subsidiary passages, and yet from the musical point of view it blends into a compact whole.

Serenade No. 1. Op. 11

Brahms wrote two serenades, No. 1, op. 11, in D, for full orchestra, and No. 2, op. 16, in A, for small orchestra. By the title "Serenade" in this connection, however, the hearer is not to expect the vocal serenade of the lover to his inamorata, much less such music as may be performed by an instrumental organization in honor of some eminent personage. The Brahms serenades are purely instrumental and in regular form, composed in several short movements and constructed concisely upon thematic material and its development.

The Serenade No. 1 is in five short movements. The first, Allegro molto, opens with sustained tones in the violins and 'cellos and the announcement of the first theme in the horns, repeated by the clarinet. After development in full orchestra, closing with a vigorous climax, the second theme enters in the first violins and bassoon and then passes to the first and second violins. It is developed at some length. Another brilliant theme follows, and this part of the movement closes with a repetition of the foregoing work. The free fantasia begins with the second theme, but depends mainly upon the first, which is elaborately developed and finally leads to the first, announced in full in the solo horn as at first. The clarinet repetition also appears, and the movement comes to a closing pianissimo in which both themes have a place. The second movement, Scherzo, opens with a theme in the strings and bassoon, which is developed at considerable length and repeated after the Trio. The third movement, Adagio non troppo, like the first, is in strict form. The opening theme is given out in the bass strings and bassoon and the usual development follows. Passage work in the first violins and violas, with a tremolo accompaniment in the remaining strings, leads to the second theme, announced in the horns. All this thematic material is worked up, and the movement closes with a short Coda. The fourth movement is composed of two light Minuets for reduced orchestra, the first being repeated after the second. The fifth movement is another Scherzo, the principal theme given out in the horns, which also have the melody in the Trio. After repetition of the trio the Scherzo is repeated, bringing the movement to its close. The last movement is a brilliant Rondo, composed of two themes, the first for the 'cellos, clarinet, and bassoon, and the second for the first violins with accompaniment by the violas, horns, and 'cellos.

Serenade No. 2. Op. 16

The second serenade of Brahms, in A major, is a greater favorite with a popular audience than the first in D, possibly because its melodious character imparts to it more of the conventional serenade quality, though one eminent German critic has said that the relations of the two are those of sister and brother, the brother evidently being the Serenade in D, which is more massively constructed and composed for full orchestra, whereas the sister serenade is written only for wood winds, horns, violas, 'cellos, and double basses. The violins, which usually do the principal part in serenade love-making, are silent.

The opening theme is given out in the clarinets and bassoons with responses in the remaining wind instruments, and after development, lead to the second, a joyous theme stated by the clarinets. The development of these two themes and the subsidiary passages close this very romantic movement. The second movement, Scherzo, is in regular form, its two fresh, charming themes beautifully interwoven, though the first dominates the movement. The third movement is an Adagio, beginning with a slow, quiet, dreamy rhythm in the strings, forming a background to a melody in the flute and clarinet of the same general character. After development of this material an intermezzo occurs, devoted to a fresh, piquant melody, and a repetition of the first part closes the movement. The fourth movement is a Minuet and Trio in usual form, which is charmingly melodious in its construction. The last movement is a brilliant Rondo, the principal theme of which is announced in the clarinet. The second theme is more expressive, and is taken in canon form in the clarinets and bassoons. Its elaboration closes the serenade. The two serenades are dignified, massive works, constructed in the sonata style, every movement precisely formal and classic, and of such length and general fashion that it is unlikely either of them will ever be heard under a fair one's window or resound to the tinklings of guitars or the jinglings of castanets.

Variations on a Theme by Joseph Haydn. Op. 56a

The theme of Haydn's which Brahms selected for these variations is the "Chorale Sancti Antoni" (the "Chorale of St. Anthony"). The variations are eight in number and close with a finale of great power. The theme itself is given out in the wind instruments, the double bassoon, 'cellos and double basses carrying the bass. It is hardly necessary to describe the construction of each variation by itself. It is almost entirely contrapuntal work and sometimes independent of the theme, so that the connection is at times difficult to trace. Like some of the older composers, Brahms evidently selected the theme because it lends itself well to this form of treatment and for a display of contrapuntal skill. The result is that after the impressive statement of the theme itself, its working up is of more interest to the trained musician than to the average concert-goer.

German Requiem. Op. 45

The "German Requiem," so called, is not a requiem in its sentiment, nor in any sense, a religious service. It might with more propriety be called a "sacred cantata." The poem is full of consolation for the mourner, of assurances of joy hereafter, of warnings against the pomps and vanities of the world, and closes with the victory of the saints over death and the grave. The work has seven numbers — two barytone solos and chorus, soprano solo and chorus, and four separate choruses.

The opening chorus ("Blessed are they that go mourning") is particularly noticeable for the richness of its accompaniment. In the Funeral March, which follows, a very graphic resemblance to the measured tread of the *cortège* is accomplished by the use of triple time. The third number ("Lord, make me to know the Measure of my Days on Earth") opens with a barytone solo, followed by two choral fugues, which are solidly constructed. They are extremely difficult to sing, and call for a chorus of unusual discipline and intelligence. The fourth, for chorus ("How lovely is Thy Dwelling-place, O Lord of Hosts"), is in striking contrast with its predecessor, being a slow movement, and very melodious in style. The fifth ("Ye now are sorrowful, grieve not"), for soprano solo and chorus, shows the composer's unusual power as a song-writer, as well as his melodious attractiveness when melody answers his purpose. In the next number, set for chorus with barytone solo responses ("Here on Earth we have no continuing Place, we seek now a heavenly One"), the character of the music changes again, and the resurrection of the dead is pictured in fugal passages of tremendous power and difficulty. After the storm comes the calm again in the Finale ("Blessed are the Faithful who in the Lord are sleeping"), which contains a reminiscence of the opening number and closes the work in a gentle, but deeply serious strain.

Triumphlied. Op. 55

"Triumphlied" ("Song of Triumph") was written by Brahms in commemoration of the victories of German arms and the reestablishment of the Empire, and is dedicated to "the German Emperor Wilhelm I." It was first performed in a complete form at Carlsruhe in 1872. The text is a paraphrase of certain verses in the nineteenth chapter of the Book of Revelation.

The scriptural selections are divided into three movements, written for double chorus (with the exception of two short barytone solos), orchestra, and organ, and are introduced by a brief instrumental prelude of a solemn but animated and exultant character, in the closing measures of which both choirs unite in jubilant shouts of ("Hallelujah! praise the Lord!"). The theme of the movement is the German national hymn

(" Heil dir im Siegerkranz "), which is worked up with consummate skill. The first part closes with a climax of power and contrapuntal effect hardly to be found elsewhere outside the choruses of Handel.

The second movement (" Glory be to God!") is of the same general character as the first. After the opening ascription, a short fugue intervenes, leading to a fresh melody alternately sung by both choruses.

The third movement, after a very brief but spirited orchestral flourish, opens with an exultant barytone solo (" And behold then the Heavens opened wide"). The choruses respond with animation (" And yonder a snow-white Horse"). Again the barytone intervenes (" And lo! a great Name hath He written"), and then the choruses take up the majestic theme (" King of Kings and Lord of Lords"), each answering the other with triumphant shouts that gather force and fire as they proceed, and closing with a mighty "Hallelujah" in which voices, orchestra, and organ join with fullest power. The work is one of extreme difficulty, as the two choirs are treated independently, and their harmonies are complicated, though blended in general effect.

Hungarian Dances

The Hungarian Dances were originally written for piano for four hands. How many of them are original with Brahms it is impossible to say. Indeed the old controversy between Remenyi and Brahms, in which the violinist accused the composer of stealing from him, may be fresh in the reader's memory. There is in fact an almost endless number of these dances, some of them modern and some very old, based upon the national Czarda which usually consists of two parts, the one melancholy, the other wild and passionate, reflecting respectively the Magyar and Gypsy spirit. In those attributed to Brahms, whether the themes are his own or not, the setting is unmistakably his. Those most frequently played belong to a set of ten, originally adapted for four-hand piano performance, afterwards arranged for piano and violin by Joachim, and at last scored for orchestra by Brahms. They are probably much different in effect from what they would be when played by a band of traveling gypsies, but they are specially interesting as showing how their effect can be enhanced when transformed into art worthy a great composer.

BRUCKNER

1824–1896

Symphony No. 2, in C Minor

1. Moderato.
2. Andante, feierlich etwas bewegt.
3. Scherzo.
4. Finale.

THE first movement of Bruckner's Second Symphony is in the ordinary sonata form, opening with a tremolo of violins and violas, accompanying the introduction and the first theme which is given out by the 'cellos, with responses from the horns. The theme is repeated by 'cellos and double basses to a more vigorous accompaniment, and leads to a climax. At its close the 'cellos give out the second theme, followed by a motive in the strings in unison which dominates the movement through the first part. Then follows the free fantasie with reentries of the themes, stated in much the same manner as in the beginning of the movement, after which, and a short passage in slow time, an elaborate Coda brings the movement to a close.

The second movement, in A flat major, is constructed upon two themes in rondo form, the first given out by the first violins with accompaniment of the other strings, and the second, or minor one, by the horn with pizzicato string accompaniment. These two themes are developed in a very skilful manner, especially the principal one by the wind instruments in the close, just before the Coda.

The third movement, in C minor, opens with a somewhat dignified and consequential theme for a Scherzo, which is at first stated in unison by the strings, wood winds, and horns, and afterwards is richly developed and leads up to a most resonant climax. The Trio is in waltz time, the theme being given out by the violas with a violin tremolo, and at its conclusion the opening of the movement is repeated and followed by a Coda.

The fourth movement, in C minor, is built up on three themes which are worked out at great length in succession and with most painstaking elaboration, the movement closing with a tremendous climax. This symphony, like all of Bruckner's, is a masterpiece of musical mechanics and mathematics.

Symphony No. 4, in E Flat. (Romantic)

1. Allegro molto moderato.
2. Andante.
3. Scherzo.
4. Finale.

The Fourth of Bruckner's symphonies was first produced in Vienna in 1881 and was performed for the first time in America in New York in 1888. Like all of this composer's symphonies, it is so elaborately constructed and full of musical complications that it is only possible, in a volume of this kind, to present a bare sketch. The first movement opens with a passage in the horns accompanied by the strings, which, several times repeated, prepares the way for the introduction of the first and second principal subjects, both of which present two themes. These, with their working up and the treatment of subsidiary ideas, constitute the learned structure of the movement which closes with a return to the horn passage of the opening.

The Andante is impressive and sombre in character, opening with a funeral march with characteristic refrains, followed by a melody for violas with string pizzicato accompaniment. After the development of this melody the march theme is restated most impressively and the movement closes with drum taps as the second theme dies away.

The Scherzo is a hunting movement, built up on two lively and graceful themes, after which is a country dance which furnishes the material for the trio. The movement closes with a repetition of the hunting scene music.

The Finale, Wagner fashion, introduces all the principal ideas of the other three movements, which are worked up and combined with the utmost skill. It is in reality a *résumé* of the whole symphony. Old forms are restated, and new forms growing out of them are presented. The workmanship is solid and the learning of the composer is everywhere apparent.

Symphony No. 7, in E Major

1. Allegro moderato.
2. Adagio: Sehr feierlich und langsam.
3. Scherzo: Allegro.
4. Finale: Bewegt, doch nicht schnell.

Bruckner's Seventh Symphony was first performed at Leipsic, December 30, 1884, and was played for the first time in America in Chicago, July 29, 1886, under Theodore Thomas' direction. The opening theme of the first movement is stated by the 'cellos, supported by the violas and clarinets. It is then repeated by the violins and wood winds, and leads up to the second theme, given out by oboe and clarinet. In the fantasia, both themes are worked up most skilfully, and are followed by the Finale, which is complicated though regular in form, and closes with an impressive climax.

The second movement, an Adagio, is based upon a most impressive theme nobly worked out, and of a nature to appeal even to the uneducated hearer. Though treated most elaborately, the contents of the Adagio are very emotional, and the coloring so beautiful as to appeal to every one. The Scherzo is in regular form, and the opening is full of spirit and vivacity. The first violins give out the theme of the trio, and the movement closes with a repetition of the first part.

The last movement is in rondo form, the violins giving out a brilliant theme, worked up in a fascinating manner, and leading into a second theme of a more solid nature, also stated by the first violins. The movement closes with a powerful climax, in which the opening theme of the first movement is heard again.

Symphony No. 9, in D Minor (Unfinished)

1. Feierlich.
2. Scherzo.
3. Adagio.

Bruckner's Ninth (and last) Symphony was written 1891-1894, and was first heard in Vienna, February 11, 1894. Its first performance in America was given at Chicago, February 19, 1904, by the Chicago Symphony Orchestra. Bruckner had designed closing the symphony with a choral movement in the manner of Beethoven's Ninth, but his death intervened and left the work unfinished.

The opening movement is so elaborate in its construction as to render it impossible to convey any intelligent description of it in the condensed form required by this volume. It contains four principal themes, each leading up to powerful climaxes. The movement, indeed, might be called a series of climaxes, for after the reconsideration of each theme and its fresh development, the movement closes with a new climax, which only the word "tremendous" can fitly describe.

The Scherzo is a relief after the tempests of the opening movement, being in dance rhythm, followed by the Trio, and a repetition of the first part. The Adagio movement consists mainly of the complicated development of two principal themes leading to another powerful climax, but closing pianissimo. The symphony is mostly interesting to musical scholars. The layman is apt to be thankful the work was left unfinished, though it would have been interesting to have had Bruckner's choral ideas.

CASELLA

1883 –

Rhapsody, Italia

ALFREDO CASELLA comes of musical parentage. His father was a violoncellist and his mother, who gave him his first instruction, a pianist. As a boy Casella disclosed remarkable love and aptitude for science, particularly for chemistry and electricity, and either of those sciences was considered as a career for him. Giuseppe Martucci, one of the principal Italian musicians in the nineteenth century, advised the boy's parents that Casella had a gift for music that was of more than ordinary importance and that he should devote himself to that art. Casella was then sent to the Paris Conservatoire, where he became a pupil in piano-playing of Diémer and in composition of Fauré. After a brilliant studentship, Casella taught for a time in the Conservatoire and later at the Accademia Santa Cecilia, at Rome.

The Rhapsody "Italia" was finished in 1909 and produced for the first time at a concert of his own works given at Paris, April 23, 1910. The score, published in 1912 with a dedication to Leon Jéhin (conductor of the Monaco orchestra) contains a preface in which it is stated that the Rhapsody endeavors to "picture musically — but without any 'program' whatever — Sicilian and Neapolitan life; the first, tragic, superstitious, passionate, as it is found under the scorching sun or in the inferno of the sulphur mines; the second the turbulent, careless, frenetic existence which may be lived amid the magic of the Gulf of Naples."

"Italia" is made up of melodies belonging to Sicily and Naples. It begins (Lento, grave, tragico, con molto fantasia) in A minor with a theme taken from the province of Caltanissetta — a theme which is sung with ferocity by a lover who has been angered by his mistress. After this has been developed Casella introduces a melody (in the wood winds, lamentoso) sung by the unfortunate men who work in the sulphur mines of the province. A third theme, also belonging to Caltanissetta, is given out by the English horn (Lento assai) and is a hymn sung in the Good Friday processions. The bassoon then brings forward a more lively tune, this being a song sung by the women who labor in the marble quarries at Catitu. Wolf-Ferrari also made use of this air in his opera "The Jewels of the Madonna." This ushers in the finale, which begins with Denza's "Funiculi-Funiculà," which, after considerable development, is followed by a motive from Mario Costa's song "Lariulà" and another from Tosti's Neapolitan ditty "Amarechiare."

F. B.

Pupazzetti, Five Pieces for Marionettes

This suite, comprising the following movements — Marcietta (Little March), Berceuse, Serenata, Notturnino and Polka — was originally composed in 1916 for piano (four hands). In its orchestral form "Pupazzetti" ("Marionettes") was published in London in 1916. In America it was first heard at a concert of the Cleveland Symphony Orchestra, Cleveland, February 15, 1923, Casella having been the conductor of it. The program book contained, on that occasion, the following matter, evidently inspired by the composer:

"Composed as an accompaniment for that favorite diversion of childhood, the Punch and Judy show, the music mirrors the spasmodic gestures and necessarily angular and fantastic motions of the little mechanical wooden dolls.

"The march portrays the procession of the little troupe as it files before the curtain at the beginning of the performance; the lullaby is a tender little scene of mother-love; the serenata evokes a fragment of Neapolitan comedy as interpreted by the 'pupazzi' as the little dolls are called in Italy; the nocturne, a short ecstatic love duet between a miniature wooden Tristan and his Isolde; the polka, which is also the finale, represents in turn the various activities of the country fair — the troupe of acrobats, the Spanish dancers, the holiday spirit of fun which calls forth all sorts of pranks, and lastly the faraway echo of a trumpet announcing the victor of the day's games; then the curtain falls on the scene now deserted by the actors."

F. B.

CHABRIER

1841 – 1894

Suite Pastorale

THE "Suite Pastorale" was drawn by Chabrier from a group of ten piano pieces written in 1880 and later scored. The first movement, "Idylle," consists entirely of a tender, graceful little theme in the solo flute with pizzicato string accompaniment, followed by its development, with the addition of some delightful subsidiary passages. The character of the second movement is indicated by its title, "Danse Villageoise," a rustic dance with a tripping theme given out by the clarinet, thence extending to other instruments. After a contrasting middle part the fanciful theme returns. The third movement, "Sous Bois," is clearly a wood visit and is full of forest stir and pastoral sentiment. The last movement, "Scherzo-Valse," is a long and brilliant dance which brings this charming pastoral story in tones to a vigorous and happy close.

Rhapsody, España

This brilliant piece came into existence as the outcome of Chabrier's travels in Spain in the Spring of 1883. The composer had written into his note-book numerous Spanish songs — music which completely fascinated him — and it was these upon which he drew when, on his return to Paris, he wrote the rhapsody, "España," which made him famous. The work was played for the first time at a concert, conducted by Lamoureux and given at the Château d'Eau, Paris, November 4, 1883.

"España" is a freely constructed fantasie upon the Spanish themes. Only one of the melodies — a motive given out by the trombones — was actually Chabrier's own. Two national dances are brought forward prominently — the jota, which is a species of waltz which, in Spain, is sung as well as danced, and the malagueña, a dance somewhat similar to the fandango, written in 3-4 time and performed with the accompaniment of castanets. The rhapsody is in F major.

F. B.

Joyeuse Marche

Chabrier's "Joyeuse Marche" was not originally composed for orchestra, but was conceived as a work for piano. The composer had been asked by the Bordeaux Conservatoire to provide it with two piano pieces for the use of the young ladies in the sight-reading classes. For this purpose Chabrier sent a "Prélude pastorale" and a "Marche française." The music proved to be too difficult for the students and both pieces were returned by the conservatory authorities to their composer. Chabrier then took them in hand and arranged them for orchestra. They were first played at Angers in 1888 and, the following year, at a concert of the Société Nationale de Musique, in Paris. The march, whose title Chabrier changed to "Joyeuse Marche," was given for the first time alone at a Lamoureux concert, Paris, February 16, 1890. It was the French master's intention to reflect in the music of the march the burlesque spirit of carnival. The piece, which was published in 1890, was dedicated to Vincent d'Indy.

F. B.

Bourrée Fantasque

The orchestral form in which this piece is so frequently heard was not given it by Chabrier, but by Felix Mottl, a German conductor (1856-1911) whose name was prominently associated with the interpretation of Wagner's music dramas at Bayreuth and elsewhere. Chabrier composed the Bourrée

Fantasque for piano in 1891 and it was published in September of that year with a dedication to Edouard Risler, a well known pianist, who frequently performed it at his recitals. The orchestral version of the work was first played, under the direction of Mottl, at Carlsruhe in 1897.

F. B.

CHADWICK

1854 –

Symphony No. 3, in F

1. Allegro.
2. Andante.
3. Saltarello.
4. Allegro molto.

MR. CHADWICK'S Third Symphony received the prize offered by the National Conservatory at the time when Anton Dvořák was its director, and is dedicated to Theodore Thomas. It is stated that the theme for the horns in unison (C, B, and A) has reference to the first three letters of the composer's name, B being known in German musical notation as H. The opening theme of the first movement is closely elaborated and leads up to its statement by full orchestra. An episode for the oboe and clarinet introduces the second subject in the horns with string accompaniment. Its development leads to the entrance of the main theme which is the foundation of the whole movement.

The second movement begins with a fresh and beautiful melody in the strings which gradually gathers intensity. The second theme, which is dramatic in character, enters in the 'cellos and basses, continually gaining in vigor. The first subject is then repeated with wood wind accompaniment and a counter theme in the violins, the Coda bringing the movement to its close.

The third movement is in Saltarello form with the Trios, and accompanying melodies in the horn, flute and oboe. The first Trio is in song style for the strings, after which the Saltarello is repeated. The second Trio is for the horns with responses by the other instruments. It is once again vigorously stated and followed by the Saltarello, a Coda bringing the close.

The last movement opens with a theme started by the horns and accompanied by the full harmony of the orchestra. An episode with trumpet calls and the repetition of the theme lead to the second subject, which is made up of two independent melodies. Development and working out of this material bring the symphony to its close.

Suite Symphonique

Mr. Chadwick's " Suite Symphonique " in E flat major enjoys the distinction of having won the prize offered by the National Federation of Music Clubs in 1910, and is dedicated to the Chicago Symphony Orchestra and its conductor, Mr. Stock. It is written in four movements. The first, Allegro molto animato, opens with a subject in the brasses and 'cellos, violins accompanying. Another part of it is given out by the clarinet, the first part returning in the trombone, tuba and basses. The clarinet with harp accompaniment gives out another theme, followed by a passage in the horns which in turn is succeeded by the second subject in the strings and wood winds. Development and recapitulation follow and the movement ends with a fortissimo of the clarinet theme mentioned.

The second movement, a romanza, begins with a theme for the saxophone which is next taken up in first violins, 'cellos and harp. An episode follows in flute and bassoon with string accompaniment. The oboe has a short passage with flute and clarinet accompaniment and after a cadenza, the first theme returns in violins and 'cellos.

The third movement, Intermezzo, begins with a theme in the clarinet, bassoon and strings, a portion of which is treated by different instruments. Both portions are developed, after which a new subject is given out in the 'cellos and bassoons. After development of this subject in humorous style, the movement closes. The Finale, an Allegro molto ed energico, closes the suite in a most vigorous manner.

Overtures, Thalia, Euterpe, and Melpomene

These three overtures are grouped together because they belong to one family, and they are presented not according to dates of composition, but rather with regard to their contents, beginning with the lighter of the three. Their subjects, as the titles indicate, are: "Thalia, the joyful muse who inspired gaiety and was the patroness of feasts, also known as the muse of comedy; Euterpe, the divinity of pleasure, of the music we now know as the folk song, also the inventor of the Greek double flute; and Melpomene, the sombre muse of tragedy, as well as of song and harmony."

The "Thalia" Overture is one of Mr. Chadwick's earlier works (1882 – 1883), and I have the composer's authority for the statement that it was written with the sub-title, "Overture to an Imaginary Comedy," and is in reality a sort of Lustspiel. It is simply constructed, with an introduction and Allegro, with the development of the introductory theme in the middle and at the end, as in the "Sonata Pathétique," but without its tragic significance. The overture is light and melodious in character and would be specially adapted for the theater when provided with a capable orchestra. It was first performed by the Boston Symphony Orchestra under Mr. George Henschel's direction in 1882, and again at the Handel and Haydn Society's Festival of 1883.

The "Euterpe" Overture, composed in 1903, was first performed in 1904 by the Boston Symphony Orchestra. It is written in the orthodox form, with an introduction and symphonic elaboration of two principal themes, its only deviation from the symphonic form being that the two themes are always heard together after the first announcement. The spirit of the overture is cheerful and optimistic throughout, as befits the nature of the charming queen of the flute. Being destitute of a program, the composer is left with more freedom in working up his music and at the same time can preserve the strict form. Hence the listener is not to suppose that he is being treated to a glimpse of an Olympian festival, in which this muse of the flute played an important part, but rather that he is hearing a classical composition laid out in classical style, with its regular introduction, its thematic material, contrasts, combinations, and subsidiary passages all woven into a symmetrical whole.

The overture to "Melpomene" was first played by the Boston Symphony Orchestra in 1886. Its tragic mood is evidenced at once in the opening measures. The first theme of the introduction is given out by the English horn and trombone and colors the whole overture. After the theme has passed to the strings and wood winds, a new subject is indicated. Chords in full orchestra prepare the way for the first theme announced by the strings. The rest of the first section is worked out in regular form and closes with a trumpet call, evidently the signal for the contest. The second theme is given out by the oboe and English horn, accompanied by the strings and wind instruments. This theme is most elaborately developed. Anon the first theme reappears and leads to a powerful climax for full orchestra. The strife is at its height, but in the Coda the tolling bells announce the end of the battle. In this work the composer has utilized the full resources of the orchestra, the brass section and percussion instruments being specially conspicuous in the dramatic climax, and at the same time he has displayed scholarly skill in the handling of the thematic material and in working up the tragic denouement.

Elegiac Overture, Adonais

The "Elegiac" Overture "Adonais" was written in 1899 and is dedicated to the memory of the composer's friend, Frank Fay Marshall, who died in 1897. It was suggested by the elegy of Shelley on the death of Keats. It bears the same title, "Adonais," but evidently is not intended to illustrate the varying phases and emotions of the poem. The inspiration must have been caught from the opening lines —

> "I weep for Adonais — he is dead!
> Oh, weep for Adonais! though our tears
> Thaw not the frost which binds so dear a head!"

but there is no further relationship between the music and the poem.

The overture, which is an Allegro, begins with an Adagio introduction in which a tender theme appears in the first violins, dominating the whole work in varied forms. This is followed by the first theme, which after development gives place to passage work of a more vigorous character, still with suggestions of the theme. At last the theme returns in the oboes, alternating with a passage in the basses and bassoons which has appeared in the passage work. The second theme is stated in the violins in unison over chords in the wood winds and harp arpeggios. The theme is followed by a passage based upon the theme in the introduction, and this in turn by a sombre hymn for the brasses, this section closing with the return of the second theme. After a brief free fantasia and recapitulation a long Coda closes with a return of the introduction and the work ends pianissimo.

Tam O'Shanter, Ballade for Orchestra

Mr. Chadwick's lively setting of Burns' well-known poem was first produced in 1915, at Norfolk, Conn. The sketch is condensed from one furnished by the composer for the original program. A brief introduction leads to the Tam O'Shanter theme, a chorus in the style of the Scotch folk tune, set forth in the horns and trombones and repeated by the strings and wood winds. It is interrupted by a thunderstorm and after it dies away, Tam's homeward journey begins in a trotting figure in the basses and 'cellos. This is followed by a choral theme based on the old Scotch tune "The Martyrs." At its close, the composer presents the revel in the church in a wild instrumental orgy. After Tam's recitative, in the horns and bassoons, silence for an instant, and then follows the wild witch chase and the tragedy at the bridge to Maggie. In the Finale, the Tam O'Shanter theme returns at first in the wind instruments and then to the divided strings and harp. But here it no longer depicts the carousals of the drunken Highlanders. It is a quiet melody with simple harmonizing. A short episode brings each fragment of the revel in combination with the trombone Chorale and the ballade ends with a reminiscence of the Tam O'Shanter theme.

Symphonic Sketches

Chadwick composed his Symphonic Sketches at various periods. The first two movements — "Jubilee" and "Noël" — were written in 1895, the last movement — "A Vagrom Ballad" — in 1896, and the third movement — "Hobgoblin" — in 1904. The work as a whole was published in 1907.

The first movement, entitled "Jubilee," is a reflection in sound of the following poem, which is printed on a fly-leaf of the score:

> No cool gray tones for me!
> Give me the warmest red and green,
> A cornet and a tambourine,
> To paint my jubilee!
>
> For when the flutes and oboes play,
> To sadness I become a prey;
> Give me the violets and the May,
> But no gray skies for me!

The movement begins exultantly with a theme given out sonorously by the full orchestra. Later a new idea is brought forward by the lower wood winds, violas and violoncellos and is developed. The first theme then returns and is worked over. The mood changes (Lento espressivo) and a quiet passage is given out by the wood winds and horns. Previous material recurs and a brilliant Coda (Presto) brings the movement to an end.

II. Noël. Andante con tenerezza, D flat major, 3-4 time. The poem which serves as the "program" of the movement is as follows:

> Through the soft, calm moonlight comes a sound;
> A mother lulls her babe, and all around
> The gentle snow lies glistening;

On such a night the Virgin Mother mild
In dreamless slumber wrapped the Holy Child,
While angel hosts were listening.

It may be mentioned in connection with the composer's inspiration that his younger son is named Noël. The music consists for the most part of a development of the subject which is set forth by the English horn four measures after the movement begins. A solo violin takes it up and there is a continuing section whose material is given to the violoncellos. After development and a fortissimo repetition of the opening theme, the movement closes tranquilly, as it had begun.

III. Hobgoblin. Scherzo capriccioso (Allegro vivace, F major, 3-4 time). The composer informed Mr. Philip Hale, the writer of the program books of the Boston Symphony Orchestra, that he had in mind "the rascally imp that frights maidens of the villagery, skims milk, mocks the breathless housewife at the churn, misleads night wanderers, disconcerts sorely the wisest aunt telling the saddest tale." The motto of the movement is Shakespeare's "That shrewd and knavish sprite, called Robin Goodfellow." The principal theme of the movement is heard, after a short introduction, in the wood winds. After this has been worked over extensively there is brought forward by the bassoons (un poco più moderato) the subject of what may be regarded as the Trio. The first part is then repeated with modifications.

IV. A Vagrom Ballad (Moderato, Alla Barla, A minor, 2-4 time). The following verse is printed on the score:

A tale of tramps and railroad ties,
Of old clay pipes and rum,
Of broken heads and blackened eyes
And the "thirty days" to come!

The movement opens with fourteen measures of introduction, which include a cadenza for the bass clarinet. A melody in A minor is given out by lower wood winds, into which a passage for muted trumpets and drum is thrown. Following a fortissimo chord for full orchestra and a pause, a new idea is heard, in D minor, by the clarinets and violas. Soon there is heard (in the xylophone) a quotation from Bach's G minor fugue for organ. Development follows and after another pause on a fortissimo chord there comes a new section (Lento misterioso) which is a cadenza for the bass clarinet. The Coda is Molto vivace.

F. B.

CHARPENTIER (GUSTAVE)

1860–

Suite, Impressions of Italy

THE name of Charpentier is not a very familiar one upon concert programs, nor was it well known to the American musical world until his romantic opera "Louise," first produced in Paris in 1900, was brought out in New York. It was during his stay in Rome (1888-1890) that he wrote the suite "Impressions of Italy." It was first performed entire in Paris in 1892, and for the first time in this country in 1893 by the Chicago Orchestra.

The suite is in five movements, and its program, affixed to the score, furnishes a sufficient musical analysis. It is presented here in condensed form. In the opening movement, "Serenade," young fellows at midnight, returning from the Osteria, are supposed to be singing serenades beneath their inamoratas' windows, accompanied by mandolins and guitars. In the second movement, "At the Fountain," we have the march of girls toward the waterfalls in the ravines, while the gay refrains of shepherds sound down from the mountain. The third movement, "On Muleback," pictures the mules trotting along to the sound of their bells. The *mulattiere* ('cello) sings a canzone, and "the sweet thirds that follow are the loving songs murmured by fair girls in the carts going up to the village." The fourth movement, "On the Summits," is a graphic and delightful Sorrentian picture. The strings in long-sustained tones furnish the background. A horn suggests a distant monastery bell. The flutes, clarinets, and harps suggest the singing of birds. The violas and 'cellos sing of poetic enthusiasm, and in the midst of their deep tones the church bells are heard, the picture fading away with their gradually diminishing sounds. The final movement, "Napoli," "is a musical picture of Naples. . . . It seems as if songs came from every street, dance rhythms, the amorous languor of violins, the amusing plunking of guitars. Calls answer to calls, military bands play loudly their brazen symphony. Dancers strike the ground with their feet and carry the rocking rhythm of tarantellas from group to group. 'Tis like the great song of a people, the hymn of Naples on its azure bay."

CHAUSSON

1855 – 1899

Symphony, B Flat Major, Op. 20

ERNEST CHAUSSON was a pupil of César Franck, whose influence is not absent from the former's works. For some time Chausson, who was a man of wealth, was a member of the composition class conducted by Jules Massenet at the Paris Conservatoire, but the ideals which were held aloft by Massenet — ideals connected with the theater — were not such as appealed to Chausson and about 1880 he came under the tuition of Franck. There was a certain similarity between teacher and pupil. Both were of the shy and diffident and modest character that made them so lovable to their friends and which, it may be added, militated against their worldly success. For both Franck and Chausson were comparatively unknown during their lifetime. The death of Chausson was of tragic suddenness. He was riding a bicycle down a hill upon his estate at Limay and, losing control of it, was dashed against a stone wall at the foot of the incline and instantly killed.

The symphony by Chausson was completed in 1890 and was played for the first time at a concert of the Société Nationale, Paris, April 18, 1891. It remained practically unknown in America until 1905, when it was given its first performance in this country at Boston, at a concert of the Boston Symphony Orchestra, December 4. The work, which was dedicated to Henry Lerolle, a well-known painter in Paris during Chausson's lifetime, was scored for three flutes, piccolo, two oboes, English horn, three clarinets, bass clarinet, three bassoons, four horns, four trumpets, three trombones, bass tuba, kettle-drums, two harps and strings.

I. The movement opens with an Introduction (Lent, B flat major, 4-4 time) whose subject is given out in the lower strings, clarinet and first horn. Important employment is given to this in the finale. The main movement (Allegro vivo, 3-4 time) sets forth its principal theme in the horn and bassoon. The full orchestra take it up. A transitional passage brings forward an upward and downward staccato figure in the wood winds of which use is made later. The second subject is given to the violoncellos and clarinet. Development now takes place, with extensive working over of the wood-wind staccato figure and of the principal theme. There is a return (in the brass) to the material of the Introduction and this is followed by the customary recapitulation.

II. (Très lent, D minor, 4-4 time.) The movement opens solemnly in the strings and wood winds. Soon a new idea is set forth by the English horn and clarinet with a triplet figure against it in the lower strings. A varied restatement of the opening material follows in the horns, the tempo is hastened and an expressive melody is given out by the violoncellos and English horn over an arpeggio figure in the strings. The violins take this up and the theme is worked up to a great climax, on which the principal theme returns fortissimo in the full orchestra.

III. (Animé, B flat minor, 4-4 time.) The movement begins with an Introduction, whose material is comprised in a foreshadowing of the principal theme of the main movement in the trumpet and wood winds against a whirling figure in the strings. The subject of the movement proper is announced by the basses — a strongly accented and energetic theme. The second subject appears in the full orchestra, a second section of it appearing in the oboe. Development now takes place, this including the working out of material in the first movement. The recapitulation follows and toward the end of the symphony the material which opened the work (Grave) returns.

F. B.

Symphonic Poem, Viviane, Op. 5

This work, whose complete title is "Viviane, symphonic poem after a legend of the Round Table," was written in 1882 and performed for the first time at a concert given at the Cirque d'Hiver, Paris, March 30, 1884, under the auspices of the Société Nationale de Musique. Later Chausson revised "Viviane" and it was performed at a Lamoureux concert, Paris, January 29, 1888. The work was heard for the first time in America at a concert of the Chicago Orchestra, Chicago, October 22, 1898. The symphonic poem is concerned with that portion of Arthurian legend, which deals with the enchanter, Merlin, and his mistress, Viviane. She is said to have brought up Lancelot in her palace, situated in the middle of a magic lake. She makes the acquaintance of Merlin, and he, infatuated by Viviane's beauty, confides to her one of his magic spells. Viviane, not believing in this charm, tries it on her lover with the result that Merlin is entrapped in a bush of hawthorn, from which his mistress is unable to release him.

Chausson's score contains the following "program":

"Viviane and Merlin in the Forest of Brocéliande. Love Scene.

"Trumpet-calls. Messengers from King Arthur scour the forest in search of the enchanter.

"Merlin remembers his errand. He fain would fly to the embraces of Viviane.

"Scene of the enchantment. To detain him, Viviane puts Merlin to sleep and binds him with blossoming hawthorns."

It will be observed that Chausson's "program" is a slight departure from the version of the legend set forth above; the composer having made use of the Amorican tale, as told by Villermarqué.

F. B.

CHERUBINI

1760 – 1842

Overture to The Water Carrier

"THE Water Carrier," known in Germany as "Der Wasserträger," in France as "Les deux Journées," and in Italy as "Il Portatore d' Acqua," was first performed at the Théâtre Feydeau, Paris, January 11, 1800, and established the fame of Cherubini. The story of the opera relates the many hair-breadth escapes of one Count Armand, President of the French Parliament, in the time of Cardinal Mazarin, who succeeds in making his escape from Paris by concealment in the water cart of a Savoyard whom he has once befriended. It is specially distinguished for the ease and grace of its introduction and the strong, vigorous character of its concerted numbers.

The overture opens with an Andante introduction, leading through a climax to the Allegro, or main section. After three measures in the strings, the full orchestra gives out the first theme, fortissimo. After the concluding melodic passage in the flute and first violins, the second theme is announced, followed by passage work in the flute, first violins, and clarinet, with full orchestral chords accentuating it. The second theme soon returns and is elaborated. A subsidiary theme, closing fortissimo in full orchestra, leads to the free fantasia, after the development of which, a long and brilliant Coda closes the overture.

Overture to Anacréon

The opera "Anacréon, ou l'Amour fugitif," was first performed at the Grand Opéra, Paris, October 4, 1803. The story is too absurd and inconsistent to be worth the telling. At the first presentation of the opera the audience was convulsed with laughter over its silliness, but the overture has survived, old-fashioned as it is, and is still a favorite in the concert-room. It opens with a slow, dignified movement in the full orchestra, followed by harmonies in the horns and wood winds several times repeated. In place of set themes it is constructed of fragments of phrases worked up by different instruments but resolving into symmetrical harmonies. After a pause, the Allegro opens in the strings alone and is elaborated with great skill. The figure passes from one group of instruments to another, and new matter is continually developed. After an episode and a pause, new material in the strings, and afterwards in the horns, is introduced. In the close of the overture a famous passage appears in the violins, culminating in a trill, and bringing the work to a brilliant close. One of the peculiar features of this overture is the introduction of the long and gradual crescendo passages which Rossini afterwards employed so often, as well as the use of the English horn.

CHOPIN

1810 – 1849

Funeral March

THE "Funeral March" of Chopin, as played in the concert-room, is an adaptation of the slow movement of Chopin's second pianoforte sonata in B flat minor, Op. 35. The work is so familiar as to need no description. The circumstances under which Chopin wrote it however, as told by M. Ziem, are of interest. Ziem, the artist, had been one evening to the studio of Polignac. There was a skeleton in the studio and among the Bohemian whimsicalities, Polignac placed it at the piano and guided its hands over the keys. In Ziem's own words:

"Some time later Chopin came into my studio, just as George Sand depicts him — the imagination haunted by the legends of the land of frogs, besieged by nameless shapes. After frightful nightmares all night, in which he had struggled against specters who threatened to carry him off to hell, he came to rest in my studio. His nightmares reminded me of the skeleton scene, and I told him of it. His eyes never left my piano, and he asked: 'Have you a skeleton?' I had none; but I promised to have one that night, and so invited Polignac to dinner and asked him to bring his skeleton. What had previously been a mere farce became, owing to Chopin's inspiration, something grand, terrible and painful. Pale, with staring eyes, and draped in a winding sheet, Chopin held the skeleton close to him, and suddenly the silence of the studio was broken by the broad, slow, deep, gloomy notes. The 'Dead March' was composed there and then from beginning to end."

CORNELIUS

1824 – 1874

Overture to The Barber of Bagdad

THE overture to "The Barber of Bagdad" is one of the most charming works of its kind in the concert repertory. The story of the opera, however, is weak and absurd. Noureddin, in love with Morgiana, the Caliph's daughter, has a secret interview with her at the opening of the work. Abdul Hassan, a garrulous barber, in the meantime is watching for him in the street. Hearing the outcries of a servant who is being chastised, he imagines Noureddin is the victim. As Abdul forces his way into the house Noureddin in alarm hides in a chest. The Caliph arrives upon the scene and discovers Noureddin, who is nearly suffocated. The barber revives him, explanations follow, and the Caliph gives the hand of Morgiana to her lover. To this silly tale Cornelius set music which created a profound excitement among musicians in Germany when it was first heard, and even had an important influence upon Wagner.

In the overture the composer has employed a *Leitmotif*, an Oriental chromatic theme, representing the barber, throughout the opera. It is followed by an allusion to a comic song by the barber, which with a song by Noureddin, calling for Morgiana, and another by Morgiana, form the introduction. The overture proper begins with a charming melody in the wood winds and muted strings, leading to another beautiful passage from a scene in the opera where the slaves sing their master to sleep. These two themes are combined and elaborated in a most skilful and fascinating manner. The overture comes to a close with a stirring and vigorous Coda. It is not only characterized by mirth and jollity, but also by extraordinary musical inventiveness and ludicrous feats of instrumentation.

DEBUSSY

1862 – 1918

Prelude to The Afternoon of a Faun

THE prelude to "The Afternoon of a Faun," suggested by the symbolic poem of Mallarmé, "L'après midi d'un Faune," was performed for the first time in Paris, in 1894. Notwithstanding the somewhat obscure text of the poem, the composer has accompanied it with delicate, expressive, and graceful music significant of the sensuous, pleasure-loving nature of the Faun. It is in effect a pastoral rhapsody without fixed form, the composer apparently having given himself up to the formless and sensuous character of the text. The principal theme is given out in the solo flute and colors the entire prelude. It is a very dreamy melody and is heard repeatedly in the wood wind tones and distant sound of horns. After the theme has had its way, the oboe and clarinet enter in a dialogue of a passionate nature. The flute theme soon returns, however, and after a subsidiary passage in the 'cello, rejoins the flute, the melody finally dying away as the charming picture disappears. The spirit which pervades the closing section is reflected in Edmund Gosse's rhapsodical interpretation of the concluding lines of the poem:

> "The delicious hour grew vaguer. Experience or dream, he (the Faun) will never know which it was. The sun is warm, the grasses yielding; and he curls himself up again after worshiping the efficacious star of wine that he may pursue the dubious ecstasy with the more hopeful boskages of sleep."

Three Nocturnes

The three nocturnes comprising this suite were written in 1897-1899. They are not nocturnes in the ordinary meaning of the term, but impressions. Though they have a program, they do not describe objects, only fantasias upon objects. Perhaps they may be more accurately defined as dreams — delicate, fleeting, elusive fancies connected in this case with the motion or rhythm of the objects. The three nocturnes are: "Clouds, and their floating across the sky; festivals, movement, rhythm dancing in the atmosphere; Sirens, the sea with its rhythm, and the song of the Sirens." It would be useless to describe this dream music in cold type. One of the best descriptions of it has been made by Bruneau, the composer:

"Here, with the aid of a magic orchestra, he has lent to clouds traversing the sombre sky the various forms created by his imagination; he has set to running and dancing the chimerical beings perceived by him in the silvery dust scintillating in the moonbeams; he has changed the white foam of the restless sea into tuneful Sirens."

Debussy himself explains the significance of these nocturnes as follows:

"Nuages." — The unchanging aspect of the sky, and the slow, solemn movement of the clouds dissolving in gray tints lightly touched with white.

"Fêtes." — The restless dancing rhythm of the atmosphere interspersed with sudden flashes of light. There is also an incidental procession (a dazzling imaginary vision) passing through and through and mingling with the aerial revery; but the background of uninterrupted festival is persistent with its blending of music, and luminous dust participating in the universal rhythm of all things."

The third Nocturne is entitled "Sirens" and was first performed at Paris in 1901. The work employed eight mezzo-soprano voices which do not, however, sing any text. Debussy's "program" was as follows: "The Sea and its innumerable rhythms; then amid the billows silvered by the moon the mysterious song of the Siren is heard. It laughs and passes."

Petite Suite

The "Petite Suite" of Debussy's was originally written for the piano, four hands, in 1889, and arranged for orchestra by

Henri Büsser in 1909. The suite is in four movements. The first ("En Bateau") opens with a theme in the flute with accompaniment in the strings muted. After development, a new theme appears in the violins and clarinets. This in turn is developed, after which the opening theme returns this time to the violins.

The second movement ("Cortège") begins with a theme in the flutes and oboes, the strings pizzicato and the harp and triangle giving the march rhythm. A counter theme is given to the lower strings, after which the march returns. After a new subject in the strings, the march closes the movement.

The third movement ("Menuet") after introduction in the wood winds opens with a theme in the first violins. The theme of the Trio is announced by the bassoon with string accompaniment and after development, the theme of the first part is given in the oboe.

The fourth movement ("Ballet") opens with a theme in the strings in unison. After a continuing section in the strings and its development, the first theme returns in full orchestra. A new subject appears in the violins to waltz time. After the recurrence of the first theme, the movement closes with suggestions of the waltz.

Gigues

"Gigues" is the first of a set of three pieces for orchestra called "Images," the other two being "Iberia" and "Rondes de Printemps." After a long introduction, the first theme is given out as a solo in the oboe d'amore. This is followed by a second theme in the bassoons. These two themes form the principal material of the piece and are worked up in the Debussy manner.

La Mer (Three Orchestral Sketches)

Debussy began the three Orchestral Sketches which he collectively entitled "The Sea," in 1903 and completed them two years later, when they were performed for the first time at a Lamoureux concert, Paris, October 15. Debussy conducted the work himself at a Colonne concert in September and a clash occurred between the admirers of the master's music and those who disliked it as being too "modern." The cat-calls, whistling and other forms of disapproval were quieted only by the appearance of the violinist Jacques Thibaud to play the D minor Chaconne by Bach.

Debussy disliked formal analysis of his works. "No fixed rule," he wrote once, "should guide the creative artist. Rules are established by works of art, not for works of art." The three pieces should, therefore, be listened to as impressionistic sketches whose titles permit the imagination to discover therein whatever the poetic sense can find. The first is entitled "From Dawn to Noon at Sea." The second is "Gambols of the Waves," and the third, "Dialogue Between the Wind and the Sea."

F. B.

Iberia (Images for Orchestra, No. 2)

Iberia was the name given to Spain by the ancient Greeks and Debussy's composition of that name represented his impressions of that country. It should be said, however, that the French master never visited Spain, except for an hour or two when he crossed the frontier to visit Saint Sebastian. His "Iberia," therefore, is a translation into sound of what he imagined Spain to be.

The work was composed in 1909 and it was performed for the first time at a Colonne concert, Paris, February 29, 1910. In America it was first heard at a concert of the Philharmonic Society of New York, January 3, 1911. "Iberia" is divided into the following sections: I. "Par les Rues et par les Chemins" ("In the streets and by the Wayside"). II. "Les Parfums de la Nuit" ("The Perfumes of the Night"). III. "Le Matin d'un Jour de Fête" ("The Morning of a Fête Day"). It should be remarked that the second movement leads without pause into the third.

F. B.

Marche Écossaise

This piece was originally written in 1891 as work for piano (four hands) and Debussy arranged it for orchestra in 1908. The theme of the march is not the creation of the French master, who took for the basis of the work a piece known as the Earl of Ross' March. The composition begins with some introductory material (Allegretto scherzando, A minor, 2-4 time), after which the opening theme is given out by the oboe and trumpet. Soon a new idea is brought forward by the wind instruments and in this a triplet figure plays an important part. The opening subject is developed and, ending fortissimo, is succeeded by a new section (Calme, F major), whose theme is announced by the English horn over a syncopated accompaniment in the muted lower strings. This is worked over. The time changes to 6-8, the tempo becomes quicker and the opening theme returns, now in 6-8 instead of 2-4. There is a Coda in A major at the end.

F. B.

DeLAMARTER

1880 –

Suite from music to The Betrothal

ERIC DeLAMARTER, born at Lansing, Mich., received much of his musical education in Chicago — he was, also, for a year a pupil in organ playing of Guilmant and Widor in Paris — and has made his career there. Since 1914 he has been organist of the Fourth Presbyterian Church and assistant conductor of the Chicago Symphony Orchestra since 1918. DeLamarter also has been active in musical journalism, having been critic on the staff of the Chicago Record-Herald, Chicago Inter-Ocean and Chicago Tribune.

The music to "The Betrothal" was composed for a production of the play of that name by Maeterlinck which was made by Winthrop Ames at the Schubert Theater, New York in 1919. The piece was a sequel to "The Blue Bird," which told of the peasant boy Tyltyl and of his search for happiness. Tyltyl and his sister appear also in "The Betrothal," in which play he goes to the homes of his ancestors and of his children-to-be in a search for his true mate. With him go his six sweethearts and a "veiled figure," who is none other than Tyltyl's destined wife.

The suite, which was published with a dedication to Winthrop Ames in 1929, contains three movements — An Overture, "The Veiled Figure" and "Dance of the Sweethearts." The overture is an expression of the light-heartedness and restlessness of youth and was written without reference to subsequent themes employed in the play. It is based on two motives, the first having a little catch of syncopation in it, the second, a brief lyric phrase. The second movement presents in the introduction the phrase which characterizes Tyltyl throughout the piece. Following this there is heard (in a solo violin) the motive belonging to the "Veiled Figure." The third movement was devised, as the composer has put it, "for a rapturous dance, with which the six sweethearts closed the first act of the play.

F. B.

DELIBES

1836 – 1891

Suite, Sylvia

THE delightful ballet "Sylvia," or "The Nymphs of Diana," from which the composer compiled this suite, was first performed in Paris in 1876. As arranged for concert purposes it is in four movements: 1. Prelude and Les Chasseresses. 2. Intermezzo and Valse lento. 3. Pizzicato. 4. Cortège de Bacchus. The first movement is devoted to the chase, which is in full action after a short prelude in the strings and dies away gradually in the distance. The second movement is a languishing waltz, succeeding a picturesque intermezzo. The third movement, pizzicato, is a dainty, piquant bit, the first violins giving out the theme accompanied by the other strings, pizzicato, and leading up to the closing movement, Bacchus' revel. It is a picture of a fantastic bacchanalian march movement in which, in the original ballet, satyrs appear, armed with javelins, whose approach is indicated by the trumpets. Maidens enter with flowers, followed by half-drunken fauns, bringing a goat for sacrifice. The revel begins in wild glee. The tempo quickens, the drums beginning and the basses and strings continuing the pranks of the mad company. The arrival of the wine-drinking god is suggested in an unexpected Largo, which as suprisingly develops into the wild delights of the revel.

DELIUS

1863 –

A Dance Rhapsody

FREDERICK DELIUS, who was born at Bradford, England, of German parentage, was originally destined for a commercial career and, indeed, went to America when he was twenty years of age, to take up the business of orange cultivation. In 1885 he made up his mind that music was really his vocation and he went to the Conservatory of Leipzig to study with Carl Reinecke and Jadassohn. In 1890 Delius settled at Grez-sur-Loing, in France, where he has remained ever since.

"A Dance Rhapsody" was composed in 1908 and was produced for the first time at a concert of the Hereford Music Festival, England, September 8, 1909. The composer was also the conductor on that occasion. The rhapsody, dedicated to Hermann Suter (1870-1926), a composer of considerable influence in Swiss music, was published in 1910. It opens with some introductory matter given out by the oboe and English horn. Following a fortissimo chord in the full orchestra, the principal subject is heard in the oboe, lightly accompanied by the lower strings and the bassoon. After development of this, there comes a new section (Vivo) whose theme is given out by the bassoons and lower strings. This, too, is subjected to development, after which the opening material is resumed.

F. B.

Life's Dance

This piece is a revised version of a work which, entitled "The Dance Goes On," had been composed in 1898 and produced in London the following year. Delius then rewrote it and the work was played, in its new form, for the first time as "Lebenstanz" at Düsseldorf, Germany, in 1904. Still later it was given at a concert in the Albert Hall, London, under the title "The Dance of Life" and the reviewer of music for the *Musical Times,* London, wrote concerning the work: "The title 'Life's Dance' written on the autograph score, more truly suggests the true character of the piece, the aim of the composer evidently being to depict some of the vicissitudes common to earthly existence." In Germany it was stated that Delius' composition was inspired by "Das Tanzlied" in Nietzsche's "Thus Spake Zarathustra": "In thine eyes, O Life, I gazed in youth! And in the unfathomable I seemed to sink therein." But the composer, who does not approve of "programs" to musical compositions lest they interfere with the listening, did not endorse this explanation of his music.

"Life's Dance" opens with introductory material (Allegro con brio, B flat minor, 6-8 time) which foreshadows the principal theme. The latter enters in the horns, the violins softly accompanying it. Development takes place and this is succeeded by a new idea (Lento) which a solo violin gives out on the G string. This leads to the second theme proper, the violas and violoncellos singing it as in a duet, the arpeggios of the harp and the tremolos of the violins accompanying it. Development of the first subject is resumed, a march-like motive being intermingled with it. The second theme is also hinted at in the first violins, but the rhythm of the first recurs. A waltz-like solo for the violin is heard and this is followed by a repetition of the opening portion of the work. There is further hearing of the first subject and a fortissimo presentation of the second in the brass. The piece ends on an unresolved chord, in the fashion of Richard Strauss' "Thus Spake Zarathustra."

F. B.

Paris: A Night Piece

Delius composed this work, which is subtitled "The Song of a Great City," in 1899-1900 and it was performed for the first time at Elberfeld, Germany, in the latter year, by the municipal orchestra of that city. In America it was first performed by the Boston Symphony Orchestra, Boston, November 26, 1910, under the direction of Max Fiedler.

No statement of the programatic significance of "Paris" is printed on the score, but Richard A. Streatfield, a friend of the composer and evidently inspired by him, gave the following explanation of the work:

"'Paris' is a musical picture of the composer's impressions of the great city by night. It is no mere exercise in musical realism, though it displays a keen sense of pictorial effect. Rather is it a personal record of the feelings engendered by the contemplation of the sleeping city. It is a study of effects rather than of causes, and in this is a peculiarly characteristic example of Delius' attitude toward music, and of his employment of its resources."

The composition is freely constructed as to form, but it may be remarked that Delius employs it in some of the street cries of Paris.

F. B.

On Hearing the First Cuckoo in Spring

This small piece for orchestra was composed in 1912 and was performed for the first time at a concert of the Philharmonic Society, London, January 20, 1914, under the direction of Willem Mengelberg. The piece contains two themes, the first original with the composer; the second the Norwegian folk song "I Ola Dalom" ("In Ola Valley") which Grieg harmonized in his "Norwegische Volksweisen," Opus. 66, for piano. "Delius," wrote Percy Grainger, "adores Norway and knows it as few non-Scandinavians do. He has spent eighteen summers there in the high hills (Jotunheim). Therefore, the advent of the spring brings for him longings for Norway and particularly for those glorious mountains and fine hillmen from which 'I Ola Dalom' hails. That is why he has used this Norwegian tune in this impression of Spring."

F. B.

DOHNÁNYI

1877–

Suite for Orchestra. Op. 19

DOHNÁNYI'S fascinating Suite for Orchestra was written in 1911 and is scored for an unusually complete orchestra. It is in four movements. The first, Andante con Variazioni, opens with an attractive theme in the wood winds, subsequently taken by the strings and treated to six variations. The second movement, Scherzo, opens with a theme in the wood winds and repeated in the strings. The Trio follows, the theme assigned to clarinet, and after development, the main theme is heard again, the movement closing with the Trio theme in the horns. The third movement, Romanza, opens with a graceful theme in the oboe, followed by a pert melody in the English horn. A third theme ensues in the strings with harp accompaniment. All this material is developed and the movement closes with the return of the second theme. The fourth movement, Rondo, opens with a theme in the strings, repeated in the wood winds. After a fortissimo phrase and the reentrance of the first theme, a new subject appears in the flute leading to a theme in the strings with 'cello accompaniment. This material is developed and the main theme reappears. This is worked up to a crescendo. The strings, wood winds and horns give out a vigorous theme, the rhythm accented by the castanets. In the closing measures the theme of the opening movement is heard.

DUKAS

1865–

Scherzo, L'Apprenti Sorcier

THE Scherzo, "L'Apprenti Sorcier," is a fanciful composition based upon Goethe's ballad "Der Zauberlehrling" ("The Magician's Apprentice") and was first performed in Paris in 1897. The work is free in form, and simply describes in a picturesque way the strange antics as recorded in the poem performed by the apprentice after he escaped from his master's service. An analysis of the music is hardly necessary, so clearly is the story told. In various fantastic ways the composer describes the river which supplies water for the bath, and particularly the apprentice's misadventure with the broom, which he bids stand upon two legs and bring the water in a pail. In an unfortunate moment he forgets the magic word, and the broom continues bringing pails of water until the house is flooded. Thereupon he seizes an axe and splits the broom in twain, which only increases his troubles, for both parts hurry off for water and empty it into the house in such quantities that the frightened amateur implores his master to return, and help him out of his plight. The composer has told the quaint story in tones, with great dexterity and strong effect.

DVOŘÁK

1841 – 1904

Symphony No. 3, in D Major. Op. 60

1. Allegro non tanto.
2. Adagio.
3. Scherzo (furiant).
4. Finale. Allegro con spirito.

DVOŘÁK'S Third Symphony was written in 1884, and was also his first published work. Notwithstanding its essentially Slavic character the regular symphonic form is not modified in any particular.

The first movement contains a rich display of musical ideas in its group of themes. The prelude to the opening theme is divided between the wind instruments, basses, and bassoons, and after four bars the subject is reached; but the key soon changes and a vigorous interruption occurs, after which the theme returns in the original time with a brilliant forte passage in the brasses. Its stay is transient, however, and the interruption occurs, vivacious in its character, which leads up to the introduction to the second theme — a thoroughly unique melody given out by the 'cellos and horns, with a picturesque string accompaniment. A duet for oboe and bassoon follows, with a melodious figure in accompaniment in the second violins and violas, and a long-sustained tone in the first violins. The theme is then repeated by full orchestra, after which all the ideas of the movement, of which there are no less than six distinct ones, are worked out in the orthodox form.

The second movement is rich in color, though gentle and dreamy in its sentiment. After a short prelude, as in the first movement, the first theme is given out by the strings with accompaniment in the wind instruments. After a short episode we reach the second part of the theme, taken by the flutes, with a refrain by the oboes. The key then changes, and another short episode leads back to the original key and principal subject. Another episode, developed from the materials of this theme, occurs and is followed by the Coda, in which there is a characteristic 'cello solo.

The third movement gives a national character to the whole symphony. It is marked "Furiant," and is in form and substance almost identical with the Slavonic dances, so many of which Dvořák has arranged. Its opening theme is fresh, piquant, and spirited, and is repeated over and over to a wild and furious accompaniment, punctuated and emphasized with all the strange accents and unusual rhythms that characterize the Bohemian and Hungarian music. The excitement reaches its climax in the Trio, in which the flutes and strings, pizzicato, carry the melody, and the piccolo gives it the genuine Slavic color. The second theme of the trio is broader and more dignified in style, and at its close the Scherzo is repeated and ends this stirring movement.

The last movement is made up of simple Bohemian melodies, treated in the most vigorous style. The opening theme is given out by the strings and clarinets, and with constantly accelerating tempo dashes on with a second theme for oboes and horns, which grows fairly furious when taken by the whole orchestra and yet shows humorous features in the peculiar entrances of the horns and trombones. The Coda opens with the first theme set forth by the horns and violas, and is developed with great skill. The movement comes to an end with a brilliant and vigorous Presto.

Symphony No. 5 in E Minor. Op. 95 (From the New World)

1. Adagio.
2. Allegro molto.
3. Larghetto.
4. Scherzo molto vivace.
5. Allegro con fuoco.

Dvořák's Fifth Symphony is one of peculiar interest, not only because of its intrinsic beauties and excellences, but also because it is in one sense a tribute to America by its utilization of melodies of negro character in the thematic treatment. After an expressive introduction, the first theme is given out by the horns and shortly the New World character of the work is illustrated by a rollicking passage for flutes and oboes, followed by a theme for flute with subdued string accompaniment, which every one will recognize as borrowed from the negro jubilee melody, "Swing low, sweet Chariot." The remainder of the movement is devoted to a conventional but most unique and complicated working up of these simple thematic materials.

After a short introduction for wood winds and brasses a most bewitching melody is given to the English horn in the second movement accompanied by muted strings. Its loveliness and pathos can hardly be overstated. After a repetition of much of the introduction the beautiful melody returns and is soon followed by a more resonant theme for flutes and oboes. This in turn is succeeded by some complicated development leading up to the conclusion, the "swan song" of which is the beautiful melody already referred to, which seems even more beautiful in its new setting.

The Scherzo is in the usual form, and besides its own themes contains reminiscences of the first movement. The last movement not only deals with its own materials but those of all the other movements, including the beautiful horn theme of the second, and closes a symphony which, if not as orthodox as some of its predecessors, is yet full of beauty and deservedly a favorite.

Overtures, In der Natur. Op. 91; Carnival, Op. 92; Othello, Op. 93

The three overtures entitled above are grouped together for the reason that they were written as a trilogy by the composer and were intended to be played together. They were styled "Triple Overture" and were described in the program of the first performance as "Nature," "Life" ("Bohemian Carnival"), and "Love" ("Othello"). The interrelation of the three seems somewhat forced, when judged by the titles, but they are connected by the link of one theme which is specially conspicuous in the first and third overtures, with a reference to it in the second.

As to the "Nature" Overture, Dvořák has left this clew to its meaning: "The composer chose in the part entitled 'Nature' to present the emotions awakened in a solitary walk through meadows and woods on a quiet summer afternoon when the shadows grow longer and longer until they lose themselves in the dusk and gradually turn into the early shades of night." The overture opens with the theme already mentioned, given out in the bassoon and violas with soft responses by the flute. It is developed in a graceful crescendo, and finally is announced fortissimo in full orchestra. After subsidiary passages the strings give out, pianissimo, a light and trifling little theme. This also is gradually worked up to a climax in which the first theme returns fortissimo. After the free fantasia, the third part begins with the first theme announced by English horn and bass clarinet. Further development follows, and the Coda opens with the first theme fortissimo in the horns and trumpets, accompanied by the violins and violas, after which the overture comes to a tranquil close.

The composer has also left a clew to the meaning of the "Carnival" Overture. He says he "imagines the lonely, contemplative wanderer reaching the city at nightfall, where a carnival of pleasure reigns supreme. On every side is heard the clangor of instruments, mingled with shouts of joy and the unrestrained hilarity of the people giving vent to their feelings in their songs and dance-tunes." The overture begins with a brilliant, vigorous theme, fortissimo, in full orchestra, describing the revelry of the people, which is freely developed. After subsidiary passages, the first and second violins introduce a second theme of a more quiet nature, a counter figure appearing in the oboes and clarinets. After its development, the opening theme returns in the violins, wood winds, and harp, and a fortissimo leads to an entirely new subject. The wanderer, mentioned in the composer's statement, accidentally encounters some surreptitious lovemaking in a quiet corner, and this gives rise to an episodic melody alternately announced in flute and violins with an accompanying figure in the English horn. The episode is a charming one, but is of short duration, and leads to the original Allegro and passages from the first theme. After a brilliant climax, the first theme returns and is developed. The revelry is then resumed, and its musical description closes the overture.

Except for the "Nature" theme, which binds the three overtures together, the relation of "Othello" to its two companions is very vague. It is rather a love poem than an overture. The "Nature" theme appears in the introduction as typical of Desdemona. The main section opens with a theme which clearly depicts the passion of Othello. It is answered by the Desdemona theme as soon as it is stated, and in the alternate statements and responses, and the transitions from the tragic wrath of the one to the piteous appeals of the other, their combinations and contrasts, the interest of the overture consists.

Overture, Husitzka. Op. 67

The "Husitzka" Overture was composed in 1883, the occasion of its composition being a commission to write a piece for the opening of the new Bohemian Theater in Prague, which replaced one destroyed by fire two years previously. As the theater was a national one, all classes of the Bohemian people contributed toward its erection, and Dvořák's overture added to the brilliancy of the dedicatory ceremonies. For the subject of his work the composer selected a stirring national event — the struggle of the followers of Johann Huss, the religious martyr — and for its main theme an impressive and defiant theme from one of the Hussite battle hymns. Around this theme in its varying forms and expression the overture is built. It depicts the alternating hopes and fears of the Hussites, the fury of the strife, and at last, in a jubilant climax, the triumphant outcome.

Overture, Mein Heim. Op. 62

The overture "Mein Heim" ("My Home") is based upon two themes from Bohemian folk songs. Both appear in the introduction, which, opening pianissimo, works up to a fortissimo. It gradually dies away, but soon through a vigorous crescendo leads to the main section of the overture, which opens with a new subject in dance time. After a brilliant development of this subject a quieter second subject appears, which is followed by subsidiary passages from the first. The first subject also appears in the Coda, closing the overture. The overture was written in 1882.

Scherzo Capriccioso. Op. 66

Dvořák wrote his Scherzo Capriccioso in the Spring of 1883, and it was published in the following year. It was played for the first time in America at a concert of the Brooklyn Philharmonic Society, November 8, 1884, Theodore Thomas having been the conductor. The Scherzo opens (Allegro con fuoco, 3-4 time) with a subject which, given out by the horns, may be regarded as the underlying basis of the work. But it is, however, introductory to the principal theme which is announced by the full orchestra. A second subject, of waltz-like character, is heard in the violins and, after some development, the material of the first part is repeated. The Trio, in D major, opens with a theme of expressive character in the English horn, this being succeeded by another subject given to the strings. The remainder of the work is made up of development of former material and a modified repetition of the Scherzo, with a Coda built upon the subject which had been heard at the opening of the piece.

F. B.

Slavonic Dances

The Slavonic Dances which Dvořák composed, in the first instance, for piano (four hands) were the works which first brought popularity to him. Simrock, the publisher who brought out the Bohemian master's earliest works, suggested that a set of Slavonic dances similar in vein to the Hungarian Dances by Brahms, would be likely to meet with favor from the public. In their original form Dvořák's Slavonic Dances were published in 1879 and so great was the success that Simrock urged the composer to arrange them for orchestra. It was the popularity of the Dances, too, which moved Dvořák to write a second series in 1886. There are sixteen of the Slavonic Dances in all.

F. B.

ELGAR

1857 –

Symphony No. 1, in A Flat. Op. 55

1. Andante. Nobilmente e semplice.
2. Allegro molto.
3. Adagio.
4. Lento. Allegro.

SIR EDWARD ELGAR'S First Symphony was finished and produced in 1908 in Manchester, England. Upon the composer's own authority, "it is written out of a full life experience and it meant to include the innumerable phases of joy and sorrow, struggle and conquest, and especially between the ideal and the actual in life. . . . It is written in a cypher to which every hearer possesses a key in his own experience."

The introduction to the first movement contains the material with which the whole structure is built. The opening theme is given out in this introduction by the wood winds and violas with staccato accompaniment in the 'cellos and double basses, and is then repeated by full orchestra. At its close the principal subject appears in the first violins, clarinets and bassoons, and is repeated fortissimo following a passage for the strings. After a climax and a new motive for the violins, the second subject appears in the first violins. After development of all the previous material, a new motive is heard in the strings and the second section is worked out. A recapitulation and long Coda bring the movement to a close.

The second movement opens vigorously in the first violins, followed by a fortissimo passage in the strings, which leads to a second subject for violas and clarinets. The opening figure reappears, followed by the fortissimo passage, at the end of which, the first theme is repeated. The Trio contains two themes, the first a duet for flutes, and the second for clarinets. After these themes are developed, and the recapitulation, a long Coda, constructed out of the first subject and the Trio, leads without stop into the third movement, the opening theme of which is the same subject as that which opened the second movement, but treated in different style, and also containing the opening theme of the symphony. After a second theme has been stated, the first returns in the strings and after development is followed by a new subject for the first violins, with which the movement closes.

The Finale opens with a slow introduction in which is heard one of the motives in the first movement. Other themes already heard are worked over and are followed by a second subject in the clarinets, violas and 'cellos. This in turn is followed by an episode, which was already suggested in the introduction. The second subject, which is in march rhythm, begins softly but reaches a climax for full orchestra. A masterly working out of the principal material of the symphony follows. The second subject is again stated and reaches a majestic climax for full orchestra. The fundamental theme dominates the close of the movement.

Symphony No. 2, in E Flat Major. Op. 63

1. Allegro vivace e nobilmente.
2. Larghetto.
3. Rondo. Presto.
4. Moderato e maestoso.

Elgar's Second Symphony was composed in 1900-1911 and first performed in London, May 24 of the latter year, and is dedicated "to the memory of His late Majesty, King Edward VII, with the gracious approval of His Majesty King George." Newman, the English critic and a close friend of Elgar, says that while the work is not written upon any program, "the dominant note of the poem is one of despondency, merging into hope at the end."

The first movement begins without introduction with a charming theme followed by four subsidiary themes which are skilfully treated. The second subject is given out by the 'cellos with a striking viola accompaniment and goes through the usual development. After a climax has been reached, a diminuendo leads to a passage for the muted strings. A very effective recapitulation of all this material brings the movement to its close.

After a short introduction for the strings, the second movement, which is somewhat in the style of a funeral march, opens with the principal theme given out in stately manner by clarinets, flutes, horn, trumpets and trombones. A passage for English horn and oboe leads to a new subject in the strings alone, followed by a motive, based upon the first theme, which, in turn, is succeeded by a new subject, given out by the horns. The development of this thematic material occupies the remainder of the movement.

A skilfully constructed Rondo takes the place of the usual Scherzo, the main theme of which is stated in the strings and wood winds. After repetition, a new passage occurs for strings and English horn. Upon the repetition of this passage a counter melody appears in the oboe. Development of this material, during which there is a long passage for strings alone, closes the Rondo.

The first and principal theme of the last movement opens in the 'cellos, wood winds and horns, and after treatment is followed by a second theme in the strings, and the third in the violins and 'cellos. The usual development follows and the symphony comes to a gradual and gentle close.

The Light of Life

"The Light of Life," sometimes called a cantata, but by the composer himself a short oratorio, the text by Rev. E. Capel-Cure, was first performed at the Worcester (England) Musical Festival, September, 1896. The libretto has for its theme the miracle of the man who was born blind. The solo parts are assigned as follows: soprano, mother of the blind man; contralto, narrator; tenor, the blind man; barytone, the Master.

The work opens with a meditation for orchestra, which is distinctly melodious — a characteristic not always found in Sir Edward Elgar's oratorios. The first vocal number is a male chorus ("Seek Him") sung by the Levites in the Temple courts, leading to a short tenor solo ("O Thou, in Heaven's Dome") in which the blind man prays for light. No. 3 is a short recitative for the narrator, leading to a chorus of the Disciples ("Who did sin?"). In No. 4, an expressive soprano solo ("Be not extreme"), the mother of the blind man declares that her son has not been punished for the sins of others. This is followed by recitative ("Neither hath this Man sinned") sung by the Master and leading to a massive but simple chorus, at times melodious, and again harmonious ("Light out of Darkness"). When this is closed, the story is resumed. The eyes of the blind man are anointed and he is told to wash in the Pool of Siloam. No. 8 ("Doubt not thy Father's Care") is an expressive chorus for sopranos and altos, followed by an ensemble, No. 9, of extraordinary instrumental effectiveness, in which the blind man is questioned by his neighbors as to the miracle. It is unusually strong and dramatic, working up through a fughetta to an eight-part climax. In No. 10 ("As a Spirit didst Thou pass") the blind man tells his story, which is followed by a vigorous choral dialogue between the Pharisees. No. 12 ("Thou only hast the Words of Life") is an arietta for the narrator. In No. 13 a new dramatic situation is brought out effectively by the orchestra in which the doubting Jews question the mother and the blind man. A beautiful solo and chorus by women ("Woe to the Shepherds of the Flock") follows, leading to a dialogue between the Master and the man He had healed, which closes with the most effective vocal number in the work — a solo for the Master ("I am the good Shepherd"). The chorus ("Light of the World"), a brief but triumphant expression of faith, closes the oratorio.

The Dream of Gerontius

"The Dream of Gerontius," poem by Cardinal Newman and set to music for mezzo soprano, tenor, and bass solos, chorus and orchestra, was first performed at the Birmingham (England) Festival of 1900. The theme of the poem is the dream of the dying Gerontius of his soul's passage to the unseen world, its reception by the angels, and the mysteries of that world.

The score is built up in the Wagnerian manner so closely that it contains no suggestions of the classical oratorio form. The orchestral prelude gives out no less than ten themes, which hold an important place in the body of the work and which must be kept in mind in order to form an intelligent idea of its meaning. The first tenor solo for Gerontius ("Jesu, Maria, I am near to Death") follows the prelude without break and this in turn is followed by a semi-chorus of devotional kind ("Kyrie eleison"). A brief tenor solo ("Rouse thee, my fainting Soul") is succeeded by a second semi-chorus ("Be merciful"), very tender and sweet in character. A longer solo for tenor ("Sanctus fortis") ensues, full of deep feeling and followed by a powerful interlude by orchestra. The voice, that of Gerontius, again comes in with a melancholy strain ("I can no more") developing into an expression of horror and dismay as in his disordered imagination he fancies himself pursued by fiends. A short chorus by the priestly assistants follows ("Rescue him, O Lord!"). As their prayer with its harmonious Amens dies away, Gerontius sings his dying song ("Novissima hora est"), and the jubilant massive chorus ("Go forth upon thy Journey") closes the first part of the oratorio.

The second part opens with an orchestral prelude significant of the soul's passage and its rest, leading to a dreamy poetical solo by the soul ("I went to Sleep, and now I am refreshed"), followed by a beautiful solo for the Angel, designated as the "Alleluia" ("My Work is done, my Task is o'er"). A dialogue ensues between the Angel and the soul and this is followed by a powerful scene, both vocal and instrumental, representing the flight of the Angel with the soul through troops of raging demons whose howls gradually die away as the Angel nears the throne of God. Another dialogue follows between the soul and the Angel to which succeeds the chorus of the Angelicals, which is so divided as to produce a most impressive effect. A third dialogue ensues, begun by the Angel ("We now have passed the Gate") followed by the chorus ("Glory to Him"). After alternating passages for the soul and the chorus, the Angelicals unite in a mighty song ("Praise to the Holiest in the Height"). As the song dies away the soul hears the voices of men left on earth, and as the Angel explains the sounds a powerful bass solo by the Angel of Agony intervenes ("Jesu! by that shuddering Dread"). At its close the Angel repeats his "Alleluia," and amid the choruses of souls in purgatory and Angelicals the Finale begins with one of the most beautiful numbers in the work, the Angel's solo ("Softly and gently, dearly ransomed Soul"), and closes with the softly diminishing chorus of the Angelicals ("Praise to the Holiest").

The Apostles

"The Apostles" was first performed at the Birmingham (England) Festival of 1903. Like "The Dream of Gerontius," it is constructed upon a series of motives, though upon a much more extensive scale, as it embodies no less than eighty distinct themes. The orchestra is unusually large, and includes a shofar, or ancient Hebrew trumpet. The characters are the Blessed Virgin and the Angel, soprano; Mary Magdalene, alto; Saint John, tenor, who is also the Narrator; Jesus, Saint Peter, and Judas, bassos.

The orchestral prelude is an epitome of the whole oratorio. The choral part is majestic in character, and the instrumental accompaniment gives out the typical themes. The first scene is the calling of the Apostles, following Jesus' night of prayer on the mountain, and introduces angelic voices declaring hope for the world, with gentle pastoral accompaniment. This leads to "The Dawn" and the chorus of the watchers on the temple roof ("It shines"), followed by the chorus within the temple ("It is a good Thing to give Thanks") accompanied by the shofar and orchestra sounding the calls which are so familiar to the Jewish synagogue. The song of the watchers is also based upon an old Hebrew melody. The scene concludes with the calling of the Apostles, introduced with the recitative ("And when it was Day"), leading into an ensemble of Apostles' themes.

The second scene is "By the Wayside," in which the Beatitudes are expressed with the simplicity and impressiveness befitting their character. The third scene, "By the Sea of Galilee," introduces Mary Magdalene in the most powerful and descriptive passage of the whole work ("O Lord Almighty, God of Israel"). Then follows a bright, tripping choral fantasy describing her past life; and lastly she sees the storm and the stilling of the sea from the tower of Magdala and describes it to a characteristic storm accompaniment. In a later passage her conversion is announced, and a solo quartet and chorus ("Turn you to the Stronghold") with an independent accompaniment bring Part I to a close.

Part II deals principally with Christ's Passion, and opens with a solemn instrumental prelude. The betrayal scene is developed at considerable length, the most beautiful feature of it being the choral passage ("And the Lord turned and looked upon Peter and he went out and wept bitterly"). Judas' remorse is impressively described in the soliloquy ("Our Life is short and tedious"), changing to a wailing farewell to life as he hears the shouts of the rabble ("Crucify him"). In the crucifixion scene ("Golgotha") the tragedy is only briefly but solemnly indicated in the instrumentation which gives expression to the cry "Eli, Eli lama sabachthani," the only vocal part being a short dialogue between Mary and John. The sixth scene, "At the Sepulchre," is in striking contrast with the last. The music describes the early morning. The song of the watchers is heard again and the first jubilant Alleluia of the angels ("Why seek ye the Living among the Dead?"). "The Ascension" closes the oratorio.

It is given to a semi-chorus of female voices, to whom the mystic chorus is assigned; a chorus of female voices in four parts; four soloists; a chorus of male voices and orchestra and organ, all uniting at the end in a mighty "Alleluia."

The Kingdom

"The Kingdom," which was written for the Birmingham Festival of 1906, is a continuation of the composer's scheme as first displayed in "The Apostles." It has four solo parts: the Virgin Mary, soprano; Mary Magdalene, alto; Saint John, tenor; and Saint Peter, bass. The chorus alternately fills the part of the disciples, the holy women and the people. In one passage there is also a mystic chorus.

The composer has constructed this work upon typical themes in the Wagnerian manner. There are seventy-eight of them in its contents, some of them from "The Apostles" appearing with the rest in the prelude called "Jerusalem." The first division of the work is called "In the upper Room," and follows the prelude without break. It opens with a quartet and chorus ("Seek first the Kingdom of God") in which the disciples call upon their followers to seek the kingdom of God and His righteousness. The Eucharist service is held, in which appears an antiphonal melody ("O sacrum Convivium"), followed by an outburst of praise and an elaborate Amen. In a second section lots are cast for a successor to Judas. There is a chorus of disciples pronouncing execration upon his memory ("Let his Habitation be desolate"), and after this a solo quartet in which the chorus eventually joins, declaring that the lot has fallen upon Saint Matthias.

The second division shows the two Marys at "The Beautiful Gate." It is a short, graceful idyllic scene in which only the two participate. Their duet ("The Singers are before the Altar") is made all the more impressive by some of the motives from "The Apostles," notably the melody sung by the watchers on the roof. The third division, "Pentecost," with its subdivision, "In Solomon's Porch," is the longest and most elaborate section of the work. The descent of the Holy Ghost and the symbolizing of "tongues parting asunder like as of fire" are brought out powerfully by the use of the mystic soprano and contralto chorus and the descriptiveness of the thrilling and picturesque accompaniment heightened by the organ. In the scene "In Solomon's Porch," where the people express their surprise at the Galileans speaking in other tongues, the composer displays an extraordinary control of technique in expressing the situation. Peter's address ("Ye Men of Judæa") follows, succeeded by an invocation to the Holy Spirit, which makes an impressive climax to the scene.

The fourth division, "The Sign of Healing," includes "At the Beautiful Gate," and "The Arrest." The music of the first section, describing the healing of the lame man at the gate and Peter and John's appeal to the people, is of a quiet, peaceful nature but changes in "The Arrest" scene where the disciples are apprehended because they proclaimed in Jesus the resurrection from the dead. Mary's soliloquy ("The Sun goeth down"), in which two Hebrew hymns are utilized, is the feature of this scene. Though first expressed in a calm, tranquil manner, with subdued accompaniment, it reaches an impassioned climax in the Finale.

The fifth division, "The Upper Room," closes the oratorio. It opens with an expression of joy by the disciples and holy women ("The voice of Joy is in the Dwelling of the Righteous"), leading to the scene of "The Breaking of Bread," which is simple, yet very expressive. After its climax the voices softly declaim the Lord's Prayer, closing upon "For ever and ever, Amen" in a powerful climax. A chorus of a solemn nature ("Thou, O Lord, art our Father") brings the oratorio to its close.

Overture, In the South (Alassio). Op. 50

In the overture under review, "conceived on a glorious spring day in the valley of Andorra," Elgar beautifully blends the joys of nature with the recollections of the past. The score has the motto: "A land which *was* the mightiest in its old command and *is* the loveliest; wherein were cast the men of Rome. Thou art the garden of the world."

The overture opens with a short, breezy theme given out by clarinet, horns, violins, and 'cellos to an accompaniment of the other strings and wood winds. Other figures are developed from this and lead to a vigorous and exultant climax. Gradually the music grows more tranquil, and the wood winds and muted strings engage in a pastoral dialogue, presenting the episode of "a shepherd with his flock and his home-made music." As it dies away the drums and double basses prepare for the entrance of the first sustained theme of the overture, the preceding ones having been fragmentary, which is given out in first violins and as solo for viola and 'cello. Another tranquil passage follows, the two forming, as it were, a sort of dreamy reverie, from which in the final working out we pass to the episode, "the relentless and domineering invading force of the ancient day and the strife and war of a later time." It is a strong tone-picture of war and violence. As the tumult dies away, the episode changes to one of charming beauty — the shepherd's melody for violin solo to the accompaniment of first violins divided into threes, four solo second violins and harps. The song is repeated in the first horn, passing to the violins and violas pianissimo throughout. Bits of other themes are woven in, after which the solo viola leads to the recapitulation, which closes this beautiful overture in an elaborate and joyous manner.

Concert Overture, Cockaigne (In London Town)
Op. 40

The concert overture, "Cockaigne," presents a panorama of London street scenes. According to the composer's program he intends to describe "the sights a pair of lovers encounter during an afternoon's stroll in that city." The overture opens with a picture of the life and animation of the streets. Then follows a section devoted to the ardor of the lovers themselves as they turn aside into one of the parks and enjoy themselves in a sequestered spot. Their loving conversation is interrupted by gamins who discover them. They seek the streets again and watch the approach of a military band whose music is heard in the distance, grows louder, and gradually dies away. Then they enter a church where the organ is being played, but as the noise from without penetrates the church the rest of the overture is of a mixed secular and religious character. Passing once more into the street, our lovers find all their former experiences repeated and intensified.

Concert Overture, Froissart. Op. 19

The "Froissart" Overture was one of Elgar's earlier works. Its motto, "When Chivalry lifted up her lance on high," is from one of Keats' poems, and indicates the general character of the music. The overture opens with a vigorous martial introduction, after which a stately first theme is given out pianissimo. Its development with new subsidiary material is very effective, and leads finally to the reappearance of the theme fortissimo. As this part of the movement dies away, the second theme, with a counter-theme in solo clarinet and first violins, appears, the former being most conspicuous in the development, at the close of which the first theme is again heard. In the closing section the second theme and its counter-theme appear, but this time the latter is given to the clarinets, the elaboration of which brings the overture to a fine concluding climax.

Suite, The Wand of Youth. Op. 1 a

The suite, "Wand of Youth," has an interesting history. In his twelfth year Elgar wrote a fairy play, "The Wand of Youth," and supplied the incidental music, the whole to be performed by members of the Elgar family. Forty years later, in 1907, he recast this music for concert purposes in two suites. The first is in seven short movements. The first, "Overture," opens with the theme in the strings, followed by full orchestra. The second theme, a graceful melody, follows, succeeded by recapitulation and a Coda based on the opening theme. The second movement, "Serenade," is introduced in the strings, the first theme announced by clarinet with accompaniment in strings and harps. This is followed by a new subject in first violins, which after its statement repeats the first theme. The third movement, "Minuet," is written in the old stately style for strings, wood winds, and horns, the violins announcing the theme. The fourth movement is a fairy rhythm called the "Sun Dance," the theme of which is announced in the wood winds. The second theme is given out by strings and clarinet and is followed by a waltz rhythm for the oboe and subsequently for first violins. After repetition of this material, a Coda closes the movement. The "Fairy Pipers" is the fifth movement, which is based upon two themes — the song of the pipers, given out by the clarinets, and a second melody by the strings. The sixth movement, "Slumber Scene" is entirely for two bassoons, one horn, and muted strings, the theme announced pianissimo in the violins. The last movement, "Fairies and Giants," a Presto, opens in the 'cellos and double basses, followed by the wood winds, which take up a light figure, repeated by the strings. After the development of this material the giants have their turn in an unmistakably portentous section of the movement as compared with the light, sprightly opening. It is followed by a repetition of the fairy music, with suggestions of the giants, and a Coda closes the suite.

Variations. Op. 36

The "Variations," Op. 36, or, as the composer himself styles the main theme, the "Enigma," was first performed in

London in 1899. The score comprises a theme and fourteen variations, and is dedicated to fourteen of his friends.

Each of the "Variations" is headed by the initials of the friend to whom it refers, but it is not easy, considering the concealed identity of the friends, to understand their idiosyncrasies from the musical descriptions. Its opening theme is strong and expressive, and the succeeding variations are sketched in a masterly manner, some of them powerful, bold, and heroic, others vivacious, animated, and tranquil, and now and then one so graceful in its melodiousness as to indicate that it represents one of the gentler sex. The final variation is one of great brilliancy and broad scoring, serving as a climax to the other thirteen. As the composer takes all his music seriously, there is very little sentiment and still less humor in these sketches. His fourteen friends, judged by their musical portraits, are fourteen serious persons, genial, refined, and intellectual.

Introduction and Allegro. Op. 47

The "Introduction and Allegro" was first performed in London in 1905. It is written for a solo quartet (two violins, viola and 'cello) and string orchestra. The composer states that he was impressed by the sound of distant singing to which the cadence of a falling third caught his fancy. "From the train of thought thus generated sprang the main theme of the work, the pseudo Welsh tune. Later on, a song heard in the Valley of the Wye reinforced the Welsh impressions and led to the completion of the work." It opens with a theme given out in all the strings, followed by another subject. After development, the Welsh melody appears in the viola. Following further treatment of the first theme and Welsh tune, the Allegro begins with a theme in the first violin. This in turn is developed and the second theme appears in the quartet, alternating with the other strings. The Welsh theme is once more suggested and followed by a fugato, introduced in the second violin. All this material is developed and the recapitulation ends with the first theme of the Allegro.

Symphonic Prelude, Polonia. Op. 76

Elgar's symphonic prelude, "Polonia" is one of the few compositions by an eminent composer, inspired by the European war. The composer says of it, "that some sort of symphonic prelude might be practical and perhaps even a useful tribute to my friend Paderewski for the concert in aid of his countrymen was the final inducement to weave into a concise orchestral movement some typical Polish themes."

After a brief introduction a martial theme by the composer himself is heard in the brasses and wood winds. After it reaches its climax three national themes are introduced. The first appears in the 'cellos and English horn, thence transferred to full orchestra; the second march tempo in the 'cellos and bassoons, then fully orchestral; and the third, "Poland is not yet lost" in full orchestra. After repetition of the martial theme, the muted violas and 'cellos give a suggestion of Chopin's G minor nocturne, followed by phrases in the violins from Paderewski's "Polish Fantasie." These are followed by the march, worked up to a vigorous climax, based upon the opening theme.

Pomp and Circumstance. Op. 39

"Pomp and Circumstance" is the stately title of several military marches. They are similar in form, being in strictly march rhythm with Trio. The first is in A minor, Allegro molto, the first part of the movement repeated after the Trio, and closes with a short Coda. The second is constructed in a larger manner, an introduction leading to the march. The Trio leads to a repetition of the first part, which is followed by the theme of the Trio. A short Coda concludes the spirited works.

ENESCO

1881 –

Suite for Orchestra. Op. 9

GEORGES ENESCO, who was born at Cordaremi, Roumania, in 1881, was educated musically for the most part in Austria and France. In the latter country he studied with Gabriel Fauré (composition) and Martin Marsick (violin) at the Conservatoire of Paris.

"Most of the creative work by Roumanians," Enesco has said, "has been done in the last fifteen years. Our music, curiously enough, is influenced not by the neighbouring Slav, but by the Indian and Egyptian folk songs, introduced by the members of those remote races, now classed as gypsies, brought to Roumania as servants of the Roman conquerors. The deeply Oriental character of our own folk music derives from these sources and possesses a flavor as singular as it is beautiful."

The suite, Op. 9, was played for the first time by Colonne's orchestra, Paris, in 1903. In America it was first heard at a concert of the Philharmonic Orchestra, New York, January 3, 1911, under the direction of Gustave Mahler. The work, which was dedicated to Camille Saint-Saëns, contains four movements: I. Prélude à l'Unisson (Modérément, C major), scored for strings and kettle-drum and leading directly into II. Menuet lent (Slow Minuet) whose principal theme is stated by a solo violin and solo violoncello in octaves. III. Intermède (Gravement, A major, 2-4 time). The movement is based, for the most part, upon the theme with which it begins in the strings. IV. Finale (Vif, C minor, 6-8 and 3-4 time). This closing section of the suite uses a constant interchange of two beats and three beats in a measure. At the opening there is a figure for the double-basses, pizzicato, which is kept up for seventy-six measures.

F. B.

Roumanian Rhapsody, A Major, Op. 11, No. 1

Enesco has written three Roumanian Rhapsodies for orchestra, of which this and another (No. 2) in D major, were played for the first time at a concert given by Pablo Casals at the Salle Gaveau, Paris, February 7, 1908. The first Rhapsody, dedicated to B. Crocé-Spinelli, is founded on Roumanian airs which appear successively and are treated in variation form rather than developed.

F. B.

Roumanian Rhapsody, D Major, Op. 11, No. 2

The second Roumanian Rhapsody by Enesco opens with a subject (Lent, D major, 4-4 time) which, although it is not the principal theme, is given considerable employment in the course of the work. The first subject is announced by the strings and twice repeated, each time more fully scored. The flute and oboe successively give out declamatory passages and suggestions of the opening measures are heard from the violins. Soon a new melody (expressif et très douloureux) is played by the English horn, while the strings play a tremolo near the bridge of their instruments. This idea is worked over and is followed by a return to the first theme fortissimo, this leading into the closing section (Vif, 2-4 time), the theme of which is played by a solo viola.

F. B.

DE FALLA

1877 –

Suite, The Three Cornered Hat

MANUEL DE FALLA, one of the most noted composers of modern Spain, was born at Cadiz, where he received his first instruction in music from Mlle. Elois Galluzo. Later he was taught in Madrid by Jose Trago (piano) and Felipe Pedrell (composition). In 1907 he went to Paris and came under the artistic influence of the modern French school—Debussy, Ravel, Dukas and others. At the outbreak of the Great War de Falla returned to Spain.

The suite "El Sombrero de Tres Picos" ("The Three Cornered Hat") is drawn from a ballet which was composed as the result of a commission given to de Falla by Serge Diaghileff, when the latter's Ballet Russe visited Spain in 1917. The ballet was produced for the first time at the Alhambra Theater, London, July 23, 1919. The story of the work, derived from a novel by Alarcon, concerns a miller and his handsome wife. The latter has been annoyed by the attentions of the Corregidor, a judge who, like most officials in Spain, wore a three-cornered hat. The action concerns the pursuit of the woman by the judge and his final discomfiture. There are three movements in the suite: I. The Neighbours (Allegro ma non troppo); II. The Miller's Dance (Poco vivo); III. Final Dance (Poco mosso).

F. B.

Suite, Love the Sorcerer

This work, like the suite "The Three Cornered Hat," is drawn from a ballet. It was conceived in 1914-15 and was given in the latter year as a choreographic fantasy for voice and small orchestra at the Teatro de Lara, Madrid. Later de Falla revised the composition and it was given as a concert piece in 1916 at Madrid under the direction of E. Fernandez-Arbos. In this revised form "Love the Sorcerer" ("El Amor Brujo") was scored for two flutes, piccolo, oboe, two clarinets, bassoon, two horns, two trumpets, kettle-drums, bells, piano and strings. A mezzo-soprano voice sings back-stage, but the voice in concert performances is often replaced by a wind instrument. Although the work is very nationalistic in character it may be said — on the authority of the composer himself — that no folk tunes have been used in it.

The story of "El Amor Brujo" is as follows: Candelas, a beautiful gypsy, has been loved by another gypsy — a fascinating, jealous, dissolute fellow — with whom Candelas has been unhappy while he lived and who, now that he is dead, is afraid that he will come back and continue to love and claim her in his old fierce caressing way. But another young man comes into the girl's life. Carmelo, a handsome, dashing swain, falls in love with her. Candelas half consents to return the man's advances, but whenever she is on the point of meeting Carmelo half-way the specter of the dead lover returns to terrify her. Finally the ghost frightens Candelas away from Carmelo. The man now bethinks himself of a means by which he can break the spell. As the specter in life was a faithless pursuer of women, it is probable that even in death he may be fascinated by one. Carmelo, who has known the ghost in the flesh, persuades Lucia, a friend of Candelas, to permit the specter to make love to her. While this ruse is being effected, Carmelo and Candelas rush into each other's arms and exchange the kiss that defeats the evil influence of the dead man and the ghost is laid for ever and a day. There are twelve movements in the suite, but these are not drawn in the sequence in which they appear in the ballet.

F. B.

FLOTOW

1812 – 1883

Overture to Martha

FRIEDRICH VON FLOTOW was one of the musicians who, born in a foreign country, exercised considerable influence upon the music of France. For a number of years he lived in Paris, and only the Revolution of 1848 drove him from that city to Germany, his native country. "Martha" is not only Flotow's most popular opera, but it has long been one of the most frequently performed works in the operatic repertory. The composition passed through several stages before it arrived at its present form. It had formed the basis of a ballet as early as the seventeenth century — its title was "Chambrières a Louer" ("Chambermaids for Hire") — and it enjoyed some success in Paris of the nineteenth century as a vaudeville entitled "La Comtesse d'Egmont." It was from the latter piece that Marzillier, ballet master of the Opéra, Paris, concocted a ballet which, under the name "Lady Henrietta, ou la Servante de Greenwich," was provided with music by Robert Burgmüller, Eduard Deldevez and von Flotow. The piece was produced February 1, 1844, and made a mild success. It was soon forgotten by everyone except Flotow, who, believing that the adventures of Lady Henrietta might form an effective opera, persuaded his friend, W. Friedrich, to turn the ballet into a libretto. Friedrich, a Viennese, wrote the text in German and under the name "Martha" the opera was produced at the Kärthnerthor Theater, Vienna, November 25, 1847, with extraordinary success. The triumph of "Martha" led to its speedy production in other cities. Three months after the Vienna première it was given in Berlin; in Prague the following month. The first production in America was in

New York in 1852, with Mme. Anna Bishop in the title-rôle.

The story of "Martha" is one of a woman of fashion, Lady Harriet Durham, and her maid, Nancy, who, bored with life at the court of Queen Anne, betake themselves to a fair at Richmond and hire out as servant-girls under the respective names of Martha and Julia. They are employed by two young farmers, Lionel and Plunkett. But the joke soon palls and the women, assisted by Lady Durham's cousin, Sir Tristram, disappear when the farmers have betaken themselves to bed. Lionel, however, has fallen in love with Martha, after she has sung to him "The Last Rose of Summer," and after various vicissitudes, proving that the course of true love runs roughly, it is shown that he is the rightful heir to the Earldom of Derby and all ends in happiness and light.

The overture to "Martha" opens with an Introduction (Andante con moto) which leads into a section (Larghetto, A major, 9-8 time) whose subject is drawn from that of the quintet in the opening act. The main movement (Allegro vivace, A minor) follows. In the middle of this the key changes to C major and there is heard the theme of the chorus sung by the servants off-stage in the opening act. A crescendo culminates in a fortissimo, upon which the subject of the Larghetto recurs in grandiose fashion. A short Coda (Allegro vivo) brings the overture to a conclusion.

F. B.

Overture to Stradella

"Stradella," opera in three acts, was written in the first instance as a musical piece to a text by Deschamps and Pacini and produced at Paris in 1837. Flotow then gave the libretto to his friend, W. Friedrich, of Vienna, to work up into a grand opera text. The work was produced at Hamburg, December 25, 1844, and in that city, as in other German towns, achieved marked success. Its triumphs in other countries, however, have been small, and at the present time the only surviving portion of the opera is the overture, which is frequently performed at concerts of the lighter music. The plot of the opera was based upon the life of Alessandro Stradella, a composer of the seventeenth century who was born either at Naples or Venice about 1645 and who, in consequence of his amorous intrigues, is supposed to have been murdered at Genoa about 1670. Much of his life-story is purely legendary, and it is upon the fiction that the various operas entitled "Stradella" have been based. The principal of these stories is concerned with the two assassins who, having been sent to murder Stradella, are so moved by his music that they refuse to take his life. Flotow's opera makes use of this incident.

The overture begins (Andante quasi Adagio, D major, 3-4 time) with the subject of the hymn "Jungfrau Maria," sung by Stradella in the last act. This is followed by the main movement (Allegro, D minor, 2-2 time), its theme given out by the violins. A bustling tutti leads to the second subject — in F major — whose melody is that of the Bell chorus, "Hört die Glocken freundlich locken," of the second act. Another sonorous tutti supervenes and there is some development of the first theme, this eventually leading to the recapitulation, in which the two subjects are re-heard. The overture closes with a fortissimo and dignified Coda.

F. B.

FOOTE

1853 –

Suite in D Minor. Op. 36

THE suite in D minor by the American composer, Arthur Foote, was first performed by the Boston Symphony Orchestra in 1896. It is in four movements: 1. Allegro energico con brio. 2. Expressivo, non troppo adagio. 3. Andante expressivo con moto, and variations. 4. Presto assai. The first movement opens at once with a bold theme, which, after development, gives place to a second and more cantabile theme sung in the strings. It is elaborated in them, as well as in the wood winds and horns, until the first theme returns. The two themes are then worked out, and the movement closes with a brilliant and vigorous Coda. The second movement is in a quieter mood, opening with a cantabile theme in the strings, extended in the wood winds and horns. The second theme is given out fortissimo by the horns, trumpets, and trombones, and, gradually subsiding, is transferred to the wood winds with string accompaniment. After its return in full orchestra the first theme is again heard, as a solo for the horns and 'cellos with accompaniment in the strings and wood winds, closing the movement. The third movement is a plain theme with seven variations, given out originally by the strings and eventually taken by the wood winds. The last movement consists of the free development of two sharply contrasted themes, at times in fugal form, and closes in a vigorous manner.

Four Character Pieces. Op. 48

The four character pieces, inspired by verses from Omar Khayyám's "Rubáiyat," were written in 1900. The composer himself has furnished the following analysis of them:

I

"Iram indeed is gone with all his Rose,
And Jamshyd's Sev'n-ring'd Cup where no one knows;
But still a Ruby kindles in the Vine,
And many a Garden by the Water blows."

Andante commodo, in B major and 3-4 time: The theme heard at the outset in the solo clarinet runs through the whole, with a contrasting counter-subject; while always there is an accompaniment persisting with a "strumming" sort of rhythm.

II

"They say the Lion and the Lizard keep
The Courts where Jamshyd gloried and drank deep:
And Bahrám, that great Hunter — the Wild Ass
Stamps o'er his Head, but cannot break his Sleep."

Allegro, in B minor and 3-4 time: The basis of this is a strongly accented theme stated at the commencement in the first violins. For this the fullest orchestra is used, and there are occasional touches of cymbal, tambourine, etc.

The middle part is as a revery:

"Yet ah, that Spring should vanish with the Rose!
That Youth's sweet-scented manuscript should close!
The Nightingale that in the branches sang,
Ah whence, and whither flown again, who knows!"

In this the accompaniment is softly given in the strings, harp, etc., the melody being sung by clarinet and flute. This dies out, and the first theme returns — ending fortissimo.

III

"A Book of Verses underneath the Bough,
A Jug of Wine, a Loaf of Bread — and Thou
Beside me singing in the Wilderness —
Oh, Wilderness were Paradise enow!"

Commodo, in A major and 4–4 time: The subject heard at the start in the strings appears in changing forms, without any other contrasting theme, and is based throughout on an organ-point on the dominant (prolonged E in the bass). It fades out in the strings in their highest positions, with a few last E's in the harp.

IV

"Yon rising Moon that looks for us again—
How oft hereafter will she wax and wane;
How oft hereafter rising look for us
Through this same Garden—and for *one* in vain!"

With strongly marked rhythm, in E minor and 6–8 time: After some chords, harp and strings pizzicato, the theme enters in the solo horn and 'cello—rises to fortissimo and, again, dies out in the E minor chord, being succeeded by the Più allegro (in B major and 3–4 time)—

"Waste not your Hour, nor in the vain pursuit
Of This and That endeavor and dispute;
Better be jocund with the fruitful Grape
Than sadden after none, or bitter, Fruit."

This next is a sort of Scherzo, toward the end of which is a reminiscence of the theme of the first piece, fortissimo. This subsides, and after a pause the first theme returns, with a wavy accompaniment in divided strings—the movement proceeding thence to an expressive pianissimo close.

FRANCK

1822 – 1890

Symphony in D Minor

1. Lento. Allegro non troppo.
2. Allegretto.
3. Allegro non troppo.

THE symphony in D Minor, which was first performed at the Paris Conservatoire, February 17, 1889, has been furnished with an analysis by the composer himself, the main points of which follow. It opens with a slow and sombre introduction, the principal motive of which is developed through thirty measures and leads to the Allegro, or first movement proper, which is energetic in style. After a reentrance of the motive of the Lento and the development of that of the Allegro, the second theme appears, and this in turn is followed by a third, which is highly developed. A return is made to the first theme which is given out fortissimo. The theme of the movement proper is resumed, leading to the conclusion of this division of the symphony.

The second movement opens with pizzicato chords for string orchestra and harp, followed by a sweet and melancholy theme given out by the English horn. This section of the movement is closed by clarinet, horn, and flute, after which the violins announce a second theme. At the conclusion of its development, the English horn and the various wind instruments take up fragments of the first motive, after which follows a Scherzo division. At the close of this sprightly Scherzo, the entire opening period, as announced by the English horn, is combined with the theme of the Scherzo, the latter being assigned to the violins.

The third movement opens brilliantly in contrast with the sombreness of the two preceding ones. The principal theme is stated in the 'cello and bassoons, and after development a new theme appears in the brasses, continued in the strings, after which a new subject occurs in the basses, followed in its turn by the theme of the second movement in the English horn. After development of the first subject of the movement in the first violins a retard is followed by a suggestion of the second movement theme in the oboe. After a pause, development of previous material leads to a climax, the full orchestra recapitulating the principal subject of the movement. The Coda follows with suggestions of the second theme in the first movement as well as its opening theme, the movement closing with its principal subject.

The Beatitudes

"The Beatitudes," written in 1870 and published in 1880, the text, a poetical paraphrase of the Gospel, by Lady Colomb, is divided into nine parts — a prologue and eight beatitudes. The prologue, an impressive number, is set for tenor solo ("Dark brooded Fear over the Land"), and celestial chorus ("Oh, blessed be He!") with orchestra.

First Beatitude

("Blessed are the poor in spirit: for theirs is the kingdom of heaven.")

The first beatitude opens with a passionate and energetic terrestrial chorus ("All the Wealth of the Earth"). The celestial chorus softly responds ("When our Hearts are oppressed"). The voice of Christ is now heard in a song ("Blessed be") of exquisite tenderness and beauty, which is taken up by the celestial chorus with a rich accompaniment, and closes the beatitude.

Second Beatitude

("Blessed are the meek: for they shall inherit the earth.")

The second beatitude, introduced by the oboe with a tremolo accompaniment of the strings, opens with the terrestrial chorus ("The Earth is dark"), followed by the celestial chorus ("Poor human Souls"). The voice of Christ closes the number with the tender strain ("Oh, blessed are the Meek").

Third Beatitude

("Blessed are they that mourn: for they shall be comforted.")

The third beatitude opens with the strongest chorus in the work ("Grief over all Creatures"). It is followed by a mother's lament over the empty cradle; the wail of the orphan over its wretched state; the sorrow of husband and wife over separation; and the slave's prayer for liberty. As the different voices unite in a farewell, the gentle voice of Christ is heard again ("Blessed are the Mourners"), followed by an inspiriting celestial chorus ("Oh, blessed forever").

Fourth Beatitude

("Blessed are they which do hunger and thirst after righteousness: for they shall be filled.")

After an impressive and mystical prelude the fourth beatitude is introduced by a dramatic tenor solo ("Where'er we stray, stern Fate enthralls us"), and concludes with another of the gentle melodies of the Christ voice ("Oh, happy he").

Fifth Beatitude

("Blessed are the merciful: for they shall obtain mercy.")

A beautiful string quartet opens the fifth beatitude, followed by an expressive tenor solo ("Like beaten Corn Sheaves"). In almost furious accord rises the appeal of the slaves ("King all glorious"), ever increasing in power and rising to a tremendous climax. The remainder of the beatitude is in striking contrast. First is heard the voice of Christ ("Vengeance belongeth"), followed by the celestial chorus for sopranos and tenors in unison ("Ever blessed are they"), which is one of the sweetest passages in the work. This in turn is followed by the song of the Angel of Forgiveness ("Holy love, sweet Pardon"), a repetition of the celestial chorus closing the number.

Sixth Beatitude

("Blessed are the pure in heart: for they shall see God.")

After a short prelude, which is scored with masterly skill, follows a chorus of heathen women ("The Gods, from us their Faces turning") succeeded by a chorus of Jewish women ("Thou, who once to our Sires appeared"), the two afterwards uniting in a mass chorus of great beauty. Four Pharisees, after brief solos, unite in a descriptive quartet ("Great God! from early youth"). Then follows an impressive song by the Angel of Death ("I gather in each Soul immortal"). The celestial chorus responds gently ("Earthly Knowledge"). The voice of Christ intervenes ("Oh, blest are the Pure") and the chorus closes ("Then purge from your Hearts").

Seventh Beatitude

("Blessed are the peacemakers: for they shall be called the children of God.")

The seventh is one of the most dramatic sections of the work. It opens with a bitter and vehemently declamatory air by Satan ("'Tis I whose baneful Spell"). The effect grows more and more passionate and furious as one after the other choruses of tyrants, pagan priests, and the multitude, enter. To them succeeds the tender voice of Christ ("Blessed are they"), followed by a remorseful wail from Satan ("Ah! that Voice") and the famous quintet of the peacemakers ("Evil cannot stay").

Eighth Beatitude

("Blessed are they which are persecuted for righteousness' sake: for theirs is the kingdom of heaven.")

The last beatitude opens with another vehement outburst from Satan ("Not yet defeated"), followed by the chorus of the just ("Hear us, Justice eternal"). Satan once more breaks out in angry denunciation ("Insensates! this wild delusion") and gives place to the Mater Dolorosa, heard in the majestic song ("Stricken with Sorrow"). Satan recognizes his fate in another remorseful song ("Mine the Doom she hath spoken"). The tender strains of the Christ voice ("O ye Righteous!") are heard. Satan in a brief passage owns His power. The voice of Christ is heard for the last time gently calling ("Oh, come, ye of my Father beloved"), and the celestial chorus brings the work to a close with a grand hosanna.

Symphonic Poem, Les Eolides

In the symphonic poem, "Les Eolides," the first of Franck's works of this class, Leconte de Lisle's poem of that name is used as the subject. It was played for the first time at a concert of the Paris Société Nationale, May 13, 1877, and was hissed. Seventeen years later it had another hearing and was received with enthusiasm. The work is written in a single movement, allegretto vivo, and the music tells its own story.

It is purely free and unconventional, the composer letting his fancy run untrammelled after the opening motive, which gives expression to the first lines of the poem, "Oh, floating breezes of the sky, sweet breaths of the fair Spring that caress the hills and plains with freshest kisses." The sentiment of the poem is admirably reproduced in this graceful and picturesque music.

Symphonic Poem, Le Chasseur Maudit

The symphonic poem, "Le Chasseur Maudit," was written in 1883 and first performed in the following year. It is based upon the familiar ballad of Bürger's, "Der wilde Jäger" ("The Wild Huntsman"), and is divided into four sections, for which the composer has provided a program. In the first movement, amid the pealing of bells, the shouts of the crowd, and the intoning of a chant, the hunting horn of the Count of the Rhine is heard as the huntsmen prepare for the chase. In the second movement the chase is in full progress over the fields and moors. A voice bids the Count listen to the pious chant, but he refuses and urges his horse forward. In the third movement he is found alone; his horse cannot move, nor will his horn utter a sound. A strong piercing theme gives out the curse, "Desecrator, be forever driven by the Evil One." In the last movement flames shoot up and the Count flies, forever pursued by demons.

GERMAN

1862 –

Three Dances from Henry VIII

EDWARD GERMAN, whose name is really German Edward Jones, received his musical training at the Royal Academy of Music, London. He began his career by playing the violin in London theaters. In 1888 he became musical director at the Globe Theater, that position having been given him by Richard Mansfield, the American actor, who was giving a season of plays there. German composed for Mansfield's production of Shakespeare's "Richard III" an overture and incidental music that attracted much favorable attention. It was the success of the English composer's music which procured for him the commission to write incidental music for a production of Shakespeare's "Henry VIII" which Henry Irving was making in 1892 at the Lyceum Theater, London. For that music he paid German a sum of $1,500. The music consisted of an overture, five entr'actes, a setting of the song "Orpheus and his Lute" and some miscellaneous incidental music. The three dances were performed in the first act of the drama, the scene being Cardinal Wolsey's reception at York Place. The popularity of the dances became very great and they are still frequently performed upon "popular" programs. The dances are as follows: I. Morris Dance. A minor, Allegro giocoso, 2-4 time. II. The Shepherd's Dance. Allegretto quasi Andantino, G major, 6-8 time. III. Torch Dance. Allegro molto, D major, 2-4 time.

F. B.

GLAZOUNOV

1865–

Symphony No. 6 in C Minor, Op. 58

1. Adagio. Allegro passionato.
2. Andante. Variatioro.
3. Intermezzo. Allegretto.
4. Andante maestoso. Scherzando.

THE first movement of Glazounov's Sixth Symphony opens with an Adagio introduction, in which a theme is announced by the 'cellos and double basses and worked up in the strings and wind instruments. Imitations on the same theme follow, reaching a fortissimo climax in full orchestra. Chromatic harmonies, with a sustained tremolo in the strings, lead to the first theme, which in reality is a development of the theme in the introduction in different rhythm. The second theme is stated in the violins and again taken up in the wood winds. Passages from the first theme then return against the second theme in a fortissimo climax. After a dramatic episode and a third part, a vigorous Coda ends the movement.

The second movement is a set of variations on a simple theme in the strings, among them a Scherzino, a Fugato and a Nocturne.

The third movement is in the form of a Scherzo and Trio and closes with the customary Coda. The final movement suggests Russian dance rhythm. Two themes are announced. The first appears in various tempi, after which the second is stated and the alternation of these two brings the movement to its close brilliantly and with great rapidity.

Symphony No. 8, E Flat Major, Op. 83

Glazounov composed this symphony at St. Petersburg in 1906, and it was published the following year. In the United States the work was heard for the first time at a concert of the Russian Symphony Orchestra, New York, November 14, 1907.

I. Allegro moderato, E flat major, 4-4 time. Following two introductory measures the bassoons and horns give out the principal theme. There is a quickening of the time and the trombones take up this theme. The second subject is heard in the oboe, a second section of it being played by the flute. Considerable employment is given later to this section. The principal subject material returns in the brass and violoncellos and this is followed by the development section. The recapitulation enters with the first theme in augmentation in the brass. The second subject is now given to the violoncellos and bassoon with a counter-theme set against it in the flute. There is development of the second section of the second subject and, later, of the first. The movement closes softly and tranquilly.

II. The second movement (Mesto, E flat minor, 3-2 time) has its chief theme in the strings. Following considerable working over of this, the second subject is heard in the flute, the remainder of the movement comprising development of both ideas.

III. The third movement (Allegro, C major, 2-4 time) brings forward the principal subject at the fifth measure in the violas. The violins take it up and work it over. A second theme is set forth later by the first and second violins and continued by the flutes. The first subject returns (più tranquillo) in the violas and bassoons in augmentation, the first violins playing a pizzicato figure above them. Development is given to the second theme and the first then returns, the movement ending brilliantly.

The Finale begins with introductory matter (Moderato sostenuto, E flat major, 4-4 time) beginning in the wind instruments. The main movement (Allegro moderato) brings forward the principal subject in the lower strings, horns and bassoons. This material, which has some affinity to the subject of the slow movement, is developed and leads to the second theme, sung by a clarinet. The violins take it up and then a return is made to the material of the introductory measures (Moderato sostenuto). The principal theme is now developed and the second also is worked over. A great climax is attained and the recapitulation is reached. The second theme in this is given to the wood winds. The Coda (Moderato maestoso) is based upon the subject which began the movement.

F. B.

Ouverture Solennelle. Op. 73

Unlike most of Glazounov's concert pieces, the "Ouverture Solennelle" has no program. It was composed in 1901, and at the time of its first performance in that year was entitled a "Festival Overture," and was evidently intended as a fitting prelude for any pageant. It opens, like others of Glazounov's compositions, with a resonant proclamation of chords in the strings and brasses, after which the wood winds and horns enter with a theme which is extended soon to the violins, answered by a short phrase in the violas, 'cellos, and bassoon. The introduction closes, as it opened, with vigorous chords. The main section begins with a melodious theme in the violins, closed by the wood winds. This is followed by the second theme, which subsequently is taken by the clarinets with string accompaniment and fully elaborated. The first theme now returns, and is worked up with subsidiary passages from the introduction. The elaboration of all this material and the Coda close the overture.

Oriental Rhapsody. Op. 29

Glazounov's "Oriental Rhapsody" abounds in melody and is characterized by a decided Oriental color. The program of the rhapsody gives a close sketch of the music. The first part opens with night in the city and the calls of the watchmen. As they die away the song of an improvisator is sung in the strings. It is taken up gradually by other instruments to a very rich accompaniment, continuously growing in intensity. As it closes, the calls of the watchmen are heard again. These again cease, and the oboe gives the signal for a lively dance, which is worked up in the percussion instruments in the most rollicking manner. As the dance comes to an end, an old man is introduced, who sings a tender melody to a sombre harp accompaniment. At its close, the watchmen's horns are heard again, and a brilliant march announces the return of the triumphant army, accompanied by the shouts of the people, who join in another animated dance, in the midst of which is heard a strain of victory. In the Finale all this material is worked up with great skill.

Symphonic Tableau, The Kremlin. Op. 30

The symphonic tableau, "The Kremlin," is purely program music, elaborately constructed and national in character. The work is in three sections. The first, "Popular Feast," is made up of several sub-sections, freely scored and descriptive of the general title. The first, an Allegro, is given out by the 'cellos and violas with a droning accompaniment in the double basses. A folk-song melody follows in the strings and wood winds. An Allegretto melody ensues for the clarinet and trumpet with string pizzicato accompaniment. After the elaboration of these episodes a new one enters in the first violins and 'cellos. The subjects already introduced follow in order, and their working out brings the first part to its close. The second part, "In the Monastery," describes a Russian church festival occasion. It opens in a serious style, with a theme in the violas and basses, followed by intonations given out by the bassoons and clarinet, the material being taken from the Greek Church liturgy. It is followed by a new subject of a different character in the clarinet, supported by the second violins and harp, which leads back to the intonations already mentioned, and is followed by the new theme, the development of which brings this part to a close. The third part, "Entrance and Greeting of the Prince," is of a sonorous and stately character. It is introduced in the horns and bassoons, and leads to the opening theme given out in unison by the strings, wood winds, and horns. The development of this material, reënforced by a new subject of a more tranquil nature, at last leads to a tremendous climax in which the principal subject is given to the basses. The Coda is constructed from this material and closes the work in a brilliant and vigorous manner.

Suite, Ruses d'Amour. Op. 61

The suite, "Ruses d'Amour," one of the most elaborate of Glazounov's dance compositions, is made up of selections from a ballet of the same name which was written in 1898. It contains five movements. The first is entitled "Introduction, Gavotte, Musette, Sarabande, and Farandole." The Introduction, based upon two melodies, is a graceful prelude to the opening scene of the ballet. Melodious themes are given out by the flutes and strings, and a brief interlude leads to a charming Gavotte and Musette. A short Sarabande follows, giving place to a lively Farandole. After the reprise the first movement closes with a brilliant climax. The second movement, "Grand Valse," based upon two themes with a Coda developed from the first theme, tells its own story. The theme is introduced in the clarinet, eventually appearing in the strings. The third movement, "Ballabile des Paysans et Paysannes," is, as its title indicates, a pastoral dance. The fourth movement, "Grand Pas des Fiancés," is a tender, graceful romanza for solo violin and 'cello. The closing movement, "La Fricassée," is a sprightly, gay piece of music, full of dash and humor, its opening subject given out by violas and 'cellos, leading to the main theme heard in the violins.

Suite, From the Middle Ages. Op. 79

The suite, "From the Middle Ages," was written in 1902. It is purely a piece of program music and freely composed in four movements. The first of these, "Prelude," suggests a castle by the seashore in which are two lovers. The second, "Scherzo," represents a Death dance in a street theater, with Death playing his violin and inviting the people to dance. The third is the graceful serenade of a troubadour. The fourth opens with the trumpets summoning the troops, and a procession of priests chanting and blessing the soldiers, their march blending with the priestly intonation, ending in a climax of popular enthusiasm as the priests' chants gradually die away.

Symphonic Poem, Stenka Razin, Op. 13

Glazounov composed his symphonic poem "Stenka Razin" at St. Petersburg in 1885. It was published in 1888 with a dedication to Alexander Borodin, who had been one of the composer's friends. Stenka Razin was a Cossack who, living in the seventeenth century, was famous for his revolt against Alexis Romanoff and for his raids which he carried on on the Volga. He was eventually captured, but Alexis pardoned Stenka on condition that he took an oath of allegiance. This the Cossack promised to do, but shortly afterward he declared himself the enemy of Tsar and of all nobles and, asserting himself to be the upholder of the liberties of the people, was able to raise an army of two hundred thousand men. Stenka Razin might, perhaps, have been successful in deposing Alexis Romanoff had he, himself, been less tyrannical and less given to robbery and violence. The Russian people realizing that the new master would be less solicitous for their happiness than the old, soon deserted Razin and, having been captured by the Tsar's soldiers, he was broken on the wheel in 1672.

The score of "Stenka Razin" gives a lengthy "program" of the work. The composition opens with an Introduction (Andante, B minor, 4-4 time) which depicts the Volga. Soon there is heard in the trombones the theme made familiar to audiences as the "Volga Boat Song," the melody which was sung by the laborers as they hauled barges up and down the river. Glazounov makes important use of this theme throughout the work. The program describes the presence on Razin's boat, whose sails were "wove of silken cloth," of the Persian Princess, made captive by the robber. She tells those around her of a dream in which she saw Stenka shot to death and she drowned in the Volga. Her dream came true. When Stenka Razin was surrounded by the Tsar's soldiers and he saw that ruin was at hand, he cried, "'Never, during the thirty years of my going up and down Mother Volga, have I made her a gift. Today I shall give her what in my eyes is the most precious of earthly treasures.' Saying this, he threw the Princess into the Volga. The savage band began to sing the praise of their leader, and they all rushed upon the soldiers of the Tsar." The main movement (Allegro con brio, B minor, 3-4 time) of the poem has its principal theme drawn from the opening subject of the Introduction. This is developed and a new idea (Allegro moderato) is given out by the clarinet. The earlier mood returns and the folk song is re-developed. The remainder of the work is concerned with material already heard, much of it stormily presented, and at the close the tempo of the Introduction returns, the folk song theme being vociferated by the brass.

F. B.

Valse de Concert No. 1, D Major, Op. 47

Glazounov composed this waltz at Peterhof, near St. Petersburg, in 1893 and published it the following year. The score was dedicated to the composer's mother, Hélène Glazounov. The Waltz begins with a short Introduction (Allegro, D major, 3-4 time) following which the principal theme (Tempo di Valse) is given out by the violas and clarinets, later to be taken up by the violins. There follows a second subject, in B flat major, which is played by the clarinet accompanied by the strings pizzicato, and the first theme then returns. A brilliant Coda brings the composition to a close.

F. B

Valse de Concert No. 2, F Major, Op. 51

This Waltz was written at St. Petersburg in 1894 and published, with a dedication to Nicolas Galkine, a well known violinist in St. Petersburg and director of the orchestra at the Alexander Theater there. The piece begins with an Introduction (Allegro, F major, 3-4 time) in which the subject of the dance is foreshadowed. The principal theme is announced (Tempo di Valse, F major, 3-4 time) by the violins. Episodical subjects are interpolated in the course of the work, the principal theme appearing at intervals in contrast to them.

F. B.

Scènes de Ballet, Op. 52

Glazounov's "Scènes de Ballet" is a suite of eight movements, written in 1894 and published the following year with a dedication to the orchestra of the Russian Opera at St. Petersburg. The first performance was given at a concert of the Imperial Musical Society, St. Petersburg, in 1895. Glazounov conducted and, as the piece was still unpublished, from the manuscript. The suite comprises the following movements:

I. Préambule (Allegro, A major, 12-8 time). This opens with an extensive Introduction. The principal subject (Allegretto, 6-8 time) being given out by the first violins and later taken up by the wood winds. II. Marionettes. After a short Introduction the principal theme (Allegro, D major 3-8 time) is heard in the piccolo and the glockenspiel. There is a middle section (Trio) in G major, with its subject in the first violins. The first part then returns in a modified form. III. Mazurka (Allegro, F major, 3-4 time). The principal theme, announced by the full orchestra, is preceded by twenty-eight introductory measures. After some episodical material has been set forth the Trio (in D major) is reached. In this the violins and horns give out the theme over a drone bass in the lower strings and bassoons. The third part of the Mazurka repeats the first with certain modifications. IV. Scherzino (Allegro, A major, 2-4 time). This movement is constructed almost completely on the material which is heard at the beginning of it in the muted strings and wood winds. V. Pas d'Action (Adagio, D major, 4-4 time). The violoncellos open the movement with a theme of expressive quality, the violins playing with them as in a duet. Most of the movement is founded upon this material. VI. Danse Orientale (Allegretto, G minor, 3-8 time). The theme is presented at the third measure by the oboe, the strings accompanying and the rhythm being punctuated by the strokes of the tambourine. VII. Valse. An Introduction (Allegro moderato, C major, 3-4 time) opens the movement, the theme shortly making its appearance in the violins. There is a Trio in A flat major, its theme being announced by the solo violin, the flute then taking up the subject. The first division of the piece is repeated and it closes with a Coda based upon the matter which had been heard in the Introduction. VIII. Polonaise. Introductory matter precedes the principal subject (Moderato, A major, 3-4 time). The latter is presented by the full orchestra. The Trio is announced by the oboe. The third part is a repetition of the first, closing with a brilliant Coda.

F. B.

GLIÈRE

1874 –

Symphony No. 1 in E Flat Major, Op. 8

1. Andante. Allegro moderato.
2. Allegro molto vivace.
3. Andante.
4. Allegro.

THE name of Reinhold Moritzovitch Glière is comparatively a new one on American concert-room programs, but the success of his first symphony gives promise that it may yet become a familiar one. The work in question was composed at Moscow in 1899, but it was not heard until 1902.

A long introduction, in which suggestions of the main theme are heard, leads to the Allegro moderato, the principal theme being stated by the oboe with string accompaniment followed by a crescendo, by the full orchestra. A phrase in the basses and 'cellos leads to the second subject, given out by the clarinet and leading up to the development.

The second movement introduces two principal themes, the first in the strings and the second combined with it in the violas and bassoon. In the Trio a theme is developed after announcement by the clarinet with string accompaniment and at its close a recapitulation of the ideas in the first part follows.

The third movement opens with a theme given out by the first violins, which is developed at considerable length. A new subject then appears in the wood winds, continued by the strings, and ending in repetition by full orchestra. The opening passages of the movement are repeated and after a climax it ends quietly.

In the Finale the theme upon which most of it is constructed is given out fortissimo by the horns, repeated in the strings and afterwards in full orchestra. It also appears during its working out, in the 'cellos and basses with responses by oboe and flute. The second subject is given out in the wood winds. The first is then developed, followed by the second in the horns and 'cellos. A crescendo follows and leads to a powerful climax. Recapitulation of all this material closes the symphony.

Symphonic Poem, The Sirens, Op. 33

Glière's symphonic poem, "The Sirens," was first produced in St. Petersburg, in 1912. The composer briefly states its program as follows: "The Sea; The Isle of the Sirens; Approach of the Vessel; The Song of the Sirens; The Shipwreck." It follows of course the old story of the enchantments of the Sirens, the allurement of mariners, and the doom of their vessels, dashed to pieces upon the hidden rocks. The symphonic poem begins with a muted passage in the violins, with basses and kettle-drum accompaniment, representing the sea. A new section in the 'cellos, second violins and horns, depicts the island itself and is followed by a passage in the flute and celeste. The approach of the vessel is indicated by a passage in muted horns and the voices of the sirens are heard in the violas and clarinet. The music becomes more and more vigorous and at last reaches a climax, suggesting the wreck, after which it gradually grows more tranquil and ends pianissimo.

GLINKA

1804 – 1857

Overture to A Life for the Tsar

A LIFE FOR THE TSAR," Glinka's first opera, was the outcome of the composer's homesickness when, in the course of a tour which he made in Germany and Italy in 1830, he determined to exploit the music of the homeland which he loved so well. On his return to St. Petersburg, Glinka approached Joukovsky, who was tutor to the tsarevitch (and a poet), to suggest a national subject which could be treated as an opera. Joukovsky proposed "Ivan Soussanine" — this later became "A Life for the Tsar" — which already had been used for a libretto in a dramatic composition by Catterino Cavos, and which had been produced with considerable success at St. Petersburg in 1799. Glinka was filled with enthusiasm for the story and he induced Baron Rosen, secretary to the tsarevitch, to work it up into an opera text. Two years were spent in accomplishing this, but the work was finished in 1836 and the first production was made December 9 of that year at the Imperial Theater, St. Petersburg. The success of "A Life for the Tsar" was enormous. The triumph meant more than a personal success for the composer; for, listening to the tunes of national character — tunes belonging to Russia alone — the patriotic fervor of the people was aroused and the Russian national school began.

The plot of "A Life for the Tsar" is concerned with the struggle between Russia and Poland at the beginning of the seventeenth century. The Russian provinces had been invaded by the Poles, for the defenses of the empire had become weak after the death of Boris Godounof. In the crisis which faced their country, the Russians elected young Michael Romanoff as Tsar and the Poles were eager to capture a ruler whose military skill was of more than ordinary worth. Unable to discover the retreat of the Tsar, the Poles pressed into their service a Russian peasant, Ivan Soussanine, and ordered him to lead them to Romanoff's hiding-place. Ivan realized that the safety of the Russian nation depended upon his courage. He consented to guide the Polish army, but previously he sent his son, Sonia, to warn the Tsar of the danger that beset him. Then Ivan Soussanine led the enemy of his country into trackless forests and through swamps in which the Poles floundered helplessly. The latter found out that they had been deceived and Soussanine paid for his strategem with his life.

The overture to "A Life for the Tsar" begins with an Introduction (Adagio ma non tanto, G minor, 2-4 time), its outstanding feature being the melody for the oboe, which is heard eight measures after the beginning of the piece. The main movement (Vivace) follows with the principal subject in the first violins. This material also is used in the transitional passage leading to the second theme. The latter, in B flat major, is introduced by the clarinet and is worked over at some length. The development then is brought forward, this being somewhat brief and concerned principally with the opening theme. The customary recapitulation follows and the overture ends with a rather lengthy Coda, which makes use of material previously heard.

F. B.

Overture to Russlan and Ludmilla

The introduction to the second of Glinka's operas, "Russlan and Ludmilla," begins with fortissimo chords in full orchestra. The first theme appears in the violins, violas and flute, accompanied by all the other instruments. After a brilliant episode in the wood winds with string pizzicato accompaniment, and other subsidiary passages, the second theme appears — a graceful melody in the violas, 'cellos and bassoon. It is thei taken up fortissimo by full orchestra and prepares the way for the concluding theme. After a short, free fantasie, the first theme reappears in the strings and introduces the third section of the overture, in which the second and concluding themes are treated. The Coda, based upon the first theme, is very brilliant and is enriched by a bell-like effect produced in the brasses.

GLUCK

1714 – 1787

Overture to Iphigenia in Aulis

THE overtures to Gluck's operas, though but two of them retain a place in the modern concert repertory, possess unusual interest because they are the preludes to the dramatic works in which Gluck introduced certain reforms which may be summed up in his own words: "My idea was that the relation of music to poetry was much the same as that of harmonious coloring and well depicted light and shade to an accurate drawing, which animates the figures without altering their outlines." As originally written, the overture had no ending, but led without interruption into the opening scene of the opera. Mozart is supposed to have written a closing section to adapt it for concert use, and Wagner made sundry revisions and also wrote a Coda to take the place of the Mozart ending. The overture begins with a slow movement, followed by an Allegro, the old method of writing overtures. The slow movement is in strict style and is divided between the strings and wind instruments. The first subject of the Allegro appears several times, followed by Episodes, each worked up in strict time and frequently repeated. Wagner sums up the contents of the overture in four subjects, the first occurring in the slow movement as an invocation for deliverance from affliction. The other three he finds in the Allegro. The second represents assertion of overbearing authority; the third, expression of womanly tenderness; and the fourth, deep sympathy. This interpretation gives the general character of the various sections of the overture.

Overture to Iphigenia in Tauris

The overture to "Iphigenia in Tauris" is not an overture in the strict sense, but a brief prelude. It is included in this collection for the reason that it introduces one of the grandest of Gluck's operas, the one indeed which settled his preeminence in the famous Gluck-Piccini war at the time when the Académie de Musique of Paris commissioned the two rivals to produce an opera on the same subject, and Gluck carried off the laurels. It was set to the text written by the poet Guillard, who based his libretto on the tragedy by Guimand de la Touche, and was first produced in 1779. The prelude simply describes a calm, peaceful sea and then a furious storm, during which Iphigenia enters with the priestesses and offers a prayer of thankfulness. The prelude is in keeping with Gluck's idea that "the overture ought to indicate the subject and prepare the spectators for the character of the piece they are to see."

GODARD

1849 – 1895

Adagio Pathétique

GODARD, who was born at Paris, obtained the greater portion of his reputation as a composer of lighter pieces for piano and for violin; but his ambitions lay upon a loftier plane and he wrote a number of operas — "Pedro de Zalamea," "Le Dante," "Jocelyn," etc. — symphonies, concertos and much chamber music. Comparatively little of this music has survived. "Jocelyn" is remembered by the little Berceuse which Godard introduced into it after the work had been completed, and which has enjoyed a great popularity in an arrangement for violin and for violoncello. Occasionally Godard's "Concerto romantique," for violin, is performed, but the French master's name is more generally associated with such piano pieces as his Second Mazurka, "Au Matin," etc.

Godard's "Adagio Pathétique," which is frequently given a place on the programs of popular symphonic concerts, was not originally written for orchestra, but is the third of a set of six pieces for violin and piano and published as Opus 120. The orchestral version was made by Ross Jungnickel and was published in 1910.

F. B.

GOLDMARK

1830 – 1915

Symphony No. 1, Ländliche Hochzeit (Country Wedding), Op. 26

1. Moderato molto. (Wedding March with Variations.)
2. Allegretto. (Bridal Song.)
3. Allegretto moderato scherzando. (Serenade.)
4. Andante. (In the Garden.)
5. Finale, allegro molto. (Dance.)

THE "Country Wedding" Symphony, written in 1876, was first performed in that year at Vienna. Its brightness, freshness, and peculiarly close interpretation of the program which it represents will always make it a favorite among concert-goers. Its program is a sketch of a country wedding. The march and procession, the nuptial song, which we may imagine sung by the friends of the happy pair, the inevitable serenade, the discourse of the lovers in a garden, interrupted by the entrance of friends whose greetings lead up to a genuine country dance in the Finale, are the various scenes in this series of cheerful pastoral pictures.

The first movement is a most decided innovation, and at once announces that the work is not in the usual symphonic form. It is a march with thirteen variations, in which the theme appears only in fragments. They are scored in the freest possible manner, the composer evidently not wishing to restrict himself to the march form. The theme, which is simple and yet quite impressive, enters in the 'cellos and basses alone in a quiet manner, and without any of the stir and brilliancy which usually characterize the march. Then follow the variations in regular order. The first horn, with an accompaniment by the other horns and a moving bass in the strings, followed by a new melody for clarinets and flutes, takes the first variation. The violins give the second in an animated manner, and the full orchestra sweeps in on the third with the utmost vivacity and good feeling. The strings again take the fourth, but the mood changes to a tender and expressive minor. In the fifth the theme returns in the basses, assisted by bassoons and horns. The sixth is also assigned to the basses, the flutes and violins weaving a fanciful accompaniment around the theme. The seventh is in the minor, and is quaintly written, the utmost freedom being allowed to all the instruments. The eighth is divided between the first violins, flutes, oboes, and clarinets. In the ninth the theme is suggested in the bass, reinforced by a new subject for flute and violin. In the tenth the first violin introduces a fanciful figure with the theme appearing in the basses and strings. The eleventh, in the minor, is characterized by an entirely fresh subject, assigned to the violin and oboe, then to clarinet and violin, and finally to the clarinet. The twelfth introduces another new theme, growing out of the first, announced by the oboe with bassoon accompaniment, the flutes and clarinets moving independently, and the violins and violas enhancing the effect in a quaint manner. With the thirteenth, which returns to the original tempo, the charming series closes. Though treated freely and fancifully, these variations never lose the "country" spirit of the work.

The second movement, "Bridal Song," is a charming melody in genuine aria form in which the oboe is prominent, the subject of the march being heard in the basses. It is short, but graceful and delicate, and admirably fills its place in the fanciful scheme of the work.

The third movement, "Serenade," comes nearer to the sonata form, and yet preserves the pastoral characteristics throughout. The prelude is somewhat elaborate, and leads up to a melody for the oboes, which is afterward worked up by the violins and other instruments.

The fourth movement, "In the Garden," is a charming picture of the lovers tenderly conversing with each other and exchanging vows of constancy and passionate utterances. It is a dreamy episode with alluring bits of color, at times, as in the solo for clarinet, rising to the very intensity of passion, while in the middle part occurs a genuine love dialogue.

The scene now changes, and in the final movements we have the dance. Oddly enough, its principal theme is in fugal form, led off by the second violins, the first coming in last. It is very brilliant and picturesque in its effect, and contains many charming episodes, among them a return to the garden music in the middle part.

Symphony No. 2 in E Flat Major, Op. 35

1. Allegro.
2. Andante.
3. Allegro quasi presto.
4. Andante assai.

Goldmark's Second Symphony was written in 1887 and was first performed at Budapest in that year. The opening theme of the first movement is stated at once, followed by a section for the strings and this in turn by a theme treated in canon form by the strings and basses. The full orchestra enters vigorously, followed by a tranquil passage for strings, leading to the second subject, which appears in the 'cellos, with accompaniment of violas and second violins, continued by the clarinet. The full orchestra then gives out the first subject and also develops the second. After development and recapitulation, the Coda opens with the principal theme in full orchestra and the movement comes to a close with a brilliant prestissimo.

The second movement opens with a theme in the strings and a passage in full orchestra leads to a second theme in the horns and wood winds, subsequently taken by the strings and followed by still another in the strings, wood winds and horns. A new subject appears in the wood winds accompanied by the strings and after its development, the first subject returns. The second theme is heard again in the brasses and the Coda closes the movement.

The third movement opens with a brilliant subject given out by muted first violins which is developed in the strings and wood winds. As it comes to a close, the Trio opens with a long trumpet solo, string accompaniment, after which another subject appears in the flutes, oboes and clarinets. This is repeated by the strings. After it is developed, the trumpet solo is heard again and the first part of the movement is repeated.

After introduction the principal theme of the Finale is stated in the first violin, followed by a passage for oboes, clarinets and bassoons, which is next taken up by the strings. After development a third subject is announced. Further development of this material leads to the Coda and closes the movement with a restatement of the principal theme.

Overture, Sakuntala. Op. 13

The overture to "Sakuntala," first produced in Vienna in 1865, marked the initial step in Goldmark's success as a composer. The story which it illustrates is that of Sakuntala by Kalidasa, the Indian poet and dramatist. Sakuntala, a water nymph's daughter, is brought up by a priest in a sacred grove and adopted as his own daughter. King Dushiante, entering the grove, sees her, falls in love with her, and they are eventually married. The King gives her a ring which will identify her as his wife when she goes to his city. In the meantime another priest, actuated by motives of revenge, magically deprives the King of all recollection of her. While washing her raiment in the sacred river, Sakuntala loses the ring. When at last she presents herself to the King he disowns her, and she is driven away. Her mother, the nymph, in pity comes for her. The ring is found by a fisherman, who brings it to the King. The sight of it restores his recollection of Sakuntala and he is filled with remorse. In a campaign against the demons he finds Sakuntala, and they are happily united.

The overture opens with a rippling melody in the violas, 'cellos, and bassoons, indicative of Sakuntala's parentage. After a few measures the clarinet and 'cellos in unison sing the first theme, a love melody with soft accompaniment of the strings and bassoons. After the working out of this material, another theme, a hunting melody, appears in second violins, violas, and horns, and after elaboration leads to a fortissimo in full orchestra. Still another and very melodious theme appears in the oboe and clarinet, leading to an outburst of harmony in full orchestra. The Allegro begins pianissimo, and ending fortissimo, closes the first part of the overture in a vigorous climax. After the free fantasia the Coda follows, based upon passages from the hunting theme and leading to a fortissimo presentation of both first and second themes. A climax, beginning with the hunting song, closes the overture.

Overture to Penthesilea. Op. 31

The overture to "Penthesilea" is a prelude to the incidents in the drama of the same name written by Heinrich von Kleist. The story is substantially as follows: Penthesilea, daughter of Mars, was celebrated for her beauty and bravery as Queen of the Amazons. She assists Priam in the Trojan War and fights against Achilles, with whom she had been in love, and is slain by him. The hero, recognizing her armor after her defeat, is so overcome by her loveliness that he sheds tears for having sacrificed her to his rage. The opening theme, given out by full orchestra, is bold and passionate, and represents the Amazons' march to battle. The development of this theme leads to a new figure with accompaniment growing out of the opening theme, and after episodical treatment returns to the original subject. A subdued passage follows, expressive of a dialogue, interrupted by a melodic phrase in the clarinet. A new theme now appears in the flute and clarinet, the strings continuing the dialogue. Several new ideas follow. The oboe has a fresh theme, supplemented in the strings, and responded to by the flute, the two at last uniting, followed by a new and joyous theme given out by full orchestra. Episodes lead back to the original subject, and at last a furious outburst indicates the battle and defeat. There is a sudden pause. Penthesilea is slain. The rejoicing of the conqueror turns to lament, and a funeral march closes the overture.

Overture, Prometheus Bound. Op. 38

The overture, "Prometheus Bound," is one of Goldmark's mature works and one of the strongest and most dramatic of concert overtures. It is based upon the familiar myth, from the Æschylus trilogy, of Prometheus' successful resistance to the purpose of Zeus to destroy the human race, his theft of the fire, and his chaining to the Scythian rock as a penalty. The composer has left no program. The overture opens with a theme suggestive of the mournful loneliness of the bound Prometheus. It is followed by a tender, plaintive strain, which has been variously interpreted, leading to passages indicating the laments of the sea nymphs. Offset against this is a more vigorous theme, evidently illustrating Prometheus' undaunted nature, and this in turn is succeeded by a fortissimo passage in the brasses, which clearly defines the wrath of Zeus, the whole closing with broad, rich harmonies in keeping with the subject.

Overture, Sappho. Op. 44

The "Sappho" Overture is based upon the old legend of the Lesbian poetess and pictures her love for Phaon, which induces her to plunge into the sea from the Leucadian promontory, but as in the case of the "Prometheus Bound" Overture, the composer has left no program. The overture is opened by broad, majestic harp phrases in a kind of march rhythm. They serve to introduce a beautiful pastoral melody for the oboe, the Sappho theme, which is further continued by the flute. As it comes to a close, the full orchestra, except heavy brasses and harps, announces a vigorous and very dramatic theme, the first theme proper. After elaboration it takes on a more melodic character as this section reaches a climax. The music now is more tragic in its nature and leads to a return of the Sappho theme in the oboe and horns. It is then taken up by the violins. The second theme is gradually worked up to a strong climax and subsides again to pianissimo, accompanied by wood winds and horns. The solo violin announces the Sappho theme with wood wind accompaniment, and after a second climax a brilliant Coda brings the overture to a close.

Overture, In Italy. Op. 49

The overture " In Italy," though one of the composer's later works, is not one of his strongest. It has no introduction, but after a few measures in bassoon, kettledrums, and 'cellos, the opening brilliant theme is given out by the wood winds, trumpets, and violins, and is then developed by full orchestra. The solo oboe has the second theme, accompanied by bassoons, horns, harp, triangle, and tambourine — a passage full of local color with subsidiary episodes in 'cellos and double basses. The theme is developed at considerable length and brings the first part of the overture to a close. An episode follows with a theme for oboe, with harp and muted string accompaniment, which is repeated by the flute. After a short passage the first theme reenters, and the first movement is recapitulated, after which the overture comes to a spirited and melodious close.

Overture, In Spring Time. Op. 36

This overture opens without introduction, the leading theme given out by the first violins with accompaniment in the other strings. After development a second theme appears in the first violins with suggestions of bird-calls in the wood winds, followed by a figure in the first violins. After development of this material, recapitulation brings back both themes which are more fully worked up. A long and somewhat complicated Coda brings the overture to a close, with suggestions of all the thematic material. " In Spring Time " was written in 1889.

GOUNOD

1818–1893

Saltarello

GOUNOD'S brilliant "Saltarello," one of the most prominent examples of this characteristic Italian dance form, was first heard in London in 1871. It is scored for very full orchestra, including fife, four horns, tuba, bass drum, cymbals, triangles, tambourine and strings. It opens with a sparkling introduction which leads up to the principal theme, kept up with great vigor and with various changes of key, until modulations take place into the key of F major, and a new theme. After this is developed, the work comes back to the original key and subject, and the Saltarello closes in brilliant fashion.

Funeral March of a Marionette

The "Funeral March of a Marionette," slight as it is, has never lost its charm. It was originally written as one of the movements of a Suite Burlesque, which was never completed. The music in the beginning is supposed to tell the listener that two of the members of the Marionette troupe have had a duel and one of them has been killed. A party of pallbearers is organized and the procession sets out for the cemetery in march time. The music soon takes on a more cheerful spirit, for some of the troupe, wearied with the march, seek consolation at a wayside inn, where they refresh themselves and also descant upon the many virtues of their late companion. At last they get into place again and the procession enters the cemetery to the march rhythm — the whole closing with the bars intended to reflect upon the briefness and weariness of life, even for marionettes.

Ballet Music from Faust

The ballet music which Gounod composed for his opera "Faust" was not written for the work as it was first produced at Paris in 1859, but for a revival made at the Théâtre Lyrique, Paris, in March, 1860—precisely a year after the opening performance. The ballet is introduced into the last act, the Brocken scene—this is frequently omitted in English and American performances—in which Mephistopheles causes the rocks of the mountainous Brocken to sink out of sight and reveal a gigantic palace, in which he shows to Faust, who is looking for his vision of ideal beauty, the most beautiful courtesans of history. Sitting on richly embroidered cushions are to be seen Cleopatra, with her Nubian slaves, Helen of Troy, attended by her maidens, Aspasia, Lais and other courtesans. The scene opens by Aspasia and Lais, at the head of other women, inviting Faust and Mephistopheles to take part in the feast which is going on. After them, Cleopatra and Helen of Troy seek to draw Faust within the circle of their fascination. This is interrupted by the apparition of Phryne, completely veiled. She signs to the others to take part in the dances which have been suspended by her appearance. Phryne also takes part in the dance, gradually dropping, one by one, the veils which have enveloped her. The triumph evoked by Phryne's beauty awakens the jealousy and anger of the others and the dance becomes a frenzied bacchanale. The courtesans return to their cushions exhausted and out of breath. Faust, subjugated by Phryne's charms, holds out his wine-cup to her. At that moment a livid light suffuses the scene and the apparition of Marguerite appears on the summit of a high rock, bathed in luminous rays. The scene gradually fades.

There are seven movements in the ballet. I. Allegretto mouvement de valse. The waltz subject is given out, after a short Introduction, by the strings. II. Adagio. Following seven introductory measures, the violoncellos announce the expressive principal theme. There is a more animated middle section, after which the first subject returns. III. Allegretto. This opens with twelve measures of Introduction, following which the strings and wood winds announce the principal subject. IV. Moderato maestoso. The movement is constructed upon the graceful theme with which it opens in the violins. V. Moderato con moto. Following a short Introduction, the strings and harp set forth the expressive subject upon which this section of the ballet is based. VI. The movement (Allegretto) opens with four fortissimo measures, after which the strings give out the principal theme. There follows a middle section which employs the material of the opening measures of the movement, after which the first subject returns. VII. Allegro vivo. The opening section is wild in character and is played by the full orchestra. A more suave melody is then played by the strings (harp accompanying), the first section then recurring. There is now brought forward a tender theme, associated with Phryne, its melody in the strings and wood winds with harp accompaniment. The opening material now returns and is continued to the end.

F. B.

Overture to Mireille

"Mireille," Gounod's eighth opera, was composed to a text by Barbier and Carré, who based it upon the poem "Mirèio" by Frédéric Mistral, the Provençal poet, who had published it in 1859 in the Provençal dialect and with a French translation. The opera was produced March 19, 1864, at The Théâtre Lyrique, Paris, but with not much more than moderate success. The story concerns the Provençal maiden Mireille, who is in love with Vincent, a poor basket-maker. The girl's father commands her to marry a rich but brutal cattle-driver, Ourrias. The latter, vowing vengeance upon his rival, wounds Vincent, but not fatally. Mireille despondently makes a pilgrimage to the church of Sainte-Marie and dies unconscious in the arms of her lover.

Gounod's "Mireille" has not been able to hold the stage, but the overture, like the introductions to many another forgotten opera, still figures in the programs of concerts. The work begins with an Introduction (Andantino, G major, 4-4 time), the wood winds giving out its subject. The main movement (Allegro, G major, 6-8 time) follows, its principal theme announced by the strings. After this has been worked over the first violins bring forward a transitional passage with new subject matter, the triangle accentuating the first beat of the measures. The second subject is set forth expressively in D major by the first violins. Development takes place, more particularly of the transitional passage and the second theme. A crescendo leads to the recapitulation of the principal subject, fortissimo, in the full orchestra, the overture ending with a Coda (animé) in 2-4 time.

F. B.

GRAINGER

1882 –

Mock Morris

PERCY GRAINGER, who was born in Melbourne, Australia, received his musical training partly in his native country and partly in Europe, where he was a student of Kwast, at Frankfort. He made his first appearance as a pianist at the age of 10 and has toured widely in America, Europe, Australia, South Africa, etc. Particularly interested in folk music, Grainger has made numerous records of folk songs in England, Norway, Denmark, etc., his enthusiasm for such music having been stimulated by his friendship with Edvard Grieg.

"Mock Morris" was written in 1910 and was played for the first time at a concert given by Balfour Gardiner, at Queen's Hall, London, April 19, 1912. The work is one of two compositions designated on the score as "Room-music Tidbits" and is written for what the composer calls a "string sixsome" (six single players) or for a string orchestra. In accordance with his liking for Anglo-Saxon words, Grainger calls the instruments for which he scored his "Mock Morris," "First fiddle, second fiddle, third fiddle, middle fiddle and first and second bass fiddles." Similarly, the nuances are set forth in English, poco a poco crescendo, for instance, being turned into "louden lots bit by bit."

The meaning of the title which Grainger gave to this composition is thus explained by the composer: "No folk music tune-stuffs at all are used herein. The rhythmic cast of the piece is Morris-like, but neither the build of the tunes nor the general lay-out of the form keep to the Morris dance-shape."

The Morris Dance, it may be said, first began to be popular in England in the reign of Henry VII and was frequently associated with May-day revels. The dancers' attire was generally adorned with little bells and frequently the dance itself was made to form part of a pageant. Although Morris Dances were suppressed by the Puritans in England. the form still survives in certain parts of the country.

F. B.

Shepherd's Hey

This piece, designated as "A Morris Dance," was begun in 1908, but not completed until 1912. The first performance was given by the Queen's Hall Orchestra, London, August 19, 1912. In the United States it was first given at a concert of the Musical Art Society, New York, in 1913. The work, which a statement on the score testifies is "lovingly and reverently dedicated to the memory of Edvard Grieg," is "set for full band by Percy Aldridge Grainger on four variants collected by Cecil J. Sharp." These variants were a tune taken from the playing of a fiddler of the Bidford Morris dancers in 1906; a tune entitled "Stow on the Wold," taken down from the playing of a fiddler in 1907; a theme contributed by W. Hathaway, of Cheltenham, England, in 1907 and a theme contributed by William Wells, Bampton, England, in 1909.

F. B.

Children's March

The "Children's March" was written in 1917, at the time its composer was serving as a musician in the U. S. army, and was frequently sung and played by the band on the march. The work, which Grainger dedicated "to my playmates beyond the hills," has thus been described by the composer:

"Though of a lively character and displaying melodies with a popular 'ring' to them (none of which, however, is actually based upon folk songs or popular tunes), this march is structurally of a complicated build, on account of the large number of different themes

and tunes employed and of the varied and irregular interplay of many contrasted sections. Tonally speaking, it is a study in the blend of piano, wind and percussion timbres — the character of the piano tone lying midway between that of the wind and the percussion (xylophone, glockenspiel, tubular bells, etc.), and, in many cases, unifying the tone colors of the two other groups."

F. B.

GRIEG

1843 – 1907

Suite, Peer Gynt, No. 1. Op. 46

THE incidental music composed by Grieg for Ibsen's well-known drama, "Peer Gynt," written in 1867, was first published as a piano duet, but was afterwards made into two suites, the selections having been chosen by the composer himself. The story of Peer Gynt, his capricious, fantastic humor and bombastic arrogance, his abduction of the rustic bride Solveig and desertion of her, his love adventures in the halls of the mountain king and his ejection from them, his return home and the lonely death of his mother, Aase, his further adventures in the desert with the Bedouin girl Anitra, and the sad plight of the pseudo-prophet, his return, old and poor, to Solveig, in whose arms he dies — all the events of the familiar drama, indeed, are well known.

The first suite comprises four movements: 1. Morning Mood. 2. Death of Aase. 3. Anitra's Dance. 4. In the Hall of the Mountain King. The first and fourth movements are written for full orchestra, but the second and third are scored without wind instruments. The first movement evidently typifies the awakening of day among the mountains and the revery of Peer Gynt, who in his sublime silliness fancies he is monarch of all he surveys. It is of a bright and cheery character, consisting of the free elaboration of a single pastoral theme, with which is interwoven a cantabile theme in the 'cellos. The second movement is an elegy, or, practically, a funeral march, describing the solitary death of Aase on the mountain side. It is made up of gloomy yet haunting harmonization, and the reiteration of its phrases is a fitting expression of the monotony of grief. The third movement gives the agility, grace, and suppleness of Anitra in the dance. It is in mazurka time. The 'cello has an independent melody running through the movement, and the use of the triangle with the string instruments gives it an Oriental effect of color. The last movement represents the episode of Peer Gynt's visit to the cavern of the gnomes and their grotesque incantations and dances. It is constructed upon a single motive, begun in the bassoons and gradually extended in full orchestra. The entire movement, with the exception of the first few bars, is a repetition of a four-measure phrase from pianissimo to fortissimo, continually increasing in intensity.

Old Norwegian Romance with Variations. Op. 51

The composition entitled above was originally written for two pianos and subsequently scored for orchestra by the composer. The introduction opens quietly, and at last presents the theme in the strings, which is subsequently varied — a quaint, simple, little Norwegian song. The variations are thirteen in number, and are so clearly worked out and so symmetrical in construction that they easily make their appeal and do not call for explanation. The final variation is the most elaborate. It begins with an Adagio molto espressivo, the strings divided into nine parts and opens in the violas, 'cellos, double basses thus divided and the bassoon. It leads to a Finale, opening with a theme in the strings, wood winds, and horns worked up in a crescendo. The main theme of the movement is then repeated and ends in a tremendous climax. The liveliest of Codas founded on this theme, and the theme itself recurring in the muted strings and wood winds, close the work.

Two Northern Melodies. Op. 63

The "Two Northern Melodies," written for string orchestra. is one of Grieg's minor compositions, but is characterized by charming melodiousness and graceful construction, as well as by unmistakable local color. The first part, "Im Volkston," is a slow movement, based upon a folk song, as its name indicates. After a few introductory measures the 'cellos take the melody, accompanied in the remaining strings. The theme is then developed in the violins, and the movement comes to a close with the theme given out fortissimo by all the strings, and a brief Coda. The second movement is extremely simple in form but is delightful in treatment. It opens with a slow, introductory melody, "Kuhreigen" ("The Cowherds' Tune"), worked up in all the strings, and closes with the "Bauerntanz" ("Peasants' Dance"), the melody of which is fascinating. The piece is a dainty bit, reflecting aspects of Norwegian life.

Suite, From Holberg's Time. Op. 40

Grieg originally composed his suite for orchestra; later he turned it into a piano composition and the latter was re-transformed into a suite for string orchestra on the occasion, in 1884, of the two hundredth anniversary of the birth of Holberg. Holberg was born at Bergen — Grieg's birthplace, too — in 1684. He died in 1754. His fame was that of the founder of modern Norwegian literature; for Holberg's comedies and other works gained for him the title of the Molière of the North. Grieg, who humorously alluded to his suite as "a peruke piece," also composed a Holberg cantata for the anniversary celebration, but later he destroyed the work. The following are the movements of "From Holberg's Time" ("Aus Holbergs Zeit"): I. Prelude. Allegro vivace, G major, 4-4 time. II. Sarabande. Andante, G major, 3-4 time. III. Gavotte, G major, 4-4 time. IV. Air. Andante religioso, G minor, 3-4 time. V. Rigaudon. Allegro con brio, G major, 2-2 time.

F. B.

Three Orchestral Pieces from Sigurd Jorsalfar, Op. 56

"Sigurd Jorsalfar" is the title of a drama by Björnstjerne Björnson which was brought out for the first time at Christiania (Oslo) in 1872. Grieg was on terms of intimate friendship with the Norwegian poet and had already composed a number of vocal works to Björnson's texts — "Bergliot," "Olaf Trygvason," etc. — when he was asked to contribute some incidental music to the production of "Sigurd Jorsalfor." "The play," wrote the Norwegian composer, "was to be produced at the Christiania Theater after such a short preparation that I was allowed only eight days in which to write and orchestrate the music. But I had the elasticity of youth and it went." Björnson took the subject of his drama from the Sagas of the Norwegian kings written by the old Icelandic historian, Snorri-Sturluson (b. 1179). Sigurd became King of Norway, together with his brother, Eystein, in 1103. The Crusades were gathering thousands of Christian knights to fight the Saracens in Palestine, and Sigurd, seized partly with religious zeal and partly with a yearning for adventure, joined the Christian hosts. He left Norway with a great army and, after he had fought many battles and gathered together much plunder, finally returned to his native land, where he died in 1130.

From his music to Björnson's drama Grieg drew two vocal pieces — "The Norse People" and "King's Song" — and the suite of three pieces for orchestra, the latter having been published in 1893 as Opus 56.

The movements are as follows: I. Prelude (In the King's Hall). Allegretto semplice, A major, 4-4 time. The piece begins with a subject set forth by the clarinet and bassoon with pizzicato accompaniment in the strings. The second part — really a Trio — is ushered in by a theme for the flute, imitated by the oboe. The third part repeats the first. II. Intermezzo (Borghild's Dream). Poco Andante, B minor, 4-4 time. The first part of the movement, which employs only strings, is made up of tranquil material, the violoncellos beginning it with a steadily moving figure over a long roll on the kettle-drum. Later the time changes to Allegro agitato and the mood to one of restlessness. After a pause there is a further change to Andante espressivo, thirteen measures in length. III. March of Homage. Allegro molto, B flat major, 4-4 time. Fanfares from trumpets and a forte chord in the full orchestra precede the principal theme (Allegretto marziale), given out by four violoncellos. A crescendo leads back to the theme, now given to the full orchestra fortissimo. The Trio opens with a subject for the first violins, accompanied by the harp and remaining strings. Suggestions of the trumpet fanfares are heard and the whole first portion of the march is repeated.

F. B.

Lyric Suite, Op. 54

Grieg's Lyric Suite is an arrangement for orchestra of four of the six pieces which the Norwegian master composed for piano as one of the books of his "Lyrische Stücke" ("Lyrical Pieces"), published as Opus 54. He was moved to do this as the result of intelligence given him in 1903 by Henry T. Finck, music reviewer for the New York Evening Post, that Anton Seidl had made orchestral arrangements of four of the pieces and had conducted them at a concert at the Metropolitan Opera House a year or two previously. Seidl had died in 1898 and Grieg requested Finck to procure the score from the conductor's widow. An examination of it did not altogether satisfy him that Seidl had carried out his intentions and he determined to rescore the pieces, having previously obtained the sanction of Mrs. Seidl, to whom Grieg sent a thousand marks in payment for her husband's score.

The suite comprises four pieces: I. "Shepherd Lad." Andantino espressivo, A minor, 6-8 time. Scored only for strings and harp. II. "Norwegian Rustic March." Allegretto marcato, D major, 6-8 time. Scored for full orchestra and concerned principally with the jaunty theme given out by the clarinet and repeated by the first violins. III. Nocturne. Andante, C major, 3-4 time. Scored for wood winds, horns, kettledrums, triangle, harp and strings. The principal thematic material is that given out by the first violins. IV. "March of the Dwarfs." Allegro marcato, D minor, 2-4 time. This movement possesses something of the character of the closing section of the first "Peer Gynt" suite ("In the Hall of the Mountain King"). The first part is based upon the gnome-like theme announced by the first violins. There is a contrasting section in the middle (poco più lento), in which a solo violin plays an expressive melody. The first part is then resumed.

F. B.

Two Melodies for String Orchestra, Op. 34

The works which Grieg published as "Two Melodies for String Orchestra" are arrangements of the songs, "The Wounded Heart" and "Springtide," which were written in 1880 to texts by A. O. Vinje. When the composer made his transcriptions he was afraid that, missing the text which had belonged to the songs, the listener would fail to grasp the significance of the music. So he changed the title of the first song to "Heartwounds" and of the second to "The Last Spring." The former (Allegretto espressivo) is in C minor, 4-4 time. The latter (Andante) in G major, 4-4 time.

F. B.

HADLEY

1871 –

Symphony No. 2 in F Minor (The Four Seasons), Op. 30

1. Moderato maestoso.
2. Allegretto con moto.
3. Andante.
4. Andante con moto.

MR. HADLEY'S Second Symphony, descriptive of the four seasons, though laid out in the formal symphonic movements, is rather a symphonic poem in sections than a symphony. The first movement (Winter) begins with a theme stated by the 'cellos, basses, bassoons and brasses with a counter melody in the violins and wood winds. After development, the second theme appears in the horns, with a syncopated passage for violins. After development and recapitulation, the movement closes.

The second movement (Spring) is monopolized by the flute theme given out at once with accompaniment of wood winds and strings. An intermezzo based upon this theme is played by the horns, accompanied by strings and wood winds, after which the opening theme returns and closes the movement.

The third movement (Summer) as stated by the composer in his program notes describes "a midnight scene on a lake surrounded by mountains." Mr. Hadley's description of this movement as well as the fourth is appended in condensed form:

"The opening chords (horns and trumpets) are treated as a motive, and designed to awaken a feeling of mystery. A fragment of an Indian Love Song is then heard from the flute answered by the oboe. The opening chords are heard again, this time from the wood winds, and are followed by the same fragment of the Love Song. The violins then take up an undulating passage, followed by some vague harmonies, and thus usher in the principal subject — the Night Motive — in the horn part. With the promulgation of this theme fortissimo by the full orchestra the majesty and glory of a perfect night are sought to be suggested. The trombones and trumpets build up a sonorous background (Night Motive). A gradual diminuendo brings calm and peace. The plaintive Indian Love Song follows. Strains, suggesting the revels at an Indian camp, interrupt the Love Song; the music works up to frenetic utterance, and then comes the Coda, combining the Night Motive and the Love Song. Toward the close the Mystery chords sound again in the wood winds, followed by harmonies in the strings divisi."

The Finale, "Autumn," opens with a figure in staccato notes, divided into four parts throughout for the violins. The incessant reiteration of these little notes suggests the falling of leaves in a forest. Underneath the dropping notes is heard a melancholy theme which the composer conceives as a symbol of destiny. It is first intoned by the 'cello, violas, bassoon and horn. The melancholy mood remains despite the introduction of instrumental voices for color effects. As this first part gradually dies away hunting music sounds nearer and nearer. It waxes merry, and by a sudden crescendo reaches three staccato chords (the Death) from the full orchestra. Then the original Andante is resumed. Just before the Coda three measures of the Hunt theme are heard and the movement ends with the Death of the Leaves and the Destiny motive.

Symphony No. 4,

North, East, South and West, D Minor, Op. 64

The first performance of Hadley's fourth symphony was given at a concert of the Litchfield County Choral Union, held in the Music Shed of Mr. Carl Stoeckel's residence at Norfolk, Connecticut, June 6, 1911. The composer was also the conductor. The symphony was published in 1912 with a dedication to Mr. and Mrs. Carl Stoeckel.

I. North (Lento, grave, D minor, 3-4 time). The opening in slow tempo is introductory and written almost entirely for the brass. The main movement (Allegro energico, D minor,

9-8 time) is given out fortissimo by the horns, but considerable use is made later of a dotted figure played two measures previously by the bassoons. There is much stormy development of the principal theme, this leading to the tranquil second subject given out by the violins (G string) with harp accompaniment. A sonorous section follows in the full orchestra and there is development. Recapitulation of the first division of the movement ensues and at the close the slow tempo of the Introduction returns.

II. East (Andante dolorosamente, B flat minor, 3-4 time). Following two introductory measures, the principal theme is heard in the oboe. An episode for the horns ensues and then a solo violin takes up the theme, the oboes continuing it. The tempo changes (Allegro non troppo) and a new subject appears in the violins, the flute and oboe presenting a continuing section of it. At the close the opening subject is reheard in the oboe.

III. South (Scherzo). Allegretto giocoso, F major, 2-4 time. The movement opens with eight measures for the horn unaccompanied. The first theme then follows in the clarinet. The horn passage and the clarinet theme return and is worked over, the clarinet then presenting a new idea. Development of the material ensues and at the end the first subject returns in the full orchestra fortissimo.

IV. West (Allegro brillante, D major, 2-2 time). The principal subject begins, without Introduction, impetuously in the full orchestra. This is followed by a transitional passage, beginning with fanfares in the brass, which leads to the more expressive second theme in the strings. There are other sections of this subject, but a more important one is heard, after two fortissimo measures in the full orchestra, in the English horn — a subject of Indian character. There follows development of this which, in its turn, is succeeded by the recapitulation, the principal subject again being heard in the full orchestra. Following the second theme, again given to the strings, but now in D major, the Indian subject recurs, this time in the clarinet. The latter theme comes back again at the close, where it is vociferated by the horns fortissimo. F. B.

Overture, In Bohemia. Op. 28

The overture "In Bohemia" was composed in 1900 at the request of the Bohemian Club and was to have been produced that summer in the Bohemian Grove, California, under its composer's direction. Mr. Hadley, having been called to Europe, the performance was postponed, but meanwhile the overture was heard in many German cities. The title has no reference to that part of the former Austrian Empire which now is Czechoslovakia, but refers to that unsubstantial domain in which true artists dwell. The work was published in 1912 with a dedication to Victor Herbert and the Bohemian Club of San Francisco.

The principal subject (Allegro con brio, E major, 6-4 time) is given out at once by the full orchestra. A quieter passage for the wood winds leads to the second theme in B flat major, heard in the first violins, oboe and horn. The original mood and tempo return and there is development followed by the customary recapitulation.

F. B.

Lucifer: Tone Poem. Op. 66

Hadley's "Lucifer" was composed in 1913-14, its programatic basis having been the five-act tragedy "Lucifer" by the seventeenth century Dutch poet, Joost van den Vondel, who produced his drama at Amsterdam in 1654. It was said that Lucifer was intended by van den Vondel to be Oliver Cromwell, whom the poet greatly detested. The score of Hadley's tone poem carries the following description of his work:

"The tone poem 'Lucifer' contains five principal subjects: first, the stately theme with which the work begins (Gabriel's trumpet announcing God's message proclaiming love and goodness to all his subjects); second, the Lucifer theme, sinister, foreboding; third, the choral-like theme, suggesting angelic voices; fourth, the calm theme personifying peace and happiness; fifth, the theme of Joy and Victory during the Battle. These contrast freely until the war-trumpets announce Lucifer, who has gathered his legions round him to fight God's angels in the heavens.

"War ensues until Lucifer, defeated, is cast down into utter darkness. Then follows the peaceful theme, the work proceeding with the choral and Gabriel's trumpet-theme enlarged and harmonized for the entire orchestra, which brings the work to a brilliant close with a fanfare of four trumpets. The work is scored for three flutes (one interchangeable with piccolo), two oboes, English horn, two clarinets, bass clarinet, two bassoons, double bassoon, four horns, four trumpets, three trombones, tuba, three kettle-drums, small drum, triangle, bass drum, cymbals, celesta, harp, organ, strings and four trumpets, which intone Gabriel's message from their respective places in the auditorium."

F. B.

HALVORSEN

1864–

Entrance March of the Boyards

JOHAN HALVORSEN is known to American and English concert-goers practically by his "Entrance March of the Boyards" alone. He has, however, composed two symphonies, two Norwegian Rhapsodies for orchestra, nine orchestral suites, etc. Born at Drammen, Norway, Halvorsen studied at the Stockholm Conservatory and then was a violin pupil of Adolf Brodsky at Leipzig. He traveled for a time as solo violinist, lived for a short period at Aberdeen (Scotland) and for three years at Helsingfors as a teacher in the conservatory. Since 1899 Halvorsen has been director at the National Theater at Oslo. In his studies, as in his later career, Halvorsen was greatly assisted by Edvard Grieg, whose niece he married.

The "Entrance March of the Boyards" was composed in 1893 and it was upon the recommendation of Grieg that Theodore Thomas gave it the first performance in America at concerts of the Chicago Orchestra, now the Chicago Symphony Orchestra, December 13, 1895. The Boyards, or Boyars, were the former military nobility of Russia. They were abolished as a class by Peter the Great. Halvorsen's march scarcely requires extended discussion. It opens with a subject in the clarinet, the violoncellos and double basses sustaining a drone bass.

F. B.

HANDEL

1685 – 1759

Israel in Egypt

"ISRAEL IN EGYPT," the fifth of the nineteen oratorios which Handel composed in England, was written in 1738, the composition of the whole of this colossal work occupying but twenty-seven days. It was first performed April 4, 1739, at the King's Theater, of which Handel was then manager. It is essentially a choral oratorio. It comprises no less than twenty-eight massive double choruses, linked together by a few bars of recitative, with five arias and three duets interspersed among them. Unlike Handel's other oratorios, there is no overture or even prelude to the work. Six bars of recitative for tenor ("Now there arose a new King over Egypt which knew not Joseph") suffice to introduce it, and lead directly to the first double chorus ("And the Children of Israel sighed"), the theme of which is first given out by the altos of one choir with impressive pathos. The chorus works up to a climax of great force on the phrase ("And their Cry came up unto God"), the two choruses developing with consummate power the two principal subjects — first, the cry for relief, and second, the burden of oppression; and closing with the phrase above mentioned, upon which they unite in simple but majestic harmony. Then follow eight more bars of recitative for tenor, and the long series of descriptive choruses begins, in which Handel employs the imitative power of music in the boldest manner. The first is the plague of the water turned to blood ("They loathed to drink of the River") — a single chorus in fugue form, based upon a theme which is closely suggestive of the sickening sensations of the Egyptians, and increases in loathsomeness to the close, as the theme is variously treated. The next number is an aria for mezzo soprano voice ("Their Land brought forth Frogs"), the air itself serious and dignified, but the accompaniment imitative throughout of the hopping of these animals. It is followed by the plague of insects, whose afflictions are described by the double chorus. The tenors and basses in powerful unison declare ("He spake the word"), and the reply comes at once from the sopranos and altos ("And there came all manner of flies"), set to a shrill, buzzing, whirring accompaniment, which increases in volume and energy as the locusts appear, but bound together solidly with the phrase of the tenors and basses frequently repeated, and presenting a sonorous background to this fancy of the composer in insect imitation. From this remarkable chorus we pass to another still more remarkable, the familiar "Hailstone Chorus" ("He gave them Hailstones for Rain"), which, like the former, is closely imitative. Before the two choirs begin, the orchestra prepares the way for the on-coming storm. Drop by drop, spattering, dashing, and at last crashing, comes the storm, the gathering gloom rent with the lightning, the "fire that ran along upon the ground." But the storm passes, the gloom deepens, and we are lost in that vague, uncertain combination of tones where voices and instruments seem to be groping about, comprised in the marvelously expressive chorus ("He sent a thick Darkness over all the Land"). From the oppression of this choral gloom we emerge, only to encounter a chorus of savage, unrelenting retribution ("He smote all the First-born of Egypt"). After this savage mission is accomplished, we come to a chorus in pastoral style ("But as for His people, He led them forth like Sheep"), slow, tender, serene, and lovely in its movement. The following chorus ("Egypt was glad"), usually omitted in performance, is a fugue, both strange and intricate. The next two numbers are really one. The two choruses intone the words ("He rebuked the Red Sea"), in a majestic manner, accompanied by a few massive chords, and then pass to the glorious march of the Israelites ("He led them through the deep") — an elaborate and complicated number, but strong, forcible, and harmonious throughout, and held together by the stately opening theme with which the basses ascend. It is succeeded by another graphic chorus ("But the Waters overwhelmed their Enemies"), in which the roll and dash of the billows closing over Pharaoh's hosts are closely imitated by the instruments, and through which in the close is heard the victorious shout of the Israelites ("There was not one of them left"). Two more short choruses — the first ("And Israel saw that great work") and its continuation ("And believed the Lord"), written in church style, close this extraordinary chain of choral pictures.

The second part, "The Song of Moses," opens with a brief but forcible orchestral prelude, leading directly to the declaration by the chorus ("Moses and the Children of Israel sang this Song"), which, taken together with the instrumental prelude, serves as a stately introduction to the stupendous fugued chorus which follows ("I will sing unto the Lord, for He hath triumphed gloriously; the Horse and his Rider hath He thrown into the Sea"). It is followed by a duet for two sopranos ("The Lord is my Strength and my Song") in the minor key — an intricate but melodious number, usually omitted. Once more the chorus resumes with a brief announcement ("He is my God"), followed by a fugued movement in the old church style ("And I will exalt Him"). Next follows the great duet for two basses ("The Lord is a Man of War") — a piece of superb declamatory effect, full of vigor and stately assertion. The triumphant announcement in its closing measures ("His chosen Captains also are drowned in the Red Sea") is answered by a brief chorus ("The Depths have covered them"), followed by four choruses of triumph — ("Thy right Hand, O Lord"), an elaborate and brilliant number; ("And in the greatness of Thine excellency"), a brief but powerful bit; ("Thou sendest forth Thy Wrath"); and the single chorus ("And with the Blast of Thy nostrils"), in the last two of which Handel again returns to the imitative style with wonderful effect, especially in the declaration of the basses ("The Floods stood upright as an Heap, and the Depths were congealed"). The only tenor aria in the oratorio follows these choruses, a bravura song ("The Enemy said, 'I will pursue'"), and this is followed by the only soprano aria ("Thou didst blow with the Wind"). Two short double choruses ("Who is like unto Thee, O Lord") and ("The Earth swallowed them") lead to the duet for contralto and tenor ("Thou in Thy Mercy"), which is in the minor, and very pathetic in character. It is followed by the massive and extremely difficult chorus ("The People shall hear and be afraid"). Once more, after this majestic display, comes the solo voice, this time the contralto, in a simple, lovely song ("Thou shalt bring them in"). A short double chorus ("The Lord shall reign for ever and ever"), a few bars of recitative referring to the escape of Israel, the choral outburst once more repeated, and then the solo voice declaring ("Miriam the prophetess took a timbrel in her hand, and all the women went out after her with timbrels and with dances; and Miriam answered them"), lead to the final song of triumph — that grand, jubilant, overpowering expression of victory which, beginning with the exultant strain of Miriam ("Sing ye to the Lord, for He hath triumphed gloriously"), is amplified by voice upon voice in the great eight-part choir, and by instrument upon instrument, until it becomes a tempest of harmony, interwoven with the triumph of Miriam's cry and the exultation of the great host over the enemy's discomfiture, and closing with the combined power of voices and instruments in harmonious accord as they once more repeat Miriam's words ("The Horse and his Rider hath He thrown into the Sea").

Saul

The oratorio of "Saul" was written by Handel in 1738. The story closely follows the Biblical narrative of the relations between David and Saul. The overture is the longest of all the Handel introductions. It is in four movements, the first an Allegro, the second a Largo, in which the organ is used as a solo instrument, the third an Allegro, and the fourth a Minuetto. It is an exceedingly graceful and delicate prelude, and makes a fitting introduction to the dramatic story which follows. The characters introduced are Saul, King of Israel; Jonathan, his son; Abner, captain of the host; David; the apparition of Samuel; Doeg, a messenger; an Amalekite; Abiathar, Merab, and Michal, daughters of Saul; the Witch of Endor; and the Israelites.

The first scene opens in the Israelitish camp, where the people join in a Song of Triumph over Goliath and the Philistines. It is made up of a chorus ("How excellent Thy Name, O Lord!"), which is a stirring tribute of praise; an aria ("An Infant raised by Thy Command"), describing the meeting of David and Goliath; a trio, in which the giant is pictured as the "monster atheist," striding along to the vigorous and expressive music; and three closing choruses ("The Youth inspired by Thee"), ("How excellent Thy Name"), and a jubilant ("Hallelujah"), ending in plain but massive harmony.

The second scene is in Saul's tent. Two bars of recitative prelude an aria by Michal, Saul's daughter, who reveals her love for David ("O god-like Youth!"). Abner presents David to Saul, and a dialogue ensues between them, in which the conqueror announces his origin, and Saul pleads with him to remain, offering the hand of his daughter Merab as an inducement. David, whose part is sung by a contralto, replies in a beautiful aria, in which he attributes his success to the help of the Lord alone. In the next four numbers the friendship of Jonathan and David is cemented, which is followed by a three-verse hymn ("While yet Thy Tide of Blood runs high") of a stately character, sung by the High Priest. In a few bars of recitative Saul betroths his daughter Merab to David; but the girl replies in a vigorous aria ("My Soul rejects the Thought with Scorn"), in which she declares her intention of frustrating the scheme to unite a plebeian with the royal line. It is followed by a plaintive but vigorous aria ("See with what a scornful Air"), sung by Michal, who again gives expression to her love for David.

The next scene is entitled "Before an Israelitish City," and is prefaced with a short symphony of a jubilant character. A brief recitative introduces the maidens of the land singing and dancing in praise of the victor, leading up to one of Handel's finest choruses ("Welcome, welcome, mighty King") — a fresh, vigorous semi-chorus accompanied by the carillons, in which Saul's jealousy is aroused by the superiority of prowess attributed to David. It is followed by a furious aria ("With Rage I shall burst, his Praises to hear"). Jonathan laments the imprudence of the women in making comparisons, and Michal suggests to David that it is an old malady which may be assuaged by music, and in an aria ("Fell Rage and black Despair") expresses her belief that the monarch can be cured by David's "persuasive lyre." The next scene is in the King's house. David sings an aria ("O Lord, whose Mercies numberless"), followed by a harp solo; but it is in vain. Jonathan is in despair, and Saul, in an aria ("A Serpent in my Bosom warmed"), gives vent to his fury and hurls his javelin at David. The latter escapes; and in furious recitative Saul charges his son to destroy him. The next number is an aria for Merab ("Capricious Man, in Humor lost"), lamenting Saul's temper; and Jonathan follows with a dramatic recitative and aria, in which he refuses to obey his father's behest. The High Priest appeals to Heaven ("O Lord, whose Providence") to protect David, and the first part closes with a powerful chorus ("Preserve him for the Glory of Thy Name").

The second part is laid in the palace, and opens with a powerfully descriptive chorus ("Envy, eldest-born of Hell!"). In a noble song ("But sooner Jordan's Stream, I swear") Jonathan assures David he will never injure him. In a colloquy between them David is informed that Saul has bestowed the hand of the haughty Merab on Adriel, and Jonathan pleads the cause of the lovely Michal. Saul approaches, and David retires. Saul inquires of Jonathan whether he has obeyed his commands, and in a simple, sweet, and flowing melody ("Sin not, O King, against the Youth") he seems to overcome the wrath of the monarch, who dissembles and welcomes David, bidding him to repel the insults of the Philistines, and offering him his daughter Michal as a proof of his sincerity. In the second scene Michal declares her love for David, and they join in a rapturous duet ("O fairest of ten Thousand fair"), which is followed by a chorus in simple harmony ("Is there a Man who all his Ways"). A long symphony follows, preparing the way for the attempt on David's life. After an agitated duet with Michal ("At Persecution I can laugh"), David makes his escape just as Doeg, the messenger, enters with instructions to bring David to the King's chamber. He is shown the image in David's bed, which he says will only enrage the King still more. Michal sings an exultant aria ("No, let the Guilty tremble"), and even Merab, won over by David's qualities, pleads for him in a beautiful aria ("Author of Peace"). Another symphony intervenes, preluding the celebration of the feast of the new moon in the palace, to which David has been invited. Jonathan again interposes with an effort to save David's life, whereupon Saul, in a fresh outburst of indignation, hurls his javelin at his son, and the chorus bursts out in horror ("Oh, fatal Consequence of Rage!").

The third part opens with the intensely dramatic scene with the Witch of Endor, the interview being preluded by the powerful recitative ("Wretch that I am!"). The second scene is laid in the Witch's abode, where the incantation is practised that brings up the apparition of Samuel. This scene closes with an elegy foreboding the coming tragedy. The third scene opens with the interview between David and the Amalekite who brings the tidings of the death of Saul and Jonathan. It is followed by that magnificent dirge, the "Dead March," whose simple yet solemn and majestic strains are familiar to every one. The trumpets and trombones with their sonorous pomp and the wailing oboes and clarinets make an instrumental pageant which is the very apotheosis of grief. The effect of the march is all the more remarkable when it is considered that, in contradistinction to all other dirges, it is written in the major key. The chorus ("Mourn, Israel, mourn thy Beauty lost"), and the three arias of lament sung by David, which follow, are all characterized by feelings of the deepest gloom. A short chorus ("Eagles were not so swift as they") follows, and then David gives voice to his lament over Jonathan in an aria of exquisite tenderness ("In sweetest Harmony they lived"), at the close of which he joins with the chorus in an obligato of sorrowful grandeur ("Oh, fatal Day, how low the Mighty lie!"). In an exultant strain Abner bids the "men of Judah weep no more," and the animated martial chorus ("Gird on thy Sword, thou Man of Might") closes this great dramatic oratorio.

Samson

The oratorio, "Samson" was written in 1741. The last chorus was dated October 29; but in the following year Handel added to it "Let the bright Seraphim" and the chorus, "Let their celestial Concerts." The oratorio was first sung at Covent Garden, February 18, 1743.

The characters introduced are Samson; Micah, his friend; Manoah, his father; Delilah, his wife; Harapha, a giant of Gath; Israelitish woman; priests of Dagon; virgins attendant upon Delilah; Israelites, friends of Samson; Israelitish virgins; and Philistines. After a brilliant overture the scene opens before the prison in Gaza, with Samson blind and in chains. His opening recitative, setting forth his release from toil on account of the feast to Dagon, introduces a brilliant and effective chorus by the priests with trumpets ("Awake the Trumpet's lofty Sound"), after which a Philistine woman in a bright, playful melody invites the men of Gaza to bring "The merry Pipe and pleasing String"; whereupon the trumpet chorus is repeated. After the tenor aria ("Loud is the Thunder's awful Voice"), the chorus recurs again, showing Handel's evident partiality for it. The Philistine woman has another solo ("Then free from Sorrow"), whereupon in a pathetic song ("Torments, alas!") Samson bewails his piteous condition. His friend Micah appears, and in the aria ("Oh, Mirror of our fickle State") condoles with him.

In answer to his question, "Which shall we first bewail, thy Bondage, or lost Sight?" Samson replies in a short, but exquisitely tender aria ("Total Eclipse: no Sun, no Moon, all dark amidst the Blaze of Noon") — a song which brought tears to the eyes of the blind Handel himself when he listened to it long afterwards. The next chorus ("Oh, first-created Beam") is of more than ordinary interest, as it treats the same subject which Haydn afterwards used in "The Creation." It begins in a soft and quiet manner, in ordinary time, develops into a strong Allegro on the words ("Let there be Light"), and closes with a spirited fugue on the words ("To Thy dark Servant Life by Light afford"). A dialogue follows between Manoah and Micah, leading up to an intricate bravura aria for bass ("Thy glorious Deeds inspired my Tongue"), closing with an exquisite slow movement in broad contrast to its first part. Though comforted by his friends, Samson breaks out in furious denunciation of his enemies in the powerfully dramatic aria ("Why does the God of Israel sleep?"). It is followed up in the same spirit by the chorus ("Then shall they know") — a fugue on two vigorous subjects, the first given out by the altos, and the second by the tenors. Samson's wrath subsides in the recitative ("My genial Spirits droop"), and the first act closes with the beautifully constructed chorus ("Then round about the starry Throne"), in which his friends console him with the joys he will find in another life.

The second part, after a brief recitative, opens with an aria by Manoah ("Just are the Ways of God to Man"), in which he conjures Samson to repose his trust in God. It is followed by the beautiful prayer of Micah ("Return, return, O God of Hosts"), emphasized by the chorus to which it leads ("To dust his Glory they would tread"), with which the prayer is interwoven in obligato form. From this point, as Delilah appears, the music is full of bright color, and loses its sombre tone. In a short recitative she excuses her misdeed, and then breaks out in an aria of sensuous sweetness ("With plaintive Notes and am'rous Moan, thus coos the Turtle left alone"). Its bewitching grace, however, makes little impression upon Samson, who replies with the aria ("Your Charms to Ruin led the Way"). In another enticing melody ("My Faith and Truth, O Samson, prove"), she seeks to induce him to return to her house, and a chorus of virgins add their entreaties. A last effort is made in the tasteful and elegant aria ("To fleeting Pleasures make your Court"); but when that also fails, Delilah reveals her true self. Samson rebukes "her warbling charms," her "trains and wiles," and counts "this prison-house the house of liberty to thine"; whereupon a highly characteristic duet ensues ("Traitor to Love"). An aria for Micah follows ("It is nor Virtue, Valor, Wit"), leading up to a powerful dissertation on masculine supremacy in a fugued chorus which is treated in a spirited manner. The giant Harapha now appears, and mocks Samson with the taunt that had he met him before he was blind, he would have left him dead on the field of death, "where thou wrought'st Wonders with an Ass' Jaw." His first number ("Honor and Arms scorn such a Foe") is one of the most spirited and dashing bass solos ever written. Samson replies with the majestic aria ("My Strength is from the living God"). The two solos reach their climax in the energetic duet between the giants ("Go, baffled Coward, go"). Micah then suggests to Harapha that he shall call upon Dagon to dissolve "those magic Spells that gave our Hero Strength," as a test of his power. The recitative is followed by an impressive six-part chorus ("Hear, Jacob's God") in the true church style. Its smooth, quiet flow of harmony is refreshing as compared with the tumult of the giants' music which precedes, and the sensuousness of the chorus ("To Song and Dance we give the Day") which follows it. The act closes with the massive double chorus ("Fixed in His everlasting Seat") in which the Israelites and Philistines celebrate the attributes of their respective deities and invoke their protection, and in which also the composer brings out with overwhelming effect the majesty and grandeur of God as compared with the nothingness of Dagon.

The third part opens with a dialogue in which Harapha

brings the message to Samson that he must repair to the feast of Dagon to delight the Philistines with some of his feats of strength. Upon Samson's refusal, Harapha sings the threatening aria ("Presuming Slave!"). The Israelities invoke the protection of God in the spirited chorus ("With Thunder armed"), closing with a prayer which changes to wild and supplicating entreaty. Samson at last yields in a tender, pathetic aria ("Thus when the Sun"), which seems to anticipate his fate. In a song of solemn parting ("The Holy One of Israel be thy Guide"), accompanied by the chorus ("To Fame immortal go"), his friends bid him farewell. The festivities begin, and in an exultant chorus ("Great Dagon has subdued our Foe") the Philistines are heard exulting over Samson's discomfiture. Micah and Manoah, hearing the sounds, are filled with anxiety, and the latter expresses his solicitude in the tender aria ("How willing my paternal Love"). But the scene suddenly changes. In a short, crashing presto the coming destruction is anticipated. The trembling Israelites express their alarm in the chorus ("Hear us, our God"), and appeal to Heaven for protection. A messenger rushes upon the scene and announces that Samson is dead and has involved the destruction of his enemies in the general calamity. Micah gives expression to his grief in the touching aria ("Ye sons of Israel, now lament"), followed by the Israelites in a sorrowful wail ("Weep, Israel, weep"). A funeral march, in the major key, intervenes, full of tender expression of sorrow — for which, after the first two representations, Handel substituted the Dead March from "Saul," and both marches are now printed in the scores for general use. As at first written, the oratorio closed with the effective chorus and solo ("Bring the Laurels"); but a year afterwards Handel made a different ending. Manoah calls upon the people to cease their lamentations, and the funeral pageant is followed by the magnificent trumpet aria ("Let the bright seraphim") — a song worthy only of the greatest artists, characterized by joyousness, brilliancy and lofty inspiration, both with voice and instrument — and the equally magnificent chorus ("Let their celestial Concerts"), which closes the great oratorio with triumphant exultation.

The Messiah

"The Messiah" represents the ripened product of Handel's genius, and reflects the noblest aspirations and most exalted devotion of mankind. Among all his oratorios it retains its original freshness, vigor, and beauty in the highest degree, in that it appeals to the loftiest sentiment and to universal religious devotion, and is based upon the most harmonious, symmetrical, and enduring forms of the art. It was begun on the twenty-second day of August, 1741, and finished on the following September 14. The text was taken from the literal words of Scripture, and the libretto arranged by Charles Jennens.

The oratorio is divided into three parts. The first illustrates the longing of the world for the Messiah, prophesies his coming, and announces his birth; the second part is devoted to the sufferings, death, and exaltation of Christ, and develops the spread and ultimate triumph of the Gospel; while the third is occupied with the declaration of the highest truths of doctrine—faith in the existence of God, the surety of immortal life, the resurrection, and the attainment of an eternity of happiness.

The first part opens with an overture, or rather orchestral prelude, of majestic chords, leading to a short fugue, developed with severe simplicity and preparing the way for the accompanied recitative ("Comfort ye my People"), and the aria for tenor ("Every Valley shall be exalted"), which in turn leads to the full, strong chorus ("And the Glory of the Lord shall be revealed")—the three numbers in reality forming one. The prophecy is announced, only to be followed by the human apprehension in the great aria for bass ("But who may abide the Day of His coming?"), written in the Sicilian pastoral style. The aria leads to the exquisitely constructed number ("And He shall purify") a fugued chorus closing in simple harmony. Once more the prophet announces ("Behold, a Virgin shall conceive"), followed by the alto solo ("O Thou that tellest"), which preludes a chorus in the same tempo. The next aria ("The People that walked in Darkness"), with its curious but characteristic modulations leads to one of the most graphic fugued choruses in the whole work ("For unto us a Child is born"), elegantly interwoven with the violin parts, and emphasized with sublime announcements of the names of the Messiah in full harmony and with the strongest choral power. The grand burst of sound dies away, there is a significant pause, and then follows a short but exquisite Pastoral Symphony for the strings, which with the four succeeding bits of recitative tells the message of the angels to the shepherds on the plains of Bethlehem. Suddenly follows the chorus of the heavenly hosts ("Glory to God"), which is remarkably expressive, and affords sharp contrasts in the successive clear responses to the fugue. The difficult but very brilliant aria for soprano ("Rejoice greatly"), the lovely aria ("He shall feed His Flock"), in which Handel returns again to the pastoral style, and a short chorus ("His Yoke is easy"), close the first part.

The second part is the most impressive portion of the work. It begins with a majestic and solemn chorus ("Behold the Lamb of God"), which is followed by the aria for alto ("He was despised") — one of the most pathetic and deeply expressive songs ever written, in which the very key-note of sorrow is struck. Two choruses — ("Surely He hath borne our Griefs"), rather intricate in harmony, and ("With His Stripes we are healed"), a fugued chorus written *a capella* upon an admirable subject — lead to the spirited and thoroughly interesting chorus ("All we like Sheep have gone astray"), closing with an Adagio of great beauty ("And the Lord hath laid on Him the Iniquity of us all"). This is followed by several short numbers — a choral fugue ("He trusted in God"), the accompanied recitative ("Thy Rebuke hath broken His Heart"), a short but very pathetic aria for tenor ("Behold and see if there be any Sorrow"), and an aria for soprano ("But Thou didst not leave His soul in

Hell") — all of which are remarkable instances of the musical expression of sorrow and pity. These numbers lead to a triumphal shout in the chorus and semi-choruses ("Lift up your Heads, O ye Gates!") which reach a climax of magnificent power and strongly contrasted effects. After the chorus ("Let all the Angels of God worship Him"), a fugue constructed upon two subjects, the aria ("Thou art gone up on high"), and the chorus ("The Lord gave the Word"), we reach another pastoral aria of great beauty ("How beautiful are the Feet"). This is followed by a powerfully descriptive chorus ("Their Sound is gone out into all Lands"), a massive aria for bass ("Why do the Nations"), the chorus ("Let us break their Bonds asunder"), and the aria ("Thou shalt break them"), leading directly to the great "Hallelujah Chorus," which is the triumph of the work and its real climax. It opens with exultant shouts of "Hallelujah." Then ensue three simple phrases, the middle one in plain counterpoint, which form the groundwork for the "Hallelujah." These phrases, seemingly growing out of each other, and reiterated with constantly increasing power, interweaving with and sustaining the "Hallelujah" with wonderful harmonic effects, make up a chorus that has never been excelled, not only in musical skill, but also in grandeur and sublimity. After listening to its performance, one can understand Handel's words: "I did think I did see all heaven before me, and the great God Himself." This number closes the second part.

If the oratorio had closed at this point, the unities would have been preserved, but Handel carried it into a third part with undiminished interest, opening it with that sublime confession of faith ("I know that my Redeemer liveth"). It is followed by two quartets in plain counterpoint with choral responses ("Since by Man came Death"), and ("For as in Adam all die"), in which the effects of contrast are very forcibly brought out. The last important aria in the work ("The Trumpet shall sound"), for bass with trumpet obligato, will always be admired for its beauty and stirring effect. The oratorio closes with three choruses, all in the same key and of the same general sentiment ("Worthy is the Lamb"), a piece of smooth, flowing harmony; ("Blessing and Honor"), a fugue led off by the tenors and bassos in unison, and repeated by the sopranos and altos on the octave, closing with full harmony on the words "for ever and ever" several times reiterated; and the final "Amen" chorus, which is treated in the severest style, and in which the composer evidently gave free rein to his genius, not being hampered with the trammels of words.

Judas Maccabaeus

The oratorio, "Judas Maccabaeus" was written in thirty-two days, between July 9 and August 11, 1746, upon the commission of Frederic, Prince of Wales, to celebrate the return of the Duke of Cumberland from Scotland after the decisive victory of Culloden. The words were taken from the narrative of the exploits of the Jewish deliverer contained in the first book of Maccabees and in the twelfth book of Josephus' "Antiquities of the Jews." It was first performed at Covent Garden, April 1, 1747. The characters represented are Judas Maccabæus; Simon, his brother; an Israelitish messenger; and Israelitish men and women.

The first scene introduces the Israelitish men and women lamenting the death of the father of Judas in the sorrowful chorus ("Mourn, ye afflicted Children"), which, after a duet for soprano and tenor, is followed by still another chorus in a similar strain ("For Zion Lamentation make"), but much more impressive, and rising to a more powerful climax. After a brief and simple soprano solo ("Pious Orgies"), the chorus sings the prayer ("O Father, whose almighty Power"), closing with a characteristic fugue on the words ("And grant a Leader"). After a short recitative, Simon, bass, breaks out in the heroic and sonorous aria ("Arm, arm, ye Brave!") which has always retained its popularity, notwithstanding its antique bravura. It is followed by the chorus in the brief but stirring number ("We come in bright array").

Five arias, a duet, and two choruses, nearly all of which are now omitted in performances, being of the same general character, and mainly apostrophes to liberty lead to the great chorus closing the first part ("Hear us, O Lord!").

The second part opens with the Israelites celebrating the return of Judas from the victories over Appollonius and Seron. An instrumental prelude, picturing the scenes of battle, leads directly to the great chorus, the best in the work ("Fallen is the Foe"). The triumphant declaration is made over and over with constantly increasing energy, finally leading to a brilliant fugue on the words ("Where warlike Judas wields his righteous Sword"); but interwoven with it are still heard those notes of victory ("Fallen is the Foe"), and the response ("So fall Thy Foes"). The Israelitish man sings a vigorous tribute to Judas ("So rapid thy Course is"). The triumphant strain ("Zion now her Head shall raise") is taken by two voices, closing with the soprano alone; but before her part ends, the whole chorus takes it and joins in the paean ("Tune your Harps"), and the double number ends in broad, flowing harmony. In a florid number ("From mighty Kings he took the Spoil") the Israelitish woman once more sings Judas' praise. The two voices unite in a welcome ("Hail Judæa, happy Land"), and finally the whole chorus join in a simple but jubilant acclaim to the same words. The rejoicings soon change to expressions of alarm and apprehension as a messenger enters and announces that Gorgias has been sent by Antiochus to attack the Israelites, and is already near at hand. They join in a chorus expressive of deep despondency ("Oh, wretched Israel"); but Simon, in a spirited aria ("The Lord worketh Wonders"), bids them put their trust in Heaven, and Judas rouses their courage with the martial trumpet song ("Sound an Alarm"), which, though very brief, is full of vigor and fire. After the departure of Judas to meet the foe, Simon, the Israelitish man, and the Israelitish woman follow each other in denunciation of the idolatries which have been practiced by the heathen among them, and close with the splendid chorus ("We never will bow down to the rude Stock or sculptured Stone"), in which vigorous repetitions of the opening phrase lead to a chorale in broad, impressive harmony, with which is interwoven equally vigorous repetitions of the phrase ("We worship God alone").

The third part opens with the impressive prayer ("Father of Heaven, from Thy eternal Throne"), sung by the priest. As the fire ascends from the altar, the sanctuary having been purified of its heathen defilement, the Israelites look upon it as an omen of victory and take courage. A messenger enters with tidings of Judas' triumph over all their enemies. The Israelitish maidens and youths go out to meet him, singing the exultant march chorus ("See the conquering Hero comes"), which is familiar to every one by its common use on all occasions, from Handel's time to this, where tribute has been paid to martial success and heroes have been welcomed. It is the universal accompaniment of victory, as the Dead March in "Saul" is of the pageantry of death. It is very simple in its construction, like many others of Handel's most effective numbers and first sung as a three-part chorus, then as a duet or chorus of virgins, again by the full power of all the voices, and gradually dies away in the form of an instrumental march. A very elaborate chorus ("Sing unto God"), a florid aria with trumpet solo for Judas ("With Honor let Desert be Crowned"), the chorus ("To our great God"), a pastoral duet with exquisite accompaniment ("Oh, lovely Peace!"), and a "Hallelujah" in the composer's customary exultant style, close this brilliant and dramatic oratorio.

Acis and Galatea

The first idea of Handel's famous pastoral, "Acis and Galatea," is to be found in a serenata, "Aci, Galatea, e Polifemo," which he produced at Naples in July, 1708. The plan of the work resembles that of the later pastoral, though its musical setting is entirely different. The story is based on the seventh fable in the thirteenth book of the Metamorphoses — the sad story which Galatea, daughter of Nereus, tells to Scylla. The nymph was passionately in love with the shepherd Acis, son of Faunus and of the nymph Symæthis, and pursued him incessantly. She too was pursued by Polyphemus, the one-eyed Cyclops of Ætna, contemner of the gods. One day, reclining upon the breast of Acis, concealed behind a rock, she hears the giant pouring out to the woods and mountains his story of love and despair. As he utters his complaints, he espies the lovers. Then, raging and roaring so that the mountains shook and the sea trembled, he hurled a huge rock at Acis and crushed him. The shepherd's blood gushing forth from beneath the rock was changed into a river; and Galatea, who had fled to the sea, was consoled.

The overture to the work, consisting of one movement, is thoroughly pastoral in its style and introduces a chorus ("Oh, the Pleasures of the Plains!") in which the easy, careless life of the shepherds and their swains is pictured. Galatea enters seeking her lover, and after the recitative ("Ye verdant Plains and woody Mountains") relieves her heart with an outburst of melodious beauty ("Hush, ye pretty warbling Choir!"). Acis answers her, after a short recitative, with another aria equally graceful ("Love in her Eyes sits playing and sheds delicious Death"). The melodious and sensuous dialogue is continued by Galatea, who once more sings ("As when the Dove"). Then in a duet, sparkling with the happiness of the lovers ("Happy we"), closing with chorus to the same words, this pretty picture of ancient pastoral life among the nymphs and shepherds comes to an end.

In the second part there is another tone both to scene and music. The opening chorus of alarm ("Wretched Lovers") portends the coming of the love-sick Cyclops; the mountains bow, the forests shake, the waves run frightened to the shore as he approaches roaring and calling for "a hundred reeds of decent growth," that on "such pipe" his capacious mouth may play the praises of Galatea. The recitative ("I melt, I rage, I burn") is very characteristic, and leads to the giant's love-song, an unctuous, catching melody almost too full of humor and grace for the fierce brute of Ætna ("Oh, ruddier than the Cherry!").

In marked contrast with this declaration follows the plaintive, tender song of Acis ("Love sounds the Alarm"). Galatea appeals to him to trust the gods, and then the three join in a Trio ("The Flocks shall leave the Mountain"). Enraged at his discomfiture, the giant puts forth his power. He is no longer the lover piping to Galatea and dissembling his real nature, but a destructive, raging force; and the fragment of mountain which he tears away buries poor Acis as effectually as Ætna sometimes does the plains beneath. The catastrophe accomplished, the work closes with the sad lament of Galatea for her lover ("Must I my Acis still bemoan?") and the choral consolations of the shepherds and their swains ("Galatea, dry thy Tears, Acis now a God appears").

L' Allegro

"L' Allegro, il Penseroso ed il Moderato," the first two movements of which contain a musical setting of Milton's well-known poem, was written in the seventeen days from January 19 to February 6, 1740, and was first performed on the twenty-seventh of the latter month at the Royal Theater, Lincoln's Inn Fields, London. The text of the first two parts is by Milton, Allegro, as is well known, chanting the praises of pleasure, Penseroso those of melancholy; Allegro represented by tenor and Penseroso by soprano, and each supported by a chorus which joins in the discussion of the two moods.

The work opens without overture, its place having originally been supplied by an orchestral concerto. In vigorous and very dramatic recitative Allegro bids "loathed Melancholy" hence, followed by Penseroso, who in a few bars of recitative far less vigorously consigns "vain, deluding joys" to "some idle brain"; Allegro replies with the first aria ("Come, come, thou Goddess fair"), a beautifully free and flowing melody, responded to by Penseroso, who in an aria of stately rhythm appeals to his goddess ("Divinest Melancholy"). Now Allegro summons his retinue of mirth ("Haste thee, Nymph, and bring with thee"), and the chorus takes up the jovial refrain in the same temper. The aria itself is well known as the laughing-song. Indeed, both aria and chorus are full of unrestrained mirth, and go laughingly along in genuine musical giggles. The effect is still further enhanced by the next aria for Allegro ("Come and trip it as you go"), a graceful minuet, which is also taken by the chorus. After a recitative by Penseroso ("Come, pensive Nun"), and the aria ("Come, but keep thy wonted State"), the first Penseroso chorus occurs ("Join with thee calm Peace and Quiet"), a short but beautiful passage of tranquil harmony. Once more in recitative Allegro bids "loathed Melancholy" hence, and then in the aria ("Mirth, admit me of thy Crew") leading into chorus, sings of the lark, "startling dull Night" and bidding good-morrow at his window — a brilliant number accompanied with an imitation of the lark's song. Penseroso replies by an equally brilliant song ("Sweet Bird that shun'st the noise of Folly"), in which the nightingale plays the part of accompaniment. Another aria by Allegro ("Oft listening how the Hounds and Horn") gives an opportunity for a blithe and jocund hunting-song for the bass, followed by one of the most beautiful numbers in the work ("Oft on a plat of rising ground"), sung by Penseroso, in which the ringing of the far-off curfew, "swinging slow, with sullen roar," is introduced with telling effect. This is followed by a quiet, meditative aria ("Far from all resorts of Mirth"), when once again Allegro takes up the strain in two arias ("Let me wander not unseen") and ("Straight mine Eye hath caught new Pleasures"). The first part closes with the Allegro aria and chorus ("Or let the merry Bells ring round!"), full of the very spirit of joy and youth; and ending with an exquisite harmonic effect as the gay crowd creep to bed, "by whispering winds soon lulled to sleep."

The second part begins with a stately recitative and aria by Penseroso ("Sometimes let gorgeous Tragedy"), followed by one of the most characteristic arias in the work ("But oh, sad Virgin, that thy Power might raise!") in which the passage ("Or bid the Soul of Orpheus sing") is accompanied by long, persistent trills that admirably suit the words. The next number ("Populous Cities please me then") is a very descriptive solo for Allegro, with chorus which begins in canon form for the voices and then turns to a lively movement as it pictures the knights celebrating their triumphs and the "store of ladies" awarding prizes to their gallants. Again Allegro in a graceful aria sings ("There let Hymen oft appear"). It is followed by a charming canzonet ("Hide me from Day's garish Eye") for Penseroso, which leads to an aria for Allegro ("I'll to the well-trod Stage anon"), opening in genuinely theatrical style, and then changing to a delightfully melodious warble at the words ("Or sweetest Shakespeare, Fancy's Child"). This is followed by three characteristic arias ("And ever, against eating Cares"), ("Orpheus himself may heave his Head"), and ("These Delights, if thou canst give") — the last with chorus.

The Dettingen Te Deum

On the twenty-seventh of June, 1743, the British army and its allies, under the command of King George II and Lord Stair, won a victory at Dettingen, in Bavaria, over the French army, commanded by the Maréchal del Noailles and the Duc de Grammont. On the King's return a day of public thanksgiving was appointed, and Handel, at that time "Composer of Musick to the Chapel Royal," was commissioned to write a Te Deum and an anthem for the occasion.

The Dettingen Te Deum is not a Te Deum in the strict sense, but a grand martial panegyric. It contains eighteen short solos and choruses, mostly of a brilliant, martial character, the solos being divided between the alto, barytone, and bass. After a brief instrumental prelude, the work opens with the triumphant, jubilant chorus with trumpets and drums ("We praise Thee, O God"), written for five parts, the sopranos being divided into firsts and seconds, containing also a short alto solo leading to a closing fugue. The second number ("All the Earth doth worship Thee") is also an alto solo with five-part chorus of the same general character. It is followed by a semi-chorus in three parts ("To Thee all Angels cry aloud"), plaintive in style, and leading to the full chorus ("To Thee, Cherubim and Seraphim"), which is majestic in its movement and rich in harmony. The fifth number is a quartet and chorus ("The glorious Company of the Apostles praise Thee"), dominated by the bass, with responses from the other parts, and followed by a short, full chorus ("Thine adorable, true, and only Son"). The seventh number is a stirring bass solo with trumpets. A fanfare of trumpets introduces the next four numbers, all choruses. In this group the art of fugue and counterpoint is splendidly illustrated, but never to the sacrifice of brilliant effect, which is also heightened by the trumpets in the accompaniments. An impressive bass solo ("Vouchsafe, O Lord") intervenes, and then the trumpets sound the stately symphony to the final chorus ("O Lord, in Thee have I trusted"). It begins with a long alto solo with delicate oboe accompaniment that makes the effect very impressive when voices and instruments take up the phrase in a magnificent outburst of power and rich harmony, and carry it to the close.

Largo

The work which, in an instrumental arrangement, has long been known to the world as "Handel's Largo" is an aria which, entitled "Ombra mai fu," originally formed part of the opening scene of the opera "Serse" ("Xerxes"), which Handel produced at London in 1738. Although the work ostensibly deals with Xerxes, the king of Persia, who invaded Greece in 480 B. C., the story in reality has nothing to do with him and the opera was, indeed, Handel's one excursion into comic music-drama.

The scene in which the aria is sung represents "a summer house near a beautiful garden, in the midst of which grows a plane tree." The character named Xerxes sings the aria lying under the tree, which he apostrophizes in his song. The best known of the instrumental arrangements of the Largo is that made for violin by Joseph Hellmesberger.

F. B.

Water Music

It was believed for many years that the so-called "Water Music" by Handel was composed for the purpose of appeasing the wrath of George I, King of England, which had been evoked by the composer when he had been permitted to visit England — George having been, at that time, Elector of Hanover — and had outstayed his leave of absence to an outrageous extent. George had succeeded to the British throne in 1714 and it was held that Handel's propitiatory music had been composed the following year as a surprise to the monarch when he made a state progress in his barge down the Thames. This would have been a romantic incident, but unfortunately it has proved to be untrue. Handel's music was not written until 1717 and the King's displeasure had long been smoothed away. Yet the "Water Music" was written for George I's progress from Lambeth to Chelsea and the facts of the affair were communicated by Frederic Bonnet, envoy from the Duke of Brandenburg to the English court, in a report which the former made to his master and dated July 19, 1717. The river party was arranged by Baron Kielmansegge for George's pleasure and the royal barge was accompanied by a large number of other boats containing members of the king's suite. On one of the barges was stationed Handel's orchestra — fifty musicians — and Bonnet states that they comprised "trumpets, hunting horns, oboes, bassoons, German flutes, French flutes à bec, violins and basses, but without voices." The music, expressly composed by Handel, so greatly charmed the king that he commanded it to be repeated "once before and once after supper, although it took an hour for each performance."

The "Water Music" was published in 1720. Of the twenty movements which comprised the work, six were arranged for modern orchestra by Sir Hamilton Harty, conductor of the Halle Orchestra in Manchester, England, and it is this edition that is generally played.

F. B.

HAYDN

1732 – 1809

Symphony No. 1 (B. & H.), in E Flat

1. Adagio. Allegro con spirito.
2. Andante.
3. Minuet.
4. Finale. Presto.

THE Symphony in E flat was composed in 1795, and is the eighth in the set written for Salomon, and the first of the Breitkopf and Härtel edition. It opens with an Adagio, introduced by a roll on the kettle-drum, with the following theme:

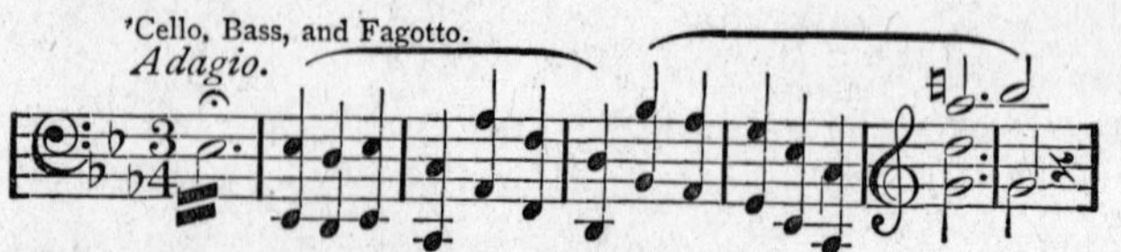

This broad and sombre melody gives the key to the whole work. It ends in a unison phrase in C minor, in a half-mysterious way on G, the fifth of the chord. Then enters the Allegro con spirito, with the following theme:

The half-step in the first group, forced in the repetition by an accidental, keeps the otherwise humorous theme within bounds. The second part is worked up in strict compliance with the sonata form, and displays Haydn's mastery in counterpoint. After a hold, the basses take up the melody of the opening Adagio, pressed into the new mould of the $\frac{6}{8}$ tempo. This middle movement is again interrupted by a hold, followed by the working-out of the second theme and closing on the dominant seventh chord and a grand pause, after which the first part is repeated. At the half-cadence the opening Adagio unexpectedly enters with its solemn roll of the drum and deep-toned melody, followed by a short Coda, Allegro.

The Andante, in C minor, opens with the following melody:

The first bar has a vein of inexpressibly sad loveliness, which also pervades the whole song, as it may be called. In the third part it is interesting to see how simply the composer accomplishes his purpose by enlivening the rhythm.

The first and third parts are then repeated in the form of variations, exquisitely worked out. The third variation, in C minor, is scored for full orchestra, and is one of the many examples we find in Haydn which show that the minor mood or minor key was for him rather the expression of the grand and heroic than of sadness or sorrow. The Coda in its simplicity, however, shows the sad undercurrent of his thought while writing this lovely Andante, although the close is in the major key.

The Minuet, with the following theme—

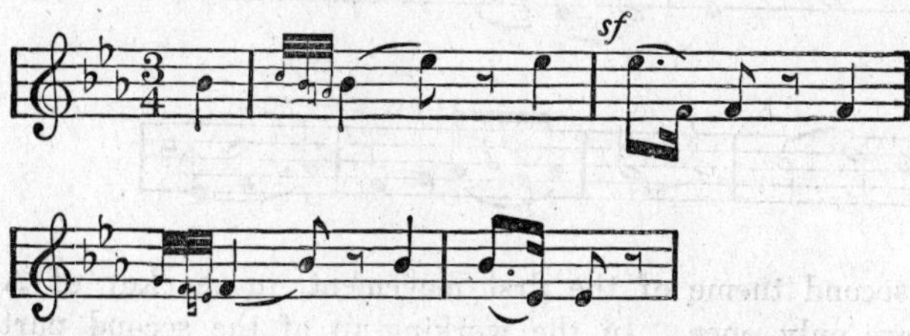

reaches far higher than the dance form, and its working-up in the second part is unusually rich in harmonic treatment. The Trio contains the flowing legato figures which Haydn so often used to offset the broken rhythm and skipping melody of the Minuet proper.

The Finale, in E flat, is founded on the following theme, with underlying figure for horns, as marked:

The whole movement is symphonic in character, and shows little of the playfulness we are wont to look for in Haydn's compositions.

Symphony No. 2 (B. & H.), in D Major

1. Adagio. Allegro.
2. Andante.
3. Minuet.
4. Finale. Allegro spiritoso.

The Symphony in D major — No. 2, Breitkopf and Härtel — was written in 1795. It has the usual Adagio introduction, in D minor, closing on the dominant pianissimo and leading into the Allegro with the following theme:

The second theme of the first movement, in the key of A, appears only once. In the working-up of the second part, the composer utilizes the four quarter-beats followed by two half-notes, given above, as a separate motive, which imparts to the whole movement a certain brusqueness and force.

The Andante, in G major, $\frac{2}{4}$ time, is based on the following lovely song written in a popular vein—

and treated in the form of variations; not, however, in the usual strict manner, but interspersed with significant and deeply effective intermezzos. The second part of the melody proceeds with the following tuneful counterpoint, using the opening bars of the Andante for an accompaniment:

The Minuet, in D major, is energetic in character, owing to its peculiar accentuation, as well as strong harmony, and yet preserves the humor and piquancy of the master's most favorite movements in a wonderful degree. The Trio has the same character, in its contrast to the Minuet proper, as that in the E flat symphony.

The Finale, in D major, Allegro spiritoso, has a flavor of country life and its enjoyments. It begins on a pedal bass for horns and 'cellos, over which runs the most natural, simple song, which however gives free play to the master's art in counterpoint.

Symphony No. 6 (B. & H.), in G Major (Surprise)

1. ADAGIO. VIVACE ASSAI.
2. ANDANTE.
3. MINUET.
4. FINALE. ALLEGRO MOLTO.

The Symphony in G major, popularly known as "The Surprise"—No. 6, Breitkopf and Härtel—was written in

1791. It has a short introductory Adagio, in which an unusual number of chromatics are employed, leading at once into the main Vivace assai, with the following for the first theme:

Daintily as it steps in, it soon develops into the full rush of life.

The Andante, in C major, the movement which gave the name of "Surprise" to the symphony, is based on this exceedingly simple melody, moving through the intervals of the chord:

It opens piano, is repeated pianissimo, and closes with an unexpected crash of the whole orchestra. Here we have the genial "Papa Haydn," who enjoyed a joke, and when in the humor for it did not think it beneath his dignity "to score" the joke; for to a friend, who was visiting him when writing the Andante, he remarked: "That's sure to make the ladies jump"; and his waggish purpose has been secured to this day. The theme is carried out in his favorite form of variations, and the movement closes with a pedal point giving the opening phrase and dying away in a pianissimo.

The Minuet seems the natural sequence of this extremely simple Andante. The sweep of the violins in the last two measures of the first part is made the motive for the second part, which is used in canon form between the violins and basses and connected with the Trio, written in the usual manner.

The last movement, Allegro molto, in G major, has this happy theme for its foundation:

The piquancy of its phrasing is in the master's happiest vein, and although worked out with less display of science than some of his other finales, it gathers new interest by the rushing violin figures that are used quite lavishly and fully sustain its joyful character.

Symphony No. 9 (B. & H.), in C Minor

1. Allegro.
2. Andante.
3. Minuet.
4. Finale. Vivace.

The Symphony in C minor — Breitkopf and Härtel, No. 9 — opens at once with an Allegro in common time:

The bold steps at the opening and the march-like rhythm of the third and fourth measures, although subdued in a dynamic sense, and never used in a military mood, give the movement a certain crispness which is effectively off-set by the second theme:

This is followed by scale runs in triplets, that alternate between the higher and lower instrumental groups and well preserve the strong character of the otherwise short movement.

The Andante cantabile, in E flat, in its idyllic theme—

betrays the composer of "With Verdure clad," and vies with that well-known melody in sweetness. It is worked out in a number of variations, among which the one in E flat minor is especially noticeable.

The Minuet is one of the popular concert numbers, and is a masterly specimen of grace and refined humor, combined with the stateliness of the old-fashioned dance. Its theme is the following:

The Trio varies from many of the previous ones in that the movement of eighth notes appears staccato throughout. and is given to the 'cellos, the violins only marking the rhythm.

The Finale vivace, in C major, is rich in the treatment of counterpoint and fugue; but a glance at the leading theme—

will show at once that it is not dry or heavy music. The

general treatment reminds us of his earlier symphonies, but much of it also shows the influence of Mozart.

Symphony No. 11 (B. & H.), in G Major (Military)

1. Largo. Allegro.
2. Allegretto.
3. Minuet.
4. Finale. Presto.

The Symphony in G major — No. 11 of the Breitkopf and Härtel edition — was written in 1794. It opens with a slow movement of broad and even pathetic character, closing on the dominant chord with a hold. The first movement proper, Allegro, starts in with the following theme, given out by the flutes and oboes:

and is repeated in ever new instrumental combinations, leading into a play of questions and answers between wind and string instruments, which Haydn's successors have made use of so often. After the half-cadence, the second theme —

enters piano. In spirit it is a lively march, and although at its first appearance it is quite subdued, the staccato marks relieve any uncertainty as to its meaning. The working-up in the second part relies chiefly on this second theme; and when the double-basses take it up, it rises to its full importance. The greater length of the movement, its ingenious harmonic treatment, the stubborn character in the sforzando strokes after the second theme appears fortissimo, the crisp staccato scales in broken thirds in the violins, stamp this Allegro as one of the most important the master has left.

The Allegretto, in C major, which here takes the place of the usual Andante, has given to this symphony the name of "The Military" and is based on an old French romanza:

In its treatment of interchanging instrumental groups, and in its quiet yet cheerful movement, it sounds like the last farewells of soldiers as they take leave of home. After several repeats, the trumpets sound the signal for falling into line, and with a few strong chords in the key of A flat, the march is resumed. The composer has made masterly use of the drums, cymbals, and triangle, in the various repeats of this simple theme, relying almost entirely on the tone-colors of the different orchestral instruments and their combination for the maintaining of the interest in the simple march theme.

The Minuet, moderato, in its form comes nearer the dance minuet in graceful groups of violin figures than any we have considered; while the Trio is worked up in a more distinct character than usual, and with its dotted rhythm remains nearer the original dance than the legato Trios of former symphonies.

The last movement, Presto, is in Haydn's happiest vein. Its theme —

is playful and charming, and the whole Finale, although not devoid of more forcible intermezzos, broken by unexpected pauses and elaborate treatment in harmonic changes, moves along in a happy and natural manner.

Symphony No. 12 (B. & H.), in B Flat

1. Largo. Allegro.
2. Adagio.
3. Minuet.
4. Finale. Presto.

The Symphony in B flat, written in 1794, is No. 12 of the Breitkopf and Härtel edition. A short Largo opens with a hold on the keynote, followed by a phrase for wind instruments reflecting the sadness of the whole Introduction.

The first movement, Allegro vivace, brings in the main theme —

at once fortissimo by the whole orchestra, and reversing the order to repeat, appears as a piano phrase. This is followed by a lively figure for violins through sixteen measures, working up into a crescendo fortissimo that reaches its climax on a whole note on A in unison, and with the grand pause following prepares the entrance of the second theme in A major, as follows:

This, with several other shorter themes, furnishes the material for the working-up of the second part. The whole scheme is broader than usual. The rhythmic, harmonic, and dynamic changes form a picture of real life pulsating with vital force.

The Adagio in F major is comparatively short, and has Italian touches of elegance in the rich ornamentation with which the melody is embellished. In character it leaves the popular vein which Haydn's slow movements generally show, and leans more toward the elegiac and sentimental.

The Minuet, although its first part inclines toward the dance form, assumes a style of its own by the stubborn assertion of a group of three notes in repeat, leading to a hold, after which a playful treatment of the same motive brings us back to the original theme.

The Finale, in B flat, Presto, opens with the following gay song —

which flows along without interruption, for even the occasional attempts at stubbornness have an undercurrent of jollity. Syncopations, pianissimo staccatos, unexpected pauses, clashes of the full orchestra, sudden transitions of key, the playful use of parts of a motive, etc., combine in making a picture of happiness and joyous life which is all the more extraordinary when we consider that Haydn wrote this work in his sixty-second year.

The Creation

Haydn was sixty-five years of age when he undertook the great work of his life. It was begun in 1796, and finished in 1798. When urged to bring it to a conclusion more rapidly, he replied, "I spend much time over it, because I intend it to last a long time." The first public performance was given in Vienna, March 19, 1799, Haydn's name-day. Its success was immediate, and rivalled that of "The Messiah."

The oratorio opens with an overture representing chaos.

Its effect is at first dull and indefinite, its utterances inarticulate, and its notes destitute of perceptible melody. Gradually instrument after instrument makes an effort to extricate itself, and as the clarinets and flutes struggle out of the confusion, the feeling of order begins to make itself apparent. The resolutions indicate harmony. At last the wonderful discordances settle, leaving a misty effect that vividly illustrates ("the Spirit of God moving upon the Face of the Waters"). Then, at the fiat of the Creator ("Let there be Light"), the whole orchestra and chorus burst forth in the sonorous response ("And there was Light"). A brief passage by Uriel, tenor, describes the division of light from darkness, and the end of chaos, introducing a fugued chorus, in which the rage of Satan and his hellish spirits, as they are precipitated into the abyss, is described with tremendous discords and strange modulations; but before it closes, the music relates the beauties of the newly created earth springing up ("at God's Command"). Raphael describes the making of the firmament, the raging of the storms, the flashing lightning and rolling thunders, the showers of rain and hail, and the gently falling snow, to an accompaniment which is closely imitative in character. The work of the second day forms the theme of ("The marvelous Work"), for soprano obligato with chorus — a number characterized by great joyousness and spirit. This leads to the number ("Rolling in foaming Billows") in which the music is employed to represent the effect of water, from the roaring billows of the ("boisterous Seas"), and the rivers flowing in ("Serpent Error"), to the ("limpid Brook"), whose murmuring ripple is set to one of the sweetest and most delicious of melodies. This leads the way to the well-known aria ("With Verdure clad"), of which Haydn himself was very fond, and which he recast three times before he was satisfied with it. It is followed by a fugued chorus ("Awake the Harp"), in which the angels praise the Creator. We next pass to the creation of the planets. The instrumental prelude is a wonderful bit of constantly developing color, which increases ("in Splendor bright"), until the sun appears. It is followed by the rising of the moon, to an accompaniment as tender as its own radiance; and as the stars appear ("the Sons of God"), announce the fourth day, and the first part closes with the great chorus ("The Heavens are telling"), in which the entire force of band and singers is employed in full, broad harmony and sonorous chords, leading to a cadence of magnificent power.

The second part opens with the aria ("On mighty Pens"), describing in a majestic manner the flight of the eagle, and then blithely passes to the gaiety of the lark, the tenderness of the cooing doves, and the plaintiveness of the nightingale, in which the singing of the birds is imitated as closely as the resources of music will allow. A beautiful terzetto describes with inimitable grace the gently sloping hills covered with their verdure, the leaping of the fountain into the light, and the flights of birds; and a bass solo in sonorous manner takes up the swimming fish, closing with ("the Upheaval of Leviathan from the Deep"), who disports himself among the double-basses. This leads to a powerful chorus ("The Lord is great"). The next number describes the creation of various animals; and perhaps nothing that art contains can vie with it in varied and vivid description. It begins with the lion, whose deep roar is heard among the wind instruments. The alertness of the ("flexible Tiger") is shown in rapid flights by the strings. A Presto ingeniously represents the quick movements of the stag. The horse is accompanied by music which prances and neighs. A quiet pastoral movement, in strong contrast with the preceding abrupt transitions, pictures the cattle seeking their food ("on Fields and Meadows green"). A flutter of sounds describes the swarms of insects in the air, and from this we pass to a long, undulating thread of harmony, representing the ("sinuous Trace") of the worm. This masterpiece of imitative music is contained in a single recitative. A powerful and dignified aria, sung by Raphael ("Now Heaven in fullest Glory shone"), introduces the creation of man, which is completed in an exquisitely beautiful aria ("In native Worth") by Uriel, the second part of which is full of tender beauty in its description of the creation of Eve, and closes with a picture of the happiness of the newly created pair. A brief recitative ("And God saw Everything that He had made") leads to the chorus ("Achieved is the glorious Work") — a fugue of great power, superbly accompanied. It is interrupted by a Trio ("On Thee each living Soul awaits"), but soon returns with still greater power and grandeur, closing with a Gloria and Hallelujah of magnificent proportions.

The third part opens with a symphonic introduction descriptive of the first morning of creation, in which the flutes and horns, combined with the strings, are used with exquisite effect. In a brief recitative ("In rosy Mantle appears") Uriel pictures the joy of Adam and Eve, and bids them sing the praise of God with the angelic choir, which forms the theme of the succeeding duet and chorus ("By Thee with Bliss"); to which the answering choir replies with a gentle and distant effect, as if from the celestial heights ("Forever blessed be His Power"). Again Adam and Eve in successive solos, join with the choir in extolling the goodness of God; and as they close, all take up the paean ("Hail, bounteous Lord! Almighty, hail!"). As the angelic shout dies away, a tender, loving dialogue ensues between Adam and Eve, leading to the beautiful duet ("Graceful Consort"), which is not only the most delightful number in the work, but in freshness, sweetness, and tenderness stands almost unsurpassed among compositions of its kind. After a short bit of recitative by Uriel ("O happy Pair"), the chorus enters upon the closing number ("Sing the Lord, ye Voices all"), beginning slowly and majestically, then developing into a masterly fugue ("Jehovah's Praise forever shall endure"), and closing with a laudamus of matchless beauty, in which the principal voices in solo parts are set off against the choral and orchestral masses with powerful effect.

HERBERT

1859 – 1924

Irish Rhapsody

VICTOR HERBERT, who is best known for his numerous comic operas, composed a number of works for orchestra of which the "Irish Rhapsody" has been the most popular. It was published in 1910 with a dedication to the Gaelic Society of New York. The Rhapsody is based upon national melodies, more particularly upon those which are contained in the "Irish Melodies" of Thomas Moore, a collection which the poet made in 1807. It begins (Allegro molto, A major, 6-8 time) with suggestions of the song "We May Roam through This World," set by Moore to the tune "Garry Owen" ("Garyone"). Soon the tempo changes to Lento and, following a cadenza for the harp, there is given out the melody "My Lodging's on the Cold Ground" which Moore used for his verse, "Believe me if all those endearing young charms." This, in its turn, is succeeded by another section (Allegro feroce, B minor, 9-8 time) the material of which is a modified version of "The Rocky Road to Dublin." This is worked over and the tune "Fague a Ballagh," which Moore set to "To Ladies' Eyes," is heard. Later this is followed by Moore's "Erin, O Erin," set to the tune "Thamama Hulla," Moore's "Come o'er the Sea," set to "Cuishlih Ma Chree," is now given out by the violoncellos and the violins follow with the poet's "Rich and rare were the gems she wore," to the tune "The Summer is Coming." There is a cadenza for the oboe which leads to "St. Patrick's Day." At the end the tune "Garry Owen" returns, the brass combining with it the theme of "Erin, O Erin."

F. B.

HÉROLD

1791 – 1833

Overture to Zampa

"ZAMPA," opera comique in three acts, was written to a text by Mélesville who based it upon the story of the "Statue Bride," in itself a variant of the "Don Juan" legend. The plot is concerned with one Zampa, a pirate, who, having betrayed his sweetheart, Albina, returns from the sea in after years and jestingly offers to wed the statue of Albina, which, when he puts a ring on its stony finger, raises its arm menacingly. Zampa forces another girl — Camille — to marry him, although she is betrothed to Alphonse. On the eve of the marriage Camille flees from the pirate, who, when he pursues her, is suddenly confronted with the statue of Albina, which seizes him and throws him and itself into the sea.

The overture begins (Allegro vivace ed impetuoso, D major, 2-2 time) with a vigorous theme in the full orchestra, drawn from a bacchanalian chorus of pirates in the opening act. Following a pause, the time changes to Andante. Rolls on the kettle-drum are answered by fortissimo chords in the wind instruments. Clarinets, horns and bassoons then give out a new theme in B flat major (Andante sans lenteur). The tempo becomes more animated and development is given to the opening theme. A crescendo then leads to a sonorous tutti (Allegro vivace assai con grandezza). This is worked over and, after a pause, is followed by a new theme, espressivo, in the clarinet, lightly accompanied by the pizzicato of the strings. A dance-like subject follows (un peu plus vite) in the first violins, the triangle marking the first beat of the measures. A forte tutti, beginning with a fanfare in the brass, succeeds this and leads to a light triplet figuration in the first violins. A development of this brings the overture to a brilliant conclusion.

F. B.

HOLST

1874 –

The Planets. Op. 32

GUSTAV HOLST, who was born at Cheltenham, England, where his father was engaged as organist and teacher of piano, received his musical education at the Royal College of Music, London. In that institution he was a pupil of Sir Charles Villiers Stanford. Holst, in addition to his studies in composition, took up the trombone and, indeed, began his career playing the instrument in the orchestra of the Carl Rosa Opera Company and in the Scottish Orchestra (Glasgow).

Holst's suite "The Planets" was produced for the first time — at least as to five of its seven movements — at a concert of the Royal Philharmonic Society, London, February 27, 1919. The work was written in 1915-1916 and, as to its significance, was astrological rather than astronomical. Astrology, it will be remembered, undertook to foretell or judge human events by studying the position of the heavenly bodies. It was a science known to and practiced by the ancient Chaldeans, Chinese, Egyptians and Persians and it was one which led to the development of astronomy.

"The Planets" demands a large orchestra for its interpretation. The work is scored for four flutes (two of them interchangeable with piccolos and one with a bass flute), three oboes (one interchangeable with a bass oboe), English horn, three clarinets, bass clarinet, three bassoons, double bassoon, six horns, four trumpets, two tenor trombones, bass trombone, bass tuba, tenor tuba, six kettle-drums, bass drum, side drum, cymbals, bells, triangle, tambourine, glockenspiel, celesta, xylophone, gong, two harps, organ, chorus of women's voices and strings.

I. Mars — the Bringer of War. (Allegro, C major, 5-4 time.) Much use is made in the movement of the barbaric rhythm set forth in the repeated G's in the strings (which play with the wooden part of the bow instead of the hair), harps and kettle-drums. An important motive is given out by the bassoons and horns at the third measure. A climax is attained and the brass announce a third idea, of which use is made later. There is extensive development and the opening motive returns *fff*, followed by fanfares in the brass.

II. Venus — the Bringer of Peace. (Adagio, E flat major, 4-4 time.) Two measures for a solo horn open the movement. The descending figure which follows in the flute is given employment later. Later, too, the key changes to F sharp major and a new theme is heard in the oboes and English horn. This is developed. The opening motive returns and is worked over.

III. Mercury — the Winged Messenger. (Vivace, 6-8 time.) The movement begins with a rapidly moving figure in the muted strings and some of the wood winds, accompanied by the harps. Soon there is heard a motive in the bassoons and harps to which employment is given later. This is developed and is followed by a subject in the two oboes and English horn, accompanied by repeated E's in the first violins. A continuing section of this, first given to a solo violin, is continually repeated by various instruments. The remainder of the movement makes use of the foregoing material and comes lightly and softly to an end with a reminiscence of the subject, previously referred to, in the two oboes and English horn.

IV. Jupiter — the Bringer of Jollity. (Allegro giocoso, C major, 2-4 time.) After five introductory measures in the first violins, a breezy tune is given out by the lower strings and horns and repeated by the trombones. Immediately afterward a strongly marked rhythm in the horns is heard and this is worked over at considerable length. The first theme recurs in the strings, piano. The time changes to 3-4 and a new idea is brought forward by the six horns, accompanied by chords in the strings. Following another recurrence of the first theme, a new section (Andante maestoso, E flat major, 3-4 time) is given out by the horns and strings. The original tempo and the accented horn theme return, the first subject then being worked over. Foregoing material is developed and the movement ends, somewhat suddenly, with the rhythm of the opening theme.

V. Saturn — the Bringer of Old Age. (Adagio, C major, 4-4 time.) Some introductory measures for the flutes and harps are followed by a phrase for the double-basses upon which a large portion of the movement is based. The brasses take up this motive (pizzicato in the lowest strings) and it is developed by other instruments. The flutes bring forward a new idea and there is a crescendo followed by a climax, the first subject recurring in the double-basses, tuba and wood winds. There is a Coda, which is really a variant of the opening subject.

VI. Uranus — the Magician. (Vivace, C major, 6-4 time.) A sonorous and portentous motive is thundered out by the brass and repeated in notes of shorter length by the tubas and kettle-drums. A staccato figure is then presented by the bassoons, which is developed. The opening motive returns in the double-basses and double bassoon and imitations of it occur in the kettle-drums and other instruments. Following a pause, a new section is brought forward, whose subject is allotted to the tubas. The music becomes more sonorous and a great climax is attained. A curious effect is made at this point by a glissando on the keys of the organ. Following this there is a sudden pianissimo and the opening subject is given out very softly.

VII. Neptune — the Mystic. (Andante, 5-4 time.) A languorous melody is played by two flutes alone, then repeated with a tremolo accompaniment in the two harps. Later the wood winds bring forward another idea (Allegretto) which is worked over. At the close a hidden choir of female voices is heard.

F. B.

Suite, Beni Mora. Op. 29, No. 1

This suite was the outcome of a vacation which Gustav Holst spent in Algeria and was composed in 1910. The first production was given at a concert given by Balfour Gardiner at Queen's Hall, London, May 1, 1912. Concerning the significance of "Beni Mora" the following statement written by Edwin Evans in the London Musical Times may be quoted:

"In a program note the composer asks the listener to 'imagine himself in the still, dry air of the desert at night. As he approaches the oasis he hears a flute in the distance and sees the dim outlines of a white-robed Arab procession wending its way from street to street. Above this flute melody are heard fragments of tunes answering one another. All grows more definite until he reaches the street of the Ouled Naïls, and pausing at different entrances he hears one dance after another, each in a different key and rhythm, amidst which the procession music remains unaltered.'"

The reader may be reminded that it is at Beni Mora that much of the scene in Robert Hichens' novel "The Garden of Allah" is laid.

The suite is divided into the following movements. I. First Dance. Adagio, E minor, 3-4 time. II. Second Dance. Allegretto, A minor, 5-4 time. III. "In the Street of the Ouled Naïls." Adagio, E minor, 4-4 time.

F. B.

HONEGGER

1892 –

Pacific (231)

ARTHUR HONEGGER, born at Havre, of Swiss-German parentage, received his first musical influences from his mother, who played the piano. He received instruction on the violin from a teacher in Havre, but more intensive training was given him at the Conservatory at Zurich, Switzerland, from Hegar, its director, Lothar Kempter and W. de Boer. Later, Honegger, who had been destined to follow the commercial pursuits of his father, determined to make music his career and he entered the Conservatory of Paris, there to study composition with Gédalge and violin playing with Capet. In 1912 he made the French capital his home and is still living there. At the time the little French coterie of composers, who were known as "The Six," were attracting considerable attention. Honegger was its most important member.

"Pacific (231)" owes its title and "program" to the enthusiasm which Honegger always has possessed for railway locomotives — an enthusiasm which he first cultivated as a boy at Havre. The work, which was composed in 1923, was first produced at Paris, May 8, 1924. Concerning the significance of "Pacific (231)" the composer caused the following to be printed on a flyleaf of his score — a quotation from an interview with him published in a Geneva journal:

"I have always had a passionate liking for locomotives; for me they are living things and I love them as others love women or horses. That which I have endeavored to portray in 'Pacific' is not an imitation of the noises of the locomotive, but the translation into music of the visual impression made by, and physical sensation of it. It sets forth the objective contemplation; the quiet breathing of the machine in repose, its effort in starting, then the gradual increase in speed, leading from the lyric to the pathetic condition of a train of 300 tons hurling itself through the night at a speed of 120 miles an hour. As subject, I have chosen the type of locomotive 'Pacific, No. 231,' for heavy trains that are of great speed."

F. B.

Rugby

Honegger wrote his "symphonic movement" "Rugby" in 1928 and it was produced for the first time at a concert of the Orchestre Symphonique, Paris, October 19, 1928. The work is connected with football, for that game was greatly favored by the composer during his adolescent years. The notion of writing a football composition occurred to him as the result of a chance remark made by a journalist who, having been informed that Honegger declared that, when he saw a game of football he could visualize its musical equivalent, wrote in his paper that the composer was at work on a symphonic work entitled "Rugby." Henry Prunières, a French critic, wrote thus of Honegger's composition:

"'Rugby' belongs in the same category with 'Pacific (231)' but in my opinion is superior to that work. 'Pacific' contains a quality of descriptive realism, especially in the locomotive theme with its whistlings and puffings, which rather shocked me. In the case of 'Rugby' all materialistic descriptions have been omitted. The different phases of the game, the tacklings, the escape of a player with the ball, the pursuits, all these incidents can be expressed by figures of geometric precision, which mysteriously find their equivalent in the play of the counterpoint. Thus there is a continuous interchange of visual and dynamic impressions, but no lyric or impressionistic matter whatever."

F. B.

Le Chant de Nigamon

This work was composed in 1917, when Honegger was in the orchestral class at the Conservatoire at Paris and it was first given under the composer's direction at a Conservatoire concert in April, 1918. The score contains the following "program":

"Tareah, the Huron, had reserved Nigamon and the other Iroquois to be burned alive. Fire was put to the faggots. When the flames began to rise, Tareah leaped across, mercilessly scalped Nigamon and his companions, and slapped them with their own hair. Then the Iroquois began their death song; but when Nigamon lifted up his voice, the others stopped to listen."

The foregoing is an extract from Gustave Aimard's book "Le Souriquet." In the development of the situation, thus described, Honegger employed three Indian themes — a war song of the Hurons, a war song of the Iroquois and an Iroquois song, "The Warrior's Last Word," which he obtained from Julien Tiersot's "Ethnographie musicale," published at Paris in 1905.

F. B.

Symphonic Poem, Pastorale d'Été

With this "Pastorale d'Été" Honegger won the Verley Prize in 1921 and the work was published the following year. The composition is scored for a small orchestra: one flute, one oboe, one clarinet, one bassoon, one horn and strings. It begins, after three introductory measures, with a theme in the horn. There is an accelerando and the second division of the piece (Vif et gai) is set forth in the clarinet. This is taken up by other wind instruments and developed. The first part then returns, the theme which had before been set forth by the horn, now being given to the bassoon.

F. B.

HUMPERDINCK

1854–1921

Prelude to Hänsel and Gretel

THE charming fairy opera, "Hänsel and Gretel," Humperdinck's masterpiece, was written in 1893, and first performed in the same year at the Court Theater, Weimar. The story concerns the adventures of Peter's, the broom maker's, children, Hänsel and Gretel, who are lost in the forest, the visit of the Sandman, the appearance of the fourteen angels, who watch over them while they sleep, their awakening by the Dawn Fairy, the discovery of the Witch's gingerbread house, the latter's discomfiture as she is preparing to bake the children into gingerbread, and their final rescue by their parents. The prelude opens with a prayer theme given out by four horns and two bassoons, which is regularly developed by the strings and other instruments, closing pianissimo. The movement now changes to a Vivace. Accompanied by the wood winds and strings pizzicato, the trumpet sounds a vigorous passage, and as it comes to a close the strings and wood winds announce a new theme of a nature clearly indicating the nightly orgies of the witch, pierced through at intervals by the trumpet blast. It gradually works up to a climax for full orchestra, leading to a very melodious theme, and this in turn to a dance tempo. These are developed, and the prelude closes pianissimo with the contents of the introduction.

Moorish Rhapsody

The "Moorish" Rhapsody was composed for the Leeds (England) Music Festival of 1898. It is in three movements:

1. Tarifa — Elegy at sunrise. 2. Tangiers — a night in the Moorish *café*. 3. Tetuan — a rider in the desert. The program is a poem written by the composer. The first movement represents a shepherd's lament over the decay of the Moorish people; the second, a scene in a coffee house at Tangiers where an old singer chants the deeds of heroes and opium dreams of the glories of Seville and Granada; and the third, a ride in the desert over an old battleground with Paradise visible on the far horizon. The first movement opens with an expressive introduction in muted first violins, beginning pianissimo, and after reaching fortissimo dying away again pianissimo. It is followed by a weird Moorish melody by English horn, eventually appearing in full harmony in the horns, bassoons, English horn, and clarinet. This leads to a figure in the 'cellos, followed by the reappearance of the first violin theme, with a counter theme in the horns. After a crescendo it dies away pianissimo. A pastoral theme is now announced in the oboe, and all this thematic material is worked out in the close. In the second movement, after a string passage, the bassoon has a unique theme which is developed in the oboe, English horn, and bassoon, and afterwards in the horns and wood winds, closing with the opening string passage. A fresh theme, in the violas, is followed by several passages, the elaboration of which describes the scene in the *café*. The third movement opens with a tone-picture of the desert and the solitary rider. The Moorish melody of the first movement again appears. It dominates the movement, and against it are heard several subsidiary themes. At the close the composer presents an effective picture of the mirage in the Coda, during which the Moorish melody is still heard.

Suite, Königskinder

The music of the "Königskinder" Suite is based upon the incidental music to a drama of the same name which has now become pleasantly familiar in this country by its operatic evolution. The play itself was first performed in 1897 and at an opera in 1910. The suite is arranged in three movements, the prelude, "the King's Son"; the "Verdorben-Gestorben," or "Ruin-Death," and the "Hellafest."

The prelude opens at once with a statement of the principal theme in the horns which is combined with another theme in full orchestra. A theme in march tempo follows, succeeded by a melody for clarinet with viola accompaniment. The first violins thereupon take up a fresh motive, the main movement is heard in the second violins, followed by a fresh one for the oboe. The development of these sprightly themes closes the prelude.

The second movement begins in the wind instruments followed by the muted strings, the theme itself appearing in the oboe. The horns next give utterance to the minstrel song with harp arpeggios. The strings follow and combine with them the material in the opening of the movement, a Coda closing.

The final movement, picturing the festivities of the people of Hellebrunn as they await their prince, opens with a march in the wood winds introducing the principal theme in full orchestra. A second theme stated by the oboe and trumpet is accompanied by the strings and leads to the children's dance for the clarinet based upon a folk song. After a repeat of the march a Coda based on the theme of the children's dance closes the suite.

D'INDY

1851 –

Symphonic Poem, Wallenstein's Camp. Part I. Op. 12

IN 1874 d'Indy produced the overture "Piccolomini" with great success at a concert in Paris. Subsequently it was altered and incorporated in the dramatic symphony, "Wallenstein," based upon Schiller's drama, and the symphony was produced as a whole in 1888. The titles of its movements are: 1. Wallenstein's Camp. 2. Max and Thekla (the remodelled overture). 3. Wallenstein's Death. "Wallenstein's Camp" is frequently produced as a concert number. It is of a cheerful, even jovial nature, and presents a picture of the amusements and revelries in the hero's camp, which forms the Scherzo of the symphony. The opening theme clearly illustrates the stir and pleasure of the camp and is very fully elaborated to suit the situation. The violins and flutes follow in a subdued passage, after which the second theme enters in the violins, but is barely announced when the rest of the orchestra joins in a waltz rhythm, with a roistering sort of accompaniment. Another elaboration follows, and is kept up until a new element is introduced by the appearance of a Capuchin monk, who preaches a sermon to the revellers which takes the form of an ingenious fugue for the bassoon. The monk's sermon, however, commands slight attention, and is lost in the humor and mockery of the soldiers, which appears in the caricaturing of the sermon by various instruments. The waltz reappears. The tuba seeks to enforce the fugue theme, but the effort is useless, and the revelry breaks out anew, but is suddenly checked as the horns, trumpets, and trombones announce in a dignified phrase the entrance of Wallenstein himself upon the scene. The opening theme of the movement reappears, and after fresh development leads up to the waltz theme. As this closes the opening theme is heard once more, and is developed into a jubilant tribute to the hero, closing the movement.

Symphonic Legend, The Enchanted Forest. Op. 8

"The Enchanted Forest" is one of d'Indy's early works, having been written in 1872. The program attached to the score sufficiently describes the music. Harold at the head of his warriors is riding through a forest in the moonlight, enlivening the time with their war songs. A troop of elves suddenly appears. Harold, who is enraptured by their beauty, is embraced by the elfin leader and finds himself deserted by his warriors, who have gone in pursuit of the elves. He resists his enchantress, however, and continues his ride alone. Stopping to drink from a spring, its magic waters overcome him, and he sinks to sleep upon a rock. There he remains for centuries, with the elves dancing about him in the moonlight. This poetical conceit d'Indy has treated with charming skill, investing his music with delicate and shifting tints of color.

Suite, Medea. Op. 47

The suite "Medea" was written in 1898 as incidental music to Catullus Mendès' tragedy of the same name. It is in five movements. The first, "Prelude," begins with a theme in the first violins and horns, which, after short development, leads to a subsidiary passage. A 'cello solo follows, accompanied at intervals by the first and second violins, richly elaborated. The opening theme resumes, and gradually leads to a lively movement in dance rhythm, in which the second violins and violas participate. The remainder of the prelude is devoted to the working up of this thematic material. The second movement, "Pantomime," consists of one theme presented at the opening in flute, clarinet, and strings, then repeated fortissimo in full orchestra, and leading in ever accelerated tempo to a dance with the melody in the flute and clarinet with pizzicato string accompaniment. After a climax the movement closes pianissimo. The third movement, "Medea waiting," begins with a tender melody for the flute over a delicate accompaniment in the muted strings and harp. By a change of time a more vigorous and passionate theme is announced in the violins and wood winds which gradually works up to full orchestral effect. The tender melody of the opening returns in the clarinet and closes the movement. The fourth movement, "Medea and Jason," opens with a solo for the horn, followed by melodies in the violins and 'cellos. The wood winds reply with a theme from the first movement. After the elaboration of this material a fresh theme appears in the violins, followed by the old theme and leading to a climax, after which the movement closes pianissimo. The last movement, "Triomphe Auroral," opens with a short introduction in which the theme from the first movement is worked up. After a pause, swift, vigorous passages occur in the harp and strings, leading to a resumption of the introductory passages, followed by a fresh episode, "Solennelle." With the development of this episode the work ends in a powerful climax.

Symphonic Variations, Istar. Op. 42

"Istar," performed for the first time at Brussels in 1897, resembles "The Enchanted Forest" as a poetic fancy, but its musical development differs from that in the earlier work. Its program supplies all needed analysis. The verses inspiring the work are taken from a Babylonian poem, "The Epic of Izdubar." Istar, the daughter of Sir, goes to the realm of death, "the abode of the seven gates," where her lover, the Son of Life, has preceded her. At the first gate the warder removes her tiara; at the second, the pendants from her ears; at the third, her necklace; at the fourth, the jewels on her heart; at the fifth, the belt about her waist; at the sixth, her rings; and at the seventh, the last veil which conceals her body. Having entered the abode of Death, she receives the waters of life and frees her lover. In constructing his work the composer has used parts of the theme in variations to signify the scene at each gate, but when Istar passes the last gate and releases her lover, the whole of the simple theme appears.

Rhapsody, Summer Day on the Mountain. Op. 61

This charming rhapsody, "Jour d'Eté à la Montagne" ("Summer Day on the Mountain"), was written in 1905 for large orchestra, with addition of pianoforte. The composer has attached a program to the score, condensed from a prose poem of Roger de Pampelonne's. The movements are, Dawn, Day, and Evening, which, instead of presenting any special scenes for illustration, are characterized by poetical and emotional expression. The Dawn movement is an appeal to nature to awake. The Day movement represents a quiet repose under the pines, amid the murmur of the breezes and the songs of birds. The Evening suggests the sunset, gradual darkening of the landscape, and slumber. The subjects are eminently adapted to the composer's style of musical thought and expression. Though the text is of the modern impressionist style, the music is not that of an impressionist, like so much that is produced by the ultra-French modern school, but rather the product of a deep thinker, a graceful colorist, and conservative composer, who does not allow himself to be carried away by the modern and somewhat morbid manner.

IPPOLITOV-IVANOV

1859–

Caucasian Sketches

IPPOLITOV-IVANOV was a pupil, at the St. Petersburg Conservatory, of Rimsky-Korsakov. He studied at the institution from 1875 until 1882. In the latter year Ippolitov-Ivanov's enthusiasm for South-eastern Russia, especially the Caucasus, was stimulated by his friendship with the two Caucasian musicians, Alichanov and Karganoff. He became in 1882 director of music of the Conservatory of Music at Tiflis, one of the principal Caucasian cities, and two years later, the conductor of its opera house. It was this residence at Tiflis that inspired the Russian composer to write his Caucasian Sketches. This work, which Ippolitov-Ivanov dedicated to I. Pitoev, president of the branch of the Imperial Musical Society at Tiflis, contains four movements: I. "Dans le Défile" ("In the Pass"), Allegro moderato, E major, 4-4 time; II. "Dans l'Aoule" ("In the Village"), Larghetto, F sharp minor, 2-4 time; III. "Dans la Mosquée" ("In the Mosque"), Adagietto, B minor, 3-4 time; IV. "Cortége du Sardar" ("March of the Sardar"), Allegro moderato, tempo marziale, E major, 4-4 time.

F. B.

JÄRNEFELT

1869 -

Prelude and Berceuse

ARMAS JÄRNEFELT is best known to concert-goers by the two pieces named above, although he has written two overtures, four orchestral suites and a number of choral works. He was born at Viborg, Finland, and, after studying at the Helsingfors Conservatory with Wegelius and Busoni, became a pupil of Becker, in Berlin, and of Massenet in Paris. He served as assistant conductor at Magdeburg and Düsseldorf and then returned to his native town in 1898 as orchestral director. In 1905 Järnefelt conducted the symphony concerts at the Stockholm Royal Theater and became director of the opera there two years later.

The " Prelude " (Praeludium) is scored for small orchestra: two flutes, two oboes, two clarinets, two bassoons, two horns, two trumpets, kettle-drums, glockenspiel, triangle, cymbals and strings. The greater portion of the piece is constructed on the theme (Allegro quasi allegretto, F major, 2-4 time) with which it opens in the oboe after three introductory measures, pizzicato, in the strings. Various wind instruments take up the subject. Later the key changes to A minor and the violins continue the theme over a drone bass. After a short passage for a solo violin the first subject returns, once more in the oboe.

The " Berceuse " was published in 1905. Its scoring is even more restricted than that of the " Prelude," the orchestra comprising only two clarinets, one bassoon, two horns, violin solo and strings. The piece is simple in construction, having been made up of the subject which, after four introductory measures in the muted strings, is played by the solo violin.

F. B.

KALINNIKOV

1866 – 1901

Symphony No. 1, G Minor

BASIL SERGEIVICH KALINNIKOV lives in the concert repertory practically only by this, the first of his two symphonies. He was the son of an official in the Russian police service in the days of the Imperial régime. Determined to enter upon a musical career, Kalinnikov betook himself to Moscow, where he entered the music school of the Philharmonic Society as a pupil of Ilyinsky and Blaramberg. In 1893 he obtained the position of second conductor at the Italian Opera, Moscow, but symptoms of tuberculosis of the lungs compelled him to leave for the warmer climate of the Crimea. He died at Jalta in 1901.

The G minor symphony was first produced at Kiev, Russia, in 1897. It was played at Vienna the following year and later at Paris and London, bringing its composer's name prominently before the musical world. The work was published in 1900 with a dedication by the composer to his friend Semjon Nikolajewitsch Kruglikow, a well-known critic in Moscow and, at the time of Kalinnikov's acquaintance with him, director of the singing school of the Moscow synod.

The symphony, which has a pronounced national flavor, begins (Allegro moderato, G minor, 2-2 time) with the principal subject in the strings, the horn entering at the fourth measure with a continuing phrase. This material is continued softly by the flute and clarinet. The second subject is given out by the horns, violas and violoncellos accompanied by a syncopated figure in the wood winds. The violins take up the theme.

The Coda, which follows, bears suggestions of the principal subject. The development, after some preliminary matter, concerns itself with the principal theme. The customary recapitulation follows (the principal subject in the oboe and bassoon) and, in its turn, is succeeded by the Coda. The slow movement (Andante commodamente, E flat major, 3-4 time) begins with some introductory measures in the harp and muted first violins. The principal theme is announced by English horn and violas. The clarinet and violoncellos take up the subject and lead to a new section (Un poco più mosso) whose theme is presented by the oboe. Development of both themes follows and the material of the Introduction recurs. The opening subject is heard once more — in the English horn — shortly before the movement comes to a close.

The Scherzo (Allegro non troppo, C major, 3-4 time) begins with the principal theme announced vigorously by the strings. The second phrase of it is given to the wood winds and, after some working over of it, the first subject returns fortissimo in the full orchestra. The Trio (subject in the oboe) follows and there is a repetition of the first division of the Scherzo. The Finale (Allegro moderato, G major, 2-2 time) draws upon material which had already been used in previous movements, opening with a sonorous presentation of the theme of the first movement. The first subject proper appears in the strings and wood winds. The second subject is allotted to the clarinet, accompanied by the strings and harp. After the first violins have taken up the theme, the opening subject recurs fortissimo, the second theme also being worked over. Development of former material now takes place. An organ point (reiteration of the note D in the basses) leads to a climax, upon which the time changes to 3-2, at which point the brass thunder out the subject of the slow movement. This leads to a closing section (Allegro con brio, G major, 2-2 time) whose spirited subject is given to the strings and wood winds. There follows more development, in which material from other movements is worked over and the subject of the Andante is again vociferated by the brass.

F. B.

LALO

1823 - 1892

Overture to Le Roi d'Ys

LALO began the composition of his opera "Le Roi d'Ys" in 1876. In April of that year an aria from it was sung at a concert of the Société Nationale by Adolphe Théophile Manoury, one of the baritones of the Opéra. But the composer went leisurely about the labor of creation. He finished sketching "Le Roi d'Ys" in 1881 and was still working upon and improving it in 1887. The opera was completed the following year. The first performance took place at the Opéra Comique, May 7, 1888. In America "Le Roi d'Ys" was heard for the first time at New Orleans, January 23, 1890.

The libretto of "Le Roi d'Ys" was written by Edouard Blau (1836-1906), who took for his story a Breton legend. This concerned the two daughters of the king of Is — or, as Blau had it, Ys — who both loved Mylio, a knight who was believed to have died in foreign service far from home. The King of Ys is waging war with Karnac, a neighbouring prince, and to bring about peace he promises to give Karnac the hand in marriage of his daughter Margared. The latter is filled with woe, for she loves Mylio, who, however, has given his heart to her sister, Rozenn. In the midst of all the perturbation brought about by the determination of the King to marry his child to Karnac, Mylio returns. He fights and defeats Karnac, but Margared, inflamed with jealousy, plots with the enemy of her father. They open the gates which keep the sea from the town of Ys. The water rushes in and in the confusion a battle takes place in which Mylio kills Karnac. The water is still rising when Margared cries "The flood will not stop until its prey is reached," and she casts herself into the sea. Saint

Corentin then appears on the surface of the waters and commands them to recede.

The overture begins with an Introduction (D major, 3-4 time) whose clarinet solo is derived from the aria "Si le ciel est plein de flammes," sung by Mylio in the opening act. A fanfare for the trumpets leads into the main movement (*Allegro,* D minor). The fiery principal theme is supposed to represent the passion of Margared for Mylio. There is heard, part of the invocation sung by Margared in the second act to the text "Lors que je t'ai vu soudain reparitre." The fanfare returns in a new version but a section of greater importance is the *Andantino non troppo,* B flat major, 6-4 time, in which there is introduced Rozenn's air, "En silence pourquoi souffrir?" The opening theme returns, there is a reminiscence of the Introduction and the overture closes with the music of Mylio's war song.

F. B.

Norwegian Rhapsody

The title "Norwegian Rhapsody" by which this piece is generally known, and, indeed, by which Lalo referred to it himself, is named on the published score merely "Rapsodie pour Orchestre." The composition grew out of a work which the French master composed for violin and orchestra and which, entitled "Fantasie Norvégienne," was intended for the great Spanish violinist Pablo de Sarasate, who had made Lalo's "Symphonie Espagnole" so popular. This "Fantasie Norvégienne" had been completed in 1875. The composer, who not only used some of the Fantasie for the orchestral Rhapsody, but who added considerable new matter, produced the latter at a concert of the Société Nationale, at Paris, April 20, 1879. The work is divided into two parts, the first beginning (Andantino, A major, 6-8 time) in the strings and leading without pause into the main movement of the part (Allegretto, A major, 2-4 time). The second division (Presto, D minor, 3-4 time) opens with its subject announced by the trumpets fortissimo.

F. B.

LIADOV

1855 – 1914

Tableau Musical, Baba Yaga. Op. 56

ANATOLE CONSTANTINOVICH LIADOV received his musical training, first from his father, who was conductor of the ballet orchestra of the Russian Opera in St. Petersburg during the Imperial régime, and from Rimsky-Korsakov at the Conservatory in the Russian capital. His "Baba Yaga" was published in 1905 with a dedication to Vladimir Stassov, one of the best and most respected music critics in Russia in the nineteenth century. The Baba Yaga of Muscovite fairy tales corresponds to the witch of western European folklore. She lives in a hut, around which she has built a fence constructed from the bones of people whom she has caught and eaten. Baba Yaga does not, however, always stay at home. She travels in a mortar, which she urges on with a pestle and, as she goes, she sweeps away the traces of her flight with a broom. It is this progress of the witch that Liadov has depicted in his work.

F. B.

Legend for Orchestra, Le Lac Enchanté. Op. 62

This piece was published in 1909. In it Liadov endeavors to set forth in sound a picture of a lake, in whose waters are reflected the shadows of a great forest and wherein dwell the water nymphs, which figure in so many Russian fairy tales. The composition opens with an undulating figure (Andante, D flat major) in the muted strings, and this constitutes its principal material.

F. B.

Legend for Orchestra, Kikimora. Op. 63

"Kikimora" was played for the first time in America at a concert of the Russian Symphony Orchestra, New York, November 16, 1910. The work, as well as "Le Lac Enchanté," was published in 1909 with a dedication to Nicolai Tscherepnin, who, like Liadov, was a pupil of Rimsky-Korsakov. The score of "Kikimora" contains the following "program," which was drawn from Sakharov's folk-tales:

"Kikimora has been brought up by a witch in the mountains and, in youth, that is, from early in the morning until late at night, has been beguiled by stories of foreign lands, told to him by the witch's magic cat. From night until the dawn Kikimora is rocked in a cradle made of crystal. In seven years the phantom grows up. Shiny and black, its head is as tiny as a thimble and its body as thin as a straw. From morning until evening Kikimora makes all manner of noises and whistles and hisses from evening until the middle of the night. Then the phantom spins until the day breaks — spins and stores up in its mind evil against all mankind."

The main movement of "Kikimora" is preceded by introductory material (Adagio, E minor, 4-4 time) which begins with mysterious passages for muted lower strings. Soon a melancholy strain is heard from the English horn and the flute and oboe give out a motive (over tremolo chords in the strings) of which use is made later. A new section (Presto) is introduced, and the key changes to E minor.

F. B.

LISZT

1811–1886

A Faust Symphony

1. Allegro. (Faust.)
2. Andante. (Gretchen.)
3. Scherzo. (Mephistopheles.)

THE "Faust" Symphony, while it is a prominent illustration of program-music, is unique in this respect, that it is not a program of scenes or situations, but a series of delineations of character. Liszt himself styles the three movements of the symphony "Charakterbilder" ("Character-pictures"), and has named them for the three leading *dramatis personæ* in Goethe's poem — Fuast, Gretchen, and Mephistopheles. He gives us no further program.

The first movement, "Faust," is intended to typify the longings, aspirations, and sufferings of man, with Faust as the illustration. Four themes are utilized in the expression of Faust's traits of character. The first, Lento, clearly enough illustrates dissatisfaction, restless longing, satiety, and aspiration. Massive chords introduce it. It changes to a monologue, passing from instrument to instrument, and then develops into an Allegro impetuoso. The second theme, which is brighter and more vivacious in character, shows the dawning of hope. A brief episode passes, in which the old feeling appears in hints of the opening theme, but soon gives way to the third theme, introduced by the horns and clarinets. The fourth and last theme now appears, foreshadowing, with its trumpet calls, the stirring activity which has taken the place of doubt in Faust's nature. After this the thematic material as set forth is worked up in genuine symphonic form.

There is as marked a contrast between the first and second movements of the symphony. After a short prelude the first theme of the Gretchen movement — a gentle, tender melody — is given out by the oboe, with double-bass accompaniment. The second theme, tells its own story of the love which has made Gretchen its victim. Between these are several charming episodes, one of them with its gradual crescendo evidently indicating her questioning of the daisy, "He loves me, he loves me not." At last the horn sounds Faust's love motive, which we have already encountered in the first movement, followed by the love-scene, which is wrought out with fascinating skill, rising to the ecstasy of passion and dying away in gentle content.

The third movement, "Mephistopheles," takes the place of the Scherzo in the regular form. It typifies the appearance of the spirit who denies, with all his cynicism and sneers. Liszt has indicated these qualities in a subtle way. Mephistopheles cannot withstand its pure influence. He leaves the field discomfited; and then by a sudden transition we pass to the purer heights. The solemn strains of the organ are heard, and a männerchor, the Chorus Mysticus, intones, *à la capella,* the chant ("All Things transitory"). A solo tenor enters with the Gretchen motive, and the symphony comes to its mystic and triumphant close.

A Symphony to Dante's Divina Commedia

1. Inferno.
2. Purgatorio. Magnificat.

Liszt's symphony to the "Divina Commedia" of Dante is in two parts, "Inferno" and "Purgatorio"; though by the introduction of the Magnificat after the Finale to the "Purgatorio," the composer also indicates the other division of the poem, the "Paradiso." The "Inferno" opens at once with a characteristic phrase for the bass instruments with a crashing accompaniment, announcing in recitative the inscription over the door of hell: "Per mi si va nella città dolente" ("Through me pass on to horror's dwelling-place"), whereupon the trombones and horns sound out the well-known warning, "Lasciate ogni speranza" ("All ye who enter here, leave hope behind"). After the enunciation of the curse the composer paints the infernal scenes with all the fury and barbarity of which apparently music is capable. Unnatural combinations, chromatic phrases, grating dissonances, and weird cries picture the horror and suffering of the damned amid which the curse appears with literally "damnable iteration." In the midst of all this din, however, there is a lull. Amid the tinkling of harps and graceful figures for the strings and flutes, the bass clarinet intones a recitative (the "Nessun maggior dolore," of the original), and the English horn replies, the two instruments joining in a dialogue which tells the mournful fate of Paolo and Francesca da Rimini. At its close the curse sounds again, and the movement comes to a close amid the shrieks and blasphemies of the damned in an Allegro frenetico which is graphic enough not to need words.

The second movement, "Purgatorio," opens with a quiet, restful theme in choral style, its soft and gentle melody picturing that period of expectancy which is the prelude to the enjoyments of Paradise. It is followed by a masterly fugue expressive of resignation and melancholy. Before it closes the first theme returns again and peacefully dies away, leading to the Finale. A solo followed by a chorus chants the Magnificat in the old classic style. All the resources of the orchestra are employed in enhancing the effect of the chant, and the work comes to a close with imposing Hosannas. For this Finale Liszt has written two endings — the one dying softly away like music heard from a distance, the other full of ecstasy and ending with a mighty Hallelujah.

Les Préludes

"What is our life but a succession of preludes to that unknown song whose first solemn note is sounded by death? Love is the enchanted dawn of every heart, but what mortal is there, over whose first joys and happiness does not break some storm, dispelling with its icy breath his fanciful illusions, and shattering his altar? What soul thus cruelly wounded does not at times try to dream away the recollection of such storms in the solitude of country life? And yet man, it seems, is not able to bear the languid rest on Nature's bosom, and when the trumpet sounds the signal of danger, he hastens to join his comrades, no matter what the cause that calls him to arms. He rushes into the thickest of the fight, and amid the uproar of the battle regains confidence in himself and his powers."

This quotation from Lamartine's "Méditations Poétiques" prefaces the score to the "Préludes," and serves as a guide to the meaning of the composition. As this work is heard, perhaps, more often than any of the other symphonic poems, and also displays Liszt's manner of thematic treatment in as clear and intelligible a way as any, we will undertake to point out to the reader the many-sided uses in which a simple motive can be employed, and will attempt it in such a way as to make it intelligible to the lay reader. The "Préludes" is based on two themes, and we present them with their variations in two groups, A and B:

Given a number of intervals at 1, by playing the eight lines through, or humming them, the reader will at once see that although they appear in very different shapes they contain essentially the same notes. The line 2 opens the composition pizzicato pianissimo by the double basses with mysterious effect, hinting at the "unknown song." The theme is then enlarged and repeated on D, running finally into a dominant chord on G, and working up in a grand crescendo to the fortissimo outbreak at 3, in which all the bass instruments carry the melody as given above, repeated with different harmonies and with ever-increasing force, until it appears after a rapid decrescendo in a l'istesso tempo in the violins, as at 4. The accompaniment of the phrase in this form is very beautiful.

Basses.
A
pp
arco.
pizz.
pp
etc. 2
Trombones.
ff
sf
etc. 3
Violins.
Espressivo cantando.
p
4
Wind instruments.
ff
etc. 5
Oboe.
Dolce espressivo.
6
7
Horns and Trumpets.
ff
8

The violins connect or lead into the different repeats with a soaring figure, while the basses have a figure somewhat like the one given at *d*, which appears in that form in the accompaniment of the pastorale. Then follows the stormy period breaking in on life's happy spring. It will not be difficult for the listener to trace the detached portions of the motive, which appear throughout in connection chiefly with chromatic runs and a superabundance of diminished seventh chords. The trumpet motive, in its form as at 5, is also brought in toward the end of that tempestuous passage.

When the skies brighten again, the motive appears in its most charming form as at 6 and 7, with an accompaniment in color and form exceedingly graceful, and flowing naturally into the Allegretto pastorale, which is built up on the motive at *d*, using the same at first with great ingenuity as a leading motive, and bringing out its pastoral character by the skilful use of oboes, clarinets, etc., while later on it is used in connection with the theme *a*, as an accompaniment at times below the melody, as indicated in *c*, *d*, and at times moving above it.

The dreamy, swinging motion of the movement is finally interrupted by two abrupt chords, and the Allegro marziale opens with horns and trumpets, as at 8, connecting with the second theme in its martial garb at *c*, and leading in triumphant measures to a repetition of the main theme, as we heard it once at 3, only reinforced with all the resources known to the modern orchestra.

To point out the varied employment of the leading motive by using it only in part or dwelling on its more characteristic intervals, by inverting it, and otherwise, would lead too deeply into technicalities; but enough has been given to show how by change of rhythm and other means of expression an apparently simple succession of intervals can be developed into a tone-poem.

Tasso, Lamento e Trionfo

The sad fate of the unhappy Italian has furnished Goethe and Byron with the material for great poetical works. Liszt says he was most impressed by the powerful conception of Byron, who introduces Tasso in prison, in a monologue, but could not confine himself to the English poet, as he wanted to portray also his final triumph. Liszt therefore called his symphonic poem, "Lamento e Trionfo," suffering and triumphant vindication being the great contrasts in the life of the poet.

The opening phrase expresses the very soul of Tasso. After its development, an accelerando leads to an Allegro strepitoso, which takes us to the prison of the poet, the harsh chords, although still formed on the triplet figure of the main theme, resembling the rattling of the chains, while the chromatic steps of the lament appear fortissimo to ever-changing, diminished seventh chords. After a repetition of the Lento, the main theme enters at an Adagio mesto, the melody being given in bass clarinet and muted 'cellos at first, and then repeated in the violins. A new melody then appears, in 'cellos and horn, repeated by the violins, which continue with an imploring motive accompanied by descending chromatics, after which the main theme reappears, this time with an instrumentation rich and full, the brasses carrying the melody and changing its character to one of stately festivity, ending in a recitative embodying the closing motive. An Allegretto follows with a theme which in its further working-up appears in the wind instruments, contrasted with a broader and more sentimental phrase in the strings. This phrase is developed to some length, after which the Allegro strepitoso reenters and closes the Lamento. From here on, the Trionfo claims its rights. The very opening of the Allegro molto con brio, although still built upon the same material, is changed by characteristic instrumentation and appropriate tempos into jubilant triumph.

Festklänge

The symphonic poem, "Festklänge," begins with a martial rhythm given out by the kettle-drums, which is taken up in the horns and other instruments, until, passing through a non-accord, it rests on a second accord of C with the C flat in the basses. This whole section, repeated a step higher, and closing on a second accord of D, with C in the basses, then runs into an Andante sostenuto, which, after a short passage in the brasses, develops a delicate treatment of a non-accord on G and A, and after eight measures returns into the first tempo, and, with a short modulation, strikes the principal theme, which is worked up to considerable length, when the rhythm of the Introduction enters in a Coda of eight measures, connecting with an Allegretto in polacca time. Its chief melody closes with a trill cadenza, after which the violins respond with a phrase based on inversion, followed by a livelier figure of a more pronounced polacca character, which appears alternately in the violins and flutes, and which predominates during the rest of the movement, until its return to the first tempo. The Allegro mosso con brio is repeated in more extended form, and with new and enriched orchestration, only to return once more to the Polacca intermezzo, treated with similar variations and leading into the last Allegro in common time. Utilizing the themes of the march movement and reiterating the more essential motives, it runs into the Coda, which by the free use of the trumpet figure at the very opening and a very forcible ascending motive in the basses brings the composition to a close in truly festive style.

Hunnenschlacht

The "Hunnenschlacht" ("The Battle of the Huns") was suggested by Kaulbach's cartoon representing the legend of the battle in mid-air between the spirits of the Huns and of the Romans who had fallen before the walls of their city. The music depicts the war of races and the final triumph of the Christian faith. The opening Allegro begins with the low rumbling of kettle-drums, and an ascending motive in the minor scale. The 'cellos start, and are soon reinforced by the other strings in unison. The diminished seventh chord is extensively employed in the brasses and further on in the double basses. At a Più mosso allegro energico assai, these chords in a somewhat altered form are made the chief motive for the first part. After a repetition of the opening theme, the 'cellos and bassoons give out the war-cry, piano, as if in the far distance, to the low rumbling of the drums. The time then changes, and a new rhythmic motive enters, closing with a short figure in the violins which enhances the wild character of the music. During the fray the trombones give out the strains of the chorale, representing the Christian warriors. The war-cry motive resounds in all the wind instruments, while the other themes to which we have drawn attention, in succession or used jointly, keep up the turmoil. Only twice appears a new feature in a succession of scale runs, fortissimo, in unison in the strings. The peculiar rhythm lends itself well to the increasing stormy character. The fortissimos grow into double fortissimos, the Agitato into a Furioso, until all the forces are engaged, and enter with the whole weight of the orchestra on an Andante, the chord being held by the higher instruments, while the basses of strings and brasses repeat the war-cry double fortissimo. They cease abruptly, and the organ takes up the old hymn ("Crux fidelis, inter omnes").

The strains of the chorale, which sound as if from afar, are interrupted by the overwhelming fanfare opening the Andante, until the "Crux fidelis" claims its right, and a very beautiful scoring of the fine old melody, set off by solo figures for the violin, oboe, and flute, leads to a peaceful and restful mood. The final Allegro grows gradually into the hymn of triumph. The war-cry resounds only mezzo forte, and in stately, solemn tempo the chorale increases in breadth of instrumentation. The stretto opens a long crescendo, and the organ finally joins the orchestral forces, dominating the grand close with long-held chords, while the orchestra accents only with abrupt chords the pompous triumphal march of the victorious legions.

Hungarian Rhapsody No. 2

Liszt wrote fifteen Hungarian rhapsodies, all of them originally for piano solo, but many of them have been scored for orchestra. Of all these the second is by far the most popular and the most frequently heard in the concert-room and is therefore selected for description. Its orchestral version was made by Herr Muller-Berghaus, though another version was also made by the composer, assisted by Franz Doppler. The two principal movements are the Lassan, or slow movement, and the Friska, or quick movement, of the conventional Hungarian Czardas, the national dance. The Lassan begins in the clarinets, violins and violas in unison, accompanied by chords in the horns, trombones and basses and is very earnest and resolute in character. A slow and mournful passage follows in the same instruments with a similar accompaniment, the theme of which, after a clarinet cadenza, appears in the flutes and oboes. In the next section, a theme of the Friska is suggested in the flute, harp and violas with a pizzicato string, triangle and bells accompaniment. The same melody is next taken in a spirited manner in the first violins and wood winds, leading to a second clarinet cadenza, after which the first part of the movement is repeated with some variations and comes to a quiet close. The Friska opens with the theme suggested in the Lassan, announced in the oboe with accompaniment in the violins, piccolo and clarinet. A crescendo follows, the time gradually growing more rapid, until a climax is reached, and the whole orchestra gives out the principal dance theme of the Friska, a dashing, brilliant melody. It is developed with the greatest energy, bringing out at the same time, some subsidiaries in the wild rush. Near the close there is a lull for an instant, and a quiet little melody is heard, based upon one of the themes, in the clarinet and bassoon. Then comes a momentary pause, followed by the fortissimo Coda, which brings this spirited work to its close.

Oratorio, The Legend of the Holy Elizabeth

The oratorio, "Legend of the Holy Elizabeth," was written in 1864, and first produced August 15, 1865, upon the occasion of the twenty-fifth anniversary of the Conservatory of Budapest. The text is by Otto Roquette, and was inspired by Moritz von Schwind's frescos at the Wartburg representing scenes in the life of the saint. The characters introduced in the oratorio are Saint Elizabeth, Landgrave Ludwig, Landgrave Hermann, Landgravine Sophie, a Hungarian Magnate, the Seneschal, and the Emperor Frederick II. The work is laid out in two parts, each having three scenes.

The first scene opens with a long orchestral introduction, working up to a powerful climax, and based mainly upon a theme from the old church service, which is Elizabeth's motive, and is frequently heard throughout the work. An animated prelude which follows it introduces the opening chorus ("Welcome the Bride"). A brief solo by Landgrave Hermann ("Welcome, my little Daughter") and another of a national character by the Hungarian Magnate attending the bride intervene, and again the chorus breaks out in noisy welcome. After a dignified solo by Hermann and a brief dialogue between Ludwig and Elizabeth, a light, graceful allegretto ensues, leading up to a children's chorus ("Merriest Games with thee would we play"). At its close the chorus of welcome resumes, and the scene ends with a ritornelle, foreboding the sorrow which is fast approaching.

The second scene, after a short prelude, opens with Ludwig's hunting-song ("From the Mists of the Valleys"). As he meets Elizabeth, a dialogue ensues, leading up to a brief chorus ("The Lord has done a Wonder"), and followed by an impressive duet in church style ("Him we worship and praise this Day"). The scene closes with an ensemble, a duet with full choral harmony, worked up with constantly increasing power and set to an accompaniment full of rich color and brilliant effect.

The third scene opens with the song of the Crusaders ("In Palestine, the Holy Land"), the accompaniment to which is an independent march movement. The stately rhythm is followed by a solo by the Landgrave, bidding farewell to Elizabeth and appealing to his subjects to be loyal to her. The chorus replies in a short number, based upon the Hungarian melody which has already been heard. Elizabeth follows with a tender but passionate appeal to her husband ("Oh, tarry! Oh, shorten not the Hour"), leading to a solo ("With Grief my Spirit wrestles"), which is full of the pain of parting. A long dialogue follows between them, interrupted here and there by the strains of the Crusaders, in which finally the whole chorus joins with great power in a martial but sorrowful style. As it comes to a close, the orchestra breaks out into the Crusaders' March, the time gradually accelerating as well as the force, until it reaches a tremendous climax. The chorus once more resumes its shout of jubilee, and the brilliant scene comes to an end.

In the fourth scene a slow and mournful movement, followed by an Allegro ominous and agitated in style, introduces the Landgravine Sophie, the evil genius of the Wartburg. The tidings of the death of Ludwig have come, and with fierce declamation she orders Elizabeth away from the castle. The latter replies with an aria ("Oh, Day of Mourning, Day of Sorrow!") marked by sorrowful lamentation. Sophie again hurls her imprecations, and a dramatic dialogue ensues, which takes the trio form as the reluctant Seneschal consents to enforce the cruel order. Once more Elizabeth tenderly appeals to her in the aria ("Thou too art a Mother"). Sophie impatiently and fiercely exclaims ("No longer tarry!"). The scene comes to an end with Elizabeth's lament as she goes out into the storm.

The fifth scene opens with a long declamatory solo by Elizabeth, in which she recalls the dream of childhood — closing with an orchestral movement of the same general character. It is followed by the full chorus ("Here 'neath the Roof of Want"), which after a few bars is taken by the sopranos and altos separately, closing with chorus again and soprano solo ("Elizabeth, thou holy One"). The death-scene follows ("This is no earthly Night"). Her last words ("Unto mine End thy Love has led me") are set to music full of pathos, and as she expires, the instrumentation dies away in peaceful, tranquil strains. A semi-chorus ("The Pain is over") closes the scene, the ritornelle at the end being made still more effective by the harps, which give it a celestial character.

The last scene opens with an interlude which gathers up all the motives of the oratorio — the Pilgrim's Song, the Crusaders' March, the Church Song, and the Hungarian Air — and weaves them into a rich and varied texture for full orchestra, bells, and drums, forming the funeral song of Elizabeth. It is followed by a solo from the Emperor ("I see assembled round the Throne") — a slow and dignified air, leading to the great ensemble closing the work, and descriptive of the canonization of Elizabeth. It begins as an antiphonal chorus ("Mid Tears and solemn Mourning"), the female chorus answering the male and closing in unison. Once more the Crusaders' March is heard in the orchestra as the knights sing ("O Thou whose Life-blood streamed"). The church choir sings the chorale ("Decorata novo flore"), the Hungarian and German bishops intone their benedictions, and then all join in the powerful and broadly harmonious hymn ("Tu pro nobis Mater pia"), closing with a sonorous and majestic "Amen."

LOEFFLER

1861 –

Dramatic Poem, The Death of Tintagiles. Op. 6

THE music of Loeffler's dramatic poem, "The Death of Tintagiles," is set to one of the three little marionette dramas by Maeterlinck and is written for large orchestra with two solo parts for *viol d'amour*.* In the drama, Tintagiles, a child and future sovereign of a legendary land, his sisters, Ygraine and Bellangère, and Aglevami, an old warrior, are found upon an island, where dwells the old queen in her gloomy castle. She is bent upon keeping Tintagiles from the throne, and at last her handmaidens find an opportunity to seize him in spite of his sister's efforts to prevent them. Ygraine herself is thrown into a dungeon. As the Queen is carrying the child past Ygraine, he struggles and implores his sister to save him. She tries to force the door, but it will not yield, and the death of Tintagiles completes the tragic scene. The symphonic poem opens with music descriptive of a storm, in the tumult of which is heard a melodious motive. As the storm subsides a passage occurs with bass clarinet accompaniment in the two *viols d'amour,* flute, clarinet and violas. A slower movement follows in which the viols (supposed to represent Tintagiles and his sister Ygraine) have a theme which soon passes to the clarinets and harps. This is succeeded by an Allegro molto, followed by an Allegro vivace, in which the storm theme and opening melody are elaborated. After the storm has entirely passed the two viols are again heard over a melody in bass clarinet and resume the passage in the opening of the movement. The development

* An ancient member of the violin family having supplementary strings which vibrate in sympathy with the strings commonly used.

of this material grows more agitated and at last becomes furious. The conclusion is very effective. The Coda begins fortissimo, and after the stroke of midnight, the bell effect being produced on the harp, subsides to a quiet Adagio. The two viols again take up their cantabile theme, and the music dies away in sustained piano chords in the trombones, trumpets, horns, and wood winds.

Symphonic Fantasia, The Devil's Villanelle. Op. 9

That Mr. Loeffler has a decided penchant for the weird and fantastic is shown by his choice of subjects for musical illustration, and particularly by that of "The Devil's Villanelle," written for orchestra and organ, after a poem by M. Rollinet. His muse is a sombre creature. In these villanelles, or couplets, followed by alternate refrains, the refrain in one case being the cheerful announcement "Hell's a-burning, burning, burning," and in the other the fateful intelligence that "The Devil prowling roves about," we have picturesque sketches of His Satanic Majesty in various shapes, prowling about on the earth and underground, skipping along the railroads, flying through the air, "floating as in a bubble, squirming as a worm, disguised as a flower, dragon fly, woman, black cat, green snake, a grand seignior, student, teacher," and in numerous other disguises, always bent upon evil designs. The final couplet, "My clock strikes midnight. If I should go to see Lucifer! Hell's a-burning, burning, burning, the Devil prowling roves about," perhaps indicates the fate of the victim whose clock has just struck. The music which the composer has set to this diabolic fantasia is absolutely of the program kind. The villanelle refrains have their corresponding musical refrains. Each couplet also has its musical representation in most characteristic tones, calling for all the resources of the orchestra. The fantasia is a tonal *mélange* thrown together with extraordinary skill, and often in very melodious style. As musical devices to explain the text they are of a most ingenious sort, but they do not leave a very good taste in the mouth.

A Pagan Poem. Op. 14

Loeffler conceived his "Pagan Poem" originally as a chamber music composition for piano, two flutes, oboe, clarinet, English horn, two horns, three trumpets (the latter played from a distance), viola and double-bass. In this form the work was completed in 1901. Later the composer made an arrangement for piano and three trumpets (1903). The present symphonic form was made in 1905-1906 and was given its first production at a concert of the Boston Symphony Orchestra, Boston, November 23, 1907. The work is scored for three flutes (the third flute interchangeable with a piccolo), two oboes, English horn, two clarinets, bass clarinet, two bassoons, four horns, four trumpets, three trombones, bass tuba, three kettle-drums, antique cymbals, gong, piano and strings. "A Pagan Poem" is based upon the eighth Eclogue of Virgil, which consists of two love songs — those of Damon and Alphesiboeus. The latter narrates a Thessalian girl's attempt to win back by magic incantations the love of her truant swain, Daphnis. Mr. Loeffler has stated that it was not his intention to present in his music a tonal picture of Virgil's verse, but to write a fantasy inspired by the latter.

F. B.

Poem, La Bonne Chanson

Concerning this work the composer caused the following to be printed on a fly-leaf of the published score:

"This 'Poem' and a symphonic fantasy, 'La Villanelle du Diable,' were written in the summer of 1901 at Dover, Mass. Mr. Wilhelm Gericke performed both works for the first time at the Boston Symphony Orchestra concerts on April 2 and 3, 1902, in Boston. Since then the 'Poem' has been reorchestrated; it was performed in the new version by the Boston Symphony Orchestra, Mr. Pierre Monteux conducting, on November 1, 1918, and March 25, 1921, at Boston. The music was suggested to the composer after reading the fifth poem in Paul Verlaine's 'La Bonne Chanson.'" The following is a translation of the poem made by Mr. Philip Hale:

"Before you fade and disappear, pale morning star — a thousand quails call in the thyme —
Turn toward the poet, whose eyes brim with love — the lark mounts skyward with the day —
Turn your face, drowned by the dawn in its blue — O the joy among ripe wheat fields —
Make my thoughts shine yonder — far off, O so far! the dew glistens on the hay —
In the sweet dream wherein my love, still sleeping, stirs — hasten, hasten; for, lo, the golden sun."

Loeffler's poem, dedicated to his wife, Elise, is a rhapsodic fantasie, having some affinity to the variation form.

F. B.

MACDOWELL

1861 – 1908

Symphonic Poem, Lancelot and Elaine. Op. 25

THE lamented composer, whose untimely and peculiarly sad death occurred in 1908, wrote the symphonic poem, "Lancelot and Elaine," in 1884. In a letter to a friend the composer says:

"It is one of the results of the fascination that so-called 'program music' had over me at the time. I can only say that if it gives the public pleasure or brings to it in any degree some remembrance of Tennyson's beautiful poem, I shall have succeeded in my aim. The name 'Lancelot and Elaine' was given to the music simply because the latter was suggested by the poem, in my most enthusiastic 'program music' days. I would never have insisted that this symphonic poem need mean 'Lancelot and Elaine' to every one."

But in spite of this seeming disclaimer, "Lancelot and Elaine" this symphonic poem will remain. The opening theme for the strings is indicated by the composer in the score as describing Lancelot and Elaine. It speedily passes over to the wood winds, accompanied in the strings. The horns shortly announce a march theme with accompaniment in 'cellos and basses describing the ride to the tournament. This is worked up to a climax, and dies away as Lancelot comes to the castle of Elaine's father. A solo for oboe with delicate accompaniment in strings and wood winds is the Elaine theme. This is followed by a vigorous announcement of the opening theme, indicating the summons to the contest. The tournament reaches its height through a vigorous crescendo, in which is heard Lancelot's motive in horns, bassoons, clarinets, and oboe, a trill in the flutes and violins announcing his victory. In the next episode Lancelot's downfall and Elaine's grief are pictured. The Lancelot theme is again taken up in violins, bassoons, and clarinets, with 'cello and bass accompaniment, representing his return to camp. A figure in full orchestra describes an interview with Guinevere. The work closes sadly, with a musical picture of the barge bearing Elaine, with the lily in one hand and in the other the message of Lancelot.

Indian Suite. Op. 48

The "Indian" Suite, completed in 1892, was first performed in 1896. Its title is closely descriptive of the contents, as appears from the following statement by the composer:

"The thematic material of this work has been suggested for the most part by Indian melodies. Their occasional similarity to Northern European themes seems to the author a direct testimony in corroboration of Thorfinn Karlsefin's Saga. The opening theme of No. 3, for instance, is very similar to the (presumably Russian) one made use of by Rimsky-Korsakov in the third movement of his symphony, 'Antar.'"

The five divisions of the suite are as follows: 1. "Legend." 2. "Love Song." 3. "In War Time." 4. "Dirge." 5. "Village Festival." The opening movement, it is said, was suggested to the composer by Aldrich's Indian legend, "Miantowona." The horns give out two themes which are purely Indian, one of them strong, the other soft. These lead to the movement proper, which is constructed from the second theme, developed in a style peculiar to Indian melodies. The second movement opens with a love song which is a reproduction of a love song of the Iowas. It is tender and plaintive, and its effectiveness is greatly increased by the beautiful accompaniment and episodes with which the composer has enriched it. The third movement is warlike in character, as is indicated by the direction, "with rough vigor, almost savagely." It is a fitting prelude to the dirge of the fourth movement, which is introduced by the tolling of bells, or an effect similar to it. The song itself is of a most mournful kind, and at times conveys the very intensity of grief, but at last dies quietly away. In the last movement the composer introduces two Iroquois themes, the first announced in the violins pizzicato and the second in the flute and piccolo with string and wood-wind accompaniment. They represent a war song and woman's dance and are typical of an Indian festival.

Suite. Op. 42

MacDowell's A minor suite was completed in Boston in 1889-1890, shortly after the composer's return to America from Germany. It had been begun at Wiesbaden and MacDowell was inspired to the music, his wife has said, by the close proximity in which they lived to the Wiesbaden Forest. "We had a tiny cottage there," wrote Mrs. MacDowell, "just on the edge of the woods, and he spent hours wandering in them. His Scotch blood had filled his mind with mysticism. Deep in his heart he half believed the old tales of spirits and fairies — of course, not in his ordinary moods, but his imagination often carried him very far, even though he might laugh at himself."

The first performance of the suite was given at a concert of the thirty-fourth annual festival of the Worcester (Mass.) Musical Association, at Mechanics Hall, Worcester, September 24, 1891. Carl Zerrahn was the conductor. At that time the suite contained four movements, but MacDowell originally intended to write an additional movement, "In October," and this was played with the remainder of the composition at Boston in 1896. The following are the movements:

I. "In a Haunted Forest": Largamente misterioso, A minor, 6-8 time; Allegro furioso, A minor, 6-8 time. II. "Summer Idyl": Allegretto grazioso, A major, 6-8 time. III. "In October": Allegro con brio, F major, 6-8 time. IV. "The Shepherdess Song": Andantino semplice, C major, 4-4 time. V. "Forest Spirits": Molto allegro, A minor, 2-4 time.

F. B.

MAHLER

1860 – 1911

Symphony No. 1 in D Major

1. Langsam schleppend.
2. Kräftig bewegt.
3. Feierlich und gemessen.
4. Stürmlich bewegt.

MAHLER'S First Symphony was finished in 1888 and was first performed at Budapest under the composer's direction. The various movements were thus described on the original program: I. Spring and no end. II. Mosaic. III. Under full sail. IV. The Hunter's funeral procession.

The first movement opens with an introduction which is intended to describe the awakening of Nature at early dawn. The cuckoo's song is heard in the clarinets and there are distant trumpet calls. A subject for the 'cellos and double basses leads into the main movement, the theme of which, given out in the 'cellos and double basses is a song of the composer's, written some time before. After the working up of this material and the reappearance of parts of the introduction a new theme appears in the horns, followed by another in the 'cellos. Development is followed by a crescendo and this leads to a recapitulation, closing the movement.

The second movement is largely constructed out of a theme announced in the wood winds. After the Trio there is a passage for violins and 'cellos, and the movement closes with a return of the first theme.

The third movement, a dead march, opens with muffled drums, followed by a subject taken from an old French canon and given out in the double basses. The oboe next takes up the theme, followed by tuba and clarinet, and during the playing of the latter the oboe enters with a counter theme. It next appears as a canon for flutes, English horn and clarinets. After a retard, the oboes enter with a new theme, a counter theme appearing in the trumpets, followed by a passage for bass drums and cymbals. A change of key ensues and introduces a folk song in the first violins. The principal subject now returns and after development, the movement closes.

The last movement opens "Stürmisch" in full orchestra, after which a theme heard in the first movement returns, which is worked up in most strenuous fashion, leading to a new passage for first violins. Parts of the introduction again appear and the movement grows more and more "stürmisch." After most elaborate development, a vigorous crescendo leads to a climax, and the end is reached in a massive display by full orchestra.

Symphony No. 4 in G Major

1. Bedächtig.
2. In gemächlicher Bewegung.
3. Ruhevoll.
4. Sehr behäglich.

Mahler's Fourth Symphony was written in 1900 and performed for the first time in Munich in 1904. It is scored for a very full orchestra, including in addition to the usual instruments, bass drum, triangle, gong, glockenspiel, and has besides a soprano part in the last movement. In the opening movement the theme is given out in the first violins, following which is a subject in the other strings. The oboe and first violins take it up, leading to new material. After a return of the first theme, a new melody appears in the flutes with pizzicato accompaniment in the double basses. Further development leads to a climax and recapitulation. The second theme is heard in the second violins, violas and oboes, and the movement closes with hints of the opening theme.

The second movement opens with a theme for the horn, followed by another for solo violin. The muted strings take up a lively melody, followed by the horn motive in horns and double bassoon. A subject for clarinets is followed by development leading to a theme in the clarinets, with harp and string accompaniment. The movement closes with development of the thematic portions.

The third movement begins with a theme in the lower strings which is also treated in the double basses. A new subject now appears in the oboe and violins, followed by a theme in the 'cellos with counter theme in the clarinets. All this material is worked up, the movement ending pianissimo.

The Finale is principally noticeable for the introduction of the soprano voice in a setting of an old Bavarian folk song, "Der Himmel hängt voll Geigen" ("The Sky hangs full of Fiddles"), orchestral interludes and fragments of themes following each stanza.

Symphony No. 8

Mahler's gigantic Eighth Symphony was first produced in this country by the Philadelphia Symphony Orchestra, March 1, 1916, under the direction of its conductor, Leopold Stokovski, and was repeated eight times. It was also given by the same orchestra in New York, April 9, 1916. That the appellation "gigantic" is not exaggerated is shown by the fact that upon these occasions in addition to the regular orchestra, celesta, pianoforte, organ and mandolin, and an extra force of four trumpets and three trombones, a total of 110 instruments, were employed. The choral force numbered 950, including three sopranos, two altos, one tenor, one barytone and one bass soloist, two mixed choruses and a boy choir. The extra four trumpets and three trombones were played from proscenium boxes to give added effect to the "Gloria" of the Latin Hymn which forms the material of the first section of the work. One can hardly call Mahler's Eighth a symphony in the old classic form and yet in its first section it retains a relation to the sonata form in the manner in which the themes are stated, and in its second section one may trace the Adagio, Scherzo, and Finale, greatly modernized. To present a detailed analysis of this involved work would require a presentation of nearly the whole score, so involved is it and so closely interrelated are the instrumental and vocal parts, the whole dominated by the main theme of the first part.

Stated in a general way this so-called symphony is a musical setting of the ancient Latin hymn, "Veni, Creator spiritus," which by some has been attributed to Hrabanus, Archbishop of Rheims, and by others to Charlemagne, and of a scene from the second part of Goethe's "Faust." The first section opens with a choral statement of the main theme, "Veni, Creator," which is then taken up in the orchestra, repeated by chorus, and followed by a second theme in the violins. Theme after theme appear with all their variations, in orchestra and chorus and solo voice, the climax of the part being reached in a mighty double fugue, which unites the various themes and leads to the main one and the close of the section.

An orchestral interlude, which has been called "a landscape in tones," leads to the second section devoted to the transfiguration of Gretchen. The philosophical sentimentalist may trace a connection between the pleading of the "Veni, Creator spiritus" and the "eternal feminine" of Goethe, and the mystic evolve many meanings out of this strange music, but the ordinary hearer will find his delight in the chorus of the Anchorites, the song of the Pater ecstaticus, the Chorus of the Angels, the Rose Chorus, the devotional hymn of Doctor Marianus, the song of the three Marys, Gretchen's supplication, and the mighty Finale devoted to the sentiment, which dominates the entire section, "the Woman Soul leadeth us upward and on," and which the composer would have us believe is but the fulfilment by the "Creator spiritus."

MASSENET

1842 – 1912

Overture to Phèdre

THE overture to "Phèdre" one of Massenet's early works, having been written in 1876, is very dramatic, and in its material closely follows the story as told by Racine in his tragedy of Phèdre, daughter of the Cretan King Minos, who becomes the wife of Theseus. In the unconventional manner of the mythological personage she next becomes enamored of Hippolytus, son of Theseus, but without any encouragement on the part of the former. Thereupon the crafty Phèdre makes Theseus jealous of his own son, and the father commits him to the vengeance of Neptune, who terrifies his horses with a sea monster while driving in his chariot. He is killed, but the skilful Æsculapius restores him to life, and Diana conveys him to Italy, where he lives happily ever after, under the protection of the charming nymph Egeria. The story, as will be observed, gives ample material for dramatic treatment. The overture opens with a massive, gloomy introduction, leading up to an impassioned theme for clarinet, suggesting Phèdre's lament over her unrequited passion. After a counter theme for oboe the opening theme is heard again, and leads to another impassioned outburst as Hippolytus is about departing. The violins in unison follow with Phèdre's declaration of love for Hippolytus, after which occur the storm and an impetuous outburst describing Neptune's wrath. This thematic material is worked up, and the overture closes with the sombre, impressive theme which opened it.

Suite, Scènes Alsaciennes

The suite "Scènes Alsaciennes" was first produced in Paris in 1882, though written some time before that. It is evidently one of those war scenes inspired at the time when Massenet was an actor in them, for he served in the Franco-Prussian War. It has to do, however, with Alsace, lost to France as the outcome of that struggle, and recalls memories of the lost province. It is divided in four movements: 1. "Sunday Morning." 2. "At the Tavern." 3. "Under the Linden Trees." 4. "Sunday Evening." Massenet has prefixed this program to the suite, which sufficiently explains its musical meaning:

". . . . . . Especially now that Alsace is enclosed by a wall, do all my former impressions of this lost country return to me. . . .

"That which I recall with happiness is the Alsatian village, the *Sunday morning* at the hour of service; the deserted streets, the empty houses with some old people sunning themselves before their doors, the filled church . . . and the religious songs heard at intervals by the passer-by. . . .

"And *the tavern,* in the principal street, with its little leaded windows, garlanded with hops and roses. . . .

"'Oho there! Schmidt, some drink!' . . .

"And the song of the foresters as they lay aside their guns! . . .

"Oho! the joyous life and the gay companions! . . .

"Again, further on, 't was always the same village, but with the great calm of a summer afternoon . . . at the edge of the country, a long avenue of *linden trees,* in whose shadow a loving pair walk quietly, hand in hand; she leaning toward him gently and murmuring softly: 'Wilt thou love me always?' . . .

"Also *the evening,* in the public square, what noise, what commotion! . . . everybody out of doors, groups of young beaux in the street . . . and the dances which rhythmize the songs of the country. . . .

"Eight o'clock! . . . the noise of the drums, the song of the bugles . . . *it was the retreat! . . . the French retreat!* Alsace! Alsace! . . .

. . . .

"And when in the distance the last roll of the drum was silenced, the women called the children from the street . . . the old folks relighted their good big pipes, and to the sound of the violins the joyous dance recommenced in more lively circlings by more crowded couples. . . ."

Suite, Esclarmonde

The suite "Esclarmonde" is based upon Massenet's opera of the same name, its subject-matter being taken from different scenes and entr'actes and arranged for the concert-room. The first number of the suite, "Evocation," opens with a unison fortissimo in the brass and wind instruments, from which it passes to full orchestra, and is carried on until a decrescendo leads to a flowing, graceful melody which works up to a grand climax, closing the movement. The second movement, "L'Ile Magique," opens with quiet, mysterious harmonies, which at last lead to an Allegro scherzando, an animated dance figure. Another charming melody follows and alternates with the other theme, closing the movement. The third movement, "Hyménée," is composed entirely of a broad, stately theme in triple time, and its development. The fourth movement, "Dans la Forêt," is divided into two sections, "Pastorale," and "La Chasse." The first section consists of a delicate melody announced in flute and oboe over a drone bass. It leads without interruption to "La Chasse," in which the violins persistently repeat a spinning figure, while the wood winds take detached phrases until the whole orchestra at last is engaged with the hunting theme, the movement closing with an impetuous Coda.

Suite, Les Erinnyes

The suite "Les Erinnyes" is made up for concert purposes from incidental music which Massenet wrote for the antique tragedy of the same name written by Leconte de Lisle in 1872. The story of the drama pertains to the murder of Agamemnon and the revenge of Orestes, his son, who slays his mother Clytemnestra. The first movement, entr'acte, is an Andante appassionato, and is composed of the elaboration of a passionate theme first given out in the violins in unison, with accompaniment in the other strings, and then repeated in ampler form. The movement leads to a Grecian dance in three sections, in the first of which the flutes give out the dance theme with pizzicato accompaniment in the strings. After the development of this theme and a counter theme, the time changes, and the music works up to a climax and closes Allegro vivo assai. The remainder of the movement partakes of the same general character and does not call for special consideration. The next movement, "Scène Religieuse," is the best known part of the suite, as it is the most frequently performed, by reason of its opportunity for an impressive 'cello solo. It depicts the funeral rites at the tomb of Agamemnon, and consists of a solemn dance rhythm. It is in reality a stately antique Minuet, the music being assigned to the strings and flutes with harp accompaniment. Its Trio is an invocation, in which the muted 'cello sings a pathetic and expressive melody, accompanied by the other strings, also muted. After the Trio is finished the first part of the suite is repeated. The Finale is composed of an agitated dance theme, or rather a series of phrases, fully and freely elaborated.

Suite, Scènes Pittoresques

Massenet composed this work, his fourth suite for orchestra, in 1873 and it was played for the first time at a Châtelet concert, Paris, March 22, 1874. The score was published two years later. For many years the "Scènes Pittoresques" enjoyed great popularity at Parisian concerts and the work has been scarcely less popular abroad. The suite contains the following movements: I. Marche. II. Air de Ballet. III. Angelus. IV. Fête Bohême.

F. B.

Ballet Music from Le Cid

"Le Cid," opera in five acts and ten tableaux, was Massenet's sixth dramatic composition. The text, written by Louis

Gallet and Edouard Blau with additions by d'Ennery, was partly based upon Corneille's play and partly on episodes invented by the librettists. The opera was produced at the Opéra, Paris, November 30, 1885, a remarkable cast having been its first interpreters; for the part of Rodrigue was sung by Jean de Reszke; Edouard de Reszke was Don Diègue; Pol Plancon, le Comte de Gormas; and Mme. Fides-Devriés, Chimène. The hero of the work is that of the Spanish legend, Rodrigue del Bivar, known as the Cid Campeador, or Fighting Chief. In the version of the legend employed in Massenet's opera, the Cid is loved by two women — the Infanta of Spain and Chimène, daughter of the Count de Gormas. The former realizes that, as a princess of Spain, she cannot marry the warrior and she resigns him to Chimène. The latter's parent, Count de Gormas, has insulted and defeated the Cid's father, Don Diégue and Rodrigue (the Cid), after a despairing self-struggle, avenges the stain on his family's honor by challenging his beloved's father and killing him. Rodrigue feels that now all chance of happiness and love has vanished. The King permits him to lead the Spanish army against Boabdil, the Moorish chieftain, and presently news comes of the Cid's death. The shock of this intelligence makes it clear to the stricken Chimène that she still loves Rodrigue. She is weeping bitterly when the King enters and announces that the Cid is not dead but is returning alive and victorious. The opera ends with the reconciliation of the warrior and Chimène.

The ballet music is drawn from the second scene of the second act, representing a gay scene in the public square at Burgos. Massenet composed this music at the hotel at Marseilles at which he stayed for some time in 1885. The motive which begins the ballet is one which the French master heard at an inn in Spain when a wedding was being celebrated with song and dance in the room underneath his. The ballet was written particularly for Mlle. Rosita Mauri, one of the most famous French dancers in the 'eighties. The suite which Massenet made up from this music comprises the following movements: I. Castellane, typical of the dance of Castille. II. Andalouse, whose music represents Andalusia, the southern division of Spain, which contains such cities as Cadiz and Seville. III. Aragonaise, dance music from Aragon. IV. Aubade. This word signifies a morning serenade. V. Madrilène, the dance of Madrid, written in two divisions, the first dreamy and langourous, the second boisterous and animated. VI. Navarraise, characteristic of the music of Navarre.

F. B.

Meditation from Thaïs

"Thaïs," written to a story by Anatole France, was produced at the Opéra, Paris, March 16, 1894, with the American soprano, Sybil Sanderson, in the title-rôle. The opera, which is concerned with the efforts made by the monk Athanaël to draw the courtesan, Thaïs, from the worship of Venus to the worship of God, pictures the struggle between Christian asceticism and Pagan sensuality. The Meditation, principally for violin solo, lightly accompanied by the orchestra, follows the close of the second act — the act in which Athanaël seeks out Thaïs in her own house and urges her to take up a life of repentance. The courtesan realizes that Death is inevitable and that the present joys are but fleeting. The Meditation pictures the thoughts of contrition and the peaceful happiness which occupy the soul of Thaïs.

F. B.

Le Dernier Sommeil de la Vierge

Massenet's sacred legend "La Vierge" ("The Virgin") was produced May 22, 1880, at one of the Concerts Historiques, given at the Opéra, Paris. The composer had won great success with two previous sacred works — "Marie Magdeleine" and "Eve" — and he looked forward to another. The fickle public, however, ruled otherwise. There was but a small sale of tickets and the majority of the audience, which had come in on passes, listened to "La Vierge" with indifference. "The work is a rather painful memory in my life," wrote Massenet in his Memoirs "Its reception was cold and only one fragment seemed to satisfy the large audience which filled the hall. They encored three times the passage which is now in the repertoire of many concerts, the prelude to Part IV, 'Le Dernier Sommeil de la Vierge.'"

F. B.

MENDELSSOHN

1809 – 1847

Symphony No. 3, in A Minor (Scotch). Op. 56

1. Introduction. Allegro agitato.
2. Scherzo. Assai vivace.
3. Adagio cantabile.
4. Allegro guerriero. Finale maestoso.

THE A minor Symphony, the third of the Mendelssohn series, is familiarly known as the "Scotch," the composer having given it that name in his letters written from Rome in 1832. The first conception of the symphony dates still farther back. In April, 1829, Mendelssohn, then in his twentieth year, paid his first visit to England. After remaining in London two months he went to Scotland, arriving in Edinburgh July 28; the next day he heard a competition of the Highland pipers, which, it may well be imagined, gave him a good idea of the national melodies. The next day he visited Holyrood. He wrote down on the spot the first sixteen bars of the introduction, announcing the theme which not only opens but closes the movements and thus gives an unmistakable clew to its meaning.

Its introduction begins with the Andante theme already mentioned, a melody of a sombre and even melancholy cast. The first theme is of the same cast. A subsidiary theme, of a tender, plaintive character, leads back to the Andante of the introduction, which closes a movement rarely equaled for its musical and poetical expression and graceful finish.

A short passage for flutes, horns, and bassoons connects this earnest, serious movement with the Scherzo, which gives us a different picture. In its form, it departs from the Minuet and Trio, and is purely a caprice, and a most lovely one; while, at the same time, it differs from all his other Scherzos in the absence of their sportive, fantastic quality. It is a picture of pastoral nature, characterized by a continuous flow of rural gaiety. Its opening theme, given out by the clarinets, dominates it throughout; for the second theme plays but a small part, though it has its place in the general working up. The first motive is frequently reiterated, and fills the movement with glowing life and spirit.

The Adagio cantabile presents still another picture. The first movement gave us the sombre tints; the second, those of rural freedom and idyllic gaiety; the third, though still infused with melancholy, is evidently a reverie in which the composer meditates upon the ancient state and grandeur of the country. Its majestic strains well prepare the way for the final movement, the impetuous first part of which is marked Allegro guerriero. The romantic sentiment disappears. In its place we have the heroic expressed with astonishing force and exuberant spirit in its three themes, which finally give place to a short second part, maestoso, colored by national melody, and closing this exquisite tone-picture of the Scotch visit.

Symphony No. 4, in A (Italian). Op. 90

1. Allegro vivace.
2. Andante con moto.
3. Con moto moderato.
4. Saltarello. Presto.

Like the A minor Symphony, the A major gets its familiar name from the composer himself, who always styles it the "Italian" in his letters. The first movement, Allegro vivace, reflects as clearly the blue skies, clear air, brightness, and joyousness of Italy as the first movement of the A minor Symphony does the sombre and melancholy aspect of Holyrood. After a moment of preparation, the violins sweep off at once in a vigorous theme to an accompaniment of horns, bassoons, clarinets, and flutes. After its development, the order is reversed; and a second theme, more restful in character, appears in the clarinets and bassoons, with string accompaniment. It is taken by the flutes and oboes, and leads the way to a new theme in the first violins and clarinets, the development of which brings us back to the first theme, closing the first part of the movement. The second part opens with a fresh, bright theme given out by the second violins and continued in the other strings and flutes, followed by an episode for the strings alone. It is finally interrupted by the wind instruments. The principal themes reappear in various forms, at last returning to the first. Toward the close of the movement an entirely new subject appears in the first violins. The Coda is full of spirit and joyous feeling, and at last the happy, vivacious movement comes to an end.

The Andante, sometimes called the "Pilgrims' March," opens with a unison phrase, followed at once by the principal theme, given out in the oboe, bassoon, and violas, and then repeated by the first violins, with an elaborate accompaniment by the flutes. After the announcement of the second theme, with a similar instrumental setting to the first, the second part opens with a bright, joyous strain from the clarinets, reinforced by the violins and flutes. At the close of its development the call is heard again, summoning attention to the development of thematic materials already presented.

The third movement is supposed to have been taken from one of his youthful works, though its identity in this respect has never been discovered. It opens with a simple but graceful melody. The trio is fresh and full of delicate fancy. At its conclusion the first theme returns, and a charming Coda constructed upon suggestions of this theme, brings the movement to a close.

If there were any doubt about the national significance of this symphony, it would be removed by the Italian Finale, Saltarello presto, evidently inspired by the Roman carnival, of which Mendelssohn was a delighted spectator. The movement is a Saltarello, a favorite dance rhythm in Italy, combined with a whirling Tarantella with astonishing skill. After a short introduction the flutes lead off in the merry dance, the other instruments soon joining as if they too had caught the mad contagion. At the close of the theme a soberer melody is given out by the violins, the wind instruments still busied with fragments of the dance measures. Soon the Saltarello returns again, this time, however, with a fresh accompaniment. At last it gives place to the rush of a Tarantella whirling gayly along until the Saltarello combines with it, and the two rhythms go on to the end, now alternating, now together, in a general terpsichorean hurly-burly.

Overture to A Midsummer Night's Dream. Op. 21

The overture to "A Midsummer Night's Dream," written in 1826, is especially interesting as being the starting-point in Mendelssohn's musical career. It was the first work to express his individuality and maturity of creative power, for when he wrote the music to the play, seventeen years later, it filled its place in the perfected scheme as freshly and fittingly as if it had been composed simultaneously with the rest. It contains all the motives of the play — the songs and dances of the fairies, the chases of the lovers, the dance of the rustic clowns, the grace of Titania, and the airiness of Puck. It leads us into the fairy realm, with all its poetic beauty, refinement, grace, and lightness; and yet this almost ethereal mixture of humor and fancy is constructed in the strongest and most solid manner. The overture opens with four sustained chords in the wind instruments, introducing us to fairy land, in which the first theme is heard. After several bars of fairy music the second theme, the hunting-horn melody, enters, and is followed by a love melody, simple but full of graceful charm. This leads up to a mock pageant, a dance by the clowns, with a humorous imitation of the donkey's bray. The horns of Theseus are heard again, and the fairy revels resumed in all their freshness and dreamy beauty. The subjects already introduced are elaborated and the exquisite fairy overture closes with a charming Coda.

Overture, Fingal's Cave. Op. 26

This overture is called in Mendelssohn's letters alternately "The Hebrides" and "The Solitary Island," and the name

"Fingal's Cave" is prefixed to the published score, while that of "Hebrides" is on the orchestral parts. It reflects the impressions made on Mendelssohn by a journey to the Western Highlands.

The overture is written in regular form and opens with a theme in violas, 'cellos, and bassoons, which occurred to Mendelssohn while in the cave, depicting the loneliness of the spot. The second theme, a beautiful Cantabile, pictures the movement of the sea, accompanied by a peculiar wavelike effect in the violins. The elaboration of this theme is an extremely vivid and poetical description of the cries of the seabirds, the wail of the wind, and the gradual lashing of the ocean into fury. As it subsides, the first subject returns again, and the effect of solitude is once more felt. This is followed by the free development and extension of the second theme. After recapitulation of this material, a short but very brilliant Coda brings this highly colored tone-picture of the solitude of the sea and the cave, as well as of the rage of the ocean, to a close. Its sentiment is sombre, even melancholy.

Overture, A Calm Sea and Prosperous Voyage. Op. 27

The overture, "A Calm Sea and Prosperous Voyage," was first performed in 1835, at a Leipsic Gewandhaus concert. It illustrates two short poems of Goethe's, "The Calmness of the Sea" and "A Prosperous Voyage." It is constructed in two sections, the first being an Adagio, and the second a Molto allegro vivace and Allegro maestoso. The Adagio opens with a phrase assigned to double basses only, and may be considered the motto of the overture, as it dominates it throughout. The calm of the sea is indicated by full harmonies in the strings, with delicate accompaniment by the wind instruments. A figure in the flute announces the change, and the voyage begins. It commences with a long prelude indicating the bustle on board and the rising of the sea. The first theme of this section is given out by the flute and wind instruments, with pizzicato string accompaniment. The second subject is of the same general character and leads to one of the most beautiful of the Mendelssohn melodies, assigned to the 'cello. The usual elaboration follows, and in the short Coda a stately passage for trumpets refers to the safe arrival and happy greetings to the voyagers.

Overture, Melusina. Op. 32

The "Melusina" Overture was written in 1833 and first performed in 1834. It was announced upon the program as "Overture to Melusina, or, The Mermaid and the Knight," but its official title is "Overture to the Legend of the Lovely Melusina." The story is a romantic one. Melusina buried her father in a mountain for ill treatment of her mother, whereupon she was made to undergo transformation into a serpent on the last day of each week as a penalty. After her union with Count Raymond, she exacted a promise from him that he would not make any inquiry into her actions on that day. Incited by jealousy, however, he concealed himself and beheld her after her transformation. This ended the happiness of both. Melusina was compelled to abandon her husband and her human form and wander as a spirit until the day of doom, when she would be released. The overture opens with a graceful theme which throughout the overture is the Melusina theme. After its development the second, or Raymond theme, is given out in the first violins and wood winds and is then developed in full orchestra. The third theme is assigned to the first violins with 'cellos an octave lower. The close of the overture sets forth Raymond's fatal discovery of his wife's secret and the dissolution of his happiness, ending with the sad cries of Melusina at the moment of her husband's death.

Overture to Athalia. Op. 71

The music to Racine's drama "Athalia" consists of an overture, a march, and six vocal pieces. The choruses were originally composed for female voices with piano accompaniment, and were completed at Leipsic in 1843. In June of the following year, and during a visit to London, Mendelssohn wrote the overture and the march with the expectation that the drama would be brought out on the stage at Berlin; and after his return thither he completed the work by rearranging the choruses for four voices and scoring them for full orchestra. The overture begins with a slow introductory movement, the melody of which is taken from a chorus for sopranos and altos near the end of the work. This is succeeded by a subject of broad, melodious character in the flutes and clarinets, accompanied by harps and strings, forming a sort of prelude to the development of the stirring incidents of the drama, illustrated by the full orchestra in a triumphant climax.

Overture to Ruy Blas. Op. 95

The overture to "Ruy Blas" was written in 1839 for the benefit of the Leipsic Theater Pension Fund, but as Mendelssohn was dissatisfied with it as well as with the play, it was not published until after the composer's death. It begins with four bars, rather slow and stately in character, leading to a suggestion of the first theme in the strings. Both are repeated with certain modifications, and then the principal theme is given out by the first violins and flutes accompanied by the other strings. The slow opening is again repeated, leading to the second theme, which is only indicated. After a few measures the theme is boldly given out by clarinet, bassoon, and 'cellos. A short episode follows, and the second subject is also developed. The various themes then appear in due order, and a vigorous Coda closes the overture.

Saint Paul

"Saint Paul," first of Mendelssohn's oratorios, was begun in Düsseldorf and finished in Leipsic in the winter of 1835, the composer being then in his twenty-sixth year. Its three principal themes are the martyrdom of Saint Stephen, the conversion of Saint Paul, and the Apostle's subsequent career. The work was first produced May 22, 1836, on the occasion of the Lower Rhine Festival at Düsseldorf.

After a long and expressive overture for orchestra and organ, the first part opens with a strong and exultant chorus ("Lord! Thou alone art God"). It is massively constructed, and in its middle part runs into a restless, agitated theme ("The Heathen furiously rage"). It closes, however, in the same energetic and jubilant manner which characterizes its opening, and leads directly to a chorale ("To God on high"), set to a famous old German hymn-book tune ("Allein Gott in der Höh' sei Ehr"), which is serenely beautiful in its clearly flowing harmony. The martyrdom of Stephen follows. The basses in vigorous recitative accuse him of blasphemy, and the people break out in an angry chorus ("Now this Man ceaseth not to utter blasphemous Words"). At its close Stephen sings a brief, but beautiful solo ("Men, Brethren, and Fathers!"); and as the calm protest dies away, again the full chorus gives vent to a tumultuous shout of indignation ("Take him away"). A note of warning is heard in the fervent soprano solo ("Jerusalem, thou that killest the Prophets"); but it is of no avail. Again the chorus hurls its imprecations more furiously than before ("Stone him to Death"). The tragedy occurs. A few bars of recitative for tenor, full of pathos, tell the sad story, and then follows another beautiful chorale of submission ("To Thee, O Lord, I yield my Spirit"). The lament for Stephen is followed by the chorus ("Happy and blest are they"), which is beautifully melodious in character. Saul now appears, "breathing out threatenings and slaughter" against the Apostles. His first aria ("Consume them all") is a bass solo which is fiery in its energy. It is followed by the lovely arioso for alto ("But the Lord is mindful of His own"). Then occurs the conversion. The voice from heaven ("Saul, Saul, why persecutest thou Me?") is represented, as was often done in the passion-music, by the soprano choir, which gives it peculiar significance and makes it stand out in striking contrast with the rest of the work. A forcible orchestral interlude, worked up in a strong crescendo, leads to the vigorous chorus ("Rise up! arise!") in which the powerful orchestral climax adds great strength to the vocal part. It is a vigorously constructed chorus, and is followed by a chorale ("Sleepers, wake! a Voice is calling"), the effect of which is heightened by trumpet notes between the lines. At the close of the imposing harmony the music grows deeper and more serious in character as Saul breathes out his prayer ("O God, have Mercy upon me"); and again, after the message of forgiveness and mercy delivered by Ananias, more joyful and exultant in the bass solo with chorus ("I praise Thee, O Lord, my God"), Saul receives his sight, and straightway begins his ministrations. A grand reflective chorus ("Oh, great is the Depth of the Riches of Wisdom"), strong and jubilant in character, and rising to a powerful climax, closes the first part.

The second part opens with the five-part chorus ("The Nations are now the Lord's") — a clear fugue, stately and dignified in its style, leading, after a tenor and bass duet ("Now all are Ambassadors in the Name of Christ"), to the melodious chorus ("How lovely are the Messengers that preach us the Gospel of Peace!") and the soprano arioso ("I will sing of Thy great Mercies"). After the chorus ("Thus saith the Lord"), and a second tumultuous chorus expressive of rage and scorn ("Is this He who in Jerusalem"), another chorale occurs ("O Thou, the true and only Light"), in which the Church prays for direction. The tenor recitative announcing the departure of Paul and Barnabas to the Gentiles, followed by the tenor and bass duet ("For so hath the Lord Himself commanded"), leads to the scene of the sacrifice at Lystra, in which the two choruses ("The Gods themselves as Mortals") and ("Oh, be gracious, ye Immortals"), are sensuous and in striking contrast with the seriousness and majestic character of the harmony in the Christian chorus ("But our God abideth in Heaven") which follows. Once more the Jews interfere, in the raging, wrathful chorus ("This is Jehovah's Temple"). In a pathetic tenor aria ("Be thou faithful unto Death") Paul takes a sorrowful leave of his brethren, and in response comes an equally tender chorus ("Far be it from thy Path"). Two stately choruses ("See what Love hath the Father") and ("Now only unto Him") close the work.

Hymn of Praise

The "Lobgesang" ("Hymn of Praise") was written at Leipsic in 1840, the occasion which gave birth to it being the fourth centennial celebration of the introduction of the art of printing. The text is not in narrative form, nor has it any particular dramatic significance. It is what its name indicates — a tribute of praise.

The symphony is in three parts, beginning with a Maestoso movement, in which the trombones at once give out the choral motive ("All that has Life and Breath sing to the Lord"). This movement, which is strong and energetic in character, is followed by an Allegretto based upon a beautiful melody, and to this in turn succeeds an Adagio religioso, rich in harmony. The opening chorus ("All that has Life and Breath") is based upon the choral motive, and enunciates the real "Hymn of Praise." It moves along in a stately manner, and finally leads without break into a semi-chorus ("Praise thou the Lord, O my Spirit!"), a soprano solo with accompaniment of female voices. The tenor in a long dramatic recitative ("Sing ye Praise, all ye redeemed of the Lord") urges the faithful to join in praise and extol His goodness, and the chorus responds, first the tenors, and then all the parts ("All ye that cried unto the Lord"). The next number is a duet for soprano and alto with chorus ("I waited for the Lord"). It is thoroughly devotional in style, and in its general color and effect reminds one of the arias, "Oh, rest in the Lord," from "Elijah," and "The Lord is mindful of His own," from "Saint Paul." This duet is followed by a sorrowful, almost wailing tenor solo ("The Sorrows of Death had closed all around me"), ending with the piercing, anxious cry in recitative ("Watchman! will the Night soon pass?") set to a restless, agitated accompaniment and thrice repeated. Like a flash from a cloud comes the quick response of the chorus ("The Night is departing"), which forms the climax of the work. At first the full chorus proclaims the night's departure; it then takes the fugal form on the words ("Therefore let us cast off the Works of Darkness"), effectively worked out.

In the Finale the male voices are massed on the declaration ("The Night is departing") and the female voices on the response ("The Day is approaching"); and after alternating repetitions all close in broad, flowing harmony. This chorus leads directly to the chorale ("Let all Men praise the Lord"), sung first without accompaniment, and then in unison with orchestra. Another duet ("My Song shall alway be Thy Mercy"), this time for soprano and tenor, follows, and prepares the way for the final fugued chorus ("Ye Nations, offer to the Lord"), a massive number, stately in its proportions and impressive in its effect, and closing with a fortissimo delivery of the choral motive ("All that has Life and Breath").

Elijah

"Elijah," the most popular of all Mendelssohn's compositions, was finished in 1846, and was first performed August 18 of that year, at the Birmingham (England) Festival. The prominent scenes treated in the oratorio are the drought prophecy, the raising of the widow's son, the rival sacrifices, the appearance of the rain in answer to Elijah's appeal, Jezebel's persecution of Elijah, the sojourn in the desert, his return, his disappearance in the fiery chariot, and the Finale, which reflects upon the meaning of the sacred narrative.

The introduction to the oratorio is prefaced by a brief, but impressive recitative — Elijah's prophecy of the drought — leading directly to the overture, a sombre, despairing prelude, picturing the distress which is to follow as the course settles down upon the streams and valleys. At last the suffering is voiced in the opening chorus ("Help, Lord!"), which, after three passionate appeals, moves along in plaintive beauty, developing phrase after phrase of touching appeal, and leading to a second chorus, with duet for two sopranos ("Lord, bow Thine ear to our Prayer"), the choral part of which is an old Jewish chant, sung alternately by the male and female voices in unison. It is followed by Obadiah's tenor aria ("If with all your Hearts"), full of tenderness and consolation. Again the people break out into a chorus of lamentation ("Yet doth the Lord see it not"), which at the close develops into a chorale of serene beauty ("For He the Lord our God"). Then follows the voice of an angel summoning Elijah to the brook of Cherith, leading to the beautiful double quartet ("For He shall give His angels charge over thee"), the melody of which is simple, but full of animation. Again the angel summons Elijah to go to the widow's house at Zarephath. The dramatic scene of the raising of her son ensues, comprising a passionate song by the mother ("What have I to do with thee?") and the noble declaration of the prophet ("Give me thy Son"), and closing with the reflective chorus ("Blessed are the Men who fear Him").

In the next scene we have the appearance of Elijah before Ahab, and the challenge of the priests of Baal to the sacrifice on Mount Carmel, set forth in vigorous recitative, accompanied by short choral outbursts. At the words of Elijah ("Invoke your Forest Gods and Mountain Deities") the priests of Baal break out into the stirring double chorus ("Baal, we cry to thee"), which is fairly sensual and heathenish in its rugged, abrupt melodies, as compared with the Christian music. At its close Elijah bids them ("call him louder, for he is a God; he talketh, or he is pursuing!"). Again they break out into a chorus of barbaric energy ("Hear our cry, O Baal!"), in the intervals of which Elijah taunts them again and again with the appeal ("Call him louder"). The priests renew their shouts, each time with increasing force, pausing in vain for the reply, and closing with a rapid, almost angry expostulation ("Hear and answer"). Then follows the calm, dignified prayer of the prophet ("Lord God of Abraham"), succeeded by a simple, but beautiful chorale ("Cast thy Burden upon the Lord"). It is the moment of quiet before the storm which is to come. He calls for the fire to descend upon the altar, and a chorus of passionate energy replies ("The fire descends from Heaven"), accompanied by imitative music, and closing with a brief movement in broad harmony. In fierce recitative Elijah dooms the priests of Baal to destruction, and after a short chorale reply sings the bass aria ("Is not His word like a Fire?"). An arioso for alto ("Woe unto them") follows Elijah's vigorous declamation. These two arias are connecting links between the fire chorus and the rain scene which ensues. Obadiah summons Elijah to help the people, and Elijah replies in an Andante passage, repeated by the chorus ("Open the Heavens and send us Relief"). Then follows a dialogue-passage between the prophet, the people, and the youth, whom he bids ("look toward the Sea") — the most striking features of which are the responses of the youth and the orchestral climax as the heavens grow black and ("the Storm rushes louder and louder"). As the deluge of rain descends, the thankful people break out into a passionate shout of delight ("Thanks be to God"), heard above the tempest in the orchestra. At first it is a brief expression of gratitude. The voices come to a pause, and Elijah repeats the tribute of praise. Then all join in a surging tumult of harmony, voices and instruments vying with each other in joyful acclamations, until the end is reached and the first part closes.

The second part opens with a brilliant soprano solo ("Hear ye, Israel"), beginning with a note of warning, and then with trumpet obligato developing into another melody of an impetuous and animated description ("I, I am He that comforteth"). The solo leads to the impressive chorus ("Be not afraid"), in which, after a short pause, the entire force of voices, orchestra, and organ join in the sublime strain, sweeping on in broad, full harmony. There is a pause of the voices for two bars, then they move on in a strong fugue ("Though Thousands languish and fall"). At its close they are merged again in the grand announcement ("Be not afraid"), delivered with impetuosity, and ending with the same subject in powerful chorale form. The scene which follows is intensely dramatic. The prophet rebukes Ahab and condemns the Baal worship. Jezebel fiercely accuses Elijah of conspiring against Israel, and the people in sharp, impetuous phrases declare ("He shall perish"), leading to the chorus ("Woe to him!"). After a few bars for the instruments, Obadiah, in recitative, counsels him to fly to the wilderness. In the next scene we behold Elijah alone, and in a feeble but infinitely tender plaint ("It is enough"), the prophet prays for death. A few bars of tenor recitative tell us that, wearied out, he has fallen asleep ("See, now he sleepeth beneath a Juniper-tree in the Wilderness, and there the Angels of the Lord encamp round about all them that fear Him"). It introduces the trio of the angels ("Lift thine Eyes to the Mountains"), sung without accompaniment—one of the purest and most delightful of all vocal trios. Chorus ("He watching over Israel") follows, in which the second theme, introduced by the tenors ("Shouldst thou, walking in Grief"), is full of tender beauty. At its close the angel awakes Elijah, and once more we hear his pathetic complaint ("O Lord, I have labored in vain; oh, that I now might die!"). In response comes an aria, sung by the angel ("Oh, rest in the Lord"), breathing the very spirit of heavenly peace and consolation—an aria of almost matchless purity, beauty, and grace. Firmly and with a certain sort of majestic severity follows the chorus ("He that shall endure to the End"). The next scene is one of the most impressive and dramatic in the oratorio. Elijah no longer prays for death; he longs for the divine presence. He hears the voice of the angel ("Arise now, get thee without, stand on the Mount before the Lord; for there His glory will appear and shine on thee. Thy Face must be veiled, for He draweth near"). With great and sudden strength the chorus announces ("Behold! God the Lord passed by"). With equal suddenness it drops to a pianissimo, gradually worked up in a crescendo movement, and we hear the winds ("rending the Mountains around"); but once more in pianissimo it tells us ("the Lord was not in the Tempest"). The earthquake and the fire pass by, each treated in a similar manner; but the Lord was not in those elements. Then, in gentle tones of ineffable sweetness, it declares ("After the Fire there came a still, small Voice, . . . and in that still, small voice onward came the Lord"); and onward sings the chorus in low, sweet, ravishing tones to the end ("The Seraphim above Him cried one to the other, Holy, holy, holy, is God the Lord!") — a double chorus of majestic proportions. Once more Elijah goes on his way, no longer dejected, but clothed with "the strength of the Lord." His aria ("For the Mountains shall depart") prepares us for the final climax. In strong accents the chorus announce ("Then did Elijah the Prophet break forth like a Fire; his Words were like burning Torches; he overthrew Kings; he stood on Sinai and heard the Vengeance of the future on Horeb"). Then comes a significant pause. The basses begin ("And when the Lord would take him away"); another brief pause, and the full chorus pictures in vivid color the coming of the fiery chariot and the whirlwind by which he was caught up into heaven. One more tenor aria ("Then, then shall the Righteous shine") and a brief soprano solo introduce the chorus ("Behold my Servant"). A beautiful quartet ("Oh! come, every one that thirsteth") follows, and the massive figure ("And then shall your Light break forth as the Light of the Morning") closes this masterpiece.

The First Walpurgis Night

It was during his travels in Italy in 1831 that Mendelssohn composed the music to Goethe's poem, "The First Walpurgis Night." The cantata was first publicly performed in Leipsic, February 2, 1843. The subject is a very simple one. The witches of the Northern mythology were supposed to hold their revels on the summit of the Brocken on the eve of the first of May (Walpurgis Night), and the details of their wild and infernal "Sabbath" are familiar to every reader of "Faust."

The cantata begins with an overture in two movements, an Allegro con fuoco and an Allegro vivace, which describes in vivid tone-colors the passing of the season from winter to spring. The first number is a tenor solo and chorus of Druids, which are full of spring feeling, rising to religious fervor in the close. The next number is an alto solo, the warning of an aged woman of the people, which is very dramatic in its style ("Know ye not a Deed so daring"). The warning is followed by a stately exhortation from the Druid priest ("The Man who flies our Sacrifice"), leading up to a short chorus of a stirring character in which the Druids resolve to go on with their rites. It is followed by a pianissimo chorus of the guards whispering to each other to ("secure the Passes round the Glen"). One of them suggests the demon scheme for frightening the enemy, which leads to the chorus ("Come with Torches brightly flashing"). In this chorus the composer has given the freest rein to his fancy, and presents the weird scene in a grotesque chaos of musical effects, both vocal and instrumental, which may fairly be called infernal, although it preserves form and rhythm throughout. It is followed by an exalted and impressive hymn for bass solo and chorus, which is a relief after the *diablerie* of the preceding number ("Restrained by Might"). Following this impressive hymn comes the terrified warning of the Christian guard (tenor), and the response of his equally terrified comrades ("Help, my Comrades! see a Legion"). As the Christians disappear, scared by the demon ruse, the Druids once more, led by their priest, resume their rites, closing with another choral hymn of praise similar in style to the first.

MIASKOVSKY

1881 –

Symphony No. 5, D Major, Op. 18

NICOLAS MIASKOVSKY, who was born at Novogeorgievsk, Poland, was intended for a military career — his father having been a general of engineers in the army. It was not until he had attended for some time one of the military colleges that Miaskovsky made up his mind that music, not war, was his true vocation. He then became a pupil of Glière and Krijanovsky. Later he entered the Conservatory of St. Petersburg and studied there with Liadov and Rimsky-Korsakov. Miaskovsky completed his studies there in 1910 and began his artistic career. This was rudely interrupted, however, by the Great War, into which the composer was thrust. It was not until 1920 that he was allowed by the Bolshevik government, which had come into power at the conclusion of the war, to resume his profession. Since then Miaskovsky has been living in Moscow as professor of composition at the Conservatory. His principal works are his symphonies, of which (in 1930) he has composed ten.

The fifth symphony was written in 1918 and played for the first time in Moscow, August 18, 1920. It was first heard in America at a concert of the Philadelphia Orchestra at Philadelphia, January 2, 1926. The first movement (Allegretto amabile, D major, 6-8 time) begins with the principal subject in the clarinet. After a working out of this theme, the second subject is introduced by the wood winds and lower strings. There comes, also, a motive for the bass clarinet, to which employment is given later. Development follows and the first theme is repeated. The movement becomes more animated and a fugato comes to notice, this being based upon the first theme. The second subject is worked over and, after a great climax, the material of the opening measures of the movement recurs. The movement ends tranquilly. The second movement (Lento, quasi Andante, B flat minor, 4-4 time) does not present its principal theme until the thirteenth measure, when it appears in the oboe over a tremolo figure in the violas. The first violins take it up and develop it. A new idea is then stated by the clarinets and bassoons. This, too, is developed and a climax attained, the first subject then returning. The third movement — really a Scherzo, though not so named on the score — begins (Allegro burlando ["burlando" means in a quizzing or joking style], G minor, 2-4 time) in the lower strings and bassoons. The principal subject appears in the clarinet and is continued by the strings Soon the oboe puts forward a new theme in C major — a folk song from Galicia which Miaskovsky heard near Lemberg when he was stationed there with his battalion during the Great War. The strings develop this tune as well as previous material. The folk song is worked over *forte* and the movement ends with a final presentation of its opening subject in the piccolo. The Finale (Allegro risoluto e con brio, D major, 4-4 time) brings forward the principal theme at once in the combined first and second violins. This is developed and is followed by a second subject in the first violins. The full orchestra repeats this theme and it is followed by a third subject, given out by the wood winds over reiterated chords of F minor in the strings. The material of the opening subject is developed and the recapitulation sets in, the first theme being presented *fortissimo*. The other subjects are considered and the symphony comes to a close with a sonorous repetition of the second theme of the first movement.

F. B.

Symphony No. 6, E Flat Minor, Op. 23

Miaskovsky wrote his sixth symphony in 1922. The pub lished score bears the following explanatory matter on a flyleaf:

"At the time of its writing Miaskovsky was deeply impressed by the passing of two persons particularly dear to his heart — Dr. M. Alexander Michailovitsch Revidzev (died in 1920), Miaskovsky's close friend during the war period (1914-1918) and the years of the revolution; and his aunt, Jelikonida Konstantinovna Miaskovsky, sister of the composer's father, who had been like Miaskovsky's second mother since his early childhood. Some portions of the Symphony No. 6 are also influenced by 'Les Aubes,' by Emile Verhaeren, the Belgian poet."

The first movement opens with a portentous introductory phrase (Poco largamente, E flat minor, 4-4 time) for the full orchestra. This serves as a "motto" theme. An ascending passage leads into the main movement (Allegro feroce, E flat minor), whose principal subject is heard in the first violins. This is developed stormily until the second subject is heard in the strings, clarinets and bassoons in G sharp minor, 2-2 time. There is a second section of this dirge-like theme, first given to the horn and then continued by a solo violin. The development begins with a statement of the portentous opening measures. The remainder of the movement is made up of development of previous material. The second movement (Presto tenebroso, 6-8 time) is the Scherzo of the work. The bass clarinet gives out the first subject, chromatic in character. Later a more somber theme makes its appearance and is followed by a short Trio (Andante moderato, 3-4 time) whose subject is given to the flute, oboe and clarinet, against a long held open-fifth in the harmonics of the strings. There is a hastening of the time and the original tempo and material of the movement is resumed. The third movement (Andante appassionato, 3-4 and 2-4 time) begins with a lengthy Introduction. The main theme begins unostentatiously with an expressive melody in the clarinet (Andante sostenuto, con tenerezza e con gran espressione). There follows a curious chord passage for the celesta and muted horns, this, in its turn, being succeeded by a more impassioned section — really the second theme — given to the violoncellos. The mood becomes more strenuous and eventually the first theme and the tranquil character of the opening measures return. The movement dies away in silence. The Finale is Miaskovsky's suggestion of the revolution, for it begins (in the horns) with a modification of the French revolutionary song "Dansons la Carmagnole." This is boisterously developed and is followed by a quieter presentation (in the brass) of the tune "Ca ira," another of the French revolutionary songs, which was sung October 5, 1789, when the Parisians marched upon Versailles. The first subject returns in the wood winds and a transitional passage leads to a portentous enunciation of the Dies Irae by the harp and basses. The orchestra comes to a passionate outburst and there is another hint of the Dies Irae. The clarinet then sings a new subject, a Russian folk song, following which "Ca ira" is reheard, as well as the first theme. The Dies Irae is thundered forth and there is stormy development of the motto theme. Following a diminuendo, Miaskovsky introduces an *ad libitum* chorus, which sings wailing and wordless phrases. The Russian folk song recurs in the first altos and the movement comes to a close with a suggestion of the opening subject of the slow movement.

F. B.

Symphony No. 7. Op. 24

This seventh symphony was composed in 1922, the year in which Miaskovsky also completed his sixth. The first performance was given in 1925 at Moscow at a concert given under the auspices of the Moscow Association for Contemporary Music, the orchestra of the Theater of the Revolution having performed the work under the direction of Constantine Saradief. In America the work was first heard at a concert of the Philharmonic Orchestra, New York, February 17, 1927. Victor Belaiev wrote of Miaskovsky's seventh symphony:

> "Composed together with the sixth symphony, it touches different experiences. The composer reflects in it on the entire chain of the events of a human life and the surrounding phenomena. There is experiences. The composer reflects in it on the entire chain of the most important of Miaskovsky's works."

The symphony is constructed in one movement. It begins with a slow Introduction (Andante sostenuto, 4-4 time) whose tonality is ambiguous. The flute plays a theme which is supposed "to symbolize nature." With a change of tempo to Allegro minaccioso ("minaccioso" means "threateningly") the main body of the movement is reached. The principal subject is given out at the ninth measure in the basses. An impulsive descending phrase heard in the strings is associated with the subject. The tempo becomes more moderate and a flute joins the first violins in a more expressive theme. Following a return to the Allegro development is given to the second subject. Sustained chords in the wind and a roll on the kettle-drum lead without pause into the second part of the symphony, the material of which opens with something of the same mood and matter as that which had begun the work. Soon a new theme is brought forward — (Lento, calmo) — a melancholy strain given to the muted first violins. The flute and the violas successively take up this subject, which betakes itself eventually in the low notes of the double bassoon. The bass tuba gives out a portentous phrase over a roll on the bass drum and there follows a dissonant fanfare from the brass. An impulsive outburst from the violins leads to a section which has much the character of a Scherzo (Allegro scherzando e tenebroso) whose theme is announced by the violoncellos, double basses and bass clarinet. The Lento recurs and is followed by an Allegro disperato in which material from Part I is reconsidered, the remainder of the symphony being concerned with this.

F. B.

MOUSSORGSKY

1835 – 1881

Fantasie, A Night on the Bare Mountain

MOUSSORGSKY began this piece in 1867 as a work for piano and orchestra. Unsatisfied with it, he left it uncompleted until 1870 when, upon being invited to collaborate in an opera-ballet, entitled "Mlada," with Borodin, César Cui and Rimsky-Korsakov, he took it up again. The ballet project came to nothing, however, and once more the manuscript was laid aside. Moussorgsky reconsidered the music a third time with a view to turning it into an "intermezzo" depicting the witches disporting themselves on the Bare Mountain, near Kiev. The work was still incomplete when Moussorgsky died at St. Petersburg in 1881 and his friend Rimsky-Korsakov took the sketch, revised, completed and orchestrated it. In its completed form "A Night on the Bare Mountain" was given its first performance at St. Petersburg, October 15, 1886. The "program" of the piece is thus set forth on a fly-leaf of the published score:

> "Subterranean sounds of unearthly voices; appearance of the spirits of darkness, followed by that of the god Tchernobog; Tchernobog's glorification and the Black Mass; the revels; at the height of the orgies there is heard from afar the bell of a little church, which causes the spirits to disperse; dawn."

Pictures at an Exhibition

The ten pieces which make up Moussorgsky's "Tableaux d'une Exposition" were written originally for piano and were the outcome of the Russian composer's friendship for Victor Hartmann, an architect who died in the summer of 1873. It was proposed to hold an exhibition of various pictures and designs in memory of the artist-architect, and it occurred to Moussorgsky to create musical reproductions of some of his friend's designs as a unique and practical method of expressing his admiration for Hartmann and his gifts. The pieces, named after the titles of Hartmann's pictures, were written for piano by Moussorgsky in the following order: Introduction. Promenade. In this section of the work Moussorgsky depicts himself walking to and fro, now stopping to examine a picture and now hurrying to look at a congenial work. Sometimes his gait becomes slower. He is thinking sadly of his departed friend. I. "Gnomes": Hartmann's drawing was of a little gnome with short and bandy legs, who jumps and sometimes crawls. II. "Il Vecchio Castello": A mediaeval castle, before which a troubadour is singing a melancholy song. III. "Tuileries": Children playing and quarreling in an alley of the Tuileries gardens. IV. "Bydlo": A Polish wagon with enormous wheels, drawn by oxen. V. "Ballet of Chickens in Their Shells": This was a sketch made by Hartmann for the staging of the ballet "Trilby." VI. "Samuel Goldenberg and Schmuyle": This represented two Polish Jews, one prosperous, the other needy. VII. "Limoges": The market-place with market women bickering. VIII. "Catacombs": In this picture Hartmann portrayed himself visiting the catacombs of Paris by the light of a lantern. IX. "The Hut on Fowls' Legs": Hartmann's design showed a clock in the form of a Baba-Yaga's (the Russian witch's) hut on the legs of fowls. Moussorgsky depicted also the progress of the hag as she sweeps onward in her mortar, which she urges forward with a pestle. X. "The Bogatyr's Gate at Kiev": The architect's drawing represented a proposed design for a gate in the old Russian massive style with a cupola in the form of a Slavonic helmet.

Various orchestral transcriptions of Moussorgsky's piano pieces have been made. The best known are arrangements of eight of the set made by M. Touschmalov (they were first performed at St. Petersburg in 1891) and a complete transcription made in 1923 by Maurice Ravel for the concerts of Serge Koussevitzky. There are also arrangements by Leonidas Leonardi and Sir Henry Wood.

F. B.

MOZART

1756 – 1791

Symphony in E Flat (Köchel 543)

1. Adagio. Allegretto.
2. Andante.
3. Minuet and Trio. Allegretto.
4. Finale. Allegro.

THE Symphony in E flat is the first of the three great works of its class composed by Mozart in the year 1788. It was written at a time when he was in sore financial straits, and yet breathes the very spirit of joy and gaiety throughout, except in the Andante movement.

The symphony opens with a short Adagio built up on solid chords by the whole orchestra, with intervening scale passages in the first violins, and subsequently in the second violins and basses, leading up to the Allegro, which is introduced by the following restful and melodious theme—

first announced in the violins, and on the repeat given over to the basses. The second theme is a cantabile melody of equal beauty and grace, divided between the violins and clarinets. The development of the movement is short, and the second theme is mainly used in association with a phrase at first employed as an accompaniment.

The Andante movement is principally based upon the following theme:

given out by the strings, which leads up to a second theme of more serious character. The second part begins with a passionate, almost impetuous theme, at the close of which there is a genuine harmonic display in which the bassoons play a very characteristic part.

The Minuet opens thus cheerfully:

The Trio sung by the first clarinet, the second playing an arpeggio accompaniment, is one of those lovely passages, lovely in its very simplicity, which are so characteristic of Mozart.

In the Finale the composer gives free rein to his humor and fancy, as well as to his skill in development. It opens with the following theme:

which is fairly fascinating by its sportive and tantalizing mood. The second theme is so similar in character as to amount to little more than an emphasis of the first, and seems to have been introduced to give more room for the merry thoughts of the composer, which are expressed in bewildering variety of development. The themes themselves count for little as compared with the fanciful, elaborate structure of which they are the foundation. The Finale in fact is a very carnival of gaiety and sunshine.

Symphony in G Minor (Köchel 550)

1. Allegro molto.
2. Andante.
3. Minuet and Trio. Allegro.
4. Finale. Allegro assai.

In Mozart's autograph catalogue the symphony in G minor is set down as written July 25, 1788, which refers probably to the day of completion. Of the sixteen symphonies written between 1773 and 1788 this is the only one in the minor key, and from this fact many authorities have attributed to it an expression of sorrow. It has always been a great favorite with composers. Schubert said: "You can hear the angels singing in it." Mendelssohn held it in high esteem; and there is a report that Beethoven scored it over for orchestra from a piano edition, though the score has never been found.

Without the Adagio, which was customary at that time, the first movement begins at once with the principal theme —

followed by a new theme which is afterward employed in the most elaborate fashion. Then follows an exquisite melody —

answered in the basses by

In the second part the principal theme is broken up into bits, shaken about in true kaleidoscopic fashion, and transparent at every turn, thus increasing its beauty.

The Andante is not based on a long cantilena, like most of his Adagios, but betrays rather a restless spirit by the short groups which are thrown from the instruments. The germ of the melody appears at the opening in the bass—

The Minuet, Allegro, opens with:

The stubborn syncopation is enforced at the beginning of the second part in the following manner—

followed by the cheery humor of the Trio.

The Finale, Allegro assai, is a work of such marvelous skill that, while the musical student can alone appreciate the genius of the master by close study of the score, yet the listener never is oppressed by its intricacies. All is clear, beautiful, and full of life and energy from the opening phrase,

which embodies the character of the whole movement, to the last note. Mozart reared this monument of orchestral writing with the modest means of what would nowadays be called a small orchestra, consisting, besides the string quartet, of two horns, a flute, two clarinets, two oboes, and two bassoons.

Symphony in C Major, Jupiter (Köchel 551)

1. Allegro vivace.
2. Andante cantabile.
3. Minuet and Trio. Allegretto.
4. Finale. Allegro molto.

Among all the symphonies of Mozart not one can equal the dignity, loftiness, and skill of the symphony in C, the last from his pen, which by common consent, as it were, has been christened the "Jupiter," both as compared with his other symphonies and with the symphonic works of other composers before Beethoven appeared with his wonderful series. It was composed within a period of fifteen days, and completed August 10, 1788.

It has no introduction, but begins at once with the principal theme of the Allegro, which is constructed upon two subjects — the first strong and bold in character at times, and again restful; and the second gay, even to the verge of hilarity. The first theme is as follows:

The second theme is given out by the strings, and its hilarity is intensified by the following episode, which dominates the whole movement, so far as its expression is concerned:

These are the materials which Mozart elaborates with marvelous skill. As the development proceeds he inverts the second theme, giving a fresh melodic subject, which enters into the combinations as clearly and individually as its companions. Thus on into the Coda, which again reveals the masterly skill of the composer and the ease with which he treated the most intricate contrapuntal difficulties.

Overture to The Marriage of Figaro

"The Marriage of Figaro," an opera buffa, was written by Mozart in 1786, the text by Lorenzo da Ponte, after Beaumarchais' comedy, "Le Mariage de Figaro," and was produced for the first time in the same year at Vienna. The story of the amorous adventures of Count Almaviva; the plot to entrap him made by the Countess, Susanna her maid, Figaro the barber, and Cherubino the page; the final reconciliation and the subsequent union of Figaro and Susanna are too well known to need retelling. The overture opens directly with a part of the first theme pianissimo, an octave passage for all the strings and bassoons, another part following in the wind instruments and announced fortissimo in full orchestra. The theme is then repeated as a whole. After an episode in full orchestra, the second theme appears in the violins and basses, with a passage for wood winds followed by another subsidiary for entire orchestra. The final theme is a graceful melody in violins and wood winds with a closing passage for full orchestra leading into the third part. A brilliant Coda closes the overture. As originally written, Mozart composed an Andante which came in the middle of the Allegro, but he afterwards cut it out and reunited the two parts of the Allegro, made the whole more compact, and gave it a lively, genial character throughout.

Overture to Don Giovanni

"Don Giovanni," an opera buffa, the text by Da Ponte, was written, with the exception of the overture, in the short space of six weeks. The overture was composed in a single evening. The opera was first produced in 1787, the year of its composition, at Prague. As has been said of the story of "The Marriage of Figaro," the adventures of the licentious Don Giovanni while in pursuit of Donna Anna, Donna Elvira, and Zerlina, and his righteous punishment after his supper at the hands of the Statue, which consigns him to the fiends of the infernal regions, is too well known to need full description. The overture, unlike that of "The Marriage of Figaro," is clearly identified with the opera by the impressive trombone chords thrice repeated in the opening Andante, which appear in the finale of the second act, in which the Statue comes to Don Giovanni's banquet, as well as by the weird modulations in the violins, the strange harmonies accompanying the Statue's warnings, and the muffled roll of drums announcing the fate of the reckless, dissolute hero. The main section of the overture is an Allegro, and in this the themes are not borrowed from the opera. The first theme begins immediately in the violins with a tremolo in the violas and 'cellos, to which the first violins reply, with vigorous phrases in the wind instruments. After the development of this material the second theme appears, beginning with chords for full orchestra, followed by a tender melody in oboe and clarinet and closing with a passage for full orchestra. The third theme begins in all the strings and wood winds, and after its development the first part of the movement closes in an animated manner. The free fantasia consists of an elaborate working out of the third theme. The Coda begins in the strings and wood winds, and, as originally written, leads to the first scene in the opera, though several concert endings have been written for it.

Overture to The Magic Flute

"The Magic Flute," officially designated as a "German opera," the text by Emanuel Schikaneder, was written in 1791 and produced in the same year in Vienna. It was the last great work of the composer. The story concerns Pamina, daughter of the Queen of Night, who has been induced to go to the Temple of Isis by Sarastro, the priest, and there learn the ways of wisdom, and her lover, Tamino, an Egyptian prince. In her efforts to revenge her daughter's loss, the Queen of Night induces Tamino to go to her rescue. He reaches the Temple with Papageno, a bird-catcher, the harlequin of the story. Both are seized and brought before Sarastro. Tamino promises to follow Pamina's example and take the vows. After various absurd and grotesque adventures the evil spirits are overcome, and Tamino and Pamina are united as the reward of their fidelity. The work is an important one as marking the first time that German opera employed all the elements of finished art. The overture opens with the stately chords for trombone which are heard before the priest's march and Sarastro's prayer, "O Isis and Osiris." The main body of the overture has but a single theme, which is wonderfully developed in fugal form.

Overture to The Elopement from the Seraglio

The overture to "Die Entführung aus dem Serail" ("The Elopement from the Seraglio"), a comic opera, was first performed in Vienna in 1782. It opens with the first theme in the violins and 'cellos, immediately taken up in full orchestra. Repetition leads to a new theme followed by the free fantasia. This leads to an episode, based upon the first aria in the opera ("Hier soll ich dich denn sehen, Constanze") which is presented with elaborate and beautiful embellishments, and is followed by the third part of the overture, treated in the regular manner and coming to a tranquil close.

Overture to La Clemenza di Tito

"La Clemenza di Tito" was the last operatic work of Mozart and is founded upon a drama by Metastasio. It was written in eighteen days to celebrate the coronation festivities of the

Emperor Leopold at Prague. The overture is made up almost entirely of melodies, and opens with majestic phrases in full orchestra followed by a beautiful theme and a succession of scale passages, the basses keeping up the figure of the introduction. After a pause, the second subject appears in the violins and at the close leads to a unison passage, whereupon the first theme reappears. The remainder of the overture is occupied with the development of this material, a spirited Coda bringing it to a close.

Overture to Der Schauspieldirektor

This little overture is a prelude to one of the lightest of Mozart's compositions, an operetta entitled "Der Schauspieldirektor," written in 1786. The main theme is stated at once in full orchestra. The second theme follows in the first violins. After development, recapitulation follows and a Coda based on the main theme closes the overture.

Requiem

Mozart's "Requiem" was written in Vienna in 1791, and was left in an unfinished state by the composer, who made suggestions and gave instructions as to its completion even upon his death-bed. It was long the popular belief that the "Requiem" was commissioned by a dark, mysterious stranger, whose appearance impressed Mozart with the conviction that he was a messenger of death; more than this, that he himself had been poisoned, and that he was writing his own death-song, upon the order of some supernatural power. It is now known that his suspicions were only the outcome of his morbid condition. After an introduction, which gives out the subject of the opening movement — a slow, mournful, solemn theme — the first number begins with the impressive strain ("Requiem æternam dona eis"), which gradually brightens in the phrase ("Et Lux perpetua"), and reaches a splendid burst of exultation in the ("Te decet Hymnus"). After a repetition of the ("Requiem æternam"), the number closes with the ("Kyrie eleison"), a slow and complicated fugue, which is sublime in its effect, though very sombre in color, as befits its subject.

The next number is the "Dies iræ," written for chorus in simple counterpoint, and very dramatic in its character, the orchestral part being constantly vigorous, impetuous, and agitated, and reaching intense energy on the verse ("Quantus Tremor est futurus"), the whole presenting a vivid picture in tones of the terrors of the last judgment. In the ("Tuba mirum") the spirit of the music changes from the church form to the secular. It is written for solo voices, ending in a quartet. The bass begins with the ("Tuba mirum"), set to a portentous trombone accompaniment; then follow the tenor ("Mors stupebit"), the alto ("Judex ergo"), and the soprano ("Quid sum miser"). From this extraordinary group we pass to the sublime chorus ("Rex tremendæ Majestatis"), once more in the church style, which closes with the prayer ("Salva me"), in canonical form.

The ("Dies Iræ") is followed by the ("Recordare"), written, like the ("Tuba mirum"), as a quartet for solo voices. The vocal parts are in canon form and are combined with marvelous skill, relieved here and there with solos in purely melodic style, as in the ("Quærens me"), while the orchestral part is an independent fugue, with several subjects worked up with every form of instrumental embellishment, the fugue itself sometimes relieved by plain accompaniment. Once more the orchestral part is full of agitation and even savage energy in the ("Confutatis Maledictis"), as it accompanies a powerful double chorus, closing at last in a majestic prayer ("Oro supplex et acclinis"), in which all the voices join in magnificent harmony.

The ("Lacrymosa") is the most elegant and poetically conceived movement in the "Requiem." It begins in a delicate, graceful, and even sensuous manner, which gradually broadens and strengthens, and at last develops into a crescendo of immense power, reaching its climax on the words

("Judicandus Homo reus"). Then it changes to a plaintive prayer ("Huic ergo parce Deus"), and closes in a cloud of gloom in the ("Dona eis Requiem"). The next number ("Domine Jesu Christe") is in pure church form, beginning with a motet by chorus in solid harmony, which runs into a fugue on the words ("Ne absorbeat eas Tartarus"), followed by a quartet of voices regularly fugued, leading to another great fugue on the passage ("Quam olim Abrahæ"), which closes the number in a burst of sacred inspiration. The ("Domine") is followed by the ("Hostias"), a lovely choral melody which leads to the ("Sanctus"), a sublime piece of harmony closing with a fugued ("Hosanna"). The ("Benedictus"), which follows it, is a solo quartet, plaintive and solemn in character, but full of sweet and rich melodies magnificently accompanied. The ("Agnus Dei") closes the work, a composition of profound beauty, with an accompaniment of mournful majesty, developing into a solemn, almost funereal strain on the words ("Dona eis Requiem"), and closing with the fugue of the opening ("Kyrie") on the words ("Lux æterna").

NICOLAI

1810 – 1849

Overture to The Merry Wives of Windsor

THE opera, "The Merry Wives of Windsor," based upon Shakespeare's comedy, was first performed in 1849. Old as it is, the opera still holds the stage and its overture is one of the most popular in the operatic class. The introduction opens with a theme announced in the basses and leading to an Allegro. The principal theme of the Allegro appears in the strings and wood winds. A subsidiary passage leads to the second theme, a very sprightly melody in first and second violins. A phrase of this also appears in dance tempo in the first violins, which in turn is followed by a fortissimo in full orchestra. After the development of this material the refrain succeeds, presenting all the subjects in new forms, and a brisk, animated Coda closes the overture.

PARKER

1863 – 1919

Hora Novissima

"HORA NOVISSIMA," the music by Horatio W. Parker, text arranged by Mrs. Parker, mother of the composer, was first performed by the Church Choral Society of New York in 1893, and has been often given since that time both in the United States and in England—in the latter country at the Worcester Festival in 1899, and by the Royal Choral Society of London in 1901. As a choral and orchestral setting it is one of the most interesting as it is one of the most ambitious works by an American composer.

The original Latin text, comprising three thousand lines upon the subject, "De contemptu Mundi," was written in the twelfth century by Bernard of Morlaix, a monk in the Abbey of Cluny, and from these Professor Parker has selected the stanzas which form the climax of the "Rhythm," as the poem is called, and picture a vision of the New Jerusalem. These thirty-five verses, of six lines each, present metrical difficulties, besides a constant uniformity in character, but the composer has overcome them with great technical skill. Of the eleven numbers, four are for solo voices. The remaining choral parts are written in plain, strong harmony, and are massive in construction.

The opening chorus ("Cometh Earth's latest Hour") is preceded by a long introduction which gives out many of the themes of the work, broadly and freely treated. This is followed by the quartet ("Here life is quickly gone"), which begins contrapuntally, develops into solid, effective harmony, and closes with a beautiful cadenza. No. 3 is a bass solo

("Zion is captive yet"), flowing in style and worked up with great rhythmical skill. No. 4 ("Most mighty, most holy") is a chorus with introduction and fugue, which reaches a vigorous climax. It is followed by the melodious soprano aria ("O Country, bright and fair"). The solo, quartet, and chorus ("Thou Ocean without Shore"), constructed of material from the opening number, closes the first part.

The second part opens with a tenor solo ("Golden Jerusalem"), most elaborately accompanied, which is followed by a rapid, jubilant, and massively constructed double chorus ("There stand those Halls"). No. 9, a contralto solo ("People victorious"), is usually the most popular number in the work. It is followed by an *a capella* chorus ("City of high Renown"), a fugue unaccompanied and in strict style, and the work comes to a close with a powerful quartet and chorus ("Thou City great and high"), in which the composer gathers up his chief themes and weaves them together fugally in a compactly and artistically finished whole. The musical work throughout is noble, dignified, and scholarly, and is a fitting setting for the text of the poem.

PIERNÉ

1863 –

Cantata, The Children's Crusade

GABRIEL PIERNÉ, born at Metz, was taken by his parents to Paris when he was seven years of age, there eventually to become a pupil of César Franck and Massenet at the Conservatoire. He was Franck's successor as organist of the church of Ste. Clotilde. In 1910 Pierné was appointed conductor of the Colonne concerts, Paris. "The Children's Crusade" was completed in 1902 and won the prize of 10,000 francs which the City of Paris offers every three years for the best work for chorus, for orchestra or for the stage. The first performance was given at one of the Châtelet concerts, Paris, January 18, 1905, under the direction of Edouard Colonne. In America the cantata was first heard, December 4, 1906, at a concert of the Oratorio Society, New York. The interest in the work was so great that a repetition of it was given December 22. The author of the text of "The Children's Crusade" was Marcel Schwob (1867-1905). The story of the work was written in 1895 and Pierné's cantata is an adaption of it, but certain characters — Innocence III, a leper, Gregory IV, a Kalander — do not appear in the musical version. The cantata was published in 1906, the American edition (with the French text translated by Henry Grafton Chapman) having been brought out the same year.

The score of "The Children's Crusade" contains the following prefatory explanation of the work:

"About that time, many children, without leader and without guidance, did fly in a religious ecstasy from our towns and from our cities, making for the lands beyond the seas. And to those who asked of them whither they were bound, they did make answer: 'To Jerusalem, in search of the Holy Land.' . . . They carried staves and satchels, and crosses were embroidered on their garments . . . and many of them came from beyond Cologne. They traveled to Genoa, and did embark upon seven great vessels to cross the sea. And a storm arose and two vessels perished in the waters. . . . And to those who asked of such of the children as were saved, the reason of their journey, these replied: 'We do not know.'"

The extract above was drawn from the Chronicles of Albert de Stade, of Jacques de Voragne and of Alberic des Trois-Fontaines. The Chronicle of Albert, Abbott of Stade, is valuable as having been a contemporaneous account of the remarkable pilgrimage made by children in the Middle Ages. The Children's Crusade was the result of the preaching of the boy, Stephen of Cloyes, who declared that while he was attending to his flocks on the hillsides, Christ appeared to him and commanded him to lead an army of children to Palestine, who should win for heaven the victories that had been denied the thousands of soldiers who had vainly struggled with the Saracens in five previous crusades. Boys and girls alike were fired with the wildest fanaticism. The protests of parents were unheeded. The children began their march to the sea in June, 1212, and 20,000 embarked at Marseilles; but hundreds had died on the way. The vessels to convey the little crusaders had been provided by some merchants, but eighteen years elapsed before the children's fate was revealed. It then became known that two of the ships had been wrecked in a storm off the rocks of the Island of St. Pietro and all the children had been drowned. A worse destiny was in store for the survivors on the remaining five vessels. The merchants who had provided the ships had been slave-dealers and the children on them were sold to the Saracens.

The cantata begins with a division entitled "The Forthsetting." The scene is a public square in a Flemish town at night. Celestial voices are heard calling to the children to set forth for Jerusalem. A Narrator describes the frenzied eagerness of the little ones to be gone. They call to their companions, Allys and Alain, to hearken to the celestial voices. The fathers vainly endeavor to restrain their children; the mothers cry and entreat them to return, but without avail. Alain, a blind child, leads his companions to their goal, saying: "What if this world I see not, Jesus I can see; the Christ I can see!" The second part is entitled "The Highway" and depicts the children on a highroad between a broad meadow bright with flowers and a strip of woods. The little ones sing of their faith in Jesus. Allys, too, sings of her faith in the Lord and Alain looks forward to seeing Him "clothed in holy light." The third part is "The Sea." The children have arrived at the Mediterranean, near Genoa. A Narrator sings of the sea and implores it to carry the little crusaders safely to their Lord. The children, Alain and Allys, greet the waters which will bear them to Jerusalem. Sailors sing of the ships which the magistrates of Genoa have ordered for the conveyance of the crusaders. They call to the children to come aboard. They embark. It grows dark as the vessels put off, the children singing of Jerusalem as the ships rock gently in the sea. The fourth part is "The Savior in the Storm." A tempest comes on and the Narrator describes the groaning of the cordage and the heaving of the sea. The sailors cry to each other as the storm overwhelms the ships. The children pray: "De profundis libera nos, Domine." Allys calls, terror-stricken, to Alain and the latter suddenly has a vision of the Lord. He is blind, but he has seen Jesus and Allys entreats him to lead her to Him. A baritone voice (the Voice from On High) is heard singing: "Suffer little children to come unto Me." Again the Celestial Voices are heard calling to the little crusaders as the ships sink beneath the waves.

F. B.

Entrance of the Little Fauns, from Cydalise and the Satyr

"Cydalise," a ballet in two acts and three tableaux, was composed in 1913 and produced at the Opéra, Paris, January 15, 1923. Two orchestral suites were arranged from the work and the first of these — from which the Entrance of the Little Fauns is drawn — was played for the first time in America at a concert of the New York Symphony Orchestra, New York,

October 18, 1925. The story of "Cydalise" was drawn from Rémy de Goncourt's "Lettres d'un Satyr." Styrax, who has been studying how to play the pandean pipes at the satyr's school, has been lazy and, in consequence, has been expelled from the school. Not altogether dissatisfied with his banishment, Styrax saunters along and, as he goes, beholds the aristocratic maiden Cydalise on her way to court in her handsome equipage. Styrax hops on behind and also is carried to court, where he finds adventures of great interest. The Entrance of the Little Fauns is a march which, in the ballet, accompanies a number of small fauns as, led by an old satyr, their teacher, they proceed to their school to learn the pan-pipes. The theme of the march is given out at the third measure by three piccolos. Later, there is heard a tune in the Lydian mode, played by three trumpets.

F. B.

PROKOFIEFF

1891 -

Classical Symphony, D Major, Op. 25

SERGE PROKOFIEFF, born at Sontsovka, in the Government of Ekaterinoslav, Russia, received his first musical instruction from his mother. Later he became a pupil of Glière and Taneiev, at Moscow, and of Mme. Essipov (in piano playing), Liadov and Rimsky-Korsakov (composition) at the St. Petersburg Conservatory. He began to compose at the age of five and a half, and a work for the stage — "The Giant" — was written at the age of seven. During his term of study at the St. Petersburg Conservatory Prokofieff wrote as many as one hundred works, including a symphony in E minor and six piano sonatas, most of which he suppressed.

The Classical Symphony was composed in 1916-1917 at St. Petersburg. Its first performance was given in the Russian capital by the State Orchestra in 1919 — the empire having by that time passed into the hands of the Bolsheviks. The symphony is dedicated to Boris Assafiev, a musical litterateur who has written under the pseudonym, Igor Glebov. Prokofieff has stated that his idea in writing the work was to put into his score that which Mozart, if he were living now, would put into one of his. The orchestra for which the symphony is written is that of the classical organization — two flutes, two oboes, two clarinets, two bassoons, two horns, two trumpets, kettle-drums and strings.

The first movement (Allegro, D major, 4-4 time) begins with the principal subject in the first violins. The transitional passage, which leads to the second theme, brings forward a new idea in the flutes. The second subject is announced by the first violins. The development section begins with a working over of the first theme in the strings. The transitional passage is then taken up and, later, the second subject. The recapitulation opens in C major in the strings, but the second theme reappears in D major, the key of the piece. The movement closes with a short Coda.

The second movement (Larghetto, A major, 2-2 time) brings forward its principal theme, after four introductory measures, in the first violins. An episode follows and the opening subject recurs. There is a second episode, not unrelated to the first, and the principal theme again is heard, the movement closing with the four measures which had been heard at its commencement.

The third movement is a Gavotte (Non troppo allegro, D major, 4-4 time) whose subject begins at once in the strings and wood winds. The first part, which contains only twelve measures, is followed by the Trio (in G major) whose subject is stated by the flutes and clarinets over a pedal-point in the lowest strings. The first division of the movement is then repeated.

The Finale (Molto vivace, D major, 2-2 time) begins with the principal theme in the strings. Following a transitional passage made of the same material, the second subject is heard, in A major, in the wood winds. Development then ensues and is followed by a recapitulation.

F. B.

Scythian Suite, Ala and Lolli, Op. 20

Prokofieff composed his "Scythian Suite" in 1914 and the work was first performed at the Imperial Maryinski Theater, St. Petersburg, January 29, 1916, under the direction of the composer. The Scythians were a nomadic race which, inhabiting the steppes in the south of Russia, were first mentioned by the Greek poet, Hesiod, who lived eight centuries before the Christian era. They were not an attractive people. Neither men nor women ever washed and the latter daubed themselves with a paste made from the dust of aromatic woods. The

Scythians possessed numerous deities — a sun-god, hearth god, a heaven-god, goddess of fecundity, etc.

The suite contains the following movements: I. Invocation to Veles and Ala. Allegro feroce, 4-4 time. This describes an invocation to the sun, named by the Scythians, Veles. Ala is the daughter of the sun-god. II. The Evil-God and Dance of the Pagan Monsters. Allegro moderato, 4-4 time. Seven pagan monsters are summoned by the Evil-God from their subterranean dwelling and they execute a frenzied dance. III. Night. Andantino, 4-4 time. The Evil-God comes to Ala in the darkness and great harm befalls her. The moonrays fall upon Ala and the moonmaidens descend to bring her consolation. IV. Lolli's pursuit of the Evil-God and the Sunrise. Tempestoso, 4-4 time. The Scythian hero, Lolli, went forth to save Ala and he fights the Evil-God. In the uneven battle with the latter, Lolli would have perished, but the Sun-God rises with the vanishing of the night and smites the evil deity. The suite closes with the delineation of the sun-rise.

F. B.

RACHMANINOV

1873 –

Symphony No. 2 in E Minor, Op. 27

1. Allegro moderato.
2. Allegro molto.
3. Adagio.
4. Allegro vivace.

RACHMANINOV'S Second Symphony was first performed at Moscow, in 1908, and in this country in the following year. After a long introduction, which is the foundation of the movement, it opens with a theme, given out by the violins. The second theme is divided between the wood winds and strings. The development begins with the first theme for solo violin in augmentation. The recapitulation introduces the first theme in the violins, the second theme somewhat changed, and a Coda closes the movement.

The second movement begins at once with a theme for the horns, continued in the violins. After this material is worked out, a new theme of a delightfully melodious character appears in the violins. The Trio is begun in the second violins, imitated by first violins, and followed by a strongly marked passage in the brasses, cymbals, and tambourines, with a beautiful effect in the violins and wood winds. The opening and second subjects reappear and a reference to the introduction to the first movement brings the second to its close.

The third movement is a majestic Adagio, opening with a theme in the first violins, followed by a second passage in the clarinet and a third in first violins and oboe. The middle section of the movement introduces the main theme of the introduction, which is treated in combination with the opening theme of the Adagio. Recapitulation of all this matter follows.

In the last movement, a short fortissimo introduction leads to the main theme, which is closely developed. It is followed by a subject in march rhythm in the wood winds, after which the main theme returns. The second subject is given out in octaves by the strings. There is a most elaborate development of this material. After recapitulation, a brilliant Coda brings the work to its close.

Symphonic Poem, Die Toteninsel, Op. 29

"Die Toteninsel" ("The Isle of Death") is based upon Boecklin's famous painting of the same name and was written in 1909. It begins with a slow and mournful phrase in the harps with accompaniment in muted strings and kettledrums, and followed by a figure in the 'cellos, which imitates the wash of the water as it breaks upon the strand of the Isle of Death. A theme follows in the horns, which is also heard in other parts of the poem. After various episodes in the strings and horn, a climax is reached, in which a majestic theme is sounded by the brasses. As it subsides, a new section of the work introduces a new theme in the strings, worked up to a climax, followed by development of the first theme of the section, reaching a new climax. A figure next appears in the second violins with accompaniment of harp and 'cellos. A phrase for oboe leads to a suggestion of the first theme. The water motive of the first section brings the work, one of the most beautiful of all symphonic poems, to its close.

RAVEL

1875 –

Orchestral Fragments from Daphnis et Chloé
(Second Series)

MAURICE RAVEL composed his ballet "Daphnis et Chloé" in 1910 for Serge Diaghilev's Ballet Russe. The first production was given June 8, 1912, at the Châtelet Theater, Paris, with the part of Daphnis mimed by Nijinsky and that of Chloé by Karsavina. Pierre Monteux was the conductor. The score was published in 1911 and two suites for orchestra were drawn from it. That which is performed most frequently is the second, which comprises the following movements: "Daybreak," "Pantomime" and "General Dance." The ballet contained parts for a chorus, which the composer intended should sing behind the scenes and without a definite text. This chorus is included in the music of the second Orchestral Fragments, but it can be replaced by instruments for which provision is made in the printed score. The following is the "argument," which is printed in French on a fly-leaf of the score, and translated into English by Mr. Philip Hale, the author of the admirable program books of the Boston Symphony Orchestra:

"No sound but the murmur of rivulets fed by the dew that trickles from the rocks. Daphnis lies stretched before the grotto of the nymphs. Little by little the day dawns. The songs of birds are heard. Afar off a shepherd leads his flock. Another shepherd crosses the back of the stage. Herdsmen enter, seeking Daphnis and Chloé. They find Daphnis and awaken him. In anguish he looks about for Chloé. She at last appears encircled by shepherdesses. The two rush into each other's arms. Daphnis observes Chloé's crown. His dream was a prophetic vision: the intervention of Pan is manifest.

The old shepherd Lammon explains that Pan saved Chloé, in remembrance of the nymph Syrinx, whom the god loved.

"Daphnis and Chloé mime the story of Pan and Syrinx. Chloé impersonates the young nymph wandering over the meadow. Daphnis as Pan appears and declares his love for her. The nymph repulses him; the god becomes more insistent. She disappears among the reeds. In desperation he plucks some stalks, fashions a flute, and on it plays a melancholy tune. Chloé comes out and imitates by her dance the accents of the flute.

"The dance grows more and more animated. In mad whirlings, Chloé falls into the arms of Daphnis. Before the altar of the nymphs he swears on two sheep his fidelity. Young girls enter; they are dressed as bacchantes and shake their tambourines. Daphnis and Chloé embrace tenderly. A group of young men come on the stage.

"Joyous tumult. A general dance. Daphnis and Chloé. Dorcon."

F. B.

Rapsodie Espagnole

It may be said, as an introduction to a discussion of this piece, that Ravel was born in the Basses-Pyrénées, near the Spanish border, and that the Spanish character of much of his music is due to the fact that his mother was of Basque origin. The "Rapsodie Espagnole" (Spanish Rhapsody) was composed in 1907 and published the following year with a dedication to Charles de Bériot, with whom Ravel had studied the piano during the years in which he attended the Paris Conservatoire. The composition was played for the first time at a Colonne concert, Paris, in March, 1908. As it is the custom in Latin countries for audiences to express in vocal form their approval or disapproval of the works which are performed at concerts or in opera houses, the occupants of the gallery at the Colonne concert, annoyed by the frigidity with which the people in the expensive seats had received Ravel's composition, were stirred to extra manifestations of applause and, having encored the Malagueña, one of their number called out to the conductor: "Play it again for the people downstairs who have not understood it!"

Ravel's Rhapsody contains the following movements: I. Prélude à la Nuit. Practically the entire movement is based on the figure which is given out at the commencement by the muted violins and violas. II. Malagueña. The malagueña is one of the dance-songs of southern Spain and is usually written in 3-8 time; Ravel's example, however, is in 3-4. The figure in the double basses, which opens the movement, is repeated for twenty-nine measures. III. Habanera. Ravel originally conceived this movement in 1895. The habanera is a Cuban dance, but is said to have been introduced into Cuba by negroes who came to that country from Africa. IV. Feria (The Fair). This movement is divided into three parts, the first and third being made from the same material, the second in slower tempo and opening with a theme in the English horn.

F. B.

Ma Mère l'Oye (Mother Goose)

The five little pieces that make up the work which Ravel called "Ma Mère l'Oye" were composed in the first instance for piano (four hands) and were written for the edification of two children — Mimi and Jean Godebski — to whom the composer dedicated his work. Even the first two interpreters of the suite were children, for "Mother Goose" was played for the first time by Christane Verger and Germaine Duramy, respectively six and ten years old, at a concert of the Société Musicale Indépendante, Paris, April 20, 1910. During the following year Ravel arranged the music in the form of a short ballet and this was produced at the Théâtre des Arts, Paris, January 28, 1912. The orchestral version was made from the piano pieces. The following are the movements of the work: I. Pavane of the Sleeping Beauty (Lent, A minor, 4-4 time). II. "Hop O' My Thumb." The score contains a quotation from Perrault's tales: "He believed that he would easily be able to find the way by means of the bread which he had scattered wherever he passed; but he was surprised to discover not one single crumb; the birds had come and eaten all." The movement is Très modéré, 2-4 time. III. "Laideronette, Empress of the Pagodes." The following is set forth as the program in the score: "She disrobed and entered the bath. At once the pagodes and pagodines began to sing and play on instruments; some had archlutes made of walnut-shells; others played on viols made from the shells of almonds — for they were obliged to proportion their instruments to their stature." Laideronette, it may be said, was the heroine of a story by Comtesse Marie Catherine d'Aulnoy (1650-1705). Cursed in her cradle by a wicked fairy, Laideronette grew up so hideous that she begged her parents to allow her to dwell alone in a distant castle, where none could see her. In one of the forests surrounding this castle Laideronette encounters a large green serpent which, perceiving the terror which it inspires in her, informs the girl that it was once handsomer than she was. Laideronette encounters strange adventures. She embarks in a little boat and is carried far out to sea, protected, however, by the green serpent, which follows her. The boat is wrecked on an island inhabited by the pagodes (the name given by the French to the little figures with movable heads) and which is ruled by an invisible monarch, really the green serpent, who had been enchanted by the same wicked fairy which had cursed the young girl. The story ends with the restoration of the serpent to human shape and of her beauty to Laideronette and the marriage of both. The tempo of the section is Mouvement de Marche, 2-4 time. IV. "Beauty and the Beast." This division of the work (Mouvement de Valse modéré, 3-4 time), is concerned with the tale, too well known to need quotation. V. "The Fairy Garden." Ravel provides no description of this movement (Lent et grave, 3-4 time).

F. B.

La Valse

"The Waltz," subtitled "A Choreographic Poem," was conceived by Ravel during the Great War and was completed in 1920. The composer's idea was to exploit the Viennese dance, as it was made famous by Johann Strauss. In November, 1920, Alfredo Casella and Ravel played "La Valse" as an arrangement for two pianos at a concert of the Schoenberg Verein. at Vienna. Later, Florent Schmitt, in reviewing the first performance of the work in Paris, declared that the composer had informed him that "La Valse" was intended to be "the apotheosis of the dance." The work, which was heard for the first time in America at a concert of the San Francisco Symphony Orchestra, San Francisco, October 28, 1921, comprises three sections, "The Birth of the Waltz," "The Waltz" and "The Apotheosis of the Waltz." The following is the program of the composition, printed on a fly-leaf of the published score:

"Whirling clouds give glimpses, through rifts, of couples dancing, The clouds scatter, little by little. One sees an immense hall peopled with a twirling crowd. The scene is gradually illuminated. The light of the chandeliers bursts forth, fortissimo. An Imperial court about 1855."

F. B.

Alborada del Gracioso

This piece was originally written for piano; for it forms the fourth number of a set of compositions for that instrument which was published in 1906 with the collective title "Miroirs." In its orchestral form the work was played for the first time at a concert of the Boston Orchestral Club, given at Jordan Hall, Boston, February 16, 1921. G. Jean Aubry, in his book "La Musique francaise d'aujourd'hui," wrote concerning the title of Ravel's piece: "'Alborada del Gracioso' is the title of one of the pieces in the set 'Miroirs'; aubade (morning serenade) of the gracioso — the word is untranslatable; something like a jester full of finesse, a wit always aroused and an irony always ready; something like Figaro."

F. B.

REGER

1873 – 1916

A Romantic Suite

THE "Romantic Suite" of Reger's has for its program poems by Von Eichendorff and was first performed in 1912 at Dresden. The first movement is a Nocturne, based on the poem, "Nachtzauber" ("Night Magic"), and begins with a theme, also heard in the Finale, in the two flutes, with clarinet accompaniment. After restatement in the first violins, a new theme in the violins leads to a passage in the clarinet. Other subjects follow, a theme in the first violins and one for the 'cellos and horns leading to a climax which gradually subsides as the movement closes.

The second movement is a Scherzo, entitled "Elfe." With muted violin accompaniment, a theme of delicate nature is heard in the wood winds, followed by another in the clarinets and violas. This in turn leads to a theme in waltz rhythm in the oboe with string and harp accompaniment. Another section is heard in the oboe followed by a theme alternating in the wood winds and strings. After development of this material, the dance dies gradually away.

In the Finale, the composer quotes two verses of a poem entitled "Morgengruss" ("Morning Greeting"). A theme from the first movement opens it, after which the 'cellos and English horn have a stately theme. A new subject for horns, continued in the wood winds, follows. After development, a new section appears with its theme in the wood winds and violas, and a crescendo leads to a climax. A passage in the horns with tremolos in the violins and violas is followed by a climax which brings the suite to a close.

A Ballet Suite. Op. 130

Reger's Ballet Suite was first performed at Bremen in 1913. It is scored in six movements: 1. Entrée; 2. Columbine; 3. Harlequin; 4. Pierrot and Pierrette; 5. Valse d'Amour; 6. Finale.

"Entrée" is based upon a march theme given out in full orchestra and developed. After a retard, a counter theme appears in the clarinets, the movement closing with the repetition of the march theme. The "Columbine" is brief and devoted to the development of a single theme. The "Harlequin" opens with a lively theme in strings and wood winds, followed by a second theme in the clarinets, and closing with the first. "Pierrot and Pierrette" is based upon a playful theme alternating between the 'cello and oboe. The "Valse d'Amour," after a short introduction, brings forward the opening theme in the first violins and 'cellos, with imitation by oboe, closing after subsidiary episodes with the first theme. The Finale is constructed upon a dance theme and closes with suggestions of the Valse d'Amour in the horns against the dance theme in the strings.

RESPIGHI

1879 –

Symphonic Poem, The Fountains of Rome

RESPIGHI composed this work — the first of three symphonic poems dealing with Rome — in 1916 and it was performed for the first time at one of a series of concerts which were given in the Italian capital under the direction of Arturo Toscanini for the benefit of artists who had been disabled in the Great War. In the United States "The Fountains of Rome" was produced at a concert of the Philharmonic Society, New York, February 13, 1919, the work having been published the previous year.

The score of the symphonic poem contains the following descriptive analysis in Italian, French and English:

"The Fountain of Valle Giulia at dawn; the Triton Fountain at morn; the Fountain of Trevi at mid-day; the Villa Medici Fountain at sunset. In this symphonic poem the composer has endeavored to give expression to the sentiments and visions suggested to him by four of Rome's fountains, contemplated at the hour in which their character is most in harmony with the surrounding landscape, or in which their beauty appears most impressive to the observer. The first part of the poem, inspired by the Fountain of Valle Giulia, depicts a pastoral landscape; droves of cattle pass and disappear in the fresh, damp mists of a Roman dawn. A sudden loud and insistent blast of horns above the trills of the whole orchestra introduces the second part, 'The Triton Fountain.' It is like a joyous call, summoning troops of naiads and tritons, who come running up, pursuing each other and mingling in a frenzied dance between the jets of water. Next there appears a solemn theme, borne on the undulations of the orchestra. It is the Fountain of Trevi at mid-day. The solemn theme, passing from the wood to the brass instruments, assumes a triumphal character. Trumpets peal; across the radiant surface of the water there passes Neptune's chariot, drawn by sea horses and followed by a train of sirens and tritons. The procession then vanishes, while faint trumpet blasts resound in the distance. The fourth part, the 'Villa Medici Fountain,' is announced by a sad theme, which rises above a subdued warbling. It is the nostalgic hour of sunset. The air is full of the sound of bells tolling, birds twittering, leaves rustling. Then all dies peacefully into the silence of the night."

F. B.

Symphonic Poem, The Pines of Rome

"The Pines of Rome," the second of Respighi's cycle of three works dealing with Rome, was composed in 1924 and produced December 14, 1924, at the Augusteo, Rome. The work was first given in America at a concert of the Philadelphia Orchestra, Philadelphia, January 15, 1926, the composer having been the conductor. To the program book of the Philadelphia concert Respighi contributed the following:

"While in his preceding work, 'The Fountains of Rome,' the composer sought to reproduce by means of tone an impression of nature, in 'The Pines of Rome' he uses nature as a point of departure in order to recall memories and visions. The century-old trees which dominate so characteristically the Roman landscape become testimony for the principal events in Roman life."

Respighi had arrived in America on a concert tour in December, 1925, and in an interview he made reference to "The Pines of Rome," and more particularly to his use of a phonograph record of the song of a nightingale in the course of the work. He declared that such employment of a phonograph record had evoked considerable discussion, but that no combination of wind instruments could quite counterfeit the bird's notes. "Not even a coloratura soprano," he added, "could have produced an effect other than artificial. So I used the phonograph." The following are the divisions of the symphonic poem: I. The Pines of the Villa Borghese (Allegretto vivace, 2-8 time). This depicts the pine grove of the Villa, with children at play. 2. The Pines near a Catacomb (Lento, 4-4 time). This opens with divided strings and muted horns. The entrance to a catacomb is in the shadow of pines. From the cavernous interior there comes the sound of a solemn chant. 3. The Pines of the Janiculum (Lento, 4-4 time). Gianicolo's Hill in the moonlight. It is in this section that the record of the nightingale's song is used. 4. The Pines of the Appian Way (Tempo di marcia). A misty dawn on the Appian Way, the road guarded by solitary pines. There is heard the sound of approaching steps. A vision of Rome's past glories appears as the trumpets blare forth and the legions of the ancient army advance in the rays of the newly-risen sun toward the sacred way.

F. B.

Symphonic Poem, Roman Festivals

"Roman Festivals" ("Feste Romane") is the last of the Roman cycle and was composed in 1928. The first production was made, under the baton of Arturo Toscanini, at a concert of the Philharmonic Society, New York, March 17, 1929. In the work Respighi recalled "visions and evocations of Roman fetes." The composer set forth the following as the program of "Roman Festivals":

"The Circus Maximus

"A threatening sky over the Circus Maximus, but the people are celebrating: Hail Nero! The iron gates open, and the air is filled with a religious chant and the roaring of savage beasts. The mob undulates and rages: Serenely, the song of the martyrs spreads, dominates, and finally is drowned in the tumult.

"The Jubilee

"Weary, in pain, the pilgrims drag themselves through the long streets, praying. At last, from the summit of Mount Mario, is seen the holy city: Rome! Rome! And the hymn of jubilation is an swered by the clangor of multitudinous church-bells.

"The October Excursions

"Fêtes of October, in the castles engarlanded with vine-leaves — echoes of the hunt — tinklings of horse-bells — songs of love. Then, in the balmy evening, the sound of a romantic serenade.

"Epiphany

"The eve of Epiphany in Piazza Navona: a characteristic rhythm of bugles dominates the frantic clamor: on the tide of noise float now and again rustic songs, the lilt of saltarellos, the sounds of the mechanical organ in some booth, the call of the showman, hoarse and drunken cries, and the stornello, in which the spirit of the populace finds expression: 'Lassátece passá, semo Romani' ('Let us pass, we are Romans')."

F. B.

Suite for Small Orchestra, The Birds

The pieces which make up this suite are not by Respighi himself, but transcriptions for small orchestra of works written by composers for the lute and the harpsichord who lived in the seventeenth and eighteenth centuries. The suite was played for the first time in 1927 by the Sociedad de Concertos Symphonicos at São Paulo, Brazil, Respighi, who was travelling at that time in South America, having conducted it. In the United States " The Birds " was first performed at a concert of the Cincinnati Symphony Orchestra, Cincinnati, in November, 1928. With the exception of the first movement — which is a Prelude, freely written around some ideas of Pasquini — each section of the suite has been given the name of a bird. I. The Prelude (Allegro moderato) not only uses music written in the seventeenth century by Bernado Pasquini, but brings forward some of the material employed in the other movements. II. The Dove. This is based upon music by Jacques de Gallot, a lute player and composer who lived at Paris at the end of the seventeenth century. III. The Hen (Allegro vivace). Here Respighi brought forward a celebrated composition originally written for the harpsichord by Jean Philippe Rameau (1683-1764). There is no mistaking the spirit of caricature in which the Italian composer has treated Rameau's work. IV. The Nightingale. The music of an anonymous English composer has been used for this movement. V. The Cuckoo (Allegro). Respighi returned to Bernado Pasquini for the material of this closing movement of his suite. The call of the bird is, of course, one of the obvious features of the music.

F. B.

REZNICEK

1861–

Overture to Donna Diana

THE opera, "Donna Diana" was first performed at Prague in 1894. The text is based upon a play of the same name by Joseph Schreyvogel, who in turn adapted his drama from a Spanish comedy. The story is substantially as follows: Princess Diana is wooed by three lovers, two of whom are most ardent in their devotion. Prince Carlos, the third, affects indifference, the more certainly to win her. Thereupon Diana regards him with favor and chides him for his indifference. She fails to impress him, and then falls more desperately in love, but he continues to resist her approaches. She then grows jealous, and informs him she is to marry the Prince of Blau. In reply he informs her that he is going to ask for the hand of Cynthie, her maid of honor. She is now overcome with mortification, and Carlos is convinced he has won the victory. At last she bestows herself upon him, vanquished by his superiority of disdain. The overture is in regular form. After a brief introduction the principal theme is given out by first violins accompanied by the other strings. It dominates the overture. After repetition, the second theme appears in the first and second violins and violas with wood wind and horn accompaniment. The development and recapitulation follow in the regular sonata form.

RIMSKY-KORSAKOV

1844 – 1908

Russian Easter Overture. Op. 36

THE "Russian Easter" Overture, based upon themes from the Russian Church service, was written in 1886. The "program" is drawn from the Sixty-seventh Psalm and the Resurrection scene in St. Mark's Gospel, closing with the exultant Resurrexit theme. "'Resurrexit,' sing the chorus of angels in heaven to the sound of the archangels' trumpets and the fluttering of the wings of the seraphim; 'Resurrexit' sing the priests in the temples in the midst of a cloud of incense, by the light of innumerable candles, to the chimes of triumphant bells." The first theme of the overture is ecclesiastical, given out by strings and clarinets, and then developed in full orchestra. The second theme, a quiet melody, is sung by violins and violas with accompaniment of wood winds and harps over a pizzicato bass. After some stately passage work, through which the notes of the trumpets are heard, the second theme returns in the oboe, clarinet and bassoon. A recitative passage in trombones, with accompaniment by the 'cellos and double bass, is followed by a repetition of the first theme. After the elaboration of this material a majestic Coda brings the work to an impressive close, in consonance with the exultant character of the extracts from the composer's program cited above.

Symphony No. 2, Antar. Op. 9

The story of "Antar" has its origin in an Arabian tale by Sennkowsky. According to the composer's program, Antar is a desert recluse, and has sworn hatred against all human beings.

One day a beautiful gazelle appears before him, and as he is about to pursue the creature he descries a monstrous bird threatening it. He turns his weapon against the bird, which flies away with piercing cries. Antar then falls asleep and finds himself transported to the palace of the Queen of Palmyra, the fairy Gul-Nazar, who is none other than the gazelle. Grateful for her rescue, she promises him the three greatest enjoyments of life — vengeance, power, and love. He awakes in the desert, but is transported anew to the palace. After a long period of happiness the fairy perceives that Antar wearies of her. She embraces him, the fire of her passion consumes his heart, and he dies in her arms. There are two motives in the suite which dominate it — a theme in the opening in violas and wood winds, called the "Antar motive," and a charming melody in flutes and horns, which is the fairy motive. The suite is in four movements, which have been thus characterized by César Cui, the Russian composer, to whom it is dedicated:

"First part: Antar is in the desert — he saves a gazelle from a beast of prey. The gazelle is a fay, who rewards her deliverer by granting him three pleasures. The whole of this part, which begins and ends with a picture of the desolate and boundless desert, is worthy of the composer's magic brush.

"Second part: The Pleasure of Vengeance — a rugged, savage, unbridled allegro, with crescendos like the letting loose of furious winds.

"Third part: The Pleasure of Power — an Oriental march. A masterpiece of the finest and most brilliant interpretation.

"Last part: The Pleasure of Love, amid which Antar expires — a delicate, poetic, delicious andante."

Capriccio Espagnol. Op. 34

The "Capriccio Espagnol" was first performed in St. Petersburg in 1887, and is dedicated to the orchestra of the Imperial opera which played it. The Caprice is constructed in five movements. The first, "Alborada," or morning serenade, is elaborated throughout from an animated motive announced in the opening in the violins. The second movement, "Variations," consists of five variations upon a theme given out by the horns with string accompaniment. The third movement, "Alborada," repeats the opening "Alborada" with change of modulation and color. The fourth movement, "Scene and Gypsy Song," is an Allegretto. The gypsy song, which is highly characteristic of the wild gypsy life, is sung by the violins accompanied by a subject given out by the horns against the rattle of the drums. Reaching a vigorous climax, it leads without pause to the last movement, "Fandango of the Asturias," which is the old Asturian dance. The theme of the dance is divided between the trombones and wood winds. The solo violin takes a variation of the theme, and the repetition of the "Alborada" forms the Coda.

Suite, Schéhérazade. Op. 35

The suite "Schéhérazade" repeats some of the stories with which the Sultana entertained the Sultan Schahriar during the Thousand and One Nights and thereby saved her life. The composer's program names the four movements as follows: "1. The Sea and Sindbad's Ship. 2. The Narrative of the Calendar Prince. 3. The Young Prince and the Princess. 4. The Festival at Bagdad. The Sea. The ship goes to pieces on a rock surmounted by the bronze statue of a warrior. Conclusion." A single theme, that of Schéhérazade, which is mostly assigned to the first violins and represents the Sultana in the narrative, links the four themes together. The first movement opens with the ocean theme, which is elaborated with an undulating, wave-like accompaniment. Four motives appear in this movement, the Sea, Wave, Ship, and Schéhérazade, and the elaboration of these principal ideas constitutes the contents of the movement. In the second movement, after the Schéhérazade motive, the bassoon over a drone bass begins the Calendar Prince's Narrative. It is then taken up in the oboe with harp accompaniment, next in the violins, and last in the wood winds and horns with pizzicato string accompaniment. A new theme now appears in trombones and trumpets as a recitative, which leads to a brilliant march rhythm, worked up in full orchestra and accompanied by fragments of the previous themes, which bring the movement to a close in an outburst of jollity. The third movement begins with a charming romanza, interrupted here and there by the Schéhérazade motive. The second theme presents the most bizarre effects, and is given an Oriental color by the fantastic use of the triangle, tambourine, cymbals, and drum. It is a veritable picture of an Arabian night. The final movement suggests the Sea motive of the opening, followed by a recitative passage in solo violin and leading to a description of the Bagdad *fêtes,* in which the preceding motives are worked up into a wild dance, which waxes more and more furious until at last the trombones produce the crash of the ship on the magnetic rocks and the fury of a storm. It gradually subsides, and reminiscences of previous developments bring Schéhérazade's story to an end.

Variations on a Russian Theme

The "Variations on a Russian Theme" first appeared in 1903 and was played for the first time in this country by the Chicago Symphony Orchestra in the same year. The theme itself is a Russian folk song found among others in a collection made by Rimsky-Korsakov and those who collaborated in the variations are Artcibouchev, Wihtol, Liadov, Rimsky-Korsakov, and Glazounov. The six variations are a March, Allegretto, Vivo, Allegretto, Andante, and Moderato Macstoso. They hardly need analysis as they follow the original theme quite closely and are mainly interesting as an exposition of the styles of the modern Russian composers.

Suite from Le Coq d'Or

"Le Coq d'Or," Rimsky-Korsakov's last opera, was written in the period 1906-1907. It had been planned to produce the work in 1907, but difficulties arose in regard to the censorship, for the libretto, which had been written by Bielsky, was a thinly veiled satire upon monarchy, and such productions were frowned upon during the régime of the Russian tsars. It was not until 1909 that, various modifications having been made in the text, "Le Coq d'Or" was authorized for public production by the censor and the first performance was given at Moscow, September 24. Rimsky-Korsakov never saw an interpretation of his work, for he had died of heart disease at St. Petersburg in June, 1908. In America the first hearing of any of the music from "Le Coq d'Or" was the suite, made from various portions of the opera, and given at a concert of the Russian Symphony Orchestra, January 19, 1911. The opera itself was produced — but in a manner entirely different from that conceived by the composer — at the Metropolitan Opera House, New York, in 1917.

The story of "Le Coq d'Or" ("The Golden Cockerel") is as follows:

King Dodon is perturbed because the continual plotting of a neighbouring ruler endangers the existence of his kingdom. As he is discussing in the royal council, with his two sons and General Polkan, his military commander, what can be done, an astrologer enters. The latter proffers a golden cockerel which, when placed upon a spire, will give warning of any danger by flapping its wings and crying "cock-a-doodle-do." At the first alarm King Dodon sends his two sons to meet the enemy; at the second he decides to take the field himself. Arrived at the scene of hostilities — a narrow gorge hemmed in by cliffs — he stumbles upon the dead bodies of his two sons and realizes that they have fought and killed each other. As Polkan encourages Dodon to continue the search for the enemy, the dawn of day shows in the immediate vicinity a tent of many colored patterns. From this there emerges the form of the beauteous Queen of Shemakha. She fools the poor king, who becomes hopelessly infatuated with her and who offers to share his throne with her. The couple, with their retainers, return to Dodon's capital. As they arrive there the astrologer appears and he demands as the price of his golden cockerel the person of the royal bride. Dodon, infuriated kills the astrologer. The queen repulses her royal consort and in the midst of the latter's agitation the cockerel is observed flying overhead. It swoops down and attacks Dodon, who falls dead.

The following are the movements of the suite and the "program" which they portray:

I. King Dodon in his Palace. This comprises the introduction to the opera and extracts from the first act — the dream of the king as he lies in his bed, in the belief that he is safe from his enemies; the cry of alarm given by the golden cockerel, announcing the coming of the foe, and the departure of the two sons of Dodon for the field of battle.

II. This comprises extracts from the second act. The scene is a wild pass, in which the army of the two princes has been lying. It is night and the moon shines weakly upon the bodies of the slain. Dodon's warriors penetrate apprehensively the dark recesses of the pass. The king discovers the corpses of his two sons, who have killed each other. A vision of the tent of the Queen of Shemakha.

III. Like the preceding movement, this comprises extracts from the second act of the opera. King Dodon with the Queen of Shemakha. Enraptured by the beauty of the queen, Dodon forgets the tragedy of his sons. With a tambourine in her hand the Queen of Shemakha begins to dance, and she invites the king to dance with her. Dodon is elderly and corpulent, but he obeys, and does not realize that the queen is laughing at him. He invites the queen to become his bride. They return to the capital in a gilt chariot.

IV. The wedding and the lamentable end of Dodon. Extracts from the third act are comprised in this section. Introduction; Wedding March; the golden cockerel kills Dodon by piercing his brain with its beak. The queen vanishes. Conclusion of the opera.

F. B.

Suite from The Tale of Tsar Saltan

The full title of Rimsky-Korsakov's opera, from which the orchestral suite has been drawn, is "The Fairy Tale of the Tsar Saltan, his Son, the famous and mighty Paladin, the Prince Guidon Saltanovich, and the Beautiful Tsarevna Lebed." The work, which was based upon a fantastic poem by Poushkin, was composed in 1899-1900 and was produced at Moscow, December, 1900. The suite had previously been played at a concert of the Imperial Musical Society, St. Petersburg. In America this music had been interpreted at a concert of the Russian Symphony Orchestra in January, 1905. The plot of the opera is as follows:

The Tsar Saltan, who was in the habit of mixing with his people in disguise, overhears the three daughters of a rich man discuss him as a possible husband. One declares that she would make him the best of bread; the second that she would weave beautiful linen for him; the third — the youngest of the sisters — that she would bear him wonderful children. The Tsar marries the third sister, Militrissa, but after he departs for the wars, the two others conspire against her and, when her child is born, convey word to Saltan that she has given birth to a monster. The Tsar sends back the command that Militrissa be put into a barrel and consigned to the sea. But the barrel is cast up on a desert island and there the child grows up a hero and a magician, supernatural power having been given him when he saved a swan from death in the jaws of a pike that had pursued it. He calls from the sea bottom a wonderful city, filled with gardens and palaces. The swan becomes a beautiful Princess, whom the Tsarevitch marries and the Tsar Saltan, returning from the wars and hearing about the wonders of the magic island, proceeds there and is reunited to his injured wife.

The suite contains three movements, each preceded by a fanfare for the trumpet, and each being prefaced by a quotation from Poushkin's poem as an explanation of it. I. "At that time a war broke out. Tsar Saltan bade farewell to his bride, mounted his horse and bade her watch well her love for him." The music of this opening section is of martial, oriental character. The farewell of Saltan to his wife is represented by a melody for the horn, taken up later by the violins. The march recurs, but grows by degrees fainter and fainter as the army recedes into the distance. II. This is the Introduction to the second act. "In the blue sky the stars are sparkling; the billows of the ocean rush surging and the barrel leaps upon the waves. In it the Tsaritsa weeps and wails, despairing of life, while the child hourly gains in growth and strength." The sighs of the Tsaritsa, the sighing of the wind and the sounds of the sea are delineated in this movement. III. The Three Wonders (Introduction to the last scene). "An island lies in the ocean; on it there rises a sublime city with golden battlements with gardens and palaces. Three wonders are there to be seen: First, a squirrel which cracks golden nuts, taking out emeralds and heaping up the golden shells, singing at the same time 'In the orchard, in the garden.' (A Russian folksong.) Second, the sea, whose waves dashing against the lonely shore, leave there thirty-three dauntless warriors, conquerors of heroes and clad in golden helmets and coats of mail. Third, the Princess Hilda, whose beauty is so great that by day she frightens away the sun and by night illumines the earth. The full moon gleams under her braided hair and on her brow a star sheds light. . . . I was there sipping mead beer and wine, but nothing came into my mouth." (The last phrase is the customary ending of Russian fairy-tales.) This movement shows the magic island with its Three Wonders. The little squirrel hops along, singing his quaint ditty. The theme of the sea recurs and there is heard the song of the dauntless warriors (in the brass, and preceded by the trumpet call). Lastly the beauty of the Princess Hilda is depicted and the work closes with a Coda, in which the trumpet call is heard for the last time.

F. B.

Scherzo, The Flight of the Bumble Bee

From The Tale of Tsar Saltan

This Scherzo is drawn from Rimsky-Korsakov's opera "The Tale of Tsar Saltan" but is not included in the suite from that work. It occurs in the first scene of the second act. The bumble bee has flown over the sea to the enchanted island, where it buzzes around a swan, which is, in reality, a princess in disguise. The Scherzo has enjoyed considerable popularity on the programs of "popular" concerts.

F. B.

ROSSINI

1792–1868

Cantata, Stabat Mater

THE "Stabat Mater" was written in 1832 but was not publicly performed until 1842, when Grisi, Albertazzi, Mario, and Tamburini were the soloists. A brilliant prelude leads to the opening chorus ("Stabat Mater dolorosa"), arranged for solos and chorus in dramatic style. It is followed by the tenor solo ("Cujus Animam"), a clear-cut melody, free of embellishment and brilliant in character. The next number ("Quis est Homo"), for two sopranos, is based upon a lovely melody, first given out by the first soprano, and then by the second, after which the two voices carry the theme through measure after measure of mere vocal embroidery, closing with a cadenza in genuine operatic style. The fourth number is the bass aria ("Pro peccatis"), the two themes in which are earnest and even serious in character and come nearer to the church style than any other part of the work. It is followed by a beautifully constructed number ("Eia Mater"), a bass recitative with chorus. The sixth number is a quartet ("Sancta Mater"), full of variety in its treatment and closing in full, broad harmony. After a short solo for soprano ("Fac ut portem"), the climax is reached in the ("Inflammatus"), a brilliant soprano obligato with choral accompaniment. The solo number requires a voice of exceptional range, power and flexibility; with this condition satisfied, the effect is intensely dramatic, and particularly fascinating by the manner in which the solo is set off against the choral background. An unaccompanied quartet in broad, plain harmony

("Quando Corpus"), leads to the showy, fugued ("Amen") which closes the work.

Overture to William Tell

The overtures to the Rossini operas, particularly those to the brassy "La Gazza Ladra" with its inane maid and magpie story, and to the showy "Semiramide," were popular for a long period, but the overture to "William Tell," his last dramatic work, is the one of the few that still retain a place upon concert programs. The story of the opera closely follows Schiller's drama and is so well known that it is unnecessary to repeat it. The introduction to the overture in the 'cellos and basses is supposed to picture the sunrise among mountain solitudes. The second part describes the fall of rain and the rapid gathering of a furious Alpine storm. As it gradually dies away, an Andante announces the shepherds' thanksgiving and the English horn sings the "Ranz des Vaches." This is followed by trumpet calls, summoning the Swiss soldiers, and their march. A brilliant Coda brings the overture to its close. The work, although in regular form, is rather a tone-picture or fantasia than an overture. Though the libretto of "William Tell" is far from dramatic and is wretchedly constructed, the overture is quite powerful, and portions of it, as in the case of the opera, are as dramatic as anything Rossini has written. It is particularly noticeable for its melodiousness as well as for its effective and significant instrumentation.

Overture to La Gazza Ladra

"La Gazza Ladra" ("The Thieving Magpie") was Rossini's twentieth opera. The work was produced for the first time at La Scala, Milan, May 31, 1817. A French play — "La pie voleuse" — was the basis of the libretto, written by Gheradini. The plot concerns a servant girl who has been accused of stealing a silver spoon and who, having been found guilty by the court of justice, is sentenced to the scaffold. As she is being taken there one of the people in the crowd observes a magpie with the silver spoon protruding from its nest. Thereafter all ends happily.

The opera won a great success at its production and this was partly due to the innovation which Rossini adopted in the overture of employing two snare drums. There was at least one member of the audience in La Scala, however, who objected to Rossini's composition. This was a young man, a student of Rolla, the leader of the orchestra, who was so scandalized by the introduction of the snare drums into the overture to "La Gazza Ladra" that he determined to wreak summary vengeance upon a composer who was so sacrilegious. He therefore armed himself with a stiletto, in the hope of meeting Rossini. The latter was so amused at the indignation of the man that he induced Rolla to bring the student to see him. Then in a tone of humility Rossini set forth his reasons for introducing snare drums into a military overture and ended by promising never to offend in a similar manner again. "For which reason, or better reasons," wrote Sutherland Edwards in his biography of Rossini (London, 1869) "Rossini never afterward began an overture with a duet for drums."

The overture to "La Gazza Ladra" begins (Maestoso, marziale, E major, 4-4 time) with a roll of the first snare drum (placed on one side of the orchestra) followed by a roll on the second (placed on the opposite side). The full orchestra then sets forth a march theme, fortissimo. This is developed and the snare drum rolls return. Five loud chords for the full orchestra lead the way into the main movement (Allegro, E minor, 3-4 time), the subject of which is given out lightly by the strings. Rossini took this theme from a duet in the third act. The subject is developed and, following the usual Rossinian crescendo, the full orchestra enters with a sonorous section. A sustained passage for the bassoons, horns and trombone leads to the second subject, in G major Another crescendo leads to the recapitulation, its principal theme being given, as before, to the strings. The second subject, heard in the clarinet, is in E major.

F. B.

Overture to Semiramide

"Semiramide," Rossini's last Italian opera, was written for the Fenice Theater, Venice, and was produced there February 3, 1823. The libretto, written by Rossi, was based upon Voltaire's tragedy "Semiramis," which, in its turn was founded upon the account of Semiramis — mostly mythical — left by Herodotus. The story concerns Semiramide — this is the Italian spelling of the name — who, assisted by her lover Assur, has murdered her husband, King Ninus. She becomes enamoured of Arsaces, the leader of her army, who, however, is in love with the royal princess Azema. The ghost of the murdered king summons Arsaces to a midnight meeting at his tomb, there to reveal to him the secret of the assassination. Assur, learning of this, hides in the tomb, with the intention of killing Arsaces; but Semiramide has learned that Arsaces, who was supposed to be a Scythian, is her own son, and she arrives in time to receive the death blow which had been intended for him. Arsaces then slays Assur and, having ascended the Assyrian throne, weds Azema.

The overture to "Semiramide," entitled "Sinfonia" on the published score, was written for flute, piccolo, two oboes, two clarinets, two bassoons, four horns, two trumpets, three trombones, kettle-drums, bass drum and strings. The work begins with introductory material (Allegro vivace, D major, 6-8 time) over a long organ-point on D in the kettle-drum. This leads into Andantino, whose subject is given out by the four horns alone, the bassoons reinforcing the harmony in the second phrase. Following this theme there comes a sonorous tutti for the full orchestra and the Andantino theme returns in the oboes and clarinets, the strings playing a pizzicato figure against it. The loud tutti recurs. Following three fortissimo chords the main movement (Allegro, D major, 4-4 time) is reached, its subject beginning in the strings. A bustling tutti succeeds this and is developed. The second subject, in A major, is given out by the clarinet and bassoon with a pizzicato accompaniment in the strings. There follows one of Rossini's characteristic crescendos and a brilliant piece of passage work for the first violins. The recapitulation brings forward the principal theme, scored as at the beginning of the overture. The second subject, now in D major, is given to the oboe and the first horn. The overture concludes with a brilliant Coda.

F. B.

RUBINSTEIN

1830 – 1894

Suite, Bal Costumé. Op. 103

THE "Bal Costumé" is a suite in six movements. The first part introduces the ballroom with its vivacious surroundings, the soft whisperings and loud conversation of the guests. The second part, a charming gavotte, illustrates shepherds and shepherdesses walking arm in arm through the hall, and is followed in the third part by a striking tarantella, which represents a merry group of Neapolitan men and women. The fourth part is Spanish throughout and full of vivid local color. It depicts an Andalusian Carmen wooed by an impetuous toreador. The fifth part may refer to Tannhäuser, as indicated by its title, "The Pilgrim and the Evening Star." The theme of the movement is a hymn-like strain accompanied by sensuous whisperings in the harp. The sixth and last part of the suite is of a military character and is intended to illustrate a drummer boy with a *cantinière.*

Ballet Music from Feramors

The opera "Feramors" was first performed in Dresden in 1863. It is founded upon Moore's "Lalla Rookh" and relates the love story of the Hindoo Princess Lalla, who has been plighted to the Sultan of Bokhara, whom she has never seen. Secretly she is in love with the singer and poet Feramors. During a journey to Delhi she meets a royal pageant of dancers and musicians who entertain her as she rests in the Vale of Cashmere. On her wedding morning she discovers that the poet and the Sultan are one and the same person. The ballet comprises four numbers. The first, "Bayaderentanz" ("Dance of the Bayaderes"), is based on two themes, the first announced in the strings with figures in the wood winds and horns, and the second, a theme marked by Oriental color, over a graceful passage for strings and marked by a strong tambourine accent. The movement is light and airy. The second movement is in waltz tempo, imitated in the wood winds. In the Trio the violins and violas have a smoothly flowing melody, the counter theme being a lovely melody for the horns. The waltz is repeated in the wood winds over phrases in horn and first violins, the accompaniment now marked in the triangle. The third movement is a second dance of Bayaderes, which is more stately and animated than the first, the Coda introducing all the rhythms of the dance, and preparing the way for the "Hochzeitszug," which is the gathering and march of the bridal procession, forming a brilliant closing picture in Oriental tones.

DE SABATA

1892–

Symphonic Poem, Juventus

VICTOR DE SABATA, born at Trieste, was precocious as a child. He played the piano at the age of four and had composed a gavotte for that instrument when he was six. He entered the Milan Conservatory at nine as a pupil in harmony and counterpoint of Saladino and, in composition, of Orefice. So rapid was de Sabata's progress that he composed an Andante and Scherzo for orchestra when he was twelve. He was graduated from the institution in 1911.

The symphonic poem "Juventus" was published in 1919 and was played for the first time at the Augusteo, Rome, January 11, 1920. There is nothing on the printed score to indicate a "program" for the work; but one is scarcely needed, for the Latin word for Youth, which the Italian composer chose for the title of his work, is sufficiently reflected in the impetuous exuberance of the composition itself. Much employment is given in the music to the figure with which it opens and to a staccato subject which appears shortly after the commencement in the strings. De Sabata employs the following large orchestra: piccolo, two flutes, two oboes, English horn, two clarinets, bass clarinet, two bassoons, double bassoon, four horns, three trumpets, four trombones, four kettle-drums, triangle, side drum, bass drum, cymbals, gong, glockenspiel, two harps, celesta and strings.

SAINT-SAËNS

1835 – 1921

Symphony No. 3, in C Minor. Op. 78

1. Adagio. Allegro moderato. Poco adagio.
2. Allegro moderato. Presto. Maestoso. Allegro.

SAINT-SAËNS' Third Symphony was written for the London Philharmonic Society; and its first performance, July 19, 1886, was conducted by the composer himself. For this occasion the composer prepared an analysis of its contents and structure for the program, which is followed in this analysis. After a slow and plaintive introduction in violins and oboes, the string quartet gives out the first theme, sombre and agitated in character, which, after transformation by the wind instruments, leads to a second subject, marked by greater repose. After a short development, presenting the two themes simultaneously, the second reappears in new and striking form, though brief in its duration. This is followed by a fresh transformation of the first theme, through the restlessness of which are heard at intervals the plaintive notes of the opening Adagio. Various episodes, introducing a gradual feeling of repose, lead to the Adagio, in D flat, the subject of which is given out in the violins, violas, and 'cellos, sustained by organ chords. It is then assigned to clarinets, horn and trombone, accompanied by the divided strings. After a fanciful and elaborate violin variation, the second transformation of the initial theme of the Allegro reappears, restoring the old restlessness, which is still further augmented by dissonant harmonies. The principal theme of the Adagio then returns, this time played by a violin, viola, and 'cello solo, accompanied by the chords of the organ and the persistent rhythm in triplets of the preceding episodes. The movement closes with a Coda, "mystical in sentiment," says the composer.

The second movement, Allegro moderato, opens with a vigorous figure, which is at once followed by a third transformation of the initial theme of the first movement, in more agitated style than the others, and limited to a fantastic character, which declares itself in a tumultuous Presto, through which flash at intervals the arpeggios and rapid scale passages of the pianoforte, accompanied by a syncopated rhythm in the orchestra, and interrupted at last by an expressive motive. After the repetition of the Allegro moderato, a second Presto is introduced, in which shortly appears a calm, earnest figure for trombones, in striking contrast with the fantastic character of the first Presto. There is an evident conflict between the two, ending in the defeat of the latter; and after a vague reminiscence of the initial theme of the first movement, a Maestoso, C minor, announces the ultimate triumph of the new and earnest figure. The initial theme of the first movement in its new form is next stated by the divided strings and the pianoforte, four hands, and taken up in organ and full orchestra. After development in three-bar rhythm, there is an episode for organ, followed by a pastoral theme twice repeated. A Coda, in which the initial theme by a last transformation appears as a violin passage, finishes this unique work.

Suite Algérienne. Op. 60

The Suite "Algérienne" has for its title on the score "Picturesque Impressions of a Voyage to Algeria." As this title suggests, it is a tone-picture, and its four movements need only brief description to convey the meaning of their contents. It opens with a prelude, "View of Algiers," in which the characteristic undulatory movement of the music indicates the sea, and other phrases the vessel approaching the harbor and glimpses of novel sights. The second movement, "Moorish Rhapsody," is in three closely connected sections. The first is brilliant in style, and is closely worked out contrapuntally.

The second is based upon an Oriental melody and is simple in construction, and the third is marked by fantastic combinations of instruments and bizarre effects. The third movement, "An Evening Dream at Blidah," a fortress near Algiers, is a quiet, romantic nocturne. In the last movement a French military march is worked up in elaborate style. A note to the score indicates that the composer not only emphasizes his joy in viewing the French garrison, but also the security felt under its protection. Judged by the pomposity of the march rhythm, the composer's joy and sense of security knew no bounds in expression.

Le Rouet d'Omphale. Op. 31

The symphonic poem, "Rouet d'Omphale" ("Omphale's Spinning-wheel"), illustrates the old story of Hercules serving as slave to the Lydian queen, and running her spinning-wheel in female attire by her side. The composition is in sonatina form, and quite short, but exceedingly naïve and graceful. It begins with a characteristic imitation of the wheel by the violins in a well-known figure. The second motive, a sombre melody in the bass, characterizes the lamenting, groaning Hercules; but Omphale soon sets him to work again, and the wheel resumes its lively, characteristic rhythm. The poem is vivacious and elegant throughout, and a good illustration of Saint-Saëns' cleverness in instrumentation.

Phaëton. Op. 39

The symphonic poem of "Phaëton" has for its story the legend of the unfortunate amateur charioteer of the sun, who, having obtained permission to drive the fiery steeds, approaches so near the earth that it is only saved from destruction by Jupiter, who interposes with a timely thunderbolt, and hurls the reckless driver into the outer limbo. It begins with a bright, pleasant melody, the driver evidently contemplating an agreeable journey. Soon another theme comes in; the chariot is taking an upward flight. Anon he loses his course.

and the first theme appears with significant chromatic changes. His indecision, fear, and despair are clearly indicated in the uncertain, abrupt and wandering character of the music. At last Jupiter settles matters with an outburst of trumpets; and the poem closes with the second theme in dirge form, singing a lament for the unfortunate victim of overcuriosity and confidence.

Danse Macabre. Op. 40

The "Danse Macabre," or "Dance of Death," is based upon a grotesque poem by Henri Cazalis, beginning "Zig et zig et zig, la Mort in cadence." Death is described as a fiddler, summoning the skeletons from their graves at midnight for a dance, the hour being indicated on the harp. The ghastly merriment, interrupted by some sombre strains, is kept up until the cock crows, the signal for the instant disappearance of the grim and clattering revelers. The poem is based upon two themes — one in dance measure, punctuated with the clack of bones, and the other a more serious strain, symbolical of night and the loneliness of the grave. The variations upon these two themes continue until the cock-crow, given out in the oboe, sounds the signal for the close. The poem, in a word, is a waltz measure set off with grotesque, but ingenious instrumentation.

Symphonic Poem, La Jeunesse d'Hercule. Op. 50

The following inscription on the score gives the program of "The Youth of Hercules": "The fable relates that Hercules on his entrance upon life saw two roads lie open before him — that of pleasure and that of virtue. Insensible to the seductions of nymphs and bacchantes, the hero chooses the paths of struggle and combats, at the end of which he catches a glimpse of the reward of immortality, through the flames of the funeral pyre."

The poem begins with a slow introduction in the muted violins, accompanied in the strings and wood winds. A roll of the kettle-drums leads to the first theme, given out in the strings. Development in the strings, wood winds, and horns leads to a subsidiary theme in the violins, with accompaniment in wood winds. The second theme opens in the flute and clarinet, then appears in the first violins, next in the harp, and finally subsides pianissimo in the horn. An Allegro follows, giving out a festive melody in the flute over a tremolo in the violas, joined by the second violins. After development, it dies away and the Andante of the first theme returns, and is extensively developed. At last it works up to a vigorous climax, when suddenly the second theme appears in opposition in the wood winds, harp, and horns. The struggle between them leads to a climax, closing with the superiority of the first theme given out in full orchestra.

Prelude to Le Déluge. Op. 45

Saint-Saëns composed his "biblical poem," "Le Déluge," in 1874 to a text by Louis Gallet. The first production was made at the Châtelet, Paris, March 5, 1876, with Furst, Jacques Bouhy, Mlle. Vergin and Mme. Nivet-Grenier as soloists. The reception of the work by the audience was mixed. The end of the second part of the composition, which depicts the Flood, was received by many with cries and whistling, but the battle between the composer's hostile critics and his supporters eventually ended in a victory for the latter and the orchestral picture of the Flood was repeated. The work as a whole is but little known, but the prelude has long enjoyed popularity in the concert rooms of Europe and America. It begins in a manner somewhat suggesting Bach. After a few introductory measures a theme, given out by the violas, is treated in fugal fashion and leads to an expressive melody for a solo violin. Arthur Hervey, in his "Saint-Saëns," wrote thus of this prelude:

"This beautiful prelude, remarkable for its simplicity and feeling, in a way presents a synthesis of the entire work, which was suggested by the passage in Genesis 'And God repented having created the world.' The solemnity of the opening chords, the mystic feeling conveyed by the fugal section, accord well with the gravity of the subject, while the lovely melody which follows is meant to suggest humanity in its original state of purity."

It may be added that the prelude is written for string orchestra.

F. B.

Marche Héroique. Op. 34

This march was written originally for two pianos and was played by Saint-Saëns and Albert Lavignac at a benefit concert given at the Grand-Hôtel, Paris, in 1871, during the Franco-Prussian war. Later in the year Saint-Saëns arranged the march for orchestra and dedicated it to the memory of his friend, Alexandre Georges Henri Regnault. The latter was a well known painter in Paris who had enlisted in the 69th battalion of the National Guard at the outbreak of the war with Prussia. In January, 1871, Regnault had participated in a sortie made by his regiment during the attack on Buzenal, a small place in the environs of Paris. He was killed there by a shot from the Prussian guns and it was not until the next day that an ambulance driver found the painter's body stretched out upon the ground with a bullet in his heart. The "Marche Héroique," in its orchestral form, was played for the first time at one of the Concerts Populaires at the Cirque d'Hiver, Paris, December 10, 1871. It was published the same year. The march is scored for two flutes, piccolo, two oboes, two clarinets, two bassoons, four horns, two trumpets, three trombones, bass tuba, kettle-drums, bass drum, side drum, cymbals, harps and strings. Seven introductory measures precede the principal theme, which appears in the wood winds with a pizzicato accompaniment in the strings. The violins take up the subject and it is worked over. The Trio (Andantino, A flat major, 3-4 time) presents its theme in the trombone, the strings accompanying with a figure which is based upon the subject of the march itself. The wood winds take up the theme. The time changes to 2-2 and, after suggestions of the march subject have been heard, the opening division of the composition is repeated with fuller scoring and comes to a close with a sonorous Coda.

F. B.

Ballet Music from Henry VIII

"Henry VIII," opera in four acts, text by Léonce Détroyat and Armand Sylvestre, was produced at the Opéra, Paris, March 5, 1883. Saint-Saëns put himself to considerable trouble to obtain the correct atmosphere for his opera. He spent considerable time in England acquainting himself with the music of the Tudor period and availed himself of a friendship with the librarian of the Royal collection of manuscripts at Buckingham Palace in order to obtain examples of music written in the time of Henry VIII. The plot of the opera was concerned with the love of the English king for Anne Boleyn and with some subsidiary matters that depart considerably from historical accuracy. The ballet music was the last part of the opera to be composed, Louis Mérante, ballet master at the Opéra, having given Saint-Saëns the scenario of the divertissements in October, 1882. The airs which the French master used for the ballet music were largely drawn from a collection of Scotch and Irish music belonging to Mme. Détroyat, the wife of his librettist. The ballet is introduced in the second act of "Henry VIII," the occasion being a fête given by the King at Richmond in honor of the Papal Legate. The following comprise the dances: I. Introduction, Moderato, E major. II. Entry of the Clans, Allegro moderato, C minor. The Scotch clans enter to the English tune, "The Miller of the Dee," Saint-Saëns evidently having confused the English Dee with the Scotch river of the same name. III. Scotch Idyll, Moderato maestoso and Allegretto, F major. The subject of this begins in the oboe. IV. Gipsy Dance, Moderato quasi Andantino, D minor. The movement begins in the English horn with a melody of Hungarian character. It is followed by a quicker section (Allegro moderato, F major) whose theme is given out by the violins. V. Gigue and Finale (Presto). The subject of this movement is the old English jig

F. B.

SCHELLING

1876 –

A Victory Ball, Fantasy for Orchestra

ERNEST SCHELLING, who was born at Belvidere, New Jersey, began his artistic career as a pianistic prodigy, for he appeared in a concert at Philadelphia at the age of four and a half. When six years old he was taken to Paris and entered the Conservatoire as a pupil of Mathias, later studying successively with Moszkowski, Huber and Paderewski. He toured in practically every European country and in North and South America. As a composer Schelling attracted attention with a Fantastic Suite for piano and orchestra, produced at Amsterdam in 1907. He followed up the success of that work with "Impressions of an Artist's Life" for piano and orchestra, and "A Victory Ball."

"A Victory Ball" was composed in 1922 and played for the first time at a concert of the Philadelphia Orchestra, Philadelphia, February 23, 1923. The composer has stated that his work was the outcome of the Great War. "I had come back from Europe," he wrote, "still very much under the impression of cataclysm, much troubled for the future, and was amazed to find that so few seemed to remember what the war really had meant, with its sacrifice of life and youth. . . . I came across Alfred Noyes' poem, 'A Victory Ball,' while in this mood and was impelled to use it as the basis of an orchestral fantasy." The poem to which Schelling referred was contained in Noyes' "The Elfin Artist and Other Poems," and depicted a ball to celebrate the victory over the enemy, with the shadows of the dead men watching the gaieties. Lawrence Gilman described Schelling's composition as "a bacchanale transversed by a vision — an apparition of troops marching on irresistibly, inexorably." The work begins with a delineation of the ball room with its dancers, the fox-trot and tango, the festivities being dramatically interrupted by the vision of the marching hosts — their approach being announced by two trumpet calls, the "Call to Arms" and "Charge." In one section of this parade the music of the Scotch highlanders with their bagpipes is heard. At the end the trumpet, heard as from a distance, sounds "Taps."

F. B.

SCHMITT

1870 -

La Péri, A Dance Poem

"LA PÉRI," composed by Florent Schmitt in 1910, was written for choreographic representation and given for the first time at one of the Concerts de Danse, presented by Mlle. Trouhanova at the Châtelet, Paris, in April, 1912. The program contained works by d'Indy, Ravel and Florent Schmitt, Mlle. Trouhanova giving dance interpretation to all. In the United States "La Péri" was first heard as a concert piece at San Francisco under the direction of Alfred Hertz, January 16, 1916. The score of Dukas' work contains a "program" of the work, of which the following is a translation made by Mr. Philip Hale:

It happened that at the end of his youthful days, since the Magi observed that his star was growing pale, Iskender went about Iran seeking the flower of immortality.

The sun sojourned thrice in its dozen dwellings without Iskender finding the flower. At last he arrived at the end of the earth, where it is only one with sea and clouds.

And there, on the steps that lead to the hall of Ormuzd, a Péri was reclining, asleep in her jeweled robe. A star sparkled above her head; her lute rested on her breast; in her hand shone the flower. It was a lotus like unto an emerald, swaying as the sea under the morning sun.

Iskender noiselessly leaned over the sleeper, and without awakening her snatched the flower, which suddenly became between his fingers like the noonday sun over the forests of Ghilan.

The Péri, opening her eyes, clapped the palms of her hands together and uttered a loud cry, for she could not now ascend towards the light of Ormuzd.

Iskender, regarding her, wondered at her face, which surpassed in deliciousness even the face of Gurda-ferrid.

In his heart he coveted her.

So that the Péri knew the thought of the king, for in the right hand of Iskender the lotus grew purple and became as the face of longing.

Thus the servant of the Pure knew that this flower of life was not for him.

To recover it, she darted forward like a bee, while the invincible lord bore away from her the lotus, torn between his thirst for immortality and the delight for his eyes.

But the Péri danced the dance of the Péris; always approaching him until her face touched his face; and at the end he gave back the flower without regret.

Then the lotus was like unto snow and gold, as the summit of Elbourz at sunset.

The form of the Péri seemed to melt in the light coming from the calix, and soon nothing more was to be seen than a hand raising the flower of flame, which faded in the realm above.

Iskender saw her disappear. Knowing from this that his end drew near, he felt the darkness encompassing him.

F. B.

SCHÖNBERG

1874 –

Verklärte Nacht. Op. 4

ARNOLD SCHÖNBERG is most widely known as a leader among the ultra-modernists. Born at Vienna, his career was uneventful until he arrived at that stage of it in which his excursions into dissonance evoked the hostile demonstrations of his audiences in the concert rooms of Vienna. For a short time Schönberg lived in Berlin, but he returned to his native city and now divides his time between it and the Prussian capital. The composer became a practitioner of the ultra-modern methods only by gradual stages. His early works are by no means bizarre and make no use of the atonality and polytonality that characterizes his later style. "Verklärte Nacht" ("Transfigured Night") belongs to Schönberg's first period. It was written, as a string sextet, in 1899. The composer made a transcription of the work for string orchestra and this was heard for the first time in America at a concert of the National Symphony Orchestra, New York, March 14, 1921. The title is concerned with the fact that Schönberg based his music upon a poem of that name written by Richard Dehmel. In it it is told how a man forgives the grievous sin of a woman who loves him and how, by his act of self-abnegation, the world seems transfigured.

F. B.

Five Pieces for Orchestra. Op. 16

Schönberg composed these pieces for orchestra in 1909 and they were published in 1912. their first performance having taken place at a Promenade Concert, London, September 3, 1912. On that occasion they were described on the program as "experiments in dissonance." The reviewer for the Musical Times of London declared that "while nobody could reasonably claim that he had not been fairly warned, almost everybody seemed bewildered, if not shocked, at the degree to which Schönberg had carried his protest against all preconceived notions of music and harmony." The Viennese composer, explaining his attitude to chord progressions that sound cacophonous to the majority of music-loving people has said: "The alleged tones which are believed to be foreign to harmony do not exist: they are merely tones foreign to our accepted harmonic system. Tonality is not a hard and fast compulsion which directs the course of music, but a concept which makes it possible for us to give our ideas the requisite aspect of compactness. Beauty does not appear until all unessential detail disappears."

When the Five Pieces were performed for the first time, no indication of any programmatic significance was given. But at a second performance of the work in London, given in 1914, Schönberg furnished the program book with titles for each movement. They are as follows: I. "Vorgefühle" ("Presentiments"). II. "Vergangenes" ("The Past"). III. "Der Wechselnde Akkord" ("The Changing Chord"). IV. "Péripétie" ("Peripeteia"). V. "Das Obbligato Recitative" ("The Obbligato Recitative").

F. B.

SCHUBERT

1797 – 1828

Symphony No. 8, in B Minor (Unfinished)

1. Allegro moderato.
2. Andante con moto.

SCHUBERT'S Eighth Symphony is but a fragment. The first two movements are complete. There are nine bars of a Scherzo, and with them the symphony stops; and yet among all of the composer's works not one is more beautiful in ideas or more perfect in form than this. No more of it has ever been found, and no one knows why Schubert abandoned it. The first page of the score is dated, "Vienna, October 30, 1822." The first performance was given at Vienna on December 17, 1865. Since that time the symphony has become one of the favorite numbers on the concert-stage.

The Allegro opens at once and without introduction with an impressive subject given out by the 'cellos and basses. At its close the oboes and clarinets take up a melodious theme pianissimo, the violins accompanying it in an agitated manner. After a short development of this theme the 'cellos enter with a melody which will never cease to fascinate the hearer with its wonderful beauty and grace of motion. After its repetition by the violins in octaves there comes a pause followed by a most passionate declaration in the minor, as if to drown the memory of the former moment of happiness. The beautiful theme again returns, however, and the first part of the movement closes with a struggle between these expressions of perfect happiness and wild passion. The second part opens with the original subject varied for the basses, which is grandly developed amid full orchestral outburst up to a powerful climax. As it dies away the first theme reenters, and is again treated with charming variety, the whole closing with another climax in which the opening subject forms the material of the Coda.

The Andante begins with an introductory passage in the horns and bassoons, the double-basses accompanying pizzicato, leading up to another lovely theme given out by the violins. After a striking development of this theme the second subject is stated in the clarinets with string accompaniment, repeated by the oboe with the addition of a new phrase, in which the flute joins. The whole orchestra follows with stately harmony, succeeded by an episode which leads up to a new treatment of the second theme in the strings. Then follows the customary repetition in brilliant detail. The Coda is full of melodious beauty, and closes this delightful work.

Symphony No. 9, in C Major

1. Andante. Allegro ma non troppo.
2. Andante con moto.
3. Scherzo. Allegro vivace.
4. Finale. Allegro vivace.

The Symphony in C, the last and culminating work of Schubert's genius, is literally his swan song. It was begun in March, 1828, and on the nineteenth of November of the same year he passed away. On the twelfth of December following his death, it was produced at the Redouten-Saal in Vienna, and was repeated in the ensuing March. It was then neglected and forgotten until 1838, in which year Schumann visited Vienna, and, finding the score, obtained permission to take it with him. He at once went to Leipsic, where Mendelssohn was at that time conducting the Gewandhaus concerts, and together the two friends and composers studied it. It did not take them long to discover its beauty, notwithstanding its length. It was performed at the Gewandhaus, March 22, 1839.

The first movement opens with an introductory Andante, the tender, fairy-like melody of which is assigned to the horns alone, afterward repeated by oboes and clarinets. After working up at some length a start is made pianissimo, and a grand crescendo, enlivened by a triplet figure, leads to the Allegro, the strings giving out the bold, decisive first theme answered by the winds in triplets. The second theme, stated in the oboes and bassoons, is in striking contrast with the first, and really establishes the rhythm of the movement. An episode growing out of this theme, and a third broad subject in which the trombones are employed with striking effect, constitute the principal material of the movement. The Coda is long and copious, closing in rather accelerated tempo marked by a repetition of the triplet figure of the initial theme.

The Andante opens with a short prelude in the strings, after which the oboe starts off with the first theme — a quaint, plaintive, bewitching strain which has every characteristic of gypsy music, closing with a significant four-note cadence which seems to have haunted Schubert throughout the rest of the work. The theme is repeated with variation and the addition of the clarinet, after which the oboe gives out a new phrase succeeded by an episode of an agitated, even furious character, after which the fascinating first theme returns. The second subject, entering pianissimo, is ingeniously treated, and closes with a charming horn episode. The opening subject then returns, this time for oboe, which soon plays its part as accompaniment for a charming solo passage for the 'cello. A change of key, and the second subject returns with fresh treatment. The horn episode is heard again, and the movement closes with the fascinating opening theme.

The Scherzo starts with a unison passage for strings, followed by a boisterous episode in the oboes and horns, in which the four beats already alluded to make themselves felt. The second subject, given out by the strings, with accompaniment of clarinets and bassoons, is light and playful in character. The trio opens with horns and clarinets, leading to a broad melody in the winds, with string accompaniment, producing a brilliant orchestral effect and with the Scherzo, da capo, the movement closes.

The Finale crowns this extraordinary work with a fitting climax, impetuous and resistless in its rush, with the four beats asserting themselves all through it. After an introduction of a most energetic and sonorous character, the first theme is announced in the oboes and bassoons, with the violins accompanying in triplets of fiery velocity. The second theme is led off by the horns, the violins still in the mad, impetuous sweep of their triplets, and the first half of the movement closes with a working-out of part of the second theme. The second part is fiery in its energy, and closes with an immense crescendo, beginning with the violas, double pianissimo, and spreading over one hundred and sixty-four measures before coming to a final rest.

Overture to Die Zauberharfe (Rosamunde). Op. 26

Little remains of the many operas and operettas Schubert composed, except the so-called overture to "Rosamunde," and even this is involved in much confusion, as Schubert never wrote an overture to that drama. The story of the overture is interesting. In 1819 a melodrama called "Die Zauberharfe" ("The Magic Harp") was written by Hofmann for the Theater an der Wien, Vienna. The managers applied to Schubert for the incidental music. He wrote it in a fortnight, and the melodrama, when produced, proved a failure. The overture was greatly praised, especially the Adagio introduction, and it was subsequently used as a prelude to his operetta, "Die Verschwornen." When the overture was published, it was called the overture to "Rosamunde," and the mistake has continued to the present time. The overture which had been previously composed for "Alfonso and Estrella" was adopted by Schubert for "Rosamunde." "Alfonso and Estrella" was written in 1823, but it was not performed until 1854. It was based upon a Spanish subject, and, though brought out by Liszt, and subsequently remodelled and revised both in book and score, it was unsuccessful. The overture to "Rosamunde," therefore, is the overture to "Die Zauberharfe."

It opens Andante with a few stately chords of introduction, followed by a beautifully melodious theme for oboe and clarinet, the cadence echoed by the strings, the strings in turn taking the theme with responses by oboe and bassoon. An Allegro vivace follows with the theme in the first violins, accompanied only by the other strings. After the repetition of this theme, tutti, the second theme, one of the most beautiful of the great master's melodies, is announced. It is repeated in flute and oboe, and in its close a new rhythm is introduced and carried through a long episode which introduces still another melody. All this thematic material reappears in the development, and the overture closes with a spirited Coda.

Serenade

Schubert's immortal "Serenade" was written in 1826. It is so familiar that it needs no analysis, nor is one necessary from any point of view. It is simply a lovely melody from first note to last, written upon the inspiration of the moment, and yet characterized by absolute perfection of finish and a grace and beauty of which one never tires. It was originally composed as an alto solo and male chorus and was subsequently rearranged for female voices only. The circumstances of its composition as told by Schubert's biographer, Von Hellborn, are of more than ordinary interest. Von Hellborn says:

"One Sunday, during the summer of 1826, Schubert with several friends was returning from Potzleinsdorf to the city, and on strolling along through Wahring, he saw his friend Tieze sitting at a table in the garden of the 'Zum Biersack.' The whole party determined on a halt in their journey. Tieze had a book lying open before him, and Schubert soon began to turn over the leaves. Suddenly he stopped, and pointing to a poem, exclaimed, "Such a delicious melody has just come into my head, if I but had a sheet of music paper with me.' Herr Doppler drew a few music lines on the back of a bill of fare, and in the midst of a genuine Sunday hubbub, with fiddlers, skittle players, and waiters running about in different directions with orders, Schubert wrote that lovely song."

Various orchestral transcriptions have been made of Schubert's song, among them those by Theodore Thomas, Offenbach, etc.

SCHUMANN (GEORG)

1866 –

Overture, Liebesfrühling. Op. 28

THE overture, "Liebesfrühling," originally entitled "Frühlingsfeier" ("Spring Festival"), was first performed in 1891 in Berlin, and is written in strictly symphonic style. It begins with an agitated movement in the wood winds. The 'cellos give out the principal theme, very passionate in character, which is subsequently extended in the wood winds. After development the theme is resumed in the violins and violas, accompanied by a melodious figure and leading to the second theme in the wood winds, the clarinet having the principal melody, accompanied by another melodious figure in the violins. After further development the recapitulation occurs, introducing the first and second themes, the overture closing with a joyous climax.

Overture to a Drama. Op. 45

Georg Schumann's "Overture to a Drama" was first performed at Cologne in 1906. The composer has left no hint as to the special drama he had in mind. Four measures lead to the first theme, given out by the strings, which, after development, is taken in full orchestra, with a subsidiary passage in flute and clarinet. A connecting passage appears in the second violins and 'cellos, with accompaniment in the clarinets and harp arpeggios, leading to the second theme, taken at first in 'cellos, clarinets and English horn, and then in full orchestra. It is next sung by clarinet over string harmony, leading to a section where a thematic passage appears in English horn and bass clarinet, anon taken in the strings. Development, recapitulation and the Coda occupy the remainder of the overture which closes with a fortissimo chord.

Serenade. Op. 34

The composer has appended the following program to the score of "Serenade," op. 34, which explains the meaning:

"The serenade before us portrays the story of a rejected lover. *First movement* — Merry procession of the participants, in which, however, the enemy and the scoffer make themselves noticeable. *Second movement* — Spookishness of the night. Secret meeting of the enemy and the scoffer. *Third movement* — Serenade. *Fourth movement* — Intermezzo, rejection. *Fifth movement* — The lover retires in anger, amidst the derision and scoffing of the enemy, and makes use of the folksongs, 'The nobleman is a millsack,' 'There lives a miller by yonder pond — run, miller, run.'"

The composer's program is but another example of the absurdly humorous vein which runs through many of his works. The opening movement, "Auf dem Wege" ("On the Way"), an Allegro, opens with a noisy introduction, evidently describing the "procession," followed, after a sprightly episode, by a lively duet between the strings and wood winds which we may infer relates to the "enemy" and the "scoffer." The noisy passage is repeated, but is finally lost during the pianissimo closing of the movement. The second movement, "Nächtlicher Spuk" ("Spookishness of the Night"), a Presto, opens with a brief introduction followed by another duet similar to that in the first, showing that the "enemy" and "scoffer" are still at their malicious work. The third movement, "Ständchen" ("Serenade"), is a delightful melody of the romantic sort for clarinet with harp accompaniment. The Intermezzo, fourth movement, is a short melodic episode which forms a transition to the fifth movement, "Finale," a burlesque Presto, which brings the whimsical "Serenade" to an end with a

Tarantella rhythm of a rollicking sort and yet brilliantly and skilfully constructed.

Variations and Double Fugue on a Jolly Theme, Op. 30

The "Burlesque Variations and Double Fugue on a Jolly Theme" hardly need explanation. Their humor is apparent in every variation as well as the composer's remarkable knowledge of orchestral resources. A brief introduction leads to an announcement of the theme in the first violins with accompaniment in the other strings. On this theme the composer has made ten variations which differ materially from each other, but all retaining the spirit of burlesque. It is manifest even in the Funeral March and the double fugue, which notwithstanding its technical character, adds its contribution of fun to the "Jolly Theme."

SCHUMANN (ROBERT)

1810–1856

Symphony No. 1, in B Flat. Op. 38

1. Andante un poco maestoso. Allegro molto vivace.
2. Larghetto.
3. Scherzo. Molto vivace.
4. Finale. Allegro animato e gracioso.

SCHUMANN'S First Symphony, in B flat, was written in 1841, and was first performed at the Leipsic Gewandhaus concerts, under Mendelssohn's direction, March 31 of that year. According to Hanslick, Schumann himself characterized it as the "Spring Symphony."

The first movement is prefaced with a brief introduction of a passionate and earnest character, its opening phrase, given out by the horns and trumpets, playing an important part in the progress of the movement. In the development there are sombre suggestions; but with a sudden change in the harmony, the flute is heard with a more cheering tone, the violins rush in, and with a grand sweep the whole orchestra opens the fresh and vigorous Allegro, its first theme being similar to that of the Andante. The second theme, prefaced in the horns and given out by the clarinet with viola accompaniment, is a unique and thoroughly characteristic melody. As it develops it gathers fresh life and force. New and piquant phrases are introduced, and blend with it, one of them forming a charming accompaniment to the first theme. The Coda is constructed freely and broadly, and works up to a climax leading at last, after a pizzicato passage, to a joyful rhythmical song given out first by the strings and then by full orchestra.

The Larghetto movement is a grand fantasie, full of passionate devotion and almost religious in its character, showing unmistakably the influence of Beethoven. Its opening theme is given out by the violins and then repeated by the 'cellos, a new and characteristic phrase appearing in the accompaniment. Again it appears in the oboes and horns, most ingeniously varied. Its treatment on each reappearance grows more elaborate, and fresh phrases wander from one instrument to another.

The beautiful fantasie finally dies away, and with slight pause the Scherzo opens with a vigorous theme which has already been indicated in the close of the Larghetto. As opposed to it Schumann has written two trios in different rhythms. The first is thoroughly original, and rich and tender in its harmony. The second is equally characteristic, and clearly enough reveals the union of Schumann's romantic style with the old minuet form. At the close of the Scherzo the first trio again appears, and the movement ends with a diminuendo.

The Finale begins with a scale passage, which is a prominent feature in the movement. Its first theme is fresh, gay, and vigorous, and after its statement leads to an interesting dialogue in which a new and lively subject and the scale passage of the opening take part. The second theme is full of joyous contentment, and in the development the first theme appears opposed to it, with freshly varied treatment, until the brilliant and powerful close is reached.

Symphony No. 2, in C Major. Op. 61

1. Sostenuto assai. Allegro ma non troppo.
2. Scherzo. Allegro vivace.
3. Adagio espressivo.
4. Allegro molto vivace.

Schumann's C Major Symphony No. 2 * was sketched in 1845 and completed in 1846. It was first performed at a

* The C major is in reality the Third Symphony, though numbered as the Second, and in order of date follows the B flat, D minor, and E — known as the "Overture, Scherzo, and Finale."

Leipsic Gewandhaus concert, under Mendelssohn's direction, November 5, 1846.

The prelude, which introduces the first movement, is in the nature of an overture to the symphony, setting forth its story. Its opening theme will be found in each of the movements, and it also foreshadows the leading theme of the first. It is given out by the trumpets, horns, and trombone, with harmonious accompaniment by the strings. After a few bars a romantic phrase appears in the accompaniment for the wood winds, which is also repeated in the other movements. As the introduction progresses the time is accelerated, and a new subject is assigned to the flutes and oboes, which leads up to the principal theme — a resolute, energetic melody followed by a vigorous phrase, already heard, but now appearing with a fresh accompaniment and leading to the second theme, of a less energetic character, which closes the first part of the movement. The second part is devoted to the elaborate development of this thematic material, which leads up to a return of the first theme, after a long organ-point in the basses, with unique wind accompaniment. In the Coda, after a treatment of associated subjects, the trumpets take up the opening of the prelude again, this time in sonorous and aggressive style.

The Scherzo shows us Schumann in one of his rare joyous moods. Its first theme is given out by the violins, to which a counter-theme is opposed, with an accompaniment in contrary motion. The Scherzo has two trios. The first is a melody in triplets, divided between the wood winds and strings. The second, which is more subdued, is taken by the strings in full harmony. In the return the trios are displaced by the first theme; and in the Coda the trumpets and horns, with scale accompaniment by the violins, again give out the theme of the prelude.

The Adagio is in marked contrast to the preceding movements, expressing tenderness and devotion instead of conflict. Without introduction the strings alone sing a passionate love-song, the oboes and clarinets subsequently adding their voices to the beautiful strain. A brief interlude leads to the second theme, assigned to the strings, accompanied by the trumpet and horns. After its statement the love-song is repeated by the violins in octaves trilling downward, the wood winds closing it. The second part closely resembles the first and closes peacefully, with no allusion to the trumpet theme of the prelude.

The Finale begins with a rapid scale-passage leading up to the martial first theme. The transition to the second theme is characterized by vigorous and striking rhythms. The theme itself, suggestive of the Adagio, is given out by the violas, 'cellos, clarinets, and bassoons, accompanied by the violin scale-passage mentioned above and the wind instruments in triplets, and gradually leads to a return of the first subject. The end of the conflict is marked by a climax in which the trumpet theme is again heard. After suggestive rests the oboe intones a simple theme, but full of joy and victory, which is worked up to a climax. It then appears broader and more freely for the strings, and from this point moves on to the close like a grand hymn of thanksgiving, the trumpet theme making its last appearance near the end.

Symphony No. 3 (Rhenish), in E Flat. Op. 97

1. Allegro.
2. Scherzo.
3. Andante.
4. Lento.
5. Allegro Finale.

The Symphony in E flat, though numbered the Third, was the Fourth in order of composition, and is familiarly known as "The Rhenish," the title being derived from the impressions of life in the Rhineland made upon the composer. It was sketched and instrumented between November 2 and December 9, 1850, in which year Schumann was the municipal director of music at Düsseldorf. Its first performance took place in that city, February 6, 1851.

The first movement opens without introduction, the first theme being at once given out by the violins. After short development it is heard again with increased animation, and leads up to a lively second theme in the oboes, bassoons, and clarinets. The elaboration of these two themes is long and skilful.

The Scherzo begins with a characteristic theme given out by the violas, bassoons, and 'cellos — a melody which is fairly replete with good-nature and old-fashioned humor. After its development a second lively theme occurs and leads up to a subject given out by the clarinets, horns, and bassoons, corresponding to the trio, and full of color. After its statement the principal theme returns and is ingeniously varied.

The Andante opens with a quiet and beautiful melody for the bassoons and clarinets. The movement is serene and sentimental throughout, and prepares the way for the succeeding Lento, the inspiration of which has been outlined by Schumann himself. It is marked "Feierlich." The composer at first superscribed the movement, "In the character of accompaniment to a solemn ceremony." This ceremony was the festivity in the cathedral of Cologne consequent upon the elevation of Archbishop von Geissel to the rank of Cardinal, which he had witnessed. When the symphony was published, however, he erased the superscription, explaining his action by saying: "One must not show the people his heart. A more general impression of a work of art is better for them; then at least they will make no false comparisons." Its foundation is a broad and unmistakably ecclesiastic harmony given out in a solemn and stately manner in the trombones, and on this foundation he builds up an elaborate contrapuntal structure which retains the same ecclesiastic form, with added richness and brilliancy. The Finale is written in strict form, and introduces new and fresh themes, with the exception of the appearance of the ecclesiastical motive, of which the principal one is the most striking.

Symphony No. 4, in D Minor. Op. 120

1. Introduction.
2. Allegro.
3. Romanza.
4. Scherzo and Finale.

Schumann's Fourth Symphony, really his Second, was originally written in 1841, but was not revised and put into its present form until 1851. Its title is "Symphony No. 4, D minor, Introduction, Allegro, Romanza, Scherzo, and Finale, in one piece," the parts passing into one another without pause, and united by the use of subjects already stated.

The Introduction opens with a theme in the violas and 'cellos of a somewhat melancholy character, and after its brief development, with a gradually accelerated tempo, the Allegro enters with a theme dry and difficult in its contents, but used with masterly effect in its development, and presenting unusual strength, in spite of its unmelodious nature. Though there is a second theme, more gracious in style, the first dominates the whole first part of the movement. After the usual repeat the second part is treated in the style of a free fantasie, with entirely new material, in which respect Schumann makes a wide departure from the established forms. It is built up mainly on two episodes — the first given out with full strength by the winds, and in the repeat by the strings, and the second by the violins. The entire second part is devoted to the elaboration of these two episodes in a bold and striking manner, and it closes with fiery emphasis, in strange contrast with the movement to which it leads.

A single chord binds it to the Romanza, which opens with a simple, plaintive, and exquisitely refined melody. It is given out by the oboes and 'cellos, with the strings pizzicato. A short phrase follows in the violas. Then succeeds a passage from the Introduction which reminds us that this tender Romanza is filling its part in the general symphonic design. A repetition of its phrase leads to a second subject given out by the strings, while a solo violin heightens the beautiful effect with a variation on the principal theme. The movement closes with the tender song that opens it.

The Scherzo opens with a strong, energetic theme in full orchestra, except trombones, which has few reminders of the ordinary Scherzo lightness and caprice. The second part, however, is more gracious, and the Trio is soft and dreamy. At its close the Scherzo reappears, followed by the Trio, in the midst of which there is a moment of restlessness, as if the instruments knew not which way to turn. Instead of leading back to the Scherzo the music diminishes in tone as if it would disappear, when suddenly the winds give out a melodious phrase leading into the Finale. The short introduction, which contains familiar material, prepares the way for the opening theme, which is also familiar, as it has appeared in nearly the same form in the first movement. At its close occurs a subject, only a bar in length, which plays an important part in the final development. The second theme is an odd mixture of fancy and frolic. After the customary reprise Schumann gives himself up to his mood, quitting the first subject altogether and elaborating the second until in the Coda we meet with a new and unexpected theme. The Finale closes presto with a genuine Italian stretta.

Overture, Scherzo and Finale, Op. 52

The "Overture, Scherzo and Finale" was first performed at the Gewandhaus Concert, in Leipzig, on December 7, 1841, at which concert the D minor Symphony of the same composer, was also played.

The year 1841 was an unusually busy one for Schumann, for his happy surroundings stimulated him to enter the field of orchestral composition, and with his usual energy he sketched in rapid succession his first Symphony in B flat, the fourth in D minor, and the Sinfonetta, as he first called his opus 52. The latter work, not having any slow movement, he revised in 1845, and then published it under the title: "Overture, Scherzo and Finale."

The Overture, though slighter than Schumann's other symphonic movements, is full of grace and spirit. It abounds in the peculiar veins of delicate feeling and fancy which distinguish his works; and it would be difficult to find a work of his which unites his most pleasing characteristics in so short a form. The Scherzo is peculiarly stamped with that individuality which gained his symphonies such high rank, and all of which contain Scherzos of extraordinary merit. The tripping dotted rhythm, 6–8 time, prevails throughout, and is relieved in the Trio by a graceful phrase in 2–4 time. Both Scherzo and Trio are repeated, closing with a reminiscence of the first movement and a few bars from the Scherzo. The Finale assumes a more legato character in the first part, while the second half introduces a new theme, which, by its obstinate and uncompromising rhythm, is in strong contrast to the former.

Overture to Genoveva. Op. 81

"Genoveva," the only opera Schumann attempted, was composed in 1847, and was first performed in Leipsic in 1850, Schumann himself conducting the work. It did not prove a success and was withdrawn after a few presentations, but the overture still retains its place on concert programs. The story, briefly told, is as follows: Genoveva is married to the Knight Siegfried and is devotedly attached to him. During his absence in the wars, Golo makes overtures to her and attempts to effect her ruin. Being repulsed, he accuses her to Siegfried of infidelity with Drago, one of the servants. When Siegfried returns, he orders her to be put to death. The attendants, to whom the execution of the penalty is intrusted, merely leave her in the forest to die. When Golo's treachery is discovered, he seeks Genoveva, finds her in the forest, and Siegfried and she are reconciled, while Golo is executed.

The introduction to the overture is exceedingly sombre in character, with marked dissonances and a plaintive passage in the violins, which may indicate Genoveva's grief at Siegfried's wrath and her banishment from the castle. The main section opens with a restless, passionate theme in the violins, with 'cello accompaniment, followed by a charming hunting passage in the horns, continued by the oboes and flutes. After the free fantasia, the violins and violas lead, fortissimo, to the third part, after the usual development. The Coda, based upon the second theme, holds its way until at last the trombones bring the overture to an exultant close.

Overture to The Bride of Messina. Op. 100

In 1850 Richard Pohl, a student friend of Schumann, sent him Schiller's tragedy, "The Bride of Messina," arranged as an opera libretto with the suggestion that he should set it to music. Perhaps remembering the fate of "Genoveva," he could not make up his mind to compose an opera upon the subject. That he was very much interested in it, however, is shown by his writing an overture to it, which was performed in Leipsic in 1851. While it is not generally considered a fitting overture to the story, yet it has many strong passages, especially the romantic second theme. As the overture is so rarely performed it hardly needs a closer description than to say it is in the ordinary form with a sombre introduction and a middle section which is deeply infused with the romantic spirit. It was also written at a time when Schumann's power of construction was visibly weakening.

Overture to Manfred. Op. 115

The music to "Manfred" was written in 1848, in the same year as the composer's opera "Genoveva," and was first performed in 1852 at Weimar. It is based upon Byron's drama of the same name, the entire music consisting of entr'actes and incidental numbers, sixteen in all. As compared with his other concert overtures it is supreme in its excellence. The overture opens with a single bar of three agitated chords, leading, after a pause, to an introduction, the oboe announcing a wild, passionate theme, continued in the violins and leading to the main section of the overture, which is reached in a powerful climax, following which the principal theme, marked "in passionate tempo," is given out. After its energetic development another theme appears, a plaintive melody, which may stand for Astarte. This is followed by two episodes, the one very vehement and the other more tranquil. The first subject reappears, marked "with more force," and is followed by a new subject in strings and bassoons. The new theme is developed with great energy and is followed by a reprise of the original subject newly developed and very impressive in character. A short Coda embodies the principal idea of the introduction, and the overture comes to a close with a passage suggesting the death of Manfred.

Paradise and the Peri

Schumann's secular oratorio, "Paradise and the Peri," was written in 1843, and first performed at the Gewandhaus, Leipsic, December 4 of that year. Its first performance in England was given June 23, 1856, with Madame Jenny Lind-Goldschmidt in the part of the Peri. The text is taken from the second poem in Moore's "Lalla Rookh," and was suggested to Schumann by his friend Emil Flechsig, who had translated the poem. The oratorio is written in three parts, for solo voices, chorus, and orchestra, the principals being the Peri, soprano; the angel, alto; the King of Gazna, bass; a youth, tenor; the horseman, barytone; and the maiden, soprano. The choruses are sung by Indians, angels, houris, and genii of the Nile, and the part of narrator is divided among the various voices.

After a brief orchestral introduction, the narrator, alto, tells the story of the disconsolate Peri at the gate, and introduces her in the first solo ("How blest seem to me, vanished Child of Air!"), a tender, beautiful melody, characterized by romantic sentiment. The narrator, tenor, introduces the angel, who delivers her message to the Peri ("One Hope is thine"), to which the latter replies in a sensuous melody, full of Oriental color ("I know the Wealth hidden in every Urn"). The narrator introduces at this point a quartet ("Oh, beauteous Land"), in which the two trebles, tenor, and bass alternate, followed by a full, powerful chorus ("But crimson now her Rivers ran"). A weird march, fairly barbaric in its effect, indicates the approach of the tyrant of Gazna, and introduces the stirring chorus of the Indians and conquerors ("Hail to Mahmoud!"). The tenor narrator describes the youthful warrior standing alone beside his native river and defying the tyrant. Once more the chorus shouts its greeting to Mahmoud, and then ensues a dialogue in recitative between the two, leading up to the youth's death and a double chorus of lamentation ("Woe! for false flew the Shaft"). The tenor narrator describes the flight of the Peri to catch the last drop of blood shed for liberty; and then all the voices join with the soprano solo in a broad, strong, exultant Finale ("For Blood must holy be"), which is one of the most effective numbers in the work.

The second part opens in the most charming manner. The tenor narrator pictures the return of the Peri with her gift, leading up to the angel's solo ("Sweet is our Welcome"), which preludes a brief choral passage for sixteen female voices. After the narrator's declaration of her disappointment, the scene changes to Egypt, and in a dainty, delicate, three-part chorus the spirits of the Nile are invoked not to disturb the Peri. Her lament is heard ("O Eden, how longeth for thee my Heart!"), and the spirits now weave a gentle, sympathetic strain with her song. A long tenor narration follows ("Now wanders forth the Peri sighing"), describing the pestilence brooding over the Egyptian plains, set to characteristic music. The scene of the maiden dying with her lover is full of pathos, and contains two exquisite numbers — the narrative solo for mezzo-soprano ("Poor Youth, thus deserted"), and the dying love-song of the maiden ("Oh, let me only breathe the Air, Love!"). The scene closes with a sweet and gentle lament for the pair ("Sleep on"), sung by the Peri, followed by the chorus, which joins in the pathetic farewell.

The third part opens with a lovely chorus of houris ("Wreathe ye the Steps to great Allah's Throne"), interspersed with solos and Oriental in its coloring. The tenor narration ("Now Morn is blushing in the Sky"), which is very melodious in character, introduces the angel, who in an alto solo ("Not yet") once more dooms the Peri to wander. Her reply ("Rejected and sent from Eden's Door") is full of despair. The narration is now taken by the barytone in a flowing, breezy strain ("And now o'er Syria's rosy Plain"), which is followed by a charming quartet of Peris ("Say, is it so?"). Once more the barytone intervenes, followed by the Peri; and then the tenor narrator takes up the theme in a stirring description of the boy nestling amid the roses, and the "passion-stained" horseman at the fountain. The alto proclaims the vesper call to prayer, and the tenor reflects upon the memories of the wretched man as he sees the child kneeling. The solo barytone announces his repentance, followed by a quartet and chorus in broad, full harmony ("Oh, blessed Tears of true Repentance!"). The next number is a double one, composed of soprano and tenor solos with chorus ("There falls a Drop on the Land of Egypt"). In an exultant, triumphant strain ("Joy, Joy forever, my Work is done!") the Peri sings her happiness, and the chorus brings the work to a close with the heavenly greeting ("Oh, welcome 'mid the Blessed!").

SCRIABIN

1872 – 1915

Symphony No. 3 in C. Op. 43

SCRIABIN'S Third Symphony, entitled "Le Divin Poème," is written in three sections, Luttes ("Struggles"), Voluptés ("Sensual Pleasures"), and Jeu Divin ("Divine Joy"), though the three sections move along continuously. In the introduction, the main theme appears in the basses answered by the trumpets and taken up in the first violins and wood winds. The first movement begins with this theme in the violins and is taken up in the basses and gradually works up to a climax. As it dies away a hymn-like theme appears in the muted strings. The second melody follows in the wood winds with violins and bass accompaniment, this in turn followed by a theme reminiscent of the "Dresden Amen" in a long tremolo, the trumpets giving out their original theme, to full accompaniment. After recapitulation the main theme appears in the horns, the violins in agitated accompaniment. The close of the section is vehement, gradually dying away and leading to the second section without halt. A slow, tender melody appears in the wood winds and horns and later in the strings, the trumpets repeating their call in the first section. This melody, growing more and more passionate, is broken by a strong passage in the horns which finally give out in unison a joyous measure, the basses sounding the trumpet call inverted, leading to the Finale. Over a lively movement in the strings, the trumpets sound a variation of their call. A second melody follows in the oboes and 'cellos against the harmony of wood winds and horns, which is suddenly interrupted by the return of the first melody. After development the episode of the unison horns and inverted trumpet call returns. Toward the close there is a return of the main theme of the first section and the section ends with the legend and the call in unison.

Le Poème de l'Extase, Op. 54

Scriabin began his "Poem of Ecstasy" at Lausanne, Switzerland, in 1907 and completed it in January, 1908. Modest Altschuler, the conductor of the Russian Symphony Orchestra, visited the composer at his Swiss villa in 1907 and has stated that Scriabin sought to express in his "Poem of Ecstasy" "something of the emotional (and therefore musically communicable) side of his philosophy of life. Scriabin is neither a pantheist nor a theosophist, yet his creed includes ideas somewhat related to each of these schools of thought. There are three divisions in his poem: 1, His soul in the orgy of love; 2, The realization of a fantastical dream; 3, The glory of his own art." It was Mr. Altschuler's orchestra which gave the first interpretation to the "Poem of Ecstasy" at New York, December 10, 1908. Dr. A. Eaglefield Hull, who wrote a work on the Russian composer, declared that the basic idea of Scriabin's work "is the ecstasy of untrammeled action, the joy in creative activity." The prolog (Andante, Lento) contains, Dr. Hull says, "two motives which may be said respectively to symbolize human striving after the ideal and the ego theme (in the clarinet) gradually realizing itself." The main movement (Allegro volante) begins with a theme which is symbolic of the soaring flight of the spirit. With this the two motives of the prolog are combined. The second subject (Lento) includes a violin solo, which is typical of human love. There is a third subject, in the trumpet, imperious in character, which is a summons to the will to rise up. The material is now subjected to development, much of it of a stormy and defiant character. A recapitulation follows, its ecstatic quality culminating in a grandiose epilogue.

F. B.

SIBELIUS

1865 –

Symphony No. 1 in E Minor, Op. 39

1. Allegro energico.
2. Andante ma non troppo lento.
3. Scherzo.
4. Finale quasi una fantasia.

SIBELIUS' First Symphony was composed in 1899 and was first brought to performance about three years later. The first movement opens with a passage for clarinet, accompanied by a roll on the drums and leading to the first theme in the first violins with accompaniment in the other strings. The development leads up through a crescendo to a climax which dies away in the violins and violas, and is followed, after developments of the first theme in the flutes, by the second theme in the wood winds, which gradually reaches a climax. A free fantasie in the first theme, with references to the second, leads up to the recapitulation. A crescendo leads to another climax, again diminishing, and a third climax closes the movement.

The second movement opens with a theme in the first violins and 'cellos, followed by a contrasting melody in the bassoons, accompanied by the wood winds. After development the horns give out another subject with harp arpeggios. The first theme reappears and reaches a climax and the movement ends.

The third movement is in the regular Scherzo form. The last movement opens with a subject based upon the clarinet melody in the first movement, followed by the first theme in the wood winds over a roll of the drums. This material is developed and leads to a fortissimo climax. after which the second theme is stated by the violins. After restatement of the first and second themes, another climax ensues and after its subsidence, the solo clarinet takes up the second theme, which is worked up to another climax, bringing the work to its close.

Symphonic Poem, The Swan of Tuonela, Op. 22

The "Swan of Tuonela" is the third part of the symphonic poem "Lemminkäinen" which is rarely played in its entirety. The score inscription sets forth "Tuonela, the Kingdom of Death, the Hades of Finnish mythology, is surrounded by a broad river of black water and rapid current, in which the Swan of Tuonela glides in majestic fashion and sings." Rosa Newmarch in her biography of the composer has sufficiently described the composition:

"The majestic but intensely sad, swan-like melody is heard as a solo for cor-anglais, accompanied at first by muted strings and the soft roll of drums. Now and then this melody is answered by a phrase given to first 'cello or viola, which might be interpreted as the farewell sigh of some soul passing to Tuonela. For many bars the brass is silent, until suddenly the first horn (muted) echoes a few notes of the swan melody with the most poignant effect. Gradually the music works up to a great climax, indicated *con gran suono,* followed by a treble *pianissimo,* the strings playing with the back of the bow. To this accompaniment, which suggests the faint flapping of pinions, the swan's final phrases are sung. The strings return to the natural bowing and the work ends in one of the characteristic, sighing phrases for 'cello."

Symphonic Poem, Finlandia, Op. 26, No. 7

The symphonic poem "Finlandia" is a tone picture of Finnish life reflected in the sentiment of an exile on his return home. The introduction begins with a brief but vigorous theme in the brasses, responded to in the wood winds, and followed by a pathetic passage in the strings. This material leads to an episode in which the opening theme appears in the strings. A change is made to Allegro and a more cheerful theme appears in the strings, followed by a second subject in the wood winds, afterwards taken by the strings, and then by the 'cello and first violin. The development of this material closes the work.

Valse Triste

The weird "Valse Triste" is part of the music which the composer wrote for a drama called "Kuolema" or "Death." The strange music is thus explained in the program of the strange story:

"It is night. The son, who has been watching beside the bedside of his sick mother, has fallen asleep from sheer weariness. Gradually a ruddy light is diffused through the room: there is a sound of distant music: the glow and the music steal nearer until the strains of a valse melody float distantly to our ears. The sleeping mother awakens, rises from her bed and, in her long white garment, which takes the semblance of a ball dress, begins to move silently and slowly to and fro. She waves her hands and beckons in time to the music, as though she were summoning a crowd of invisible guests. And now they appear, these strange visionary couples, turning and gliding to an unearthly valse rhythm. The dying woman mingles with the dancers; she strives to make them look into her eyes, but the shadowy guests one and all avoid her glance. Then she seems to sink exhausted on her bed and the music breaks off. Presently she gathers all her strength and invokes the dance once more, with more energetic gestures than before. Back come the shadowy dancers, gyrating in a wild, mad rhythm. The weird gaiety reaches a climax; there is a knock at the door, which flies wide open; the mother utters a despairing cry; the spectral guests vanish; the music dies away. Death stands on the threshold."

SINIGAGLIA

1868 –

Overture, Le Baruffe Chiozotte. Op. 32

THE overture to "Le Baruffe Chiozotte" was first performed in 1907, and was inspired by Goldoni's comedy of that name, the story of which is quite simple, being but a picture of life in the fishing village of Chiozzo, with its quarrels among the gossiping women, an episode of the quarrel between the lovers Lucietto and Tita Nane, the interference of the magistrate, who reconciles the lovers, silences the gossips, and restores order, after which the mercurial crowd indulges in a feast of good things and a dance. The overture opens with a theme given out fortissimo in full orchestra. After elaboration a second theme appears in the oboe, eventually extending in the first violins, and carried on with gradually increasing tempo until another theme appears, suggesting that of the opening. With each new theme the time accelerates, and now a tripping passage occurs in the wood winds, leading to a repetition of the second and taken in the violins. The third theme reappears, followed by the first, which is repeated. A brief Coda closes the lively and animated overture, which is as breezy as the picturesque scenes it describes in tones.

Suite Piedmontesi, Op. 36

The "Suite Piedmontesi" of Sinigaglia is not only interesting in itself but also because it is rare that the Italian writers give themselves to composition for the orchestra.

The suite is written in four movements. The first, an Allegretto ("Over Woods and Fields") opens with a theme, which is heard again in the Finale and is followed by a subject in the clarinet and oboe. After a change of time, a new theme appears in the horn, repeated by the 'cello. The solo violin next brings out a new subject, followed by still another theme in the muted first violins. After another change of time a subject is stated in the flute, English horn and harp, after which the horn theme already mentioned returns in the clarinet with string accompaniment, followed by the recurrence of the violin solo, which closes the movement.

The second movement ("A Rustic Dance") opens with an introduction, after which the leading theme is given out in solo violin and oboe. After development, a new theme appears in the violas, 'cellos and wood winds. An episode in the violas and bassoons, leading after development to a repetition of the first theme, closes the movement.

The third movement ("In the Sacred Mountains") begins with a charming theme given out in the horns, with accompaniment in the double basses and 'cellos, following which a bell motive is heard leading to a theme in the clarinet. It is repeated in the violins and the bell motive recurs. The first theme is again heard in much amplified form and with very effective harp accompaniment. The bell motive returns and gently closes the movement.

The final movement ("Piedmontese Carnival") begins after a brief introduction with the opening theme of the first movement given out fortissimo in full orchestra. After a subject in the trumpet and first violins, and another in the trombone and strings, as well as some subsidiaries, have been developed, the first subject ends the movement in spirited style.

SMETANA

1824–1884

Symphonic Poem, Má Vlast

UNDER the general title of "Má Vlast" ("My Fatherland") Smetana, the Bohemian composer, left a cycle of six symphonic poems, dedicated to the city of Prague, entitled "Vyšehrad," "Vltáva," "Sárka," "Zčeskjáh lukûv a hájûr" ("From Bohemia's Fields and Groves"), "Tábor" ("The Hussite Fortress"), and "Blańik," the mountain in which the Hussite warriors sleep, awaiting the resurrection. Of these six the "Vyšehrad," "Vltáva," and "Sárka" are the three usually performed in the concert-room.

The "Vyšehrad" is the first in the cycle, its program in brief being "Thoughts engendered in the poet's mind on beholding the famous fortress and reflecting upon the glorious life there in its palmy days, its subsequent important struggles and final ruin." The movement is free in its form. The introduction begins with a stirring national subject in two harps. After a few measures the remaining instruments take the melody one after the other, the harps still combining, interwoven with trumpet calls gradually increasing in power and leading to a climax in full orchestra. As it dies away, the strings take up an Allegro subject, which is a modification of the original theme in fugal form, bringing this section to a brilliant close. A melodious second subject follows, which is skilfully elaborated. In the conclusion the opening subject returns in modified form."

The second poem, "Vltáva," better known as "The Moldau," is the most beautiful of the series for its melodic charm. It describes the River Moldau, the scenes through which it flows, natural beauties, historic spots, the revels of the wood and water nymphs, and the Rapids of Saint John. It begins with a delicate rippling passage in flutes, with pizzicato accompaniment in the violins and harp, picturing most vividly the movement of the water. It is next taken in the strings over a beautiful melody in first violins, oboe, and bassoon, horns and harp joining in the harmony. Hunting calls are now heard in the horns over the river motive, and as they die away a lively wedding dance is worked up to a climax of gaiety. As it in turn subsides, the wood winds announce sustained harmonies, and the flute with strings, horn, and clarinet accompaniment give out the nymphs' dance, which is followed by an impressive passage in horns, trombones, and tuba. The ripple of the river is heard again, and gradually leads up to the description of the rapids, reaching a powerful fortissimo. Then with extended decrescendo the movement, which is one of expressive beauty throughout, comes to a close.

"Sárka," the third of the poems, is based upon the story of the Bohemian Amazon. Disappointed in love, she swears vengeance upon the whole race of men. The knight Ctirad takes the field against her, and as his warriors are advancing finds Sárka bound to a tree. She cunningly pretends to have been maltreated by her sisters. Overcome by her beauty and desiring to possess her, he sets her free. During a carousal of his soldiers, Sárka gives a horn signal, to which her companions in the forest respond. Falling upon the soldiers, sleeping after their revels, they slay them all. The poem opens with a theme for violins describing Sárka's rage against men. A second subject of a light, simple character describes the march of Ctirad's warriors through the forest. This is interrupted by a sudden outcry twice heard. A duet for 'cello and clarinet follows, giving place evidently to a love passage, which is freely developed and followed by a fanfare, introducing another theme of a jubilant character. As it dies away, a lovely melody is sung by the clarinets, describing Sárka's summons to her sisters. The concluding part of the movement is marked Frenetico, and is indeed a frenzy of instrumentation, portraying Sárka's revenge.

Overture to The Sold Bride

"Die verkaufte Braut" ("The Sold Bride"), one of the most successful and beautiful of modern operas, was first produced in 1895. Its overture was first known as "Lustspiel," or "Comedy Overture," and is considered the gem of the work. The story of the opera is a simple one. Hans, the step-son of the peasant Micha, after being driven from home, returns and falls in love with Marenka. Her mother consents to the proposal of Kezal, the marriage broker, that she shall marry Wenzel, Hans' half-brother. Then the broker offers a bribe to Hans if he will abandon his claim. Hans agrees provided Marenka will marry "the son of Micha." Marenka is grieved at the seeming abandonment, but at last Hans reveals himself and all are happy. The first theme of the overture is announced in the violins, violas, 'cellos, and wood winds in unison, with a stately accompaniment of chords in the brasses with tympani. This theme is most ingeniously elaborated in fugal form and worked up to a climax, after which it is given out in unison as in the beginning. The second theme is announced in the oboe with clarinet, bassoon, horn, and second violin accompaniment. It is very brief, and is followed by a charming theme in violins and 'cellos. The first theme then returns in the wood winds, and next in the strings, whereupon the fugal elaboration is resumed, leading to a fortissimo. After further development the first theme returns in the same form as in the beginning. Further development follows, after which the Coda, based on the first theme, brings the overture to an animated close.

SOWERBY

1895 –

Overture, Comes Autumn Time

LEO SOWERBY, who was born at Grand Rapids, Michigan, received his musical training at the hands of Arthur Olaf Anderson (composition) and Calvin Lampert (piano). In 1921 he was awarded the Prix de Rome, the first American composer to win it. The overture "Comes Autumn Time" was in the first instance composed for organ and, in that form, was produced by Eric DeLamarter at an organ recital given at the Fourth Presbyterian Church, Chicago, in October, 1916. Mr. Sowerby then arranged the piece for orchestra and it was performed for the first time the following year at a concert of Sowerby's works given in Chicago under the direction of DeLamarter. The score, which was published with a dedication to Alice DeLamarter in 1920, contains on a flyleaf the poem "Autumn" by Bliss Carman, beginning: "Now when the time of fruit and grain is come."

The work begins (Joyously, animato e giocoso) with the principal theme in the bass clarinet, horns and lowest strings. A transitional passage for the wood winds leads to the second subject, which is announced by the flutes and celesta, the harp and clarinet lightly accompanying it. The development section mainly is concerned with the principal theme. In the recapitulation the second subject makes its appearance first, the principal theme following later. The overture closes with a Coda of brilliant character, based on the second theme with occasional suggestions of the first.

SPOHR

1784 – 1859

Overture to Jessonda

THE overture to the opera "Jessonda," the text by Edouard Gehe, and based upon Lemière's "Veuve de Malabar," was first produced in 1823. The story in brief is as follows: Jessonda, the widow of a Rajah, has been devoted to the flames. Although she was forced to marry, and had previously pledged her hand to a Portuguese officer, she obeys the custom of the country and accepts her fiery doom. At this time the Portuguese are besieging the city, and the officer, her lover, hearing of her intended sacrifice, scales the walls with his followers and rescues the would-be victim. The overture begins with an introduction in which tender harmonies in the wood winds and horns are followed by melodious passages in the horns, and afterwards in clarinets and bassoons, with a pizzicato accompaniment in the strings, the subject being subsequently employed in the scene of the Rajah's funeral. A short transition for full orchestra leads to the second theme, which is announced in the horns, with a counter theme in the first violins, all of which material is regularly developed. After elaboration the first theme reappears and is developed, and then leads to a return of the second theme in the clarinet and bassoon. After further development an animated Coda closes the overture.

STANFORD

1852 – 1924

Symphony No. 3, in F Minor (Irish). Op. 28

1. Allegro moderato.
2. Allegro molto vivace.
3. Andante con moto.
4. Allegro moderato.

STANFORD'S so-called Irish Symphony was completed in 1887, and was first performed June 27 of that year in one of Herr Richter's London concerts. The first movement opens with a melodious theme in the string quartet, unison and pianissimo, supported in the winds. After a short development it is repeated in a powerful crescendo in full orchestra. A phrase from the theme is then treated, and leads to the second, given out in the 'cellos in cantabile style and then taken up in the violins. The usual repetition follows, and closes the first part. The second part opens with a working-up of the first theme, followed by the second with ingenious variations. Both themes also appear in the Coda closing the movement.

The second movement, which takes the place of the customary Scherzo, begins at once with a first theme in jig-like movement in the first violins. After its development a short episode follows, given out by the wood winds, which leads up to a genuine peasant melody. The Trio opens with an attractive theme, leading to the Coda, in which the jig returns, closing the movement in spirited style.

The slow movement after some introductory harp arpeggios opens with a sombre, pathetic theme in the flutes and clarinets, several times repeated, and assigned to various instruments until the oboe appears with a second theme, the accompanying figure of which is based upon the old Irish song, "The Lament of the sons of Usnach." Fresh subjects follow with elaborate treatment, leading to a general pause, which prepares the way for the "Lament" theme. A reminiscence of the beginning of the movement and the harp arpeggios furnish the close.

The Finale is based upon two Irish songs — the first of which ("Remember the Glories of Brian the brave") constitutes the first theme. After its development a fresh modulation leads up to the second theme in string orchestra with bassoons, horn, and contrabasses, pizzicato, followed by a melodious figure which prepares the way for further treatment of the thematic material already presented. The second of the Irish themes mentioned above is now given out by three trumpets pianissimo with tremolo accompaniment of violins. After the development of this theme occurs the ordinary reprise, and a skilfully treated Coda concludes the symphony.

STOCK

1872–

Symphony in C Minor

1. Adagio. Allegro ma non troppo.
2. Scherzo.
3. Andante cantabile.
4. Finale.

THE Symphony in C minor, the first work of this kind by Frederick A. Stock, conductor of the Chicago Symphony Orchestra, was finished in 1909 and first performed by that orchestra December 31 of that year. The composer has briefly described the program of his work as illustrating human life with its sorrows and joys, the struggle against fate, despair at the futility of existence, and the hope of final victory. The first movement pictures various phases of the struggle; the second, the joys of life; the third, reminiscences of happiness; and the fourth, the motto, "Vorwärts, aufwärts" ("Forward, upward").

The first movement has an Adagio introduction in which the principal theme is stated, followed by a suggestion of the second subject in solo viola, 'cello, and oboe, the trombones holding the opening motive against it. Three chords in full orchestra and a kettle-drum roll introduce the main movement, Allegro ma non troppo. The principal subject is heard in the 'cellos and double basses, eventually reinforced by violas and wood winds. The theme is then taken in first violins and higher wood winds with a subsidiary passage in the basses and lower wood winds. The second subject is next suggested accompanied by development of the first, which at last is given out in full orchestra. After elaborate treatment of the two themes development follows, closing with an outburst in full orchestra and recapitulation. The principal theme is stated briefly in full orchestra, the second entering in the violas and English horn, with the 'cellos pizzicato against it. It is then taken by the violins and leads to the Coda, opening with the second theme in the oboe against the first in the English horn and tuba. The two themes are elaborately treated, at last reaching a climax, and the first movement comes to its close with the principal theme prestissimo.

The opening theme of the Scherzo appears in the wood winds continued in the strings. In its treatment a subsidiary theme occurs for solo violin. Development of this material follows, with the subsidiary theme in a second form. The second subject is given out in the 'cellos and violas, supported by the lower wood winds, horns, and harp. After development, recapitulation begins with a repetition of the first theme in full orchestra. The second follows at once fortissimo in the brasses and 'cellos. In the Coda the opening theme is elaborately treated, leading to a climax. There are suggestions of the subsidiary theme and the second, a Presto closing the movement with a development of the first theme.

The third movement opens with a subject in the first violins. A climax is reached and the second enters in the 'cellos and first horn. After elaboration the brasses give out the first theme and another climax occurs, followed by recapitulation, in which, after elaborate treatment of the two themes, the music grows more and more intense, at last reaching a fortissimo, the movement finally closing tranquilly.

The principal theme of the last movement, illustrating the "Upward" of the motto, is given out in unison in the violins and violas and is followed by a suggestion of the opening theme in the first movement in the violas. This is presented at once in full orchestra and developed, after which the second subject enters in the first violins. The "Forward" motive, which occurs in the introduction, is played by solo trumpet, violas pizzicato. In the treatment of this material a tremendous climax is reached. The development begins quietly with the opening notes of the principal theme of the first movement in fugal form beginning in the 'cellos. The development is most elaborate and leads to an intense climax, followed by recapitulation. The Coda is equally elaborate in its presentation of the "Upward" and "Forward" themes, and with a final statement of the second theme of the opening movement, the symphony closes.

Symphonic Variations

The score of "Symphonic Variations," the earliest work of this composer, was first performed by the Chicago Symphony Orchestra, of which at the time of its composition Mr. Stock was a member, and of which, since the death of Theodore Thomas, he has been conductor. It is dedicated to Mr. Thomas. It is based upon a theme from which he has developed thirteen variations and a Finale. The theme is given out in the 'cellos and basses in octaves, accompanied in bass clarinet and bassoons. The first variation is for all the strings, harp, and deeper wood winds. In the second, the theme is strongly accentuated, mainly in the trumpets and heavier brasses, with imitations in the rest of the orchestra and interruptions from the strings and lighter wood winds. The third is lively in character, a solo clarinet and violins having a duo with pizzicato string accompaniment. In the fourth, the theme appears as a chorale in the deeper strings and wood winds, the fifth being treated exclusively for wind and percussion instruments. The sixth is constructed of fragments of the theme in the strings, leading to a climax, gradually closing pianissimo. The seventh is a lyric intermezzo, followed by strong rhythmical passages in the eighth and ninth. The tenth is a Valse lento, and the eleventh a Marziale, scored for brasses and drums alone. The twelfth is in strong contrast to the Marziale, and the last, elaborated contrapuntally, works up to a vigorous climax, subsiding to pianissimo with rolls on the kettle-drums. The Finale begins with soft harmonics in the deeper wind instruments, after which the theme reappears. Its exposition leads to an impressive restatement, closing the work.

Symphonic Waltz

The "Symphonic Waltz" was written at Mr. Stock's summer home at Winona Lake in 1907. The following cheery statement by the composer concerning the significance of his work will be of interest:

"Some years ago Theodore Thomas played a very meritorious work by Alexander Ritter, which also was called a 'Symphonic Waltz'; and this title made such a deep impression upon the writer of these lines that after that time he contemplated most seriously composing first a 'Symphony' and then a 'Waltz.' But it happened that he was unable to complete the symphony before the commencement of this season, and for this reason he thought it best to combine these two titles and compose something that would suit them both — and the listener as well.

"As to the waltz itself, we don't think that it should stand in need of either comparison or analysis, although it is meant to be symphonic — or at least pretends to be so. It is written in the key of D major and in 3-4 time, just like the 'Beautiful Blue Danube' by Johann Strauss, but the themes are treated in more elaborate fashion. We trust fully what is good in it will make itself felt in true waltz-like fashion — let us say spontaneously, and that its pretentious title will fully protect it against undue or unbecoming popularity.

"Frequently we have been asked to whom the waltz was to be dedicated — a question which until now has not been answered satisfactorily. It is not more than natural that a composer should feel inclined to dedicate all the good things he writes (and in his opinion, of course, all his things are good, and more than that) to his own beloved self, and so the writer of this waltz had at first intended to do — when the happy thought occurred to him that it would be more appropriate, and also more unique, to dedicate the work under discussion (in whose behalf too much has been said already) 'To all his friends.'"

Symphonic Sketch, A Summer Evening

This nature sketch was written by Mr. Stock at Twin Lakes, Wis., and was originally intended to be the second movement of a suite to be called "The Seasons." At the opening, after an introduction, the principal theme is suggested in the clarinet, eventually leading to the principal subject in the first violins and violas. A continuing section is given in the oboes and shortly is taken up by two solo violins with a flute passage imitating the song of the nightingale. The main theme is then sung in the horns and 'cellos, with a counterpoint against it in the violins, violas, and some of the wood winds. A solo passage for the strings, based on the first theme, leads to a solo for first violin over which the quail is heard in the oboes and the cuckoo in the clarinet. At last a climax is reached, the sketch closing pianissimo.

STRAUSS

1864–

Symphony in F Minor

1. Allegro ma non troppo, un poco maestoso.
2. Scherzo. Presto.
3. Andante cantabile.
4. Allegro assai, molto appassionato.

RICHARD STRAUSS, so well known by his operas and symphonic poems, has written three symphonies, of which the one in F minor is best known. It opens with two phrases in the wood winds, leading to the first theme in the first violins and violas. After slight development, the first subsidiary leads to a melodious subject in full orchestra. The second theme appears in the clarinet and bassoon, repeated by violins, and is briefly developed. The first theme then returns and closes the first part of the movement. A free fantasie follows, leading to a climax, and the third part begins in the clarinet and bassoon, and closes with a long Coda.

The Scherzo is noticeable for the appearance of a cantabile theme. The Trio begins with a theme in the violas, 'cellos, clarinets, and bassoons, the flutes, oboes, horns, and violins at the same time carrying a subsidiary figure. The Scherzo repeats after the Trio and the movement closes with a short Coda.

The first theme of the third movement appears in the strings and is subsequently developed in the wood winds and horns. The second is a trumpet call over the other brasses in harmony, each call followed by passages in the strings and wood winds. The third is a plaintive melody in the horns and bassoons, with string accompaniment, and is at once followed by the fourth in the first violins and 'cellos. These themes are worked up in the second part of the movement, the first, with suggestion of the trumpet call, furnishing the material for the Coda.

The last movement opens with a discordant effect between the violins and violas on the one hand and the wood winds on the other. Two themes elaborately developed follow in regular course, with their subsidiaries, and the Coda recalls the themes in the preceding parts.

An Alpine Symphony

The so-called "Alpine Symphony" in reality a symphonic poem, was first produced in Berlin in 1915, by an orchestra of extraordinary size, the score calling for one hundred and sixteen instruments. It is program music from first to last and is played continuously. Pictorial descriptions follow each other rapidly. In the opening Lento night begins in the muted strings and bassoons followed by the Mountain motive in the brasses. After development sunrise appears in the orchestra fortissimo. This is introductory to the main movement, "The Ascent," which opens with a theme in the lower strings dominating the whole work. Hunting horns signal the "Entrance to the Forest." This is followed by a section "Wandering by the Brook," and soon we arrive at the "Waterfall," imitated by rolls on the cymbals. Other divisions, "Apparition," "On Flowery Meadows," and "On the Alm," follow, and by this time the hearer is "Lost in the Thicket and the Underwood" of the low strings and wood winds. After emerging therefrom one finds himself "On the Glacier" and experiences "Dangerous Moments," but at last reaches "the Summit," the feat being celebrated by four trombones set off against the other wind instruments and strings tremolo. The oboe in a tender sort of melody brings some relief, but now the scene changes. Clouds indicated by scale passages in the muted strings appear but are dispersed by the sun, as set forth by first violins and organ. An "Elegie" follows in the strings supported by organ. The kettle-drums and bass drum announce the approach of a storm which bursts in musical fury, rather than grandeur, by the crashes, howls, and groans of the full orchestra accentuated by wind and thunder machines. At last the distracted traveler begins his descent, the sun sets, and night comes on by the use of the same material which opened the work.

Tone Poem, Don Juan, Op. 20 *

"Don Juan," the first published of Richard Strauss' tone-poems, was written in November, 1880, and performed for the first time at Weimar, near the close of the same year. The subject of the work is taken from a poem of the same name, written by the Hungarian poet, Lenau. The hero is a Don who is in love with the feminine principle. He is devoted to the adoration of the whole feminine world rather than the pursuit of the individual. At last he becomes pessimistic. The pursuit of beauty palls. "Now it is o'er, and calm all round, above me; sheer death is every wish; all hopes o'ershrouded." At last he is satisfied to give up life itself. In the illustration of this story, Strauss' music opens with a variety of restless themes, occasionally melodious in bits, but more frequently discordant without resolution. Don Juan makes his appearance to a somewhat brilliant melody. This is followed by desultory love episodes, some of which musically are as unsatisfactory to the hearer as the episodes themselves were to the hero. They invariably end in a restless manner. Don Juan in desperation plunges into a gen-

* In presenting the analysis of "Don Juan," as well as of the remaining tone-poems by Richard Strauss, no attempt will be made to consider them in detail. The instrumentation is much too complicated and the whole orchestral scheme too involved and unusual to allow it without occupying undue space as well as voluminous notation. The analysis in each case therefore will present a general view of the works.

eral carnival of feminine and vinous revels, depicted by music intended to be bacchanalian, but unintelligible without a detailed program. The debauch closes in a manner indicating the hero's fate, and at last his end is announced by the trumpet.

Macbeth. Op. 23

Although "Macbeth" was the first tone-poem composed by Strauss, its opus number follows that of "Don Juan." Contrary to his usual custom, the composer has furnished no key to its contents except the title and occasional hints in the score. He evidently did not intend a setting of the drama, but rather musical portraits of Macbeth and Lady Macbeth, and these portraits, it must be confessed, are presented in the loudest of colors. After a motive which runs through the whole work, given out by the violins, the personal motive of Macbeth appears. It is accompanied by a counter theme and leads to a third theme, the meaning of which is left to the imagination. This prepares the way for a vigorous passage in flutes and clarinets which the score annotation intimates is the Lady Macbeth motive. The motive soon yields to a more passionate one given out by the violins. This, when thoroughly developed, gives place again to the Lady Macbeth motive. The latter, however, makes but a brief reappearance and is succeeded by a sweet and very gracious melody by the violins, which at last joins itself to another of somewhat similar character, the two progressing through unique development to the close.

Tod und Verklärung. Op. 24

"Tod und Verklärung" ("Death and Transfiguration") was written in 1889 and first performed at Eisenach in June of the next year. The composer has given the clew to its meaning in a poem by Alexander Ritter, printed on the flyleaf of the score, though, singularly enough, the poem was written after the author had heard the music. The poem describes the sleep of a sick man "who a moment since with death wildly, desperately has struggled"; the renewal of the struggle, life and death wrestling for supremacy and silence again; the delirium in which the events of his life pass in review in the mind of the sufferer; then the final struggle, followed by the transfiguration, in which he triumphs over death. The opening of the musical description is a Largo, low toned in color and restless, but with occasional melodious episodes. It is followed by strangely discordant passages evidently intended to represent the renewal of the struggle, but at this point the music assumes a more melodious character as the memories of youth come back. In the final struggle the musical fury begins again, growing more and more indefinite and discordant until the end comes and the din ceases. The transfiguration music which closes the work is extremely impressive and full of that majestic beauty which is at Strauss' command — when he elects to display it.

Till Eulenspiegel. Op. 28

"Till Eulenspiegel" was first performed at Cologne, November 5, 1895. The music represents the eccentric career of a roving Merry Andrew, the droll tricks which he played, and his final expiation upon the gallows for practical jokes which at last became too brutal to be endured. In the old legend of Till, however, he does not come to the gallows, but escapes it by trickery. Strauss, however, ruthlessly sacrifices him in the close with explosive music. The themes in this work typify the hero in various situations, and their development shows the droll tricks which he plays. His ride through the market-place and the dismay of the market-women as their wares are scattered are accompanied by imitative music. Unctuous themes display him as a clerical imposter and tender passages in the violins, clarinets, and flutes tell of his love episodes. Characteristic music shows him fooling the university doctors. At last ominous tones in the trombones and horns indicate his approaching doom. He pays no attention to them, however, until hollow rolls of the drum announce his arrest. His fear then is clearly indicated. The bassoons, horns, trombones, and tubas unmistakably tell of his death, and his soul takes its flight to twitterings of the flutes. A brief sort of in memoriam episode closes the music, as droll as the tricks of its subject.

Thus Spake Zarathustra. Op. 30

"Thus Spake Zarathustra," though based upon a philosophical subject, is one of the most popular of the Strauss tone-poems, perhaps because it has been heard more frequently than the others. It was inspired by a "prose poem" of the same name, written by Friedrich Nietzsche. The details of the philosophical story of Zarathustra, or Zoroaster, as he is more familiarly known, are too involved for use in this connection and perhaps are not needed for enjoyment of the music, which is very impressive and grows upon the listener by successive hearings. Strauss has liberally annotated his score with the headings of chapters in the Nietzsche text.

The work opens with a stately theme in trumpets leading to a powerful climax in full orchestra and organ which is the most impressive feature of the tone-poem. Then follow new themes under the headings of "Back World's Men" and "Great Longing," the music descriptive of Zarathustra's "going down" to teach the doctrine of the Overman and the "Longings" of those in the Back World for higher things. Another theme, given out by the violins, sings of their "Delights and Passions," followed by the "Grave Song"—a tender melody in the oboe which is worked up in conjunction with the "Longings" theme. The despair of science is treated as a fugal episode based upon the opening motive, followed by furious and at times dissonant outbursts in the full orchestra. An episode, "The Convalescent," is devoted to an optimistic view of humanity. This is followed by the jubilations of the Overman expressed in the "Dance Song," which is anything but terpsichorean in character. "To the general" it must be "caviar." At last twelve strokes of the bell usher in the "Song of the Night Wanderer" and a short passage — the very spirit of perplexity and doubt — being set in two keys, involving a mysterious discord, closes this extraordinary music which illlustrates such vague and mystic philosophical gropings.

Don Quixote. Op. 35

"Don Quixote" is absolute program-music and program-music run wild in which Strauss has well-nigh exhausted the ordinary orchestral effects and invented new ones. It is written in variation form and personal motives are assigned to Don Quixote, in the 'cello, and to Sancho Panza, in the viola, the first appearing in the introduction which describes knightly feeling and the hero's resolve to become a knight. But as Don Quixote pursues his studies of chivalry and realizes the duties as well as the pleasures it entails, he turns out a madman as explained by the most incoherent of dissonances.

His journey now begins and a series of pictures describing his adventures follows, in variation form. It first depicts his attack upon the windmills, the rushing of the air represented in violin trills and strange wood wind effects, and his own downfall in the wood winds emphasized in the ever-useful kettle-drums. In the second he makes his furious onslaught upon the herd of sheep whose frightened bleating is clearly discernible in the muted brasses. The third noisily tells of the dispute of the knight and his squire over chivalry. In the fourth we behold him making his attack upon the pilgrims as they chant their ecclesiastical music, mistaking them for robbers. The fifth and sixth tell of his longings for his Dulcinea and the trick which Sancho plays upon him by pointing out a homely peasant woman as the real object of his raptures. In the seventh occurs the absurd episode of the supposed journey of the Don and his squire through the air, the wind effect being made in harp, kettle-drum, flutes, and an ingenious wind machine. The eighth, a Barcarole, describes the ride to the enchanted boat, and the ninth his encounter with the two priests. In the tenth he has his last adventure with the Knight of the White Moon, which ends his knightly career. In the Finale his reason returns, but a shiver in the violins tells of his rapidly approaching death. It is followed by strange harmonies, and at last the 'cello marks the end of his follies and of his life.

Ein Heldenleben. Op. 40

"Ein Heldenleben" ("A Hero-Life") was first performed at Frankfort, March 3, 1899. It tells the story of a hero, his struggles with mankind, with love, with the enemy on the battle-field, his development of high thought, his intellectual and peaceful achievements, and at last his departure from the world.

There is no introduction. The opening theme, horn and strings, describes the characteristics of the hero, and other motives referring to attributes of his nature also appear and are worked up to an impressive climax. The contests with his fellow-men are depicted in a genuine illustration of philosophy and ethics in music. The love-music is charming throughout and closes with a duet in violin and oboe. The fourth section of the work describes the clash and fury of battle, which concludes with a splendid song of victory whose pealing harmony is fairly majestic. Then follows the hero's peace conquests in which the composer has introduced themes from nearly all his tone-poems, his opera "Guntram," and some of his songs. The last section relates to the hero's passage from this world, preluded with reminiscences and closing with a mighty outburst in the whole orchestra — fit tribute to the passing of a hero. The work is grand in its conception and treatment, and in some passages rises to inspiration.

Sinfonia Domestica, Op. 53

"Sinfonia Domestica" ("Domestic Symphony") describes a day in family life. It contains three themes, one for the father, one for the mother, and one for the child, and subsidiary themes are accepted as representing "the sisters, the cousins, and the aunts." It is a far step downwards from "Zarathustra" and "Heldenleben," and has not even the dignity of "Don Quixote" in the sheep episode, or the air ride. It lacks both quality and dignity. A great conductor, to whom Strauss sent this work, and who had introduced most of his tone-poems in America, made to the author the pertinent criticism that a composer should never intrude his personality or his domestic affairs upon the public. He should have remembered Schumann's words: "A composer must not show his heart to the public."

Symphonic Fantasia, From Italy. Op. 16

"From Italy," the first of Strauss' orchestral tone-poems, was written in 1886, after the composer had made a visit to Rome. It is divided into four movements: 1. "On the Campagna." 2. "Amid Rome's Ruins." 3. "On the Shore of Sorrento." 4. "Neapolitan Folk Life." The opening movement describes the solitude of the Campagna, with incidental allusions to historical events of which it has been the scene. After a somewhat extended introductory passage a theme is given out by the first violins and 'cellos, with accompaniment in clarinet, bassoon, and horn, with figures in the second violins and violas, and chords in harp. After development the clarinet takes the theme, with responses in horn and bassoon, the movement dying away softly. The composer has given this additional program note to the second movement: "Fantastic pictures of vanished splendor. Feelings of sadness and longing in the midst of brightest surroundings." It is constructed in sonata form with two themes. In the opening, the strings give out chords sustained against a figure in the trumpets, which constitutes the principal theme of the movement. Following the development the first violins have a fresh melody, which is worked up in the strings and wood winds, leading to a fortissimo chord in full orchestra, interrupted by trombone and trumpet, suggesting the opening theme. The latter is then taken in the 'cellos and extends to full orchestra, and is developed, the movement ending with a recapitulation of the first and second themes. The third movement is absolutely free in its construction, and evidently is intended for a description of the sea rippled by the wind. It is scored almost entirely for the strings, against which are heard boat songs and bits of melody in the wood winds. The last movement is a gay Allegro, opening with clashes of cymbals. It is constructed mainly upon a Neapolitan folk song, given out in the violas and 'cellos with horn and bassoon accompaniment, the brasses and kettle-drums accenting the time. Another theme follows in the first violins and 'cellos, after the development of which the folk song reappears in the bassoon, then passes to English horn, and thence to first and second violins, flute, and oboe. After its development the Coda closes the work with suggestions of the folk song.

Love Scene from Feuersnot, Op. 50

"Feuersnot" ("The Need of Fire"), Strauss' second opera, was produced November 21, 1901, at Dresden. The libretto, written by Ernst von Wolzogen, was based upon an old Dutch legend which Strauss had discovered in Wilhelm Wolff's "Niederländische Sagen" (1842). The story concerns one Kunrad, a mysterious individual who lives a life of solitude and of whom little is known. Outside his house children are gathering wood from various householders, for it is the custom on Midsummer eve to build bonfires, over which lovers leap. The children knock at Kunrad's door and he determines to forego his solitude and to take part in the festivities. As he goes out Kunrad's gaze falls on the burgomaster's lovely daughter, Diemut. He celebrates his return to the world by kissing her on the mouth. Diemut, furious at this affront, goes into her father's house and, seating herself at her balcony, nurses a scheme of vengeance. From the street below Kunrad sees the girl and asks to be allowed to come up to her. Diemut, looking over the balcony, perceives the basket in which wood has been let down to the children. She tells the man that if he will get into the basket she will draw him up. Kunrad does as he is bid, but when half-way up, Diemut, pretending that she can pull no more, leaves him dangling. The crowd now derides the young man; but Kunrad, too, is angry. He is a magician and, weaving a spell, he calls upon magic aid and every light and fire in the town becomes extinguished. Meanwhile, he climbs up the rope into Diemut's balcony and tells the crowd below that this punishment which he has brought about has been the result of Diemut's hoax and only by her penance can the fires be lit again. Diemut has secretly loved the young wizard and she appears at the balcony and draws him into the room. It is at this point that the Love Scene begins. The music begins slowly and tranquilly, but gradually increases in longing and passion. When the latter is at its greatest height, every fire is rekindled in the town.

F. B.

STRAVINSKY

1882–

Suite from the Ballet L'Oiseau de Feu

IGOR STRAVINSKY (born at Orianienbaum, near St. Petersburg) was a pupil of Rimsky-Korsakov, who was not altogether approving of the ultra-modernistic tendencies which Stravinsky disclosed even in his student period. It was concerning the music in "L'Oiseau de Feu" ("The Fire Bird") that Rimsky-Korsakov said, after his pupil had played it to him: "Look here; stop playing this horrid thing, otherwise I might begin to enjoy it."

"L'Oiseau de Feu" was written as a ballet and produced for the first time at the Opéra, Paris, June 25, 1910, by the company directed by Serge Diaghilev. The Fire Bird was mimed and danced by Mlle. Karsavina; Fokine was Ivan Tsarevich, and Boulgakow, the Immortal Kastcheï. The story of the ballet, which was arranged for Stravinsky by Michel Fokice, was drawn from Russian fairy-lore. Upon the same story Rimsky-Korsakov wrote his opera "Kastcheï the Immortal." The plot is concerned with Ivan Tsarevich who, wandering in the night, discovers in the darkness the Fire Bird plucking apples made of gold from a silver tree. He captures the Fire Bird, but when she entreats him for her release, permits her to escape, after receiving from her a glowing feather. As the dawn comes Ivan perceives thirteen maidens emerging from an ancient castle and, after plucking the golden apples, throw them to each other. The castle is the home of the monstrous Kastcheï, who turns into stone every traveler that approaches his domain. Ivan endeavors to penetrate the stronghold and after entering the gate, is confronted by a horde of monsters.

Kastcheï tries to petrify the young man, but the Fire Bird suddenly arrives and wards off the ogre's magic. The company of monsters breaks into an infernal dance. The charms exercised by the Fire Bird prevail and Kastcheï is defeated and killed. The castle suddenly vanishes and its beauteous prisoners are freed. One of them, the lovely Tsarevna, is united in marriage to Ivan.

Stravinsky originally scored his ballet for a very extensive orchestra. In 1919 he issued the concert suite, having scored it for a somewhat smaller instrumental aggregation: two flutes, two oboes, English horn, two clarinets, two bassoons, four horns, two trumpets, three trombones, bass tuba, kettle-drums, bass drum, cymbals, triangle, xylophone, harp, piano and strings.

The suite begins with the Introduction to the ballet, this leading without pause into "The Fire Bird and her Dance." The second movement is "Dance of the Princesses." The third is the "Infernal dance of the Subjects of Kastcheï." The fourth section is entitled "Berceuse" and leads without pause into the finale, whose music in the ballet is concerned with the disappearance of Kastcheï's castle and the revivification of its petrified occupants and the general rejoicing of the multitude at the defeat and death of the monster.

F. B.

Suite from the Ballet Petrouchka

Stravinsky composed his ballet "Petrouchka" in 1911, the work having been completed at Rome in May. The scenario was by Alexandre Benois, to whom the composer dedicated the work. The first performance was at the Châtelet, Paris, June 13, 1911, and the principal dancers were Tamar Karsavina and Nijinsky, respectively the Ballerina and Petrouchka. The ballet is concerned with the existence of the lower classes in Russia, among whom passion and jealousy and misery and death are common. Petrouchka is a puppet or polichinelle, whose characterization is at once humorous and tragic. He and other characters — the Moor, the Ballerina — are also puppets for whom the Old Charlatan has found souls. The scene is the Admiralty Square, St. Petersburg, on Shrovetide, in 1830, during the progress of a carnival. The music describes the bustle of the fair and the sounds of a hand-organ are heard. The Old Charlatan, with his puppet show, draws attention to his entertainment by playing florid passages on the flute. The curtain of the puppet show rises and discloses the Ballerina, the Moor and Petrouchka. The latter strives to win the love of the Ballerina, but he is sensitive and shrinking and has less success in winning the fancy of his lady than the Moor, who is callous and brutal. The merriment of the fair reaches a climax. Coachmen and nursemaids dance folk dances; a showman in charge of a performing bear crosses the scene; masqueraders rush in; a drunken merchant plays the accordion. In the midst of the revelry the curtains of the puppet show suddenly part and Petrouchka, the Moor and the Ballerina dart out. Petrouchka is pursued by the jealous Moor, who stabs him with his saber. The crowd watches Petrouchka's dying agonies, but the Old Charlatan holds him up before the crowd and shakes him to show that Petrouchka is only a puppet after all. The people disperse and the showman is left alone, dragging Petrouchka toward the puppet theater; but, looking up, he perceives the specter of the slain doll rise above the booth with livid face and threatening gestures. The Old Charlatan rushes in a panic from the stage. At the time "Petrouchka" was produced it was freely stated that the action of the puppet play hid a symbolic meaning — Petrouchka representing the Russian people, suffering from the misery and tragedy of Czarism, the latter represented by the cruel Old Charlatan, and the Moor his brutal agents, the Cossacks.

The following are the various sections of the suite: I. Fair in Festival Week; Russian Dance. II. Petrouchka at home. III. Toward Evening; Dance of the Nurses; Dance of Coachmen and Grooms.

F. B.

Symphonic Poem, Chant du Rossignol

The composition of his "lyric play" "Le Rossignol" ("The Nightingale") was begun by Stravinsky in 1909. Having completed the first act, the composer ceased from further labor on the work, in consequence of the indisposition which he felt, to cultivate the lyric drama. "I can write," he said to M. D. Calvocoressi, "music to words, namely, songs; or music to action, namely, ballets. But the co-operation of words, music and action is a thing that daily becomes more inadmissible to my mind. And even if I should finish 'The Nightingale,' I do not think that I shall ever attempt to write another work of that kind." Stravinsky returned to "Le Rossignol," however, and completed it in 1914. The work, whose text was based upon Hans Christian Andersen's fairy tale, was produced at the Opéra, Paris, in May, 1914, Emile Cooper having been the conductor. At a later period Stravinsky turned the opera into a ballet which, with choreography by Massine, was performed at the Opéra, Paris, February 2, 1920. In this ballet version Stravinsky changed the title to "Chant du Rossignol" and made considerable alterations in the inner economy of the piece, giving the voice parts to instruments and revising the instrumentation. As a symphonic poem "Chant du Rossignol" was first performed at a Koussewitzky concert, Paris, October 26, 1922. In America it was first given by the Philadelphia Orchestra, Philadelphia, October 19, 1923. When the symphonic poem was given at Philadelphia Mr. Lawrence Gilman, the editor of the admirable program books of the Philadelphia Orchestra, drew attention to the fact that although no programmatic explanations were printed on the published score, Stravinsky had authorized the use of a "program" which would make the symphonic poem intelligible to the listener. In giving quotation to this, it should be stated that although the matter is set forth in three main sections, the music is played without any pauses:

(a) *The Palace of the Chinese Emperor.*—Extraordinary preparations had been made for the reception of the Nightingale, whose world-wide reputation as an incomparable singer had won for it a command performance at court. The palace had been elaborately decorated. The walls and floors, which were of porcelain, shone in the rays of a hundred thousand golden lamps. The corridors were adorned with the loveliest bell-flowers, which tinkled merrily in the currents of air stirred by the running about of the excited courtiers through the halls and rooms. . . . The Nightingale was placed on a golden perch in the great hall. A Chinese March announced the ceremonious entrance of the Emperor.

(b) *The Two Nightingales.*—The Nightingale sang so beautifully that tears came to the eyes of the Emperor. . . . Even the lackeys and the chambermaids showed the liveliest satisfaction—which is saying a great deal, for these persons are not easily pleased. . . . A trumpet fanfare announced the arrival of the envoys from the Emperor of Japan, bearing as a gift to the Emperor of China a mechanical nightingale. . . . As soon as the artificial bird had been wound up, it began to sing, at the same time moving its tail, which glittered with gold and silver. . . . It had quite as great a success as its rival; and besides, it was much prettier to look at, as it was covered with diamonds, rubies, and sapphires. . . . But where was the real nightingale? No one had noticed it flying out of the window, back to its green woods by the sea. The emperor, wishing to compare the two singers, was furious. He decreed the banishment of the real nightingale, and ordered the mechanical nightingale to be placed on a silk cushion beside his bed. . . .

One hears the song of the fisherman, who has recovered his lost friend.

(c) *Illness and Recovery of the Emperor of China.*—The poor Emperor could scarcely breathe. He opened his eyes and saw Death seated beside him, wearing the monarch's golden crown, and holding in one hand the royal golden sword and in the other the royal standard. From behind the folds of the heavy velvet curtains, grotesque and spectral heads peered out. They were the Emperor's good and evil deeds . . ., reminding him of things that caused the sweat to run down his brow. "Music! music!" cried the emperor, "so that I may not hear what they are saying! . . . Little golden bird, sing! — sing!" But the mechanical nightingale was silent. . . . Suddenly from the window came the sound of sweetest singing: it was the real nightingale. As it sang, the ghostly heads became paler and paler. . . . Even Death listened and begged the Nightingale to continue. The Nightingale consented, but made Death promise to yield up the Emperor's sword, his banner, his golden crown. And Death relinquished each of these treasures for a song, whilst the Nightingale went on singing. It sang of the quiet churchyard where the white roses grow, where the elder-tree scents the air, and where the grass is moistened by the tears of those who are left behind. Then Death longed to be in his garden and floated out through the window like a cold, white mist. . . . The Emperor fell into a calm and refreshing sleep. The sun was shining in upon him when he awoke strong and well. — *Funeral March:* The courtiers, visiting the chamber to look upon their supposedly dead ruler for the last time, stood aghast, for the Emperor was sitting up in bed, and greeted them with a cheerful "Good morning!" as they entered.

The Fisherman, whom the Nightingale has rejoined, sings anew his song.

F. B.

Le Sacre du Printemps

"Le Sacre du Printemps" ("The Rite of Spring"), Pictures of Pagan Russia, was composed in 1912 and finished in 1913 at Clarens, Switzerland. In that work, which Stravinsky intended to be performed as a ballet, the composer advanced considerably beyond the methods of employing harmony which he had used in earlier works. Not only did he discard the ordinary formulae of music, but he widened the boundary of key or tonality and made rhythm one of the most important factors in delivering his message of art. Changes of time abound in the score, occasionally such times as 3-4, 2-4, 3-8, 4-4, 5-4, 6-8, 7-8 following each other in succession. The first performance of "Le Sacre du Printemps" was given by the Diaghilev Ballet Russe at the Théâtre des Champs Elysées, Paris, May 29, 1913. Pierre Monteux conducted the orchestra and Nijinsky and Mlle. Pilz were the principal dancers. In July of the same year Stravinsky's ballet was produced in London. One of the music reviewers, unable to find approval for the Russian composer's innovations, testified that "the music baffles verbal description. To say that much of it is hideous as sound is a mild description. There is certainly an impelling rhythm traceable. Practically it has no relation to music at all, as most of us understand the word." In Paris the reception of "Le Sacre du Printemps" at its production was uproarious, yells of execration being mingled with cries of "bravo" from those who were in favor of the work. Yet at a concert production of the score, given in 1914 at the Casino de Paris, the music was applauded with considerable enthusiasm. In America "Le Sacre du Printemps" was given its first hearing at a concert of the Philadelphia Orchestra, Philadelphia, March 3, 1922.

Stravinsky's composition presents as its subject the worship of the manifestations of nature by prehistoric Russians. "The embryo is a theme," Stravinsky explained, "which came to me when I had completed 'The Fire Bird.' As this theme, with that which followed, was conceived in a strong, brutal manner, I took as a pretext for developments, for the evocation of the music, the Russian prehistoric epoch, since I am a Russian. But note well that this idea came from the music; the music did not come from the idea. My work is archetonic, not anecdotal; objective, not descriptive construction."

The composition is in two parts — I. "The Fertility of the Earth." II. "The Sacrifice." The piece opens with a slow introduction which, it is said, portrays "the mystery of the physical world in spring." Stravinsky used wood-wind instruments here, for their "dryness conveys a more austere expression of truth," and he distrusts the "facile expressiveness of the strings." On the rise of the curtain the action begins with a "Dance of the Adolescents," this being an incantation rite, consisting of vigorous stamping on the ground. A dance tune for flutes follows and a mock abduction, with rapidly changing rhythms in the orchestra. There is then set forth a horovod entitled in the score "Rondes Printanières" (Spring Rounds), this being given out by the clarinet. The main portion of the dance is based on a subject which, previously, had been announced by the trumpets. Another ceremonial follows: "Games of the Rival Cities." An aged sage enters, his function being to consecrate the soil for its coming renewal. A sacred dance follows, this "Dance of the Earth" bringing the first part of the work to an end.

The second division begins with an introduction, "The Pagan Night," the music being gloomy and acrid. This introductory matter leads to the "Mystic Circle of the Adolescents," in which girls dance and play, pausing while the one

who is selected for the sacrificial offering is set apart. The chosen victim is then glorified. Then begins the final ceremony, for the sacrificial victim must dance herself to death

F. B.

SVENDSEN

1840–1911

Symphony No. 1, in D Major. Op. 4

1. Molto allegro.
2. Andante.
3. Allegretto scherzando.
4. Maestoso. Allegro assai con fuoco.

THE first of Svendsen's two symphonies is the one most frequently performed. It opens with a brilliant theme in full orchestra, in dance rhythm. The second theme, in strong contrast, is given out in the wood winds and repeated in the violins. After a somewhat abrupt close, the whole first part is repeated. The free fantasia begins in the flute, with tremolo accompaniment in the violins, and a brilliant development closes the movement.

The second movement is romantic in character, opening with a graceful melody in the first violins with accompaniment in the remaining strings. After brilliant development it returns as a horn solo, strings pizzicato, and next appears in the violins and oboes with accompaniment of flutes and clarinets. The second theme is introduced in the strings, the wood winds accompanying in counter subjects.

The third movement is marked by the dance spirit. Theme after theme of a sparkling, dancing character appears and leads up to a climax which engages the brasses. As the climax subsides, the first theme reappears, followed by the others in brilliant recapitulation and treatment. The fourth movement begins with a short introduction on a theme which later becomes the regular second theme. The whole movement is based upon Scandinavian songs, which are worked up brilliantly in a climax at the close.

The Carnival in Paris. Op. 9

Svendsen composed this work at Bayreuth in 1873, but it was not published until 1877. When "The Carnival in Paris" was played for the first time in England at a Crystal Palace concert in October, 1880, Sir George Grove, the writer of the program books for the Crystal Palace concerts, thus discussed the work:

"This piece is obviously a representation of the fun and frolic of Mardi Gras, or Shrove Tuesday, to which narrow dimensions the carnival at Paris has now shrunk. Mr. Svendsen has lived in the French capital for some time and would naturally be struck by the peculiar features of the day, to which there is nothing analogous in his native Norway. The bustle, color and picturesque effect of the scene as depicted will strike everyone and do not need any attempt at minute elucidation of scenes, circumstances or persons, all of which, in the absence of any labels by the composer must be merely conjecture."

It may be added that Svendsen did not have to depend upon his imagination for a picture of the Carnival in Paris; for, a year after he finished his studies at the Conservatory of Leipzig, he betook himself to the French capital and lived there for two years, playing in Musard's orchestra and at the Odéon. "The Carnival in Paris" is scored for two flutes, two oboes, two clarinets, two bassoons, four horns, two trumpets, three trombones, bass tuba, kettle-drums, tambourine, cymbals and strings.

F. B.

Legend for Orchestra, Zorahayda. Op. 11

"Zorahayda" belongs to the period of Svendsen's creative activity in which, from 1872 until 1877, he lived in Oslo — then called Christiania — as the conductor of the Christiania Musical Association. The score was published in 1882. The composer took the story which is the foundation of his work from a tale in Washington Irving's "Alhambra" which is entitled "The Legend of the Rose of the Alhambra." In order to elucidate the music Svendsen caused the following quotation from Irving's tale to be printed on a flyleaf of the published score:

. . . . On a clear summer night Jacinta was sitting alone in one of the halls of the Alhambra. Reclining by a fountain of alabaster, she wept; sobs burst from her breast, and her tears fell softly into the transparent water. . . .

But little by little the water became troubled, and in the midst of a wavering vapour appeared the pale phantom of a young and beautiful woman bearing in her hand a silver lute. Her apparel, resplendent with gems, was that of a Moorish princess.

"Mortal daughter," said she in a voice tender and harmonious, "why do you weep? Wherefore do you trouble the silence of the night with your plaints?"

"I weep for a lover who has abandoned me!"

"Dry your tears; thy sorrows may soon come to an end. . . . But listen further. You see before you the hapless Zorahayda. Like yourself I have known the torments of unhappy love. A Christian cavalier, one of your ancestors, stole my heart away. I had promised to embrace his faith and to follow him to his native land. But at the critical moment of departure my courage failed, I hesitated, and — retained a captive in the palace, I died a pagan after a life of suffering. Since then the Genii of Evil have had full power over me, and I must remain under their enchantments until the day when the pure hand of a Christian shall break the magic spell which holds me a prisoner here. . . . You can deliver me. . . . Will you? . . . Speak!"

"Yes, I will," responded Jacinta all of a tremble.

"Approach then. Plunge your hand into the water of the fountain; baptize me according to your faith, and my soul will find eternal repose."

Jacinta advanced, caught the water in the palm of her hand, and sprinkled it over the head of the phantom. . . . Then Zorahayda, her countenance transfigured, laid her silver lute down gently by the fountain, folded her white arms over her bosom, and, smiling on the young girl with a tenderness ineffable disappeared. . . .

Jacinta seemed to waken from a dream. But on beholding at her feet the silver lute her doubts vanished, and on remembering Zorahayda's prediction her features were illuminated with hope and joy.

Svendsen has, in addition to the foregoing explanation, provided the hearer with a more detailed statement of the meaning of his work. The various situations are thus enumerated in a "program" placed at the head of the score:

Solitude and melancholy of Jacinta — Appearance of Zorahayda — She predicts for Jacinta the end of her troubles, and tells her of her own unhappiness. Baptism alone will bring her repose — Jacinta sprinkles the sacred water over her head — Disappearance of Zorahayda — Joy of Jacinta over the remembrance of the prediction

F. B.

TAYLOR

1885 –

Suite, Through the Looking Glass

DEEMS TAYLOR is a self-taught composer. His first activities were in the field of journalism, his most notable contribution to it having been made as music reviewer for the New York World. He resigned from that position in 1921 to devote himself to composition. The suite "Through the Looking Glass" was originally written in 1917-1919 for flute, oboe, clarinet, bassoon, horn, piano and strings. In that form it was produced at a concert of the New York Chamber Music Society, New York, February 18, 1919. Taylor then reconstructed his work for full orchestra and it was heard for the first time in its new form at a performance of the New York Symphony Orchestra, Walter Damrosch, conductor, March 10, 1923.

"The suite," wrote the composer in the program book of the concert, "needs no extended analysis. It is based on Lewis Carroll's immortal nonsense fairy-tale, 'Through the Looking Glass and What Alice Found There,' and the five pictures it presents will, if all goes well, be readily recognizable to lovers of the book. There are four movements, the first being subdivided into two connected parts."

The movements of the suite are as follows: I. Dedication. In this Taylor endeavored to express the poetical preface — "Child of the pure, unclouded brow and dreaming eyes of wonder" — with which Lewis Carroll began his tale. This leads without pause into the second division of the movement, "The Garden of Live Flowers," descriptive of the looking-glass country garden of flowers which talked to each other

II. "Jabberwocky." In this section the music first delineates the frightful beast, the Jabberwock. There is a little march signalizing the approach of the hero, who enters into battle with it — the fight being delineated in a short fugue, whose subject is given out by the double basses. "Finally," says Mr. Taylor, "his vorpal blade (really the xylophone) goes 'snicker-snack' and the monster, impersonated by the double bassoon, dies a lingering and convulsive death." III. "Looking-glass Insects." Here are set forth the various insects — the Gnat, the Bee-elephant, the Rocking-horse fly, the Snap-Dragon fly and the Bread-and-Butter fly. The composer informs his listeners that there are several themes, "but there is no use trying to decide which insect any one of them stands for." IV. "The White Knight." Two themes are employed in this movement, "the first," wrote the composer, "a sort of instrumental prance, being the knight's own conception of himself as a slashing, dare-devil fellow. The second is bland, mellifluous, a little sentimental — much more like the knight as he really was."

F. B.

TCHAIKOVSKY

1840–1893

Symphony No. 2 in C Minor. Op. 17

1. Allegro vivo.
2. Andantino marciale.
3. Scherzo.
4. Moderato assai.

TCHAIKOVSKY'S Second Symphony, sometimes called the "Little Russian Symphony," was written in 1872, and was first performed in Moscow. It is considered the most national of all this composer's works, as it is based largely upon Russian themes. After a long introduction, founded upon a melody, elegiac in style, the main part of the movement begins with a theme given out by the violins, accompanied by the remaining strings, which, after development in full orchestra, leads to a second theme in oboe, accompanied by clarinets and bassoons, then passing to the violas and 'cellos with a counter theme in violins. After a short free fantasie the recapitulation begins, closing with the Coda and bits of the beautiful melody of the introduction.

The second movement opens in the kettle-drums which furnish an accompaniment to the first theme, borrowed from a march in the composer's unpublished opera, "Undine," and stated in the clarinets and bassoons. The first violins furnish the second theme, repeated by bassoons and 'cellos. The two themes are beautifully elaborated, and the movement closes with the kettle-drum beats which began it.

The first violins have the opening theme of the Scherzo, followed by a chromatic passage in second violins and violas, which leads to the second theme in the first violins. After its embellishment and the return of the first theme the Trio follows, based on a theme in wood winds and horns, most elaborately worked up. The movement ends with a repetition of the Scherzo and Coda.

The Finale is exceedingly brilliant. Its first theme, a little Russian song called "The Crane," is given out in the first violins, followed by a second original theme, also in violins. These two themes, the first being mainly dominant, are beautifully worked up to a powerful climax, the symphony closing with a Coda full of vitality and brilliancy.

Symphony No. 4, in F Minor. Op. 36

1. Andante sostenuto. Moderato con anima.
2. Andantino in modo de canzona.
3. Scherzo. Pizzicato ostinato.
4. Finale. Allegro con fuoco.

The Fourth Symphony was written in 1878, and was regarded by Tchaikovsky as his finest work. It stands almost alone in that composer's music for its humorous characteristics, which are all the more strange when it is considered he was mentally depressed while writing it. The first movement opens with a somewhat stately introduction, at the close of which the first theme enters in the first violins and 'cellos to the accompaniment of the other strings and horns. After a vigorous development, a quiet passage occurs, leading to a subsidiary plaintive theme in the clarinets, after which the second theme enters in the 'cellos. It is not long, however, before the first theme is heard again and it soon assumes the chief importance. This section is most elaborately worked up, and the movement finally comes to a close with the utmost vigor and brilliancy.

In the second movement, one of the most fascinating Tchaikovsky ever wrote, the canzona, or song, is given out by the oboe, accompanied by the strings pizzicato. The song is next taken up by the 'cello with accompaniment of wood winds, horns, and basses. It next passes to the strings, the accompaniment continually growing fuller and richer until a strong climax is reached. The bassoons and 'cellos now take the song in unison, the former soon followed by the violins, the flutes and clarinets furnishing a graceful accompaniment. After a brief episode the violins once more take up the song, followed by one group of instruments after another until the beautiful melody dies away in the bassoons.

The third movement is unique for its pizzicato string accompaniment which runs through the whole movement whenever the strings are playing. When they are not, the same effect is produced by the wood winds and brasses. The opening theme is most brilliant, and is given out by the violins. The second is slower and is stated in the oboes and bassoons. After its statement the clarinets take the theme faster, accented by the piccolos and accompanied by the brasses. Then the first theme returns in the first violins, alternating with the wood winds. The second theme is touched upon once more, after which the movement closes pianissimo.

The Finale is a brilliant Allegro. The full orchestra gives out the first theme, quickly followed by the second in the wood winds. After the repetition of the first the third is stated in the full orchestra. The movement is devoted to the development of these three themes, and in the treatment the effect runs from double fortissimo to pianissimo, the movement coming to its close with a crescendo of tremendous energy.

Symphony No. 5, in E Minor. Op. 64

1. Andante. Allegro con anima.
2. Andante cantabile.
3. Valse.
4. Finale.

The Fifth Symphony was written in 1887, and reflects one of the sad moods of the composer. The introduction is based upon an exceedingly sombre theme which is prominent through most of the work. It leads to an Allegro which is more animated in character and is based upon two subjects, one of them melancholy in color but the other bright and vigorous. after their development, however, the sombre theme of the introduction reappears, finally dying away in the bassoons.

The second movement is in the form of a romance, the melody being given out by solo horn, then passing to 'cello and afterwards to the strings. The theme is one of exceptional beauty and is followed by new themes for oboe and clarinet, the development of which is serious in character, leading to a tremendous climax, the whole orchestra joining in the opening theme. The second part of the movement is based upon the same themes and works up to a similar climax, the theme returning fitfully, the movement closing with a Coda based upon the second theme.

In place of the conventional Scherzo the composer has given us a very graceful and poetical waltz based upon two themes, its flow being interrupted occasionally by the reentrance of the principal theme of the first movement.

The Finale has a long introduction in which the principal theme is heard again. After being worked up to a grand crescendo it disappears. After an impetuous subsidiary theme is developed the second theme is given out, first in the wood winds and then in the violins. From this point to the close these two themes are treated, but the ominous theme of the introduction is continually prominent. The situation clears up at last, however, and the symphony ends with a vigorous climax.

Symphony No. 6, in B Minor (Pathétique). Op. 74

1. Adagio. Allegro non troppo.
2. Allegro con grazia.
3. Allegro molto vivace.
4. Finale. Adagio lamentoso.

The Sixth Symphony, which the composer named the "Pathetic" after its first performance, was written in 1893. He left no program for it. Indeed, he wrote to a friend that the program must remain a riddle to every one, and to the same friend: "I love it as I have never loved any other of my musical creations."

The first movement opens with an introduction in which one of the figures of the first theme is given out by the bassoons against a droning bass and most ingeniously worked up. The second theme is a melody which is developed quietly and slowly. As it ceases the powerful first theme returns and is developed with furious energy. As the storm dies away, the beautiful second theme returns and the movement closes in the quietest of pianissimos.

The second movement is in striking contrast with the first. It has little of the conventional Scherzo character, as it is set to the dance rhythm, the principal theme being given out by the 'cellos with pizzicato accompaniment in the strings and alternating chords in the wood winds and horns. The second theme is of a plaintive sort, but it is soon replaced by the sparkling first, and the movement ends placidly and cheerfully.

The third movement opens with a truly vivacious theme alternately taken in the strings and wood winds. The strings finally usurp the theme and the wood winds develop a counter theme. The contest between these two at last ends in a grand march movement, introduced in the brasses and gradually taken up in the whole orchestra with magnificent power and almost barbaric effect.

The last movement, Adagio lamentoso, is well named. It is the apotheosis of sorrow and despair. Few composers would have the courage to end a symphony with an Adagio, still fewer with an Adagio so gloomy that it has been called "suicide music." It has no regular form and well-nigh defies analysis. It is a succession of mournful outcries, despairing laments, and wretched hopelessness, and yet is worked up with great dramatic power. Its intensity is tragic. It is a relief when its last measures die away pianissimo.

Symphony after Byron's Manfred. Op. 58

1. Manfred is wandering about in the Alps.
2. The Spirit of the Alps appears.
3. Pastorale.
4. The Underground Palace of Arimanes.

"Manfred," described as "a symphony in four scenes," was written in 1884. Its scenes are based upon Byron's "Manfred" but in the *dénouement* the composer's hero evidently is reconciled to heaven and does not die rebellious. The first movement opens with a theme which dominates the whole symphony, given out by bassoons and bass clarinet, and typical of Manfred's wretchedness and anguish of soul. The second mournful phrase, bassoons, horns, oboe, and clarinets, represents his appeal for forgetfulness. Then ensue sinister, foreboding passages, broken figures, and weird effects descriptive of his futile incantations and interwoven with them the mournful love subject, recalling the lost Astarte.

The second movement, which may stand for the Scherzo, is almost entirely devoted to Manfred's invocation of the Spirit of the Alps, and is a most charming piece of nature-painting in music. The music vividly paints the rush of the water over the rocks, the reflection of the sunlight, the appearance of the rainbow, and at last the vision of the Spirit, singing her fascinating song, first violins with harp accompaniment. The pastoral movement which follows is equally restful and beautiful, but amid its quiet harmonies is heard the gloomy motive which represents Manfred as well as his motive of longing for forgetfulness.

The second and third scenes are gratefully restful after the gloom of the first and fourth scenes. The opening theme of the final scene suggests Manfred's invocation. Suddenly the shrill trills of the strings and wood winds and the weird tones of the brasses and cymbals mark the beginning of the Spirit's orgy in which Manfred is a participant. The orgy becomes a veritable delirium, and after its close the motives of invocation and despair as well as of Astarte follow each other and at last are united with impressive power. A reference is made to the "Dies Iræ" with organ accompaniment. Manfred's death follows after a powerful climax.

Symphonic Fantasia, The Tempest. Op. 18

The "Tempest" Fantasia, one of Tchaikovsky's earliest works, was written in 1872 and is dedicated to M. Stassov, who suggested Shakespeare's "Tempest" as a subject for musical description. The program furnished by Stassov is as follows: "The sea. Ariel, spirit of the air, raising a tempest at the bidding of the magician Prospero. Wreck of the vessel conveying Ferdinand. The enchanted isle. The first shy awakening of love between Ferdinand and Miranda. Ariel. Caliban. The enamored pair give themselves up to the magic of love. Prospero divests himself of his power of enchantment and quits the island. The sea." The program so exhaustively states the contents of the fantasia that a detailed analysis seems unnecessary. The sea, both in calm and storm, is forcibly described. The Ariel theme, which is graceful and sprightly, dominates the fantasia throughout, and contrasts strongly with the heavy, ungraceful figure with which the 'cellos and basses represent Caliban, and the impressive and sombre one which does the same service for Prospero. Although in a letter to Stassov the composer writes that nothing could have suited him better, that he was full of enthusiasm and could think of nothing else, the work falls below the standard of his subsequent dramatic efforts, notably "Francesca da Rimini," which shortly followed it.

Fantasia, Francesca da Rimini. Op. 32

The Fantasia "Francesca da Rimini," based upon passages from the fifth canto of Dante's "Inferno," was written in 1876. It was first conceived as an opera, but the plan was abandoned when the librettist imposed certain unsatisfactory conditions. Impressed by his reading of the canto, however, and inspired in some degree by Gustav Doré's drawings, the composer decided not to abandon the subject altogether, and cast his music in the form of a fantasia, appending the following program to his score:

"Dante arrives in the second circle of hell. He sees that here the incontinent are punished, and their punishment is to be continually tormented by the cruelest winds under a dark and gloomy air

Among these tortured ones he recognizes Francesca da Rimini, who tells her story.

"'. . . There is no greater pain than to recall a happy time in wretchedness; and this thy teacher knows. But if thou hast such desire to learn the first root of our love, I will do like one who weeps and tells.

"'One day, for pastime, we read of Lancelot, how love constrained him. We were alone, and without all suspicion. Several times that reading urged our eyes to meet, and changed the color of our faces. But one moment alone it was that overcame us. When we read of how the fond smile was kissed by such a lover, he, who shall never be divided from me, kissed my mouth all trembling. The book, and he who wrote it, was a Galeotto. That day we read in it no farther.'

"While the one spirit thus spake, the other wept so that I fainted with pity, as if I had been dying; and fell, as a dead body falls."

The fantasia opens Andante lugubre, describing "the cruelest winds under a dark and gloomy air" which greet Dante and Virgil as they arrive upon the second circle and the spectral figures they encounter. After this appalling picture is presented there is a lull, and horns, cornet, and trombones give out a theme announcing the meeting with Francesca and Paolo. The episode is very tender and at the same time passionate. A short recitative leads to the second section of the fantasia, Andante cantabile non troppo. After the theme of the first section a beautiful melody is given out by English horn and harps, evidently suggesting the relation of Francesca's meeting with Paolo and her sudden love. It is interrupted by the reappearance of the spectral forms, and the lovers are lost in the horrible storm which breaks out afresh, above which, however, is heard the love-song of Francesca.

Suite No. 1. Op. 43

The first of Tchaikovsky's suites was written in 1880, and as originally constructed consisted of five movements: 1. Introduction and fugue; 2. Divertimento; 3. Intermezzo; 4. Scherzo; 5. Gavotte. After its publication the composer added another movement, "Marche Miniature," inserted between the Intermezzo and Scherzo. As generally performed in the concert-room, the Scherzo and Gavotte, which are in the usual form of those movements, are omitted. The Introduction and fugue, scored for full orchestra without trombones, opens with a long, animated, and melodious theme, given out by bassoons, accompanied in the muted strings, and then passes to all the violins with wind instrument accompaniment. After the development of this material a fugue follows, opened in first oboe, first clarinet, and second violin, with responses in second oboe, second clarinet, and violas. The fugue is simply constructed, and its episodes bring the movement to a close.

The second movement, Divertimento, opens with a quaint theme in clarinet, followed by a passage in full orchestra and kindred passages in the wood winds, with pizzicato string accompaniment. The second section opens with an extended melody for oboe, accompanied by strings, passing to the horns. The development of this material, with a return to the first theme, closes the Divertimento.

The Intermezzo is the favorite number of the suite by reason of its melodious character. The first subject is announced in first violins, violas, bassoon, and flute, with accompaniment of strings and horns. After repetition, the second theme appears in a kind of duet for 'cellos and bassoon with pizzicato accompaniment. It next appears in the violins, violas, and 'cellos with contrapuntal accompaniment in the wood winds. The leading theme and duet are repeated and gradually lead back to the first theme, which is worked up to an intense climax. A Coda, based upon fragments of the first theme, closes the movement.

The "Marche Miniature" is a fantastic number, both in its scoring and the instruments employed, which are the piccolo, flutes, oboes, clarinets, violins, triangle, and bells. In the opening, the theme is given out by the piccolo, with pizzicato string accompaniment. It then passes to the flute. An episode appears in the strings and bells. The development of the main theme and the quaintness of the accompaniment impart a strange fascination to the music, which closes with a repetition of the principal subject.

Suite No. 3. Op. 55

The Suite No. 3 was written in 1884, the same year in which the composer's "Manfred" Symphony was produced. It is in four movements, viz.: 1. "Elegie"; 2. "Valse Melancholique"; 3. "Scherzo"; 4. "Tema con Variazione." The Elegie and Valse are scored for full orchestra, and the Scherzo further employs triangle, drum, and tambourine. The Elegie and Valse are regular in form, but of a peculiarly emotional and impressive character, and are scored with the composer's extraordinary mastery of orchestral technique. The Scherzo is in the usual scherzo form and does not call for special analysis. The "Theme and Variations" is the masterpiece of the suite. The theme is given out by the first violins with detached chord accompaniment. The variations are twelve in number. The first is opened by the strings in unison. The second is also for all the strings in unison, with a light, tripping accompaniment by the other instruments. In the third the melody is given to the first flute in the first and third sections. In the second section the second clarinet has the melody, accompanied by the other reeds. The fourth introduces a change of theme for full orchestra. The second section of the theme is also for full orchestra. The fifth treats of the theme contrapuntally. The sixth gives the theme in the form of quaver triplets. The seventh presents it in a stately chorale. In the eighth it is taken by English horn with string accompaniment. In the ninth it appears for the violins, accompanied by clarinet and four horns. In the tenth it is almost wholly assigned to a violin solo in Capriccio form. In the eleventh it is sustained by the double basses and bassoon with passages for other instruments. In the twelfth it appears as a showy Polacca, most elaborately embellished, which brings the suite to a close.

Overture Fantasia, Hamlet. Op. 67

The "Hamlet" Fantasia followed not long after Tchaikovsky's "Manfred" Symphony and is fittingly dedicated to

Grieg. It opens with a long introduction, describing Hamlet's grief over the death of the King, in the 'cellos and violins, which have a very dramatic theme, worked up to a climax, and followed by twelve successive strokes in the muted horns, representing the midnight hour and followed by the ghost theme in the horns, trombones, tuba, and double basses, accompanied by trumpet calls and string tremolos. These lead up to the main section of the fantasia. The opening theme, sombre and agitated, represents Hamlet's indecision and yet resolute purpose, and is followed by the second theme, which indicates the grace and pathos of Ophelia, given out by the wood winds with string accompaniment, thence extending to the strings. This is followed by a march rhythm in the brasses, repeated in the strings and wood winds. The first theme returns by a short transition. In the third section of the overture the thematic material is worked up with great intensity, with a subsidiary passage in oboe, followed by the second theme. The Coda is long and agitated, and is constructed mainly upon the second theme and march. This is worked up to a strenuous climax, after which the first theme reappears and the fantasia comes to a close, pianissimo.

Overture Fantasia, Romeo and Juliet

The Overture Fantasia, "Romeo and Juliet," one of Tchaikovsky's earlier works, was written in 1870 and is dedicated to his friend Balakirev, the Russian composer, who suggested the subject to him. When his friend made the suggestion, he also accompanied it with a program which the composer followed, and which will serve for an analysis of the work. It was to be in sonata form and the scheme as follows: "First, an introduction of a religious character, carried out by a chorale, representation of Friar Laurence, followed by an Allegro in B minor (Balakirev suggesting most of the tonalities), which is to depict the enmity between the Montagues and Capulets. There is to follow the love of Romeo and Juliet (second subject, the melodic passage assigned to English horn), succeeded by the elaboration of both subjects. The so-called 'develop,' that is to say, the putting together of the various theme in various forms, passes over to what is called in technical language the 'recapitulation,' in which the first theme, Allegro, appears in its original form, and the love theme (D flat major) now appears in D major, the whole ending with the death of the lovers."

Suite, Caisse Noisette. Op. 71a

The "Caisse Noisette" Suite is a fascinating trifle as compared with most of Tchaikovsky's works, though it is exceedingly graceful in its style and skillful in construction. It was originally written as a fairy ballet in fifteen numbers, and from them the composer arranged the suite. It is laid out in three parts, viz.: 1. "Overture Miniature." 2. "Danses Characteristique," comprising "Marche," "Danse de la Fée Dragée," "Trepac," "Danse Russe," "Danse Arabe," "Dance Chinoise" and "Danse des Mirlitons." 3. "Valse des Fleurs." The overture, bright and dainty, is scored without 'cellos and double basses, which, to a degree, determines its character. The march is divided into a military theme, given by the wind instruments, alternating with a second phrase given by the strings, and a middle movement which might be called the Trio, and which is built up on a similar exchange between flutes and violins. The "Danse de la Fée Dragée" is another bit of instrumental legerdemain, at the close of which the fairy seems to dart out of sight. The dance theme is given to a "celesta" (a keyed instrument with steel plates in the place of wires) or a piano. The "Russian Dance" has all the characteristic monotonous swing which is peculiar to the popular melodies of the Slav. The "Danse Arabe" is not less characteristic. Minor in mood, the melody sings along in thirds with those florid cadences which are the *sine qua non* of Arabic music. In utter contrast is the following "Danse Chinoise," a kind of caricature which seems to answer the purpose and is given by the piccolo and flute. "Les Mirlitons" is furnished with a kind of "staccato polka," cleverly worked up, while the "Danse des Fleurs" is a waltz, having in parts a Strauss-like swing.

Suite, Mozartiana. Op. 61

The "Mozartiana," written in 1887, is the fourth of Tchaikovsky's orchestral suites. In the following note, appended to the score, the composer states its general character:

"A large number of the more admirable small compositions of Mozart, for incomprehensible reasons, are very little known, not alone to the public, but even to a large proportion of musicians. The author of the arrangement of the suite, having for its title 'Mozartiana,' desires to give a new impulse to the study of the little master works which in succinct form contain incomparable beauties."

To carry out this scheme Tchaikovsky has arranged four pieces from Mozart's least known works, a Gigue, Minuet, Prayer, and Theme and Variations for full orchestra except heavy brasses, which would have been incongruous, and has elaborated them with the highest skill, which changes them from their original graceful simplicity into tone-pictures full of a novel charm and color.

Marche Slave. Op. 31

The "Marche Slave" was written by Tchaikovsky in 1876, during the war between Turkey and Servia. It opens with a theme in the bassoons of a somewhat melancholy character, which is soon changed by trumpet flourishes and the strains of the Russian National Hymn, into an impressive march, purely Slavic in rhythm and color. It was first played at a concert given for the benefit of the wounded and though a "piece of occasion" and comparatively short, it is one of Tchaikovsky's most successful minor works. It bears some relation to the "1812 overture," but is a more enthusiastically patriotic composition than the latter.

Overture, 1812. Op. 49

According to one of Tchaikovsky's biographers, Nicholas Rubinstein in the spring of 1880 suggested to the composer that he should write a *pièce d'occasion* for the consecration of the Temple of Christ in Moscow. "In addition to the church festivity Rubinstein wished to organize a musical one which should embody the history of the building of this temple, that is to say, the events of the year 1812. Tchaikovsky's fantasia or overture was to be performed in the public square before the cathedral by a colossal orchestra, the big drums to be replaced by salvos of artillery." The composition was finished in 1880, but no account is left of the proposed startling performance, which reminds one of the Gilmore Jubilee achievements. The overture opens with the subject of the old Russian Hymn, "God, preserve Thy people," parts of it being developed in wood winds, violas, and 'cellos alternately. The material is worked up to a climax in full orchestra, followed by a more quiet passage. The main section of the overture follows, representing the battle of Borodino, in which the Russian National Hymn intermingles with the "Marseillaise" amid peals of artillery. The movement reaches a deafening uproar, above which the Russian Hymn rises triumphant. A Coda, with the hymn in the basses and peals of bells, closes this unique and somewhat startling work.

The "Overture Triomphale," by Tchaikovsky, one of his earlier works, foreshadows his "1812" overture by reason of his use of the Danish National Hymn, much in the same manner as he has treated the "Marseillaise" in the "1812."

Andante Cantabile from String Quartet. Op. 11

This slow movement of Tchaikovsky's first string quartet has achieved popularity largely through its performance with string orchestra by symphonic organizations. The quartet, in D major, was composed in 1871. The Andante cantabile has a curious history. When Tchaikovsky was about to commence the composition of his slow movement a plasterer was at work on the outside of the house in which he lived. On several successive mornings the Russian master heard the man singing a melody of plaintive charm and this so haunted the composer that he sought out the plasterer and asked him to sing the words. The music was that of a Russian folk song and the latter, which Tchaikovsky incorporated into his slow movement, may be found in Rimsky-Korsakov's collection of national Russian songs.

F. B.

THOMAS

1811 – 1896

Overture to Mignon

AMBROISE THOMAS' "Mignon" was the nineteenth stage work of that composer. The opera was written to a text by Jules Barbier and Michel Carré, who based it upon Goethe's "Wilhelm Meister." They had previously submitted the "book" to Meyerbeer, who declined it. The opera was produced at the Opéra Comique, Paris, November 17, 1866. In America it was first heard at the Academy of Music, New York, November 22, 1871.

The overture to "Mignon" is not built on the classic model, but is a freely constructed movement which makes use of themes drawn from the opera itself. A short Introduction, in which the flute, clarinet and harp figure prominently, leads to a statement of the air, "Connais tu le pays," which is sung in the first act by Mignon. The second theme of which Thomas made use is the polonaise, "Je suis Titania," sung by Philine in the second act.

F. B

TURINA

1882–

La Procesión del Rocio

JOAQUIN TURINA, born at Seville, obtained his education in music from Jose Trajo, at Madrid, and from Vincent d'Indy, in Paris. Having lived for fourteen years in the French capital, he returned to Spain in 1914 and took up his residence at Madrid.

"La Procesión del Rocio" was composed in 1912 and was given its first performance by the Orquesta Sinfonica, of Madrid, in March, 1913. The piece represents the procession which takes place in June of each year at Triana, a suburb of Seville — this being known as "Procesión del Rocio" (Procession of the Dew) and which is held in honor of the Virgin, whose image is carried on a silver car drawn by oxen. The greatest families of the town take part in the parade and Triana is *en fête*. The composition is divided into two sections, not, however, separated by any pause. The first presents Triana in festal spirit. Dances are set forth, these being interrupted by the arrival of the Procession (this forms the second division), which is announced by players on a flute and a drum. A religious theme is given out several times and culminates in a climax with the sounding of the Royal March and the clanging of bells. The dances and the festal songs are resumed, but their jubilant sounds gradually diminish and finally die away altogether.

F. B.

VAUGHAN WILLIAMS

1872 –

A London Symphony

RALPH VAUGHAN WILLIAMS, born at Down Ampney, Gloucestershire, England, received the greater part of his education at the Royal College of Music, London, which institution he entered in 1890. He took the degree Bachelor of Music in 1894 and Doctor of Music in 1901, both from the University of Cambridge. After leaving the Royal College of Music in 1896, Vaughan Williams received some instruction in composition from Max Bruch in Berlin, and still later (in 1908) from Ravel, in Paris.

"A London Symphony" was composed in 1912-1913 and the work was produced for the first time March 27, 1914, at a concert in Queen's Hall, London. The composer then made a revision of his symphony and it was again brought forward in 1918. A third and final revision was undertaken and "A London Symphony" was presented to the world in its present form by the London Symphony Orchestra, in London, May 4, 1920. In America the work was first heard at a concert of the New York Symphony Society, New York, December 30, 1920. The score was published in London under the auspices of the Carnegie United Kingdom Trust with a dedication to George S. K. Butterworth, a composer who, like Vaughan Williams, had studied at the Royal College of Music and who was killed in 1916 during the Great War.

At the time "A London Symphony" was given for the first time in America the program contained a description of the work by Albert Coates, who was the conductor of it. Although this description bears an apparently intimate relationship to the music, the composer, who is a friend of Coates, has not given his sanction to it.

The first movement opens with a picture of London at daybreak, with the ancient Thames "calm and silent under the heavy gray dawn," and with the sound of Big Ben (the Westminster chimes) striking the half-hour. Suddenly the mood changes (Allegro risoluto) and there are heard the bustle and turmoil of the Strand. Once more the scene changes as the composer takes his listeners to that quiet part of London which is typified by one of the by-streets that lead to the river. The mood again becomes one of impetuosity as the listener is again brought back to the Strand. The second movement pictures the district of the metropolis known as Bloomsbury in the cold and damp dusk of a day in November. Over the district there broods, says Mr. Coates, "an air of shabby gentility, a sad dignity of having seen better days." A musician is playing his fiddle in the murky twilight and in the distance the cry of the lavender vendor is heard — for London, like Paris, has its street criers. The movement ends with the old fiddler playing his tune. The third movement (Allegro vivace) is a picture of the city late on Saturday night on the Thames Embankment. On the other side of the river are the London slums and from these there are heard the noises of the costermongers with their barrows, making the streets look like a fair, the coster girls dancing their "double-shuffle" jig, the sounds of an accordion and a street organ. Suddenly the mood changes and the hoary Thames again comes into view and "the picture fades into fog and silence." The fourth movement shows London in a crueler aspect — for it is the London of the unemployed and the unfortunate. The opening bars set forth (Maestoso alla marcia) the "Hunger March." Once more the noise and bustle of the streets are set forth — it is the city seen through the eyes of those who are suffering and cold and dejected. The music comes to an abrupt pause and the sound of Big Ben is heard again. What follows is an epilogue "in which," says Mr. Coates, "we seem to feel the great deep soul of London."

F. B.

Pastoral Symphony

This symphony was completed at London in 1921 and it was performed for the first time at a concert of the Royal Philharmonic Society, London, January 26, 1922. In America it was first heard at the Festival of the Litchfield County Choral Union, given in the music shed on the grounds of Carl Stoeckel, Norfolk, Connecticut, June 7, 1922. Vaughan Williams was the conductor on the latter occasion. When his Pastoral Symphony was given for the first time in London, the composer contributed the following note about it to the program:

"The mood of this symphony is, as its title suggests, almost entirely quiet and contemplative — there are few fortissimos and few allegros. The only really quick passage is the Coda to the third movement, and that is all pianissimo."

There is no "program" to the work. "The passionate analyst, remembering another 'Pastoral' Symphony and its candid sub-titles," wrote Mr. Lawrence Gilman, "finds himself, in the presence of Vaughan Williams' score, on a starvation diet, unless he chooses to be satisfied with mere music for sustenance." The composer himself has stated that he prefers the music to suggest whatever images come to the individual mind. It may be said, however, that Vaughan Williams, a fervid folk song enthusiast, has made use in this work, as in many others, of the modal peculiarities of old English folk tunes. There are no actual folk songs employed in the symphony. The first movement (Molto moderato) begins with the principal subject in the harp and lowest strings, with the flutes in a wavy figure of consecutive fifths against it. Soon a subsidiary subject is heard in the English horn. This material is worked over and soon the second theme is given out by the clarinet with a triplet figure accompanying it in the flutes. There are episodic ideas set forth in the remainder of the movement, but the main thematic material is that which has just been set forth. The second movement (Lento moderato) begins with a chord of F minor in the muted strings with the theme, in F major, played above it by a solo horn.

The violins answer this melody and soon a solo viola is heard in a contrasting phrase. The mood becomes more animated and the second theme is given out by a trumpet, a cadenza being part of its material. The violas and clarinet take up the theme and later the first subject is given out by the full orchestra. The second theme again comes to notice and the movement comes to a close in the violins alone. The third movement (Moderato pesante; presto) corresponds to the Scherzo of the classical symphony. It begins in the horns and the double basses and bassoons. A continuing section is heard in the trumpets and trombones (poco animato) and there is a third idea, set forth by the flute. The mood is robust, almost wild. The opening theme returns and the brass instruments bring back their rollicking melody. The Coda begins with a few measures of the first subject (Presto). "It is all sheer fairyland," wrote A. E. F. Dickinson, "and everything has a new and magical touch about it." In the Finale a wordless solo voice (soprano or tenor) is employed at the opening, this being set against a dull roll on the kettle-drum. The second subject follows immediately in the wood winds and harp (Moderato maestoso), and is in the Lydian mode — the scale which corresponds to the modern F major, but with B natural instead of B flat. An agitated episode succeeds this, the subject, sung at the beginning of the movement by the voice, now returning in the orchestra. The violoncellos, and after them, the flute sing a theme related to the first subject. The violins bring forward a more impassioned mood and this culminates in a recapitulation of the first subject (molto largamente) by the strings and wood winds in unison. Reminiscences of material in previous movements occur, the violins climb to a high A and the distant voice of the singer is heard again in the opening theme. The symphony then sinks gently into silence.

F. B.

VERDI

1813 – 1901

The Manzoni Requiem

THE history of "The Manzoni Requiem" is of more than ordinary interest. Shortly after Rossini's death, in 1868, Verdi conceived the idea of a requiem in his memory, to be written by many hands, which should be performed in the cathedral of Bologna on each centenary of the composer's death, but upon no other occasion and at no other place. The project met with favor. The work was laid out in thirteen numbers and assigned to thirteen Italian composers, Verdi taking the ("Libra me"), which was to be the last number in the work. Each of the composers finished his task; but when the parts were joined in a complete requiem they were found to be so dissimilar in treatment, and the whole work so incoherent and lacking in symmetry and unity, that the scheme went no further. About this time, 1873, Alessandro Manzoni, the founder of the romantic school in Italian literature, died, and was universally mourned by his countrymen. The requiem which had been intended for Rossini was now written by Verdi for his friend, the great Italian patriot and poet. It was performed for the first time at Milan, May 22, 1874, the anniversary of Manzoni's death.

The "Requiem" opens, after a few measures of prelude, with the chorus chanting the appeal for rest, *sotto voce*, the effect being carried as pianissimo as possible until the basses, by an abrupt change of key, give out the theme of a fugue ("Te decet Hymnus"), written in pure religious style. The introductory ("Requiem") is repeated, and leads to the ("Kyrie"), the theme of which is stated by the tenor, and in turn taken up by the other soloists, the chorus shortly joining, a double sextet interwoven with it, and the whole closing pianissimo, as the ("Requiem") opened.

The second part, the "Dies Iræ," is in strong contrast with the first, and is more broadly and dramatically worked up, and with freer accompaniment. The opening chorus is one of startling power. The tenors and basses open the number, immediately followed by the four parts announcing the "Day of Wrath" in high, sustained notes, while the second sopranos, altos, and tenors accompany them with immense sweeps of sound that rise and fall like the waves. There are nine numbers in this part, the most effective of them being the Adagio trio ("Quid sum miser") for soprano, alto, and tenor, upon which Verdi has lavished his melodious inspiration. The trio is continually interwoven with the chorus shouting fortissimo the ("Rex tremendæ Majestatis"), until it takes another form in the prayer ("Recordare"), a duet for soprano and alto in Verdi's best operatic vein. An effective tenor solo ("Ingemisco"), followed by a solemn and majestic bass solo ("Confutatis"), leads to the stirring measures of the "Day of Wrath" again, and closes this part in a powerful ensemble, both vocal and dramatic.

The offertory ("Domine Jesu") is a quartet with three motives — the first Andante, the second Allegro, and the third Adagio in Gregorian form, the three themes being admirably worked up and accompanied. The ("Sanctus"), the fourth part of the mass, is an impressive Allegro double chorus, followed by the ("Agnus Dei"), a duet for soprano and alto which is full of melodious inspiration, illustrated with charming instrumental color. The sixth part is the ("Lux æterna"), a trio for alto, tenor, and bass which leads to the ("Libera"), the final division and the climax of the work. In its general effect it is a soprano obligato with chorus. After a monotone recitative and solo the ("Dies Iræ") is repeated, likewise the ("Requiem æternam"), which forms the introduction of the mass, and the ("Requiem") closes with a fugue of majestic proportions, ending with the same pianissimo effect which characterizes the opening of the work.

WAGNER

1813 – 1883

Overture to Rienzi

WAGNER completed the book of "Rienzi," based upon Bulwer's novel, in 1838, and began the music in the autumn of that year. It was finished in 1839, and performed for the first time in Dresden in 1842. The overture is in the regular form, for "Rienzi" was written before Wagner had taken his new departure in music, and is based upon some of the themes in the opera. It opens with a slow movement, announced in trumpet calls, introducing after a few measures an impressive theme in the strings, Rienzi's Prayer for the People. This is repeated by wood winds and brasses with accompaniment in violins and violas. At the close of the repeat the main section begins with the theme sung by the chorus at the end of the first act, in which occurs also the battle hymn assigned to the brasses fortissimo, and combined with the theme of Rienzi's Prayer. An episode based on the theme of the slow movement leads to the second subject, sung in the finale of the second act. In the reprise, the second subject is connected with a counter theme in the trombones. A Coda of most vigorous intensity, founded on the battle hymn, closes the overture.

Overture to The Flying Dutchman

The romantic opera "The Flying Dutchman," conceived by Wagner during a storm which overtook him on a voyage from Riga to Paris, was written in 1841, and was first produced at Dresden in 1843. The overture characterizes the persons and situations in the opera and introduces motives which Wagner ever after used so freely and so skilfully. It opens with the "Curse weighing upon the Dutchman" motive, given out in unison by bassoons and horns, accompanied in the violins tremolo, picturing waves in motion, and passages in violas and 'cellos depicting increasing waves and the approaching storm, through which are heard suggestions of the Curse and motive and signals of distress. As the storm subsides the second motive is announced, "The Message of the Angel of Mercy," personifying Senta, which is heard in the opera at the close of each stanza of Senta's ballad. Impressive passages are stated in the horns and trombones, and the Curse motive is again announced, followed by the third motive, "The Personification of the Dutchman." The storm rages anew, fortissimo, and in its lulls is heard the jovial Sailors' Song on a passing vessel. The storm continues, but the Senta motive returns persistently, alternating with the Curse motive. Finally ensues the wreck scene — then silence.

Overture to Tannhäuser

Wagner first conceived the idea of writing "Tannhäuser und der Sängerkrieg auf Wartburg" ("Tannhäuser and the Singers' Contest at the Wartburg") while visiting the castle of Wartburg in Thuringia in 1842, and the opera was first produced in Dresden in 1845. The story of Tannhäuser's love for Elizabeth, his yielding to the seductive influences of Venus and his chanting her praises in the singers' contest, his penitential pilgrimage to Rome and struggle with the sirens as he returns, and his final expiation and pardon by the side of Elizabeth's bier, is a familiar one to every concert-goer. The overture is one of the great masterpieces in that class of musical composition and is here described in Wagner's own words:

"At its commencement the orchestra rehearses the song of pilgrims, which, as it approaches, grows louder and louder, and at length recedes. It is twilight; the last strain of the pilgrims' song is heard. As night comes on, magical phenomena present themselves;

a roseate-hued and fragrant mist arises, wafting voluptuous shouts of joy to our ears. We are made aware of the dizzy motion of a horribly wanton dance.

"These are the seductive magic spells of the Venusberg, which at the hour of night reveal themselves to those whose breasts are inflamed with unholy desire. Attracted by these enticing phenomena, a tall and manly figure approaches; it is Tannhäuser, the Minnesinger. Proudly exulting, he trolls forth his jubilant love-song as if to challenge the wanton magic crew to turn their attention to himself. Wild shouts respond to his call; the roseate cloud surrounds him more closely; its enrapturing fragrance overwhelms him and intoxicates his brain. Endowed now with supernatural powers of vision, he perceives, in the dim seductive light spread out before him, an unspeakably lovely female figure; he hears a voice which, with its tremulous sweetness, sounds like the call of sirens, promising to the brave the fulfilment of his wildest wishes. It is Venus herself whom he sees before him. Heart and soul he burns with desire; hot, consuming longing inflames the blood in his veins; by an irresistible power he is drawn into the presence of the goddess and with the highest rapture raises his song in her praise. As if in response to his magic call, the wonder of the Venusberg is revealed to him in its fullest brightness; boisterous shouts of wild delight re-echo on every side; Bacchantes rush hither and thither in their drunken revels, and, dragging Tannhäuser into their giddy dance, deliver him over to the love-warm arms of the goddess, who, passionately embracing him, carries him off, drunken with joy, to the unapproachable depths of her invisible kingdom. The wild throng then disperses and their commotion ceases. A voluptuous, plaintive whirring alone now stirs the air, and a horrible murmur pervades the spot where the enrapturing profane magic spell had shown itself, and which now again is overshadowed by darkness. Day at length begins to dawn, and the song of the returning pilgrims is heard in the distance. As their song draws nearer, and day succeeds to night, that whirring and murmuring in the air, which but just now sounded to us like the horrible wail of the damned, gives way to more joyful strains, till at last, when the sun has risen in all its splendor, and the pilgrims' song with mighty inspiration proclaims to the world and to all that is and lives salvation won, its surging sound swells into a rapturous torrent of sublime ecstasy. This divine song represents to us the shout of joy at his release from the curse of the unholiness of the Venusberg. Thus all the pulses of life palpitate and leap for joy in this song of deliverance; and the two divided elements, spirit and mind, God and nature, embrace each other in the holy uniting Kiss of Love."

Prelude to Lohengrin

The romantic opera, "Lohengrin," was finished in 1847 and first performed at Weimar in 1850, under Liszt's direction. The story of Lohengrin and Elsa, of Ortrud and Telramund, of the Swan boat and Elsa's death, does not need retelling for any concert-goer. The prelude to the opera takes for its subject the descent of the Holy Grail, the mysterious symbol of the Christian faith, and the Grail motive is the key to the whole composition. This mysterious motive is developed in various groups of instruments in a gradual crescendo, leading to a brief decrescendo. It is first announced in the far, airy distance in the violins pianissimo, then passes to the wood winds, thence to the violas, 'cellos, horn, and bassoon, and reaches its climax in exultant outbursts in trumpets and trombones, after this dying away gradually and closing pianissimo in the flute and muted violins.

Prelude to Tristan und Isolde

The opera, "Tristan und Isolde," was begun in 1857 and completed in 1859, during the period in which Wagner was engaged upon his colossal "Nibelung Trilogy," and was first produced in 1865 in Munich. It is peculiarly interesting, as being the first opera in which Wagner broke entirely loose from the conventional operatic form. In a Prelude of this kind, based entirely upon motives and their development, musical analysis without frequent use of notation would be of little service. The recital of the themes must tell its contents. These begin with the "Love Confession," always followed by the motive of "Desire." After their repetition the theme of the "Glance" follows, which explains its own meaning, and after its development in various forms occur the motives of the "Love Philtre" and "Death Potion," the one extremely passionate, the other sombre and mysterious. These are followed by a motive growing out of the "Glance," and an overpoweringly passionate crescendo, after which the motive "Deliverance by Death," with its development, closes the Prelude. In the concert-room the Prelude is usually coupled with the "Liebes-Tod" ("Love Death"), the closing scene in which Isolde apostrophizes the dead body of her lover.

Prelude to Die Meistersinger von Nürnberg

"Die Meistersinger," Wagner's only comic opera, occupied the attention of the composer at intervals during twenty years. It was finished in 1867, and was first produced at Munich in 1868 under the direction of Hans von Bülow. The story concerns the love of Walther, a noble young knight, and Eva, daughter of Pogner, a wealthy goldsmith, his entering the lists to become a Mastersinger, which he must do to win her hand, and which he accomplishes with the help of Hans Sachs, by outdoing Beckmesser with his beautiful "Prize Song." It is clearly apparent both from the music and the text that the opera was partly intended as a satire upon Wagner's critics, who had charged that he was incapable of melody. It is easy to see that these critics are symbolized by the pedantic Beckmesser and that in Walther we have a personification of Wagner himself.

The Prelude is composed of some of the principal themes, two of them symbolizing the corporation of the Mastersingers, the others various phases of the love of Eva and Walther. It opens with the Mastersinger's motive, a noble march movement of heavy chords, which is repeated. Immediately following it a gentle motive, "Waking Love," occurs. This leads to a second Mastersinger motive, another march rhythm known as the "Banner" motive, from the banner carried by the Mastersingers upon which King David was represented playing the harp. This is worked up at considerable length and leads by a short episode to another very melodious motive, called "Love Confessed," which is related to the "Prize Song." It is followed by an agitated motive called "Impatient Ardor," which in development is worked up with a counter theme from the singing contest. In the Finale the "Mastersingers," "Banner," and "Love Confessed" motives are ingeniously woven together by various groups of instruments, the rest of the orchestra supplying most ornate elaboration, the whole coming to an imposing climax, which closes the **Prelude.**

The Nibelung Trilogy Preludes

The "Nibelung Trilogy" consists of the introduction ("Rheingold") and the music-dramas, ("Die Walküre," "Siegfried," and "Die Götterdämmerung.") The dramatic poems were written as early as 1852. The music to "Rheingold" and "Die Walküre" was composed between 1852 and 1856; that of "Siegfried," begun in 1856, was not finished until 1869; that of "Die Götterdämmerung" between 1867 and 1876, in which latter year the entire Trilogy was performed at Bayreuth.

The prelude to "Rheingold" consists of a single chord varied with masterly skill, which fills the entire prelude and is constantly expanded yet never loses its character. It constitutes a tone-picture of water in its primeval repose, its gradual undulations and gathering force leading, as the curtain rises, to the opening scene — the bed of the Rhine and the life of the Rhine Daughters. Though the movement is designedly monotonous, such is the skill manifested in its construction that it never becomes tedious.

The prelude to "Die Walküre" is very brief, and describes the rising and subsidence of a furious storm. It is mainly constructed on a simple subject, repeated and varied, and leads to the scene where Siegmund suddenly appears in Hunding's hut.

The prelude to "Siegfried" is constructed upon the principal themes of the music-drama, among them the "Forge," the "Ring," the "Sword," the "Dragon," and other motives which are familiar to opera-goers, and introduces the scene in Mime's forge upon Siegfried's arrival, preceded by his horn calls.

There is no regular prelude to "Die Götterdämmerung," a prologue taking its place, which is divided into two scenes, that of the Norns weaving the fates of gods and men, and Brünnhilde's farewell to Siegfried as he sets forth for new adventures.

Prelude to Parsifal

"Parsifal," a "Bühnenweihfestspiel" ("Festival Acting Drama"), was completed in 1879, and was first produced at Bayreuth in 1882, seven months before the composer's death. The subject of the work is taken from the cycle of the Holy Grail myths, to which "Lohengrin" belongs, and concerns Parsifal, the King of the Grail and father of Lohengrin. Like Siegfried, Parsifal represents free human nature, and its impulsive, spontaneous action. He is styled in the text "Der Reine Thor" ("The Guileless Fool"), who, bearing out the old mythical idea, overcomes the evil principle and gains the crown by dint of pure natural impulse.

The Vorspiel opens with the symbolic motive of the "Eucharist," at first unaccompanied, and then repeated with arpeggio accompaniment. After a pause the same motive reappears, but in the minor, followed by another pause. The second motive, the Grail, now appears, and is extended, followed by the motive of Faith, which is developed in an impressive manner, the Grail motive occasionally joining it. After a drum passage, followed by a tremolo of the strings, the Eucharist motive reappears, followed by the Lance motive. After brief development the Eucharist motive leads directly to the opening scene of the dialogue between Gurnemanz and his two companions of the Grail.

Eine Faust Ouverture

"Eine Faust Ouverture," written in 1840 and rewritten in 1855, was originally intended as the first movement of a symphony based upon Goethe's drama. The symphony scheme, however, was abandoned, Wagner at that time being busy with his opera, "The Flying Dutchman." After several changes the overture was published with its present title. It has to do with Faust alone, before he has encountered Mephistopheles or met Marguerite. The following motto from Goethe's "Faust," which Wagner at one time used, probably explains its exact significance:

> "The indwelling spirit
> Whose temple is my heart, who rules its powers,
> Can stir the bosom to its lowest depths,
> But has no power to move external nature,
> And therefore is existence burdensome,
> And death desirable, and life detested."

It begins with a slow introduction, the opening subject given out by the tuba and double basses in unison, accompanied by pianissimo rolls on the kettle-drums. The 'cellos respond with a phrase several times heard in the overture. The first violins follow with a new theme, which, through its development, leads to the quick movement, the first violins opening with the theme last stated, accompanied in bassoon and horn. After somewhat complicated development the second theme, a beautifully expressive melody, appears in the wood winds and is developed, and a short transition leads to the free fantasia based upon the second theme. The first theme returns again and is elaborately developed. The concluding section of the overture begins with the first theme, fortissimo, which is subjected to new development, and the overture closes with a very dramatic Coda. The work is a wonderful picture of the restlessness of the soul, its aspirations, and its struggles with destiny.

Siegfried Idyl

The "Siegfried Idyl" was written in 1871 as a birthday gift to the composer's wife and named for his son, Siegfried, who was born while he was composing the music. The thematic material is largely drawn from "Siegfried" in the "Nibelung Trilogy," including the motive from the love scene in the third act, phrases from Wotan's Farewell and Brünnhilde's Address. With them an old German cradle-song is interwoven. The various motives are worked up with consummate skill and with as much care as if the Idyl had been written for a large orchestra. The score calls only for the strings, one flute, one oboe, two clarinets, two horns, one trumpet, and one bassoon. The first performance of the Idyl was given upon the steps of Villa Triebscheu at Lucerne, by some Zurich musicians invited for the purpose, Hans Richter among them playing the trumpet, and Wagner himself conducting the serenade to his wife.

Waldweben

"Waldweben" ("Forest Weaving") is an arrangement by Wagner himself for concert purposes of fragments of the second act of "Siegfried," describing the reveries of Siegfried amid the rustle of the forest, his slaying of the dragon, and his discovery that he can understand what the birds are saying to him after he has tasted the blood of the monster. It is one of the most delightful of the Wagner concert arrangements, though mainly repeating the music of the drama itself.

Träume

"Träume" ("Dreams"), a favorite little number on concert-programs, is a song which Wagner wrote as "a study to 'Tristan und Isolde,'" and which was arranged for orchestra many years ago by Theodore Thomas, who lent it an added charm and effect. The song is a miniature impression of "Tristan und Isolde," a mere sketch, yet drawn in exquisite line and infused with dreamy sentiment. It may have aided in depicting that mighty outburst of passion in the great music drama of Isolde's love.

Huldigungs Marsch

"Huldigungs Marsch," or "March of Homage," was written in 1864 for Ludwig II of Bavaria and was at first scored for military band. Subsequently Wagner began its arrangement for orchestra, a work which, owing to interruptions, was finished by Raff. The march begins with an introduction in march time leading to a stately theme in the wood winds and horns. This is followed by parts of another theme in the violas, 'cellos, horns and bass clarinet, with sustained harmonies in the brasses. As the time quickens, the trumpets and trombones give out a march theme with drum rolls. A fortissimo in full orchestra leads to the march proper, which opens with a brilliant theme of festal character in the wood winds and horns with string accompaniment. After development, the second theme is given out by the trombones, and after fragments of the first theme, it returns with tremendous force in all the brasses fortissimo against rolls of the drums and brilliant runs in the wood winds. The first theme now returns fortissimo in full orchestra and is further developed, and at last, after a powerful climax, leads to a return of the opening passage in the introduction. A brilliant Coda closes the march.

Kaiser Marsch

The well-known "Kaiser Marsch" was written in celebration of the German victory over France in 1870 and was first played in Berlin in 1871. It opens with a majestic theme in full orchestra which is developed with genuine "Sturm und Drang." After this subsides, the brasses and kettle-drums prepare the way for the second theme in the wood winds, which leads to the first phrase of the Martin Luther Chorale, "Ein' feste Burg," in full harmony in all the wind instruments against a powerful string accompaniment. This material is next developed, giving a picture of battle, until at last the brasses once more sing the Chorale, against the tumult signifying victory. A fanfare leads to the return of the first theme which is given out in full orchestra fortissimo. At the return of this theme a unison chorus is written, but it is rarely sung.

Bacchanale from Tannhäuser

This Bacchanale was an addition which Wagner made for the production of his opera "Tannhäuser" in Paris in 1861, sixteen years after the work had first been given at Dresden. The Paris production had been arranged through the patronage of Princess Metternich, who persuaded Napoleon III, who had never previously heard of Wagner nor of "Tannhäuser," to permit a performance of the opera to be given in Paris. Immense preparations were made for the production. No fewer than 164 rehearsals were held, but it was in connection with the ballet scene that disaster fell upon "Tannhäuser" in France. It had always been the custom to put a ballet in the second or third acts of operas given in Paris, so that the subscribers to the great national institution could make their leisurely way to the Opéra after dinner and in time to see the dancers — a portion of the composition which was of most importance to the gentlemen of the Jockey Club. No persuasion could prevail upon Wagner to put a ballet in the second or third act of "Tannhäuser," nor in any other place than that in which it would be appropriate and fitting—the first act. In order to show the German master that Paris could not be trifled with, the Jockey Club and other subscribers came to the first performance armed with whistles, rattles and other noise-making implements and but little of Wagner's music was permitted to be heard. Two other representations were given and at each bedlam was let loose; Wagner therefore withdrew his score and "Tannhäuser" thereafter was silent, as far as Paris was concerned, for more than thirty years.

Even before the fiasco of the production occurred, Wagner had had great difficulty in making the dancers of the Opéra understand what he required in the Bacchanale. His idea was to surround Venus, lying in her grotto in the Hörselberg with Tannhäuser at her feet, with bacchantes and fauns dancing before them. There were to have been two tableaux — "The Rape of Europa" and "Leda and the Swan" — but the dancers were reluctant to omit as much of their costumes as would be consistent with the mythological era. Artists' models, who might be less particular about exposing their persons, were suggested, but finally the tableaux were omitted altogether. When the composer urged upon Petipa, the ballet master, that the motions of the satyrs and bacchantes must not be of the traditional operatic kind, but frenzied and sublime, the latter said: "If I were to tell my dancers a word about this, and endeavor to give them the attitude you mean, we should have the can-can at once and would be lost."

F. B

WEBER

1786 – 1826

Overture to Euryanthe

WEBER'S "Euryanthe" was first performed in Vienna in 1823, and met with failure, though the overture has remained popular from that day to this. The story of the opera is concerned with the love troubles of Adolar and Euryanthe, and the intrigues of Lysiart and Eglantine against them, which are at last happily overcome. The libretto is of the most inane character and was largely responsible for failure of the opera. The opening theme of the overture is announced in all the wood winds, supported by the full power of the orchestra, after a brilliant introduction, signifying Adolar's reliance upon the faithfulness of Euryanthe. The second theme is a graceful melody suggesting Adolar's hope as he looks forward to a meeting with her. A tutti full of color leads to a Largo in the muted violins, accompanied by violas, which gives expression to certain revelations made by Eglantine. After a pause on the last note of the Largo, the basses give out an episode which has no connection with the opera, but which leads back to the first subject, most brilliantly elaborated. The return of the second theme and an effective Coda close the overture.

Overture to Oberon

"Oberon" was written in 1826, two acts of it in Germany and the last in England. The story upon which it is founded appears in a collection of French romances under the title of "Huon de Bordeaux." It is substantially as follows: Oberon, the Elfin King, having quarreled with his fairy partner, can never be reconciled until he finds two lovers constant to each other under all circumstances. Puck ranges the world in quest of them. The two lovers are Sir Huon, a young knight of Bordeaux, and Reiza, daughter of the Caliph of Bagdad. The story relates their trials and temptations, through all of which they remain constant, thereby securing the forgiveness of Oberon. The overture is characteristic of the opera and opens with an Adagio sostenuto of fairy music with the magic horn of Oberon summoning the fairies. A few notes lead to a short passage from a fairy chorus in the flute. A march theme is then given out, played in the Court of Charlemagne, and introducing the hero, which is twice answered in the muted strings. The fairy music continues until a fortissimo chord in full orchestra leads to the Allegro, the subject of which is taken from the quartet in the opera, "Over the Dark Blue Waters." The horn call is heard again, whereupon the clarinet gives out the theme of Sir Huon's song, "From Boyhood trained," followed by a passage from Reiza's magnificent scena, "Ocean, thou mighty Monster," and a reference to the chorus sung by the spirits when they are directed by Puck to raise the storm which wrecks the lovers' bark. The conclusion of the overture is of the most tumultuous and brilliant character. As a complete work it is one of the most remarkable combinations of fantasy and technical skill in modern music.

Overture to Der Freischütz

The opera, "Der Freischütz" was composed in 1819-1820, and is specially famous as purely German in subject and treatment. Its music was originally connected by spoken dialogue. The libretto was written by Friedrich Kind, and is based upon a German legend by Apel. Max, the lover of Agatha, daughter of Kuno, can only win her hand by victory in a shooting contest. Caspar, also a lover of Agatha, who has sold himself to the fiend Zamiel for some unerring bullets cast under magic influences, conspires to deliver Max to the fiend instead of himself. Max loses his skill in shooting and having been defeated by Kilian, abandons all hope. While in this despondent mood, Caspar induces him to cast the magic bullets in hope of propitiating Zamiel. Max succeeds well with six of his bullets and fires the seventh at a dove flying past. As he fires, Agatha appears to him as the dove, and he fancies he has killed her, but Zamiel has directed the shot to the heart of Caspar and claims his victim, while Max is rewarded with the hand of Agatha.

An impressive Adagio opening of the overture is followed by a beautiful horn quartet, which does not appear in the opera, and seems to have no connection with it, though some have thought it is intended to signify the happiness of simple woodland life. It is followed by the prelude of the story, the contract between Zamiel and Caspar, described by tremolos in the strings, weird tones in the clarinet, and drum beats. This closes the Adagio and leads to an Allegro, taken from Max's scena, closing the first act. Short passage work follows, leading to the episode of the Incantation music in full orchestra, in which the composer reaches the supreme height of wild, weird, and almost supernatural music. A beautiful contrast follows in the clarinet, which takes up the aria sung by Agatha when she meets her lover in the second act. This continues until phrases of the Incantation music break in again. Once more the beautiful Agatha theme is introduced, leading to the free fantasia. It is based upon fragments of the "Incantation" and leads to the third section of the overture, which opens with the first theme, followed by phrases from Max's aria in the first act. At its conclusion, phrases from the introduction reappear, and a decrescendo leads to the Coda, which begins with an impressive fortissimo chord in full orchestra, followed after a brief transition by a second. A short pause ensues, after which the full orchestra sings a phrase from the superb Agatha aria. The development of the second theme rises to a climax, which closes the overture.

Overture to Abu Hassan

The one-act opera, "Abu Hassan," the text written by Franz Heimer, was finished in 1811, and was first produced in the same year at Munich. The story is based upon a well-known tale in the "Arabian Nights." The opera was written in Weber's youth, but is full of spirit and delightful melodies. It opens with a sprightly theme, pianissimo, which, after development, is followed by a fortissimo passage. The second theme, also of a vivacious character, follows, and in turn is succeeded by a graceful passage. A third theme, of a grandiose nature, closes the opening section, and is followed by the free fantasia, which leads to the return of the first theme. In the concluding section the first theme is followed by the grandiose theme alluded to above, and a brilliant, sprightly Coda closes the overture.

Jubilee Overture

It was during his directorship of the opera at Dresden in 1818 that Weber was commissioned to compose a cantata in honor of the fiftieth anniversary of the accession to the throne of the King of Saxony. He wrote the cantata called "The Jubilee" in eleven days, but owing to Italian cabals against him it was not performed on that occasion. When Weber found it was not to be given, he wrote the overture known as "The Jubilee," which is entirely distinct from the cantata. It opens with a bold and striking Adagio, in which a passage for the basses leads to the principal movement. After the development of the first theme, which is taken fortissimo in full orchestra, an episode leads to the second theme, a light dance rhythm. This theme is developed at considerable length and leads to the free fantasia. In the concluding section the opening themes are repeated. After further development the first subject repeats, and the violins finally lead to a vigorous intonation of the national anthem, "Heil dir im Siegerkranz," which is played fortissimo by the wind instruments with string accompaniment.

Invitation to the Dance. Op. 65

The "Invitation to the Dance," the most brilliant example of dance music yet written, was composed by Weber in 1811, and dedicated to his wife, Caroline. It opens with a slow introduction, the "Invitation," repeated by various groups of instruments, and leading to the main section of the work, a waltz theme of a most fascinating character. The second theme, graceful and languishing in style, follows, and after skilful development is followed by an episode and a new theme. This, too, is fully developed, and leads to the third part, constructed upon phrases from the previous theme. A vivacious Coda is followed, after a pause, by the slow movement of the introduction repeated. It is related in the biography of Weber, by his son, that while the composer was playing the piano version of the "Invitation" to his wife, he gave her the following program of the piece:

"Bars 1–5, first appearance of the dancers. Bars 5–9, the lady's evasive reply. Bars 9-13, his pressing invitation. Bars 13-16, her consent. Bars 17–19, he begins conversation. Bars 19–21, her reply. Bars 21–23, speaks with greater warmth. Bars 23–25, the sympathetic agreement. Bars 25–27, addresses her with regard to the dance. Bars 27–29, her answer. Bars 29–31, they take their places. Bars 31–35, waiting for the commencement of the dance. The conclusion of the dance, his thanks, her reply, and their retirement."

Fresh, graceful, and spirited, the work is the very apotheosis of the dance. Riehl says of it: "It marks the transition of modern dance music. The waltz had been previously a sort of mere animated minuet, but Weber threw a fiery allegro into the dance. The world ran faster, why should not people dance faster? . . . Weber was the founder of the dance music expression of deep feeling, and of a school of which Richard Strauss afterwards was an acolyte."

WOLF

1860 – 1903

Symphonic Poem, Penthesilea

WOLF'S symphonic poem, "Penthesilea," based upon Kleist's tragedy of that name, was written in 1883. The opening movement describes the preparations for a campaign, with Penthesilea, the Amazon, in command, as indicated by a motive suggesting her personality. It is styled in the score, "The Departure of Amazons for Troy." As she takes the lead, a march theme introduced by trumpet flourishes is heard. After a contrasting passage the march is resumed, and dies away as the Amazons enter their encampment. The second movement, "Penthesilea's Dream of the Feast of Roses," is of a tranquil nature, the flute, oboe, and violins singing her reverie with viola accompaniment. The reverie grows more and more animated and comes to its close with Penthesilea's awakening. The title of the final movement, "Combats, Passions, Frenzy, Annihilation," well describes its musical contents. Two motives at the outset contend with each other — Penthesilea's determination to conquer, and the softer yearnings of her heart. These, after development, reach a climax, the motive of yearning last appearing in the wood winds and a tremolo of the violins. The desire for conquest breaks out again, and the trombones give out the motive of annihilation over a different treatment of the Penthesilea motive in the violins and wood winds. The tumult at last subsides, and as it dies away an expressive viola solo indicates the reappearance of Penthesilea in a more tranquil mood. After a short passage the orchestra once more breaks out in a repetition of the opening phrases and works up to a terrific climax, indicating her desire for revenge and destruction. After a pause the tumult again subsides, and the poem ends with her death.

WOLF-FERRARI

1876 –

The New Life

ERMANNO WOLF-FERRARI, born at Venice, was practically self-educated in music until his seventeenth year, when he went to Munich to study with Joseph Rheinberger. Much of the influence surrounding him was German, for the composer's father, a painter, had been a native of Weinheim, in Baden, and much of Wolf-Ferrari's self-study had been made with German music. The Italian influence became stronger when the composer, dissatisfied with Rheinberger's conservative teaching, returned to Italy and was directed in his studies by Verdi. Wolf-Ferrari is better known as a composer of operas than of symphonic works for the concert-room.

"The New Life" ("La Vita Nuova") was completed in 1901 and was produced for the first time at a concert of the Porges Choral Society, Munich, March 21, 1903. It was the success which waited upon this production which resulted in Wolf-Ferrari being appointed director of the Liceo Benedetto Marcello, the principal music school of Venice. The cantata is based upon the poems written by Dante and which were inspired by Beatrice Portinari. These were written between 1292 and 1294. It is of interest to state that Dante saw the maiden who inspired his verses only once or twice and it is probable that she scarcely knew him. Eventually she married Simone de' Bardi and she was scarcely twenty-four years of age when, on July 9, 1290, she died. But neither her marriage nor her death lessened Dante's adoration of Beatrice. The poems which he had written in her honor were published with the title "La Vita Nuova."

The following description of Wolf-Ferrari's cantata is published in the score:

Wolf-Ferrari divides the whole work into two parts. The first is preceded by a prologue. Between the two parts there is an Intermezzo. Next to the chorus, the solo baritone representing the person of the poet, is played by the composer in the foreground, while naturally the soprano solo of Beatrice stands back. Only in the prologue does it play a more prominent part, after which it disappears, not to return until the close, where it has but a few words to sing. The orchestra is no longer used as an accompaniment. In some parts the composer works out the feelings and ideas created in him by the words into short, independent passages for the orchestra; such are the *Angels' Song,* the *Preludio,* the *Intermezzo* and the Instrumental Melodrama, "*Beatrice's Death.*"

The Prologue, glorifying Love as the conqueror of Death, leads us on, as it were, through mighty portals (Soli, double chorus, boys' voices, organ and orchestra) to the first part, which describes Love in relation to Life in still more worldly strains, indulging even in pure joy of life and delight in the glories and beauties of Nature; till at the close the music bursts into strains transcending Earth and all that is earthly. It treats of the Canzone which tells of Angels pleading to the Almighty Father to take Beatrice's soul, whose glory shines unto Heavenly heights. The answer of God is sung by the full chorus in Palestrinian strains, in which plain language it conveys the idea of that "All-pervading, All-embracing" Power. An *Intermezzo* which then follows casts the first shadows of Death over the poem. It is the transfigured, sombre glorification of Sorrow, and is founded upon the two sonnets which owe their origin to the death of Beatrice's father.

The second part (in which the Angel of Death is represented in sombre harmonies [strings], and Beatrice by the solo-violin), in a thrilling scene, describes the death of Beatrice. A part sung by the chorus is followed by a baritone solo (quasi recitativo) of thrilling effect, depicting the poet a martyr to his sorrow, his eyes red with weeping; the piano accompaniment with its colorless tone producing an almost supernatural effect. The poet's early vision is changed to reality — has become an event — a description of the earthquake (with the plain triad in C minor) and forms the culminating point of this part, which contains dramatic elements bearing us up to mystic heights, and terminating with the words: "She lives in Light," pointing to the glorious union of thoughts on Eternity and Love.

The introduction of the pianoforte is a novelty; the instrument being used in solo parts and as an orchestral instrument. Once, in the Angels' Song, it is introduced together with two harps, the strings and seven kettle-drums, which the basses in the movement repeat in natural pitch. A "*Leitmotiv*" appears at the close of each part, and in the prologue the boys' voices introduce the Love greeting with the words: "We gladly hail her Lord, whose name is Love!"

F. B.

Overture to The Secret of Susanne

"The Secret of Susanne," an intermezzo in one act, was written to a text by Enrico Golisciani. The work was first produced at the Hoftheater, Munich, December 4, 1909, the Italian text having been turned into German by Max Kalbeck. The opera was conducted by Felix Mottl. In America "The Secret of Susanne" was first given by the Chicago Opera Company at Philadelphia, March 29, 1911. The story of the opera is concerned with the Countess Gil, who, unknown to her husband, is given to smoking cigarettes. When the count sniffs tobacco smoke in his house he suspects his wife of having entertained a male friend and his jealousy leads him to violent outbursts of indignation. Later the truth comes out and all ends happily.

The overture (Vivacissimo, D major, 2-4 time) opens at once with the principal subject in the first violins. After this has been developed, a second theme is brought forward, this having a certain relationship to the first. Soon both subjects are combined, the first in the wood winds and trumpet and the second in the violins.

F. B.

Intermezzo from The Jewels of the Madonna

"I Giojelli della Madonna," opera in three acts, was produced at Berlin, December 23, 1911. In America it was first given by the Chicago Opera Company, Chicago, January 16, 1912. The work, written to a libretto by E. Golisciani and C. Zangarini, is concerned with Genarro, a young worker in iron, living in Naples, and his love for Maliella. The latter despises the honest Genarro and has become infatuated with

Rafaele, the leader of the Camorra, who boasts that for her sake he would steal the jewels from the statue of the Madonna which is borne through the streets of Naples at a religious festival. Genarro hears of this idle bragging and determines to win the favor of the girl by stealing the jewels himself and giving them to her. The penalty of the theft is death. Maliella appears in the den of the Camorra beseeching Rafaele to save her from Genarro. The Camorrists perceive the Virgin's jewels upon the girl's neck and all turn from her in horror. Maliella realizes that she has lost love as well as honor and she drowns herself in the sea. Genarro, too, awakens to the desperate nature of his crime and he takes his own life with a stiletto.

The Intermezzo separates the first and second acts of "The Jewels of the Madonna." It was not, originally, part of the work, but was an afterthought.

F. B.

APPENDIX

THE ORCHESTRA

THE word "orchestra," which originally designated the space occupied by players, has come to signify the players themselves, when combined for the production of operas or of such large works as are described in this volume. The old orchestras, which were much smaller than those of the present time, comprised the string quintet (first violins, second violins, violas, violoncellos, and double basses, flutes, oboes, clarinets, bassoons, horns, trumpets, kettle-drums, and sometimes trombones). In the modern orchestras the following instruments are also included: English horn, bass clarinet, double bassoon, tuba, harp, bass and snare drums, cymbals, triangle, castanets, carillons, gong and xylophone; and sometimes the string sections are greatly strengthened to allow of subdivision.

The modern orchestra is divided into these four families or sections: strings, wood winds, brasses, and percussion instruments, or "the battery." The string section includes first violins, second violins, violas, violoncellos, and double basses, which correspond to the tones of the human voice as follows: first violins, soprano; second violins, alto; violas, tenor; violoncellos, barytone; and double basses, bass.

The wood-wind section includes clarinets, flutes, oboes, bassoons (these played in pairs), bass clarinets, double bassoons, English horns, and piccolos.

The brass section includes horns (usually called French horn), trumpets (or their substitutes, cornets), trombones, tubas, and bass tuba. The percussion instruments are the kettle-drums, or tympani, bass and snare drums, triangle, cymbals, tambourine, castanets, carillons, xylophone, and gong.

The harp, though one of the most ancient of instruments, belongs to no family. It is a comparatively recent addition to the orchestra and might be called the hermit thrush of the harmonious aggregation.

The violins are divided into firsts and seconds, the seconds only differing from the first in that they are employed to fill out the harmony by supplying the alto voice. The violin is familiar to every one. It has four strings raised above the belly of the instrument by means of a bridge, and changes of pitch are effected by stopping the strings with the fingers, thus shortening them. In addition to its natural tones, caused by pressure, it is capable of sweet, flute-like over-tones, called "harmonics," produced by the player touching the strings at certain points. Pizzicato tones are made by plucking the strings with the fingers, and the softer tones by affixing an appliance called the "Sordino," or "mute," to the bridge. The viola is only a larger form of the violin, tuned a fifth lower, which fills in the harmony with a deeper tone, corresponding to the tenor voice. The violoncello, commonly abbreviated into 'cello, is the barytone of the string family. It is usually coupled with the double basses as a reinforcement, but often has important solo work assigned to it. It has a very sympathetic and almost human quality of tone, as deep as that of the double bass, as sombre as that of the viola, and as rich as that of the violin. It is the most satisfying singer in the orchestra. The double bass, or contra bass, or in vulgar parlance the "bull fiddle," is really the bass singer of the whole orchestra, though not so boisterous as some of its bass companions in other sections. It has a deep, broad, rich tone, and is even capable of producing beautiful harmonics. Its pizzicatos also are impressive, but the mute is not usually employed.

In the wood-wind section, the clarinet, one of the oldest of instruments, holds first place by virtue of its tone and the demands composers make upon it. Unlike the oboe, English horn, and bassoon, it is played with a single reed. It is the richest in tone of all the wood winds. Its lower tones are somewhat coarse and hollow, but the others are warm, brilliant, and powerful, and it almost equals the flute in ornate and rapid facility. The bass clarinet is an octave deeper and is of different shape, having a bell mouth. The clarinet and bassoon are the real wood-wind foundation. Every one knows the flute, oldest and most bird-like of all instruments. It is the only one of the wood winds played from a side mouth-hole, for which reason it is sometimes called the traverse flute. The beak flute, like the flageolet, for instance, is a flute with a mouthpiece. The flute tone is gentle and sweet, and the instrument is peculiarly adapted for trills and rapid passages. The piccolo is only a small flute of higher range and more piercing tone. It produces the highest, shrillest, and most penetrating tone in the orchestra. The oboe is a double reed instrument. Some of its tones are weak and others shrill and nasal, but the general quality is plaintive and pastoral and very tender, even melancholy when the subject is at all sombre. In the hands of an expert player it can be made effective even as a solo instrument, and concertos have been written for it. It is a modest little instrument, but very dignified, for it gives out the A for the orchestra's tuning. The English horn, or *cor anglais,* is often mistaken by those unfamiliar with instruments, who seek for it in the brass section. It is all the more mystifying, for it is neither English nor horn. It is the alto oboe, of deeper tone, a fifth below, and partakes of the oboe's plaintive quality. The bassoon is not a dignified instrument in form or quality. It has a double reed like the oboe. Its higher and medium tones are not unmusical, when they fit into the general harmony, but its lower tones are deep and guttural and coarse. It sometimes affects an air of dignity, but it is more at home in the grotesque and is usually played by elderly, serious persons. As a solo instrument it is uncouth and uncanny. The double bassoon is an octave lower. It is to the bassoon what the double bass is to the 'cello.

In the brass section the French horn holds the leading place. It is really an evolution from the old hunting-horn. It has a smooth, rich, velvety tone, and the full harmony of a quartet of horns is exceptionally beautiful. Its "open" tones are made by blowing and manipulation of the lips and the "closed" tones by closing the bell of the instrument with the hand. The trumpet is not often heard in small orchestras, its place being taken by the B flat cornet, which has not so pure or brilliant a tone but is more easily played and is extremely facile in every kind of tonal utterance. The cornet is so well known by its frequent use as a solo instrument in bands, big and little, that it needs no detailed description. The trombones usually appear in triple array, alto, tenor, and bass. Soprano trombones have been made, but they have not proved effective. Every concert-goer is familiar with the two tubes sliding in and out, by which the pitch is varied. Its compass is a little more than two octaves and in the hands of a finished player its tone is majestic and impressive, and at the same time it is capable of delicate and melodious effect. The tuba, which has taken the place of the ophicleide, belongs to the saxhorn family, one of the seven. It has a deep, noble tone and is the dominating bass of the brasses.

The percussion family is easily distinguishable by its noise, when it has a chance to make it, but it adds rich color to instrumentation. The kettle-drums, or tympani, ordinarily two in number, one high, the other low, though sometimes three and four are used, are metal basins headed with skin. They are tuned to sound certain notes by the use of screws and are specially serviceable in accentuating rhythm, heightening effect, and adding color. The bass drum is used for certain sonorous effects and with its neighbors, the kettle-drums, is happy in a thunder storm or cannonading. The snare drum supplies the military features and aids march rhythm. The cymbals are metal disks clashed together to heighten effect. The triangle is metallic, of the shape its name indicates, and is played with a little bar of the same metal. The carillons are small bars of steel, which, when struck with a mallet, give out bell tones, and a somewhat similar effect is produced upon strips of wood constituting the xylophone. The gong is used in dirges or tragic *dénouements.* The castanets and tambourine are instruments for dance-music which are too familiar to need description.

GLOSSARY

The subjoined definitions of the terms most frequently used in this volume may be of use to readers.

Adagio, very slow.
Adagio ma non tanto, slow but not too slow.
Affetuoso, with tender expression.
Allegretto, somewhat quick.
Allegro, quick, lively.
Allegro assai, Allegro molto, very quick.
Amabile, amiable, graceful.
Andante, slow.
Andantino, somewhat quicker than Andante.
Appassionato, passionate.
Aria, a vocal form, employed in operas and oratorios.
Arpeggio, playing the notes of a chord consecutively.
Augmentation, writing a theme in notes of longer duration than those employed in its original presentation.

Berceuse, a cradle song.
Bourrée, an old French dance of lively character, in 4-4 time, beginning on the fourth beat.
Bridge passage, see Transitional passage.
Brio, vivacity, spirit.

Cadenza, an ornamental passage of brilliant character.
Canon, a form of composition in which a theme, given out by one voice, is imitated exactly by other successive voices. This exact imitation is called "canonic."
Cembalo, the Italian name for the harpsichord, the 18th century instrument which preceded the pianoforte. Its wire strings were not struck with hammers, as with the pianoforte, but plucked by quills.
Chaconne, a slow dance, probably Spanish in origin.
Coda, the concluding section of a piece, or of a division of a piece.
Commodo, conveniently, leisurely.
Con, with.
Concerto, the name originally given to any concerted composition for voices or instruments. In modern times, a work of brilliant character for a solo instrument (sometimes more than one) with orchestral accompaniment.
Counterpoint, the art, process and result of fitting two or more melodies together simultaneously.
Crescendo, becoming louder.

Deciso, in a bold or decided manner.
Decrescendo, becoming softer.
Development, working out; free fantasy.
Diminuendo, same as decrescendo.
Diminution, writing a theme in notes of shorter duration than those which had been employed in the original presentation. Opposed to augmentation (q.v.).
Disperato, desperately.
Doloroso, sadly.
Drone Bass, so called from the lowest tube of the bagpipe, the tone of which sounds continuously, see Organ-point.

Entr'acte, music played between the acts of an opera or drama. Synonymous with Intermezzo.

Episode, a digression from the principal subject; a contrasted theme.

Fanfare, a flourish of trumpets.
Fantasie, Fantasia, a composition in which the composer gives free scope to his ideas without formal restrictions.
Feierlich, in a stately manner, as befitting a festival.
Feroce, with ferocity.
Figure, figuration, a melodic or rhythmic pattern.
Finale, the closing movement of a symphony or sonata or chamber music composition; also the closing portion of an act in an opera.
Forte, loud.
Fortissimo, very loud.
Free fantasia, the name sometimes given to the development section of the sonata form (q.v.).
Fugato, in the style of a fugue (q.v.).
Fugue, a composition in strict style in which a subject, set forth at the beginning, is answered by other parts and contrapuntally developed.

Gavotte, an old dance form of lively character, written usually in 4-4 time and beginning on the third beat.
Gigue, Giga, an old dance form, very lively in character, written usually in 6-8 time. The English Jig is derived from it.
Giocoso, joyful.
Giusto, exact, precise.
Glissando, the sliding of the finger between notes on the same string of a violin, violoncellos, etc.; also the rapid sliding of the fingers along the strings of a harp, or the keys of the piano.
Grave, very slow; also heavy, deep.

Harmonics, the name given to the flute-like tones produced on a bowed instrument and on the harp by lightly touching the strings instead of pressing them.
Harmony, a combination of simultaneous tones.
Harpsichord, see Cembalo.

Imitation, the repetition of a motive or phrase in some other part than that which has first established it.
Interlude, a piece, usually short, played between acts, movements or stanzas.
Intermezzo, see Entr'acte.

Lamentoso, mournfully.
Langsam, slow.
Largo, slow, noble, broad. Slower than Lento.
Larghetto, slow, but not so slow as Largo.
Legato, smoothly. The opposite of Staccato.
Lento, Lent, slow.
Lydian Mode, one of the medieval scales corresponding to the octave F to F on the white keys of the piano.

Maestoso, majestic.
Marcato, marked, accented.
Marziale, martial, in the style of a march.
Melody, a succession of tones, rhythmically and symmetrically arranged, as opposed to harmony.
Minuet, a dance form in 3-4 time.
Misterioso, mysteriously.
Modérément, moderately.
Mosso, animated; *poco mosso,* a little animated.
Mute, a device of wood or metal placed upon the bridge of a stringed instrument to deaden the sound; also a pear-shaped pad introduced into the bell of a horn, trumpet or trombone to modify the tone.

Opera, a dramatic composition intended for stage representation and including all musical resources — the orchestra, chorus, soli, duets, trios, etc.

Oratorio, a sacred work for solo, chorus and orchestra, generally, but not always based upon a scriptural narrative.

Organ-point, a note constantly repeated or sustained in one part, usually the bass. Also called Pedal-point, see Drone Bass.

Overture, literally means the opening movement of a larger work, such as an opera, oratorio, suite, etc. In modern music the name is frequently given to independent pieces for orchestra, usually written in sonata form (q.v.).

Passacaglia, originally a dance, but turned into a variation form by Bach and Handel. It is practically identical with the Chaconne.

Passage, Passage-work, a general term for any short division of a piece, a phrase. Passage-work denotes usually passages made up of runs and bustling ornamental figures.

Pedal-point, see Organ-point.

Percussion instruments, are those in which the sound is produced by being struck. They include drums, cymbals, triangle, tambourine, xylophone, etc.

Phrase, a short passage or figure.

Pianissimo, very soft.

Piano, soft.

Più, more; *Più mosso,* more animated; *più forte,* more loudly.

Pizzicato, an effect produced by plucking the strings of such instruments as the violin, viola, violoncello and double bass with the finger instead of playing with the bow.

Poco, a little.

Polonaise, a Polish composition usually classed among the dance forms, but in reality a march. It opened the great balls of the Polish kings and nobility — the dancers parading around the room in couples

Postlude, a concluding phrase, composition or church voluntary.

Praeambulum, a prelude or introduction.

Presto, quick.

Prestissimo, very quick.

Quasi, almost.

Recapitulation, the final division of a movement in sonata form (q.v.), in which the first portion of the movement is repeated. Sometimes called the Reprise.

Recitative, a species of declamation, usually for voice, but sometimes used in instrumental music.

Reprise, see Recapitulation.

Rhythm, the arrangement of accented and unaccented, and of long and short sounds, the melody of monotone.

Rigaudon, or *Rigodon,* a lively French dance in 4-4 time resembling the Bourrée.

Ritornello, an instrumental prelude, interlude or postlude.

Rondo (Rondeau), a form originally derived from a dance-song, in which the principal theme recurs at the end of each division of the piece.

Sarabande, a slow dance form, of Spanish origin, in 3-4 time.

Scherzando, playfully.

Scherzino, a little Scherzo (q.v.).

Scherzo, a movement of playful or humorous character generally, though not always in 3-4 time.

Sehr, very; *Sehr langsam,* very slow; *Sehr schnell,* very quick;

Sehr ruhig, very quiet; *Sehr lebhaft,* very lively.

Semplice, simple.

Solo (*pl. soli*), a passage or composition for a single voice or instrument.

Sonata, a composition written for one instrument or for two instruments, containing several movements, the first movement (and sometimes others) usually written in Sonata Form (q.v.). A similar work for three instruments is called a Trio; for four, a quartet; for orchestra, a symphony.

Sonata Form, the plan or design of the first movements of sonatas, trios, quartets, symphonies and, generally, of concertos and overtures. It comprises three divisions — I. the Exposition, in which the principal subject and second subject are presented; II. the Development, in which they are worked out; III. the Recapitulation, in which they are repeated.

Sostenuto, sustained.

Staccato, detached or short.

Subject, a theme or melody.

Suite, a composition containing a series of movements.

Symphonic Poem, a term first used by Liszt for a large orchestral composition illustrative of some episode or story and usually free in form.

Symphony, a composition similar to a Sonata (q.v.), but written for orchestra and generally comprising four movements: I. an Allegro in Sonata Form (q.v.); II. A slow movement; III. A Minuet or Scherzo; IV. Finale, usually an Allegro in Sonata Form.

Syncopation, temporary displacement of the natural accent.

Tanto, so much, or as much; *Adagio ma non tanto,* slow but not too slow.

Tarantella, an Italian dance, quick in tempo and wild in character, in 6-8 time.

Tempestuoso, tempestuous, boisterous.

Tenebroso, darkly, gloomily.

Tenerezza, tenderness or delicacy.

Theme, a subject or melody.

Transitional passage, the passage in the Sonata Form which leads from the principal subject to the second subject. It is sometimes called Bridge Passage.

Très, very; *très lent,* very slow; *très vite,* very quick.

Tremolo, the reiteration of one note, or more than one note, accomplished on stringed instruments by the rapid to and fro motion of the bow.

Trio, the name given to the middle and contrasting portion of Minuets, Gavottes, Scherzos etc. Also works written for three instruments or voices.

Triplet, a group of three notes to a beat of the measure.

Tutti, literally, all; applied particularly to passages played by the entire orchestra.

Vivace, lively, quick.

Vivacissimo, very quick.

Vivo, quick, animated.

Volante, flying — a rapid, delicate manner of execution.

Vorspiel, Prelude or Introduction.

Wood wind, that division of the orchestra which comprises the flutes (piccolo), oboes (English horn), clarinets (bass clarinet) and bassoons (double bassoon).

Xylophone, an instrument consisting of graduated wooden bars, struck with wooden hammers.

INDEX